Codex 32.

WITH THE FLAG TO PRETORIA.

Drawn by Max Cowper.]

THE CROWNING OF A GREAT CAREER.

Her Majesty Queen Victoria bestowing an Earldom on Lord Roberts at Osborne, January 2, 1901. A pathetic interest attaches to this act, which was the last of importance carried out by Her Majesty in person. It is known that Lord Roberts was greatly moved by this interview, and it is safe to assume that the Queen herself realised that it marked the end of her reign.

WITH THE FLAG
TO PRETORIA

A History of the Boer War of 1899-1900

BY H. W. WILSON

Author of "Ironclads in Action," &c. &c.

ILLUSTRATED MAINLY FROM PHOTOGRAPHS AND AUTHENTIC SKETCHES
TAKEN IN SOUTH AFRICA

VOL. II.

LONDON
PUBLISHED BY HARMSWORTH BROTHERS, LIMITED
1901

MAJOR BABTIE, C.M.G., V.C., R.A.M.C.

THE ROLL OF HONOUR.

V.C.'s OF THE WAR.

Captain W. N. CONGREVE	Rifle Brigade	Colenso	December 15, 1899.
Corporal G. S. NURSE	Royal Field Artillery	,,	,, ,, ,,
Captain H. L. REED	,, ,, ,,	,,	,, ,, ,,
Lieut. Hon. FREDERICK HUGH SHERSTON ROBERTS	King's Royal Rifles	,,	,, ,, ,,
Major WILLIAM BABTIE	Royal Army Medical Corps	,,	,, ,, ,,
Major EDMUND JOHN PHIPPS-HORNBY	Q Battery, R.H.A.	Koorn Spruit	March 31, 1900.
Sergeant CHARLES PARKER	,, ,,	,, ,,	,, ,, ,,
Gunner ISAAC LODGE	,, ,,	,, ,,	,, ,, ,,
Driver HORACE HARRY GLASOCK	,, ,,	,, ,,	,, ,, ,,
Captain ERNEST BECKWITH TOWSE	Gordon Highlanders	Magersfontein, Dec. 11, 1899, Mt. Thoba, Ap. 30, 1900.	
Captain CHARLES FITZCLARENCE	Royal Fusiliers	Mafeking	Oct. 14 & 27, Dec. 26, 1899.
Lieutenant Sr JOHN P. MILBANKE, Bart.	10th Hussars	Colesberg	January 5, 1900.
Sergeant H. R. MARTINEAU	Protectorate Regiment	Mafeking	December 26, 1899.
Trooper H. E. RAMSDEN	,, ,,	,,	,, ,, ,,
Captain MATTHEW FONTAINE MAURY MEIKLEJOHN	Gordon Highlanders	Elandslaagte	October 21, 1899.
Second Lieutenant JOHN NORWOOD	5th Dragoon Guards	Ladysmith	October 30, 1899.
Sergeant-Major WILLIAM ROBERTSON	Gordon Highlanders	Elandslaagte	October 21, 1899.
Captain CONWYN MANSEL-JONES	West Yorkshire Regiment	Pieters Hill	February 27, 1900.
Corporal F. MCKAY	Gordon Highlanders	Johannesburg	May 29, 1900.
Captain WILLIAM ENGLESON GORDON	,, ,,	Doornbosch Fontein	July 11, 1900.
Captain DAVID REGINALD YOUNGER*	,, ,,	,, ,,	,, ,, ,,
Private C. WARD	2nd Yorkshire Light Infantry	Lindley	June 26, ,, 1900.
Corporal J. SHAUL	Highland Light Infantry	Magersfontein	December 11, 1900.
Sergeant ARTHUR HERBERT LINDLEY RICHARDSON	Strathcona's Horse	Wolvespruit	July 5, 1900.
Private J. H. BISDEE	Tasmanian Imperial Bushmen	Warmbad	September 1, 1900.
Lieutenant FRANCIS NEWTON PARSONS	Essex Regiment Paardeberg, Feb. 18, 1900, & Driefontein, Mch. 10, 1900.		
Lieutenant GUY G. E. WYLLY	Tasmanian Imperial Bushmen	Warmbad	September 1, 1900
Corporal H. J. KNIGHT	1st Liverpool Regiment	Vanwyk's Vlei	August 21, 1900.
Major E. D. BROWN	14th Hussars	Geluk	October 13, 1900.
Lieutenant E. T. INKSON	Royal Army Medical Corps	Relief of Ladysmith	February 24, 1900.
Lieutenant A. C. DOXAT	3rd Imperial Yeomanry	Zeerust	October 20, 1900.
Sergeant T. LAWRENCE	17th Lancers	Essenbosch Farm	August 7, 1900.
Private A. E. CURTIS	2nd East Surrey Regiment	Relief of Ladysmith	February 23, 1900.
Sergeant H. ENGELHEART	10th Hussars	Koorn Spruit	March 13, 1900.
Private WM. HEATON	1st King's Liverpool Regiment	Leuwkloof	August 23, 1900.
Corporal FRANK HOWARD KIRBY	Royal Engineers	Near Pretoria	June 2, 1900.
Quarter-Master W. ROBERTSON	Gordon Highlanders	Elandslaagte	October 21, 1899.

* Killed while performing act for which the V.C. would have been awarded.

CAPTAIN MEIKLEJOHN, V.C.

TROOPS ENGAGED IN THE WAR.

REGULAR ARMY.

IN CAPE COLONY AND NATAL IN SEPT. 1899 (N.=Natal).

CAVALRY (2 Regiments).
5th Lancers. N.   18th Hussars. N.

ARTILLERY (4 Batteries=24 guns).
13th, 67th, and 69th Field Batteries. N.
10th (Mountain) Battery. N.

INFANTRY (7½ Battalions).
1st Roy. Irish Fusiliers. N.   1st King's Liverpool. N.
1st Leicestershire. N.   2nd King's Royal Rifles. N.
1st King's Royal Rifles. N.   1st Loyal North Lancashire.
2nd Dublin Fusiliers. N.   2nd Yorks. L. Infy. (one-half).

SENT TO SOUTH AFRICA BEFORE THE OUTBREAK OF THE WAR. (Arrived on the eve of, or just after the commencement of, hostilities.)

CAVALRY (3 Regiments).
5th Dragoon Guards. N.   19th Hussars. N.   9th Lancers.

ARTILLERY (6 Batteries=36 guns).
18th, 62nd, and 75th (from home). ⎫
21st, 42nd, and 53rd (from India). N. ⎬ Field Batteries.
                                   ⎭

INFANTRY (9½ Battalions).
1st Devonshire. N.   2nd Rifle Brigade. N.
1st Gloucestershire. N.   1st Northumberland Fusiliers.
1st Manchester. N.   1st Royal Munster Fusiliers.
2nd Gordon Highlndrs. N.   2nd Yorks. L. Infy. (one half).
2nd Berkshires.   1st Border Regiment. N.

THE ARMY CORPS (Despatched Oct.–Nov. 1899).

CAVALRY (8 Regiments).
6th Dragoon Guards.   2nd Dragoons.
10th Hussars.   6th Dragoons.
12th Lancers.   13th Hussars.
1st Dragoons.   Household Cavalry Regiment.

MOUNTED INFANTRY (8 Companies).

ARTILLERY (19 Batteries=114 guns).
G, P, R, O Horse Artillery Batteries.
7th, 14th, 66th, 63rd, 64th, 73rd, 74th, 77th, 79th, 4th,
38th, 78th Field Batteries.
37th, 61st, and 65th Howitzer Batteries.

INFANTRY (32 Battalions).
3rd Grenadier Guards.   1st Royal Inniskilling Fus.
1st Coldstream Guards.   2nd Royal Irish Rifles.
2nd Coldstream Guards.   1st Connaught Rangers.
1st Scots Guards.   1st Royal Dublin Fusiliers.
2nd West Surrey.   2nd Royal Fusiliers.
2nd Devonshire.   2nd Royal Scots Fusiliers.
2nd West Yorkshire.   1st Royal Welsh Fusiliers.
2nd East Surrey.   2nd Royal Irish Fusiliers.
2nd Royal Highlanders.   1st Royal Scots.
1st Highland Light Inf.   2nd Northumberland Fus.
2nd Seaforth Highlanders.   2nd Somersetshire Light Inf.
1st Argyll and Sutherland.   2nd D. of Cornwall's L. Infy.
2nd Cameronians.   1st Welsh Regiment.
3rd King's Royal Rifles.   2nd Northamptonshire.
1st Durham Light Infantry.   2nd Shropshire Light Inftry.
1st Rifle Brigade.   1st Gordon Highlanders.

Total under SIR R. BULLER'S *command*, November 30.
13 Regiments Cavalry.   49 Battalions Infantry.
8 Companies Mounted Inf.   29 Batteries Artillery.

ORDERED OUT, OCT. 31, 1899.

ARTILLERY. 4th Mountain Battery.

INFANTRY (3 Battalions).
1st Suffolk.   1st Derbyshire (Sherwood
1st Essex.   Foresters).

ORDERED OUT, NOV. 11, 1899 (Fifth Division).

CAVALRY. 14th Hussars.

ARTILLERY (3 Batteries). 19th, 20th, & 28th Field Batteries.

INFANTRY (8 Battalions).
2nd Royal Warwick.   2nd Royal Lancaster.
1st Yorkshire.   2nd Lancashire Fusiliers.
2nd Dorsetshire.   1st South Lancashire.
2nd Middlesex.   1st York and Lancaster.

ORDERED OUT, DEC. 4 (Sixth Division).

ARTILLERY (3 Batteries). 76th, 81st, & 82nd Field Batteries.

INFANTRY (8 Battalions).
2nd Bedfordshire.   2nd East Kent.
1st Royal Irish.   2nd Gloucestershire.
2nd Worcestershire.   1st West Riding.
2nd Wiltshire.   1st Oxfordshire Light Infy.

ORDERED OUT, DEC. 14 (Seventh Division).

ARTILLERY (3 Batteries). 83rd, 84th, & 85th Field Batteries.

INFANTRY (8 Battalions).
2nd Norfolk.   2nd Cheshire.
2nd Lincolnshire.   1st East Lancashire.
1st King's Own Scott. Bord. 2nd South Wales Borderers.
2nd Hampshire.   2nd North Staffordshire.

ORDERED OUT IN DEC.—JAN.

CAVALRY (4 Regiments).
17th Lancers.   7th Dragoon Guards.
8th Hussars.   16th Lancers.

ARTILLERY (18 Batteries=108 guns).
A, J, M, Q, T, U Horse Artillery Batteries.
5th, 9th, 17th, 2nd, 8th, 44th, 39th, 68th, 88th Field Batteries.
43rd, 86th, 87th Howitzer Batteries.

INFANTRY (10 Battalions).
2nd Grenadier Guards.   1st Royal West Kent.
2nd Scots Guards.   1st South Stafford.
2nd East Yorkshire.   2nd Manchester.
1st Leinster.   1st Royal Sussex.
1st Worcestershire.   1st Cameron Highlanders.

Total Regular Cavalry, Artillery, and Infantry, April, 1900.

18 Regiments Cavalry, at war strength about - - -	9,558 men,	— guns.
8 Companies Mounted Infantry	1,048 „	— „
57 Batteries (=342 guns) - -	10,260 „	342 „
86 Battalions Infantry - -	86,860 „	— „
	107,726 „	342 „

TECHNICAL TROOPS—REGULARS.

ENGINEERS.
5th, 6th, 7th, 8th, 9th, 10th, 11th, 12th, 17th, 20th, 23rd,
26th, 29th, 31st, 37th, 38th, 42nd, 45th, 47th Companies.
1st Telegraph Division.   1st Field Park.
A, C Bridging Battalions.   Nos. 1, 2, 3 Balloon Sections.
Field Troop.

ARTILLERY.
Ammunition Columns.—1st, 2nd, 3rd, 4th, 5th, 6th, 7th,
8th, 9th, 10th, and 11th Division Columns ; two de-
tached columns ; 1st Brigade Division Column, Natal.
Ammunition Park.
Garrison Artillery.
Eastern Division : Companies Nos. 5, 6, 10.
Southern Division : Companies Nos. 14, 15, 16, 36.
Western Division: Companies Nos. 2, 6, 10, 14, 15, 17, 23.

ARMY SERVICE CORPS. Companies Nos. 3–17, 19–38, 40–45.

ROYAL ARMY MEDICAL CORPS.

MILITIA.

(31 Battalions Infantry = about 20,626 men.)

3rd Royal Scots.	4th Scottish Rifles.
3rd West Surrey.	3rd East Lancashire.
3rd East Kent.	4th East Surrey.
3rd Royal Lancaster.	3rd West Riding.
4th Royal Lancaster.	4th South Staffordshire.
6th Royal Warwickshire.	3rd South Lancashire.
3rd Norfolk.	3rd Welsh.
4th Somersetshire.	4th Derbyshire.
4th West Yorkshire.	4th Middlesex.
4th Bedfordshire.	9th King's Royal Rifles.
3rd Yorkshire.	4th North Staffordshire.
6th Lancashire Fusiliers.	3rd Durham Light Infantry.
4th Cheshire.	4th Argyll and Sutherland.
3rd South Wales Borderers.	3rd Leinster.
3rd King's Own Scottish Borderers.	3rd Royal Munster Fusiliers.
	5th Royal Dublin Fusiliers.

VOLUNTEERS AND IRREGULARS.

I.—BRITISH.

IMPERIAL YEOMANRY.

1st Battalion : 1st and 2nd (Wiltshire), 3rd (Gloucestershire), and 4th (Glamorgan) Cos.

2nd Battalion : 5th (Warwickshire), 21st and 22nd (Cheshire), and 32nd (Lancs) Cos.

3rd Battalion : 9th and 11th (Yorks.), 10th (Notts), and 12th (S. Notts) Cos.

4th Battalion : 6th (Staffordshire), 7th (Leicestershire), 8th (Derbyshire), and 28th (Beds) Cos.

5th Battalion : 14th and 15th (Northumberland), 13th (Shropshire), and 16th (Worcestershire) Cos.

6th Battalion : 17th (Ayrshire), 18th (Lanarkshire), 19th (Lothian), and 20th (Fife and Forfar) Cos.

7th Battalion : 25th (W. Somerset), 26th (Dorsetshire), 27th (Devonshire), 48th (N. Somerset) Cos.

8th Battalion : 23rd (Lancs), 24th (Westmoreland and Cumberland), and 77th (Manchester) Cos.

9th Battalion : 29th (Denbighshire), 30th (Pembrokeshire), and 31st and 49th (Montgomery) Cos.

10th Battalion : 37th and 38th (Bucks), 39th (Berks), and 40th (Oxon) Cos.

11th Battalion : 23rd (E. Kent), 24th and 25th (Midx.), and 36th (W. Kent) Cos.

12th Battalion : 41st (Hants), 42nd (Herts), and 43rd and 44th (Suffolk) Cos.

13th Battalion : 45th (Dublin), 46th and 54th (Belfast), and 47th (Lord Donoughmore's) Cos.

14th Battalion : 53rd (E. Kent), 58th (Northumberland), 62nd (Middlesex), and 69th (Sussex) Cos.

15th Battalion : 56th and 57th (Bucks), 58th (Berks), and 59th (Oxon) Cos.

16th Battalion : 63rd (Wilts), 66th (Yorks.), and 74th (Dublin) Cos.

17th Battalion : 50th (Hants), 60th (N. Irish), 61st (S. Irish), and 65th (Leicestershire) Cos.

18th Battalion : 67th, 70th, 71st, and 75th (Sharpshooter) Cos.

19th Battalion : 51st, 52nd, 68th, and 73rd (Paget's Horse) Cos.

20th Battalion : 72nd and 76th (Rough Riders), and 78th and 79th Cos.

20 Battalions, each four Companies of 116 men (one three Companies) = 79 Companies = 10,195 Officers and Men.

VOLUNTEERS.

One Company attached to each Battalion of Regulars, 9,187 men.

City of London Imperial Volunteers (1 Battalion Infantry, 1 4-gun Battery Artillery, and Mounted Infantry), about 1,600 men.

II.—COLONIAL.

SOUTH AFRICA.

Bechuanaland Rifles.	Kimberley Regiment.
Bethune's Mounted Infantry.	Kitchener's Horse.
Border Horse.	Komgha Mounted Volunteers.
Border Mounted Rifles.	Lock's Horse.
Border Scouts.	Montmorency's Scouts.
Brabant's Horse :	Natal Volunteer Brigade :
1st Regiment.	Natal Carbineers.
2nd Regiment.	„ Field Artillery.
British South Africa Police.	„ Mounted Rifles.
Cape Garrison Artillery.	„ Royal Rifles.
Cape Medical Staff Corps, A, B, and C Cos.	„ Vol. Medical Corps.
Cape Mounted Rifles.	„ Vol. Veterinary Cps.
Cape Pioneer Railway Regt.	Nesbitt's Horse.
Cape Police.	Orpen's Horse.
Capetown Highlanders.	Prince Alfred's Own Artillery.
Grahamstown Volunteers.	Prince Alfred's Vol. Guard.
Commander-in-Chief's Bodyguard.	Protectorate Regiment.
	Queenstown Rifle Volunteers.
Diamond Fields Artillery.	Rhodesian Protectorate Reg.
District Mounted Rifles.	Rimington's Guides.
Duke of Edinburgh's Rifles.	Robert's Light Horse.
Durban Light Infantry.	South African Light Horse.
East London Police.	Stellenbosch Mounted Inftry.
Eastern Province Horse.	Struben's Scouts.
French's Scouts.	Tembuland Mounted Rifles.
Frontier Mounted Rifles.	Thorneycroft's Mounted Inf.
Gatacre's Scouts.	Transkei Mounted Rifles.
Griqualand East Mounted Rifles.	Tucker's Scouts.
	Uitenhage Volunteer Rifles.
Herschel's Mounted Rifles.	Umvoti Mounted Rifles.
Imperial Light Horse.	Warwick's Scouts.
Imperial Light Infantry.	
Imperial Yeomanry Scouts.	Mounted Rifle Clubs :
Kaffrarian Rifles.	Xalanga.
Kenny's Scouts.	Nquamakwe.
Kimberley Light Horse.	Engcobo.
	T'somo.

Town Guards.—Dordrecht, E. London, Grahamstown, Hoppesia, Kimberley, King William's Town, Kokstad, Mafeking, Naauwpoort, Port Elizabeth, Queenstown, and Uitenhage.

CANADA.

Mounted Infantry (3 Regiments): Royal Canadian Dragoons (1st and 2nd Battalions), and Strathcona's Horse.
Artillery (3 Batteries): C, D, and E.
Infantry (2 Battalions) : 2nd and 3rd Battalions.

AUSTRALIA.

New South Wales : Imperial Bushmen (6 Companies, A—F), Mounted Infantry, Infantry, and Lancers.
New Zealand : Mounted Rifles (2 Contingents), and Rough Riders (3 Contingents).
Tasmania : Infantry and Imperial Bushmen.
Queensland : Mounted Infantry (4 Contingents).
South Australia : Infantry and Mounted Infantry.
Victoria : Mounted Infantry (2 Contingents), Mounted Rifles (7 Companies), and Infantry.
W. Australia : Mounted Infantry.

CEYLON CONTINGENT.   LUMSDEN'S HORSE.

Total of Troops (Combatants of the three arms only).

	Men.	Horse, Field, and Mountain Guns.
Regulars	107,726	342
Militia	20,626*	—
Imperial Yeomanry	10,195	—
City Imperial Volunteers	1,600	4
Volunteers	9,187*	—
Colonial Troops	39,966*	30
	189,300	376

* Only rough estimate can be given.

CONTENTS OF VOL. II.

—◆-I-◆—

CHAPTER XXIV.—THE HALT AT BLOEMFONTEIN.

CHAPTER XXV.—THE RELIEF OF MAFEKING.

CHAPTER XXVI.—THE SIEGE OF MAFEKING.

CHAPTER XXVII.—BLOEMFONTEIN TO PRETORIA

CHAPTER XXVIII.—OPERATIONS IN THE OUTLYING DISTRICTS.

CHAPTER XXIX.—GENERAL BULLER'S ADVANCE INTO THE TRANSVAAL.

CHAPTER XXX.—THE ADVANCE TO KOMATI POORT.

CHAPTER XXXI.—SOME LESSONS OF THE WAR

WITH THE FLAG TO PRETORIA.

VOL. II.

SIR ALFRED MILNER AND STAFF.

Lieut.-Col. Hanbury Williams   Lieut. Chas. Mitchell Wood   Geo. Vandeleur Fiddes   Sir Alfred Milner   Osmond Walrond   Duke of Westminster
(Military Secretary).   (son of Sir Evelyn Wood, and   (Imperial Secretary).   (High Commissioner   (Private Secretary).   (Aide-de-Camp).
A.D.C. to Sir Alfred Milner).   of South Africa and
Governor of Cape Colony).

KIMBERLEY PEOPLE WAITING TO DRAW THEIR RATIONS OF MEAT IN THE EARLY MORNING (5.30 TO 7.30).

[Photo by Evans.

The rations were reduced to ¼ lb. of meat for each adult and 2 oz. for each child, and for this supply people of all classes had to await their turn. The house on the right is the one in which Mr. Labram, the engineer who made Kimberley's one powerful gun, was killed.

WITH THE FLAG TO PRETORIA.

CHAPTER XVII.

THE SIEGE OF KIMBERLEY.

Mistaken optimism of the Cape Government—The situation at Kimberley—Garrison—Food and water supplies—Defences—Skirmishing commences—First days of siege—Surrender demanded—Boer proclamation garbled by the military authorities—Dodging the shells—Sorties—Red tape absurdities—Death of Scott-Turner—Non-combatants ordered to be ready to leave their homes—News of Magersfontein defeat—Food supply restricted—"Long Cecil"—Second bombardment—Boer artillery greatly strengthened—Shell-proof shelters—Death of Mr. Labram—Mr. Rhodes' abortive appeal for relief—Seeking safety in the mines—The pillar of cloud approaches—Relief force arrives—Losses in the siege—Results of the relief.

SO far back as June, 1899, it had been generally recognised in Kimberley that war was inevitable. The proximity of the town to the Free State and **Mistaken optimism of the Cape Government.** Transvaal kept its inhabitants in close touch with what was going on within the Boer republics and opened all eyes to the reality of the danger. On June 12 the Mayor of the town made strong, but fruitless, representations to Mr. Schreiner, urging that Kimberley was defenceless, that the military force there numbered only 500 volunteers, and that the artillery was quite inadequate. He begged, therefore, for rifles and cannon. But Mr. Schreiner, like the British Government, was blind to the danger. He assured the Mayor that "fears of invasion from the Boer republics are absolutely groundless." In a still later despatch he again told Kimberley there was no ground for alarm. And though for this action he has been bitterly, perhaps justly, attacked, it must be remembered that he was not more to blame for his optimism than the British Government, which had treated warning after warning in precisely the same fashion.

Mr. HENDERSON,
Mayor of Kimberley during the greater part of the siege.

With its suburbs Kimberley totalled in 1899 nearly 50,000 inhabitants, and was in point of population the second city of Cape Colony; in point of wealth the first, though the wealth was concentrated in the hands of a small group of capitalists. It had grown up with the prosperity of the diamond mines, the property of the famous De Beers Company, which had its works there—which was controlled by the man of all most hated by the Boers, Cecil Rhodes—and in which some thirty millions of British capital was invested. The town was for these and many other reasons likely to be attacked by the Dutch—not less on account of the wealth of its mines and the resources afforded by its engineering works than because it had once been Free State territory. Sound arguments, sentimental, military and political, existed to induce the burghers to attempt its capture.

[Photo by Elliott & Fry.

THE HON. WILLIAM PHILIP SCHREINER, Q.C., C.M.G.,

Is the son of a German pastor and an Englishwoman. He was born at the Cape in 1857, educated at the Cape University and Downing College, Cambridge; called to the Bar in 1882, and returned to South Africa to practise; Attorney-General in Mr. Rhodes' second ministry, 1893; Premier of the Cape, 1898, resigned office, 1900; married a sister of Mr. Reitz, many years President of the Orange Free State; though connected with the Africander Bond party, a supporter of Sir Alfred Milner. The author of "The Story of an African Farm" is his sister.

On September 13, 1899, Lieutenant-Colonel Kekewich arrived on special service, to take command of and organise the defences of Kimberley. He had

The situation at Kimberley. been preceded by a number of Imperial officers, the most distinguished of whom was Major Scott-Turner. Already the state of things was highly critical. For "political reasons" nothing had been done to secure the town, yet the forces of the Free State near the border were now mobilised and openly threatening to cut the railway which linked Kimberley with the north and with the sea. On the 18th the construction of earthworks and the equipment of volunteers began, but little progress had been made when in the first days of October the Free Staters drew close to the place. It was notorious that at this date they could have rushed it almost without an effort, and only that extraordinary good fortune which watches over the British Empire prevented them from making the attempt. In early October the outlying British detachments were concentrated, and on October 12 the Boers at last actually began the war by their attack upon the armoured train at Kraaipan. Two days later they appeared at Spytfontein, to the south of Kimberley, broke the railway, and cut the telegraph, just in time to prevent an order reaching Colonel Kekewich to send his handful of regular infantry south, and just after Mr. Rhodes had arrived from Capetown. At this

Garrison. moment the available force in the town was as follows:—

REGULARS.

1st North Lancashires (4 companies), 444 men.
23rd Company Garrison Artillery, 93 men with six muzzle-loading 7-pounder guns.
7th Field Company, Royal Engineers, 51 men.

Regulars, 588; Irregulars, 2,072.

VOLUNTEERS AND IRREGULARS.

Cape Police (from the north), 376 men with two 7-pounders.
Diamond Fields Artillery, 93 men with six 7-pounders.
Diamond Fields Horse, 148 men.
Kimberley Regiment, 299 men.
Town Guard, 1,156 men.

During the war the total strength of the irregulars was gradually raised till at the close of the siege they numbered over 4,000. Thus it will be seen that Kimberley practically provided for its own defence. The Town Guard, however, as a raw undisciplined levy without trained officers, required some weeks of service before it could be risked under fire. It behaved remarkably well, and displayed steadiness and courage. The intelligence of its members made good in great degree the want of

THE GUNS CAPTURED BY THE BOERS AT KRAAIPAN, WHEN THE ARMOURED TRAIN WAS DESTROYED, October 12, 1899.

discipline and experience, and had it been tested in action it would probably have been found to be perfectly capable of fighting the Boers in their own way. The artillery was of wretched, antiquated pattern, with so short a range that it could effect little or nothing against the Boer guns. The defences were earthworks at the most important points, supplemented by barbed-wire fences, barricades, and a thick, almost impenetrable thorn hedge surrounding the town. The enormous heaps of "tailings" round the shafts afforded fine positions for a defending force, and mines were planted in all directions, connected by wires with our works. The Boers feared these even more than they feared our rifles.

But the gravest question was the food supply. Yet, again, that curious good fortune, which appears in all the larger issues of this war to have been upon our side, intervened. In the first place the De Beers Company, notwithstanding Mr. Rhodes' opinion—that war was inconceivable—had laid in immense stocks of coal, provisions, and arms. In the second place a handful of well-to-do inhabitants had foreseen trouble and accumulated stores of tinned food. Then Kimberley did a large business in food stuffs with the neighbouring districts, so that its merchants had their shops and warehouses full, while in the goods yards of the railway were tons and tons of food and forage, much of it originally intended for Mr. Kruger's and Mr. Steyn's forces, and detained by Colonel Kekewich. The new crop of mealies had just been stored within the town, and large shipments of grain and forage from the south and west had just arrived, and the farmers had emptied their barns and granaries to make room for the new crops. The De Beers Company owned great herds of cattle and oxen for the supply of their employés. Lastly, when the line to the north was cut at Kraaipan, all the trains between that place and Kimberley were run south to Kimberley, and in this way nearly 1,000 bags of maize, intended

Food and water supplies.

[Photo by W. & D. Downey.

THE RIGHT HON. CECIL J. RHODES, P.C., &c.

THE DEFENCES AT THE RESERVOIR, AND ONE OF THE GUNS.

for the Transvaal, were brought from under the very muzzles of the Boer guns at Border Siding. Thus a combination of circumstances and the foresight of individuals made good the negligence of two governments and enabled Kimberley to hold out for 124 days without any extraordinary privations.

Not less important than the food supply was the water supply. The water works and pumping station were at Kamfer's Dam, to the north of the town, and three-and-a-half miles from it, but the water was drawn from the River Vaal at Riverton, eighteen miles away. So distant a point could not be held, but fortunately in the Premier Mine at Wesselton, a suburb three miles to the east of Kimberley, were most copious springs which the De Beers Company was able to pump for the use of the inhabitants into the water mains already existing. To supplement this, there was also a large reservoir for use in the extremest emergency. Thus the citizens were spared the horrors of thirst and the results of an insufficient water supply, deadly to a large town in a hot climate.

The ground round Kimberley generally favoured the defence. It was open and level, with no commanding positions for the enemy's siege guns. The line held by the garrison was about eleven

Defences.   miles in extent, including Kimberley itself, its suburbs of Beaconsfield and Kenilworth, and a strong post at Wesselton, where a number of regulars were stationed to guard the all-important Premier Mine. The defences were connected by telephone and telegraph with the centre of the town, where, on the lofty headgear of the De Beers mines, was built a conning tower. On this conning tower Colonel Kekewich kept watch by day; at its foot he slept

by night, with a speaking tube from his room to the officer at the top. From it, by means of a fine telescope, he could watch the movements of the Boers and of his own men, and direct the defence. A flag was hoisted on the headgear whenever the Boers shelled the town; a pennant was the indication

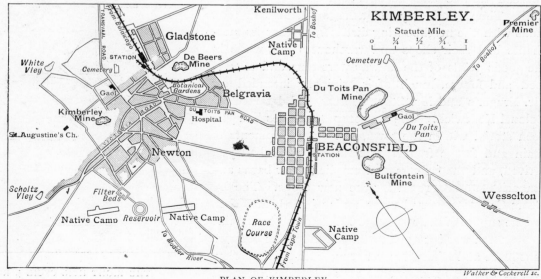

PLAN OF KIMBERLEY.

that the Colonel was watching over the safety of those committed to his charge. As a signal to the defenders of the town to repair to their posts, the "hooters" of the mines were blown at the outset, but it was found that these, with their strident note of alarm, so terrified the nervous among the women that the practice was speedily discontinued.

Skirmishing commences. On October 15 there was skirmishing both to the north and south of the town. On the north the Boers seized Riverton and cut the water pipes. A reconnoitring force went out from Kimberley, but speedily

Photo by Capt. F. J. W. Porter.

THE CONNING TOWER, DE BEERS MINE.

[Photo by J. R. Browning, Exeter.

COLONEL KEKEWICH.

Lieutenant-Colonel Kekewich joined the service in 1874 when 20 years of age. He was promoted from the East Kent in 1890 to a majority in the Inniskillings, and in 1898 appointed to command the First Loyal North Lancashire Regiment. He served in the Perak Expedition, 1874; the Nile Expedition, 1885, and was at Suakin in 1888. For some years he was military secretary to the commander-in-chief at Madras.

retired as the Boers were in some strength. On the south a train pushed down to Spytfontein station, and was fired upon by the enemy with three guns, but without sustaining any damage. That same day martial law was proclaimed, and a mixed military and civil court was appointed to try offenders. A curfew law was put into force, and no one was allowed out in the hours of darkness. The place, however, was full of spies, who gave the Boers full information of every movement. It is even said that at the close of the siege an underground wire was traced from one of the Boer positions to a house in Kimberley, from which the inhabitants promptly fled. This would explain much, as, while the Boers knew everything of our doings, we knew little or nothing of what they were about.

First days of siege. On the 18th the police detachments from Vryburg and Fourteen Streams returned to Kimberley, effecting their retreat with great skill. The Fourteen Streams men retired from their camp by night, leaving lights burning in the tents. At dawn the Boers surrounded

Major Louis Seymour.   Dr. Smartt.   Mr. Rhodes.

[*Photo by Bennett.*

MR. RHODES AT FORT RHODES, KENILWORTH.

the camp, and poured a terrific fire into it for two hours. Then with awe, expecting to find a sea of corpses, they sent a native into it to reconnoitre. Great was their chagrin when they found that they had been simply wasting their ammunition, and that the birds had flown. The early days of the siege were pleasantly exciting to the great mass of the population of Kimberley. Rumours of all kinds passed from mouth to mouth; nothing was too absurd to be credited. Only two days after communications with the south had been broken a great crowd gathered round Beaconsfield station, as it was said that a gigantic naval brigade had engaged and beaten the Boers at Spytfontein, and was on its way to their relief. Little was seen of the enemy; an occasional sniping interchange of fire was the only sign of the Boers' presence, though, as a matter of fact, Free State commandos to the strength of four or five thousand were in the neighbourhood. We have already pointed out the enormity of the mistake made by the Boers in laying actual siege to the town, instead of working south along the railway and invading Cape Colony, when they could have cut the place off every whit as effectually from hope of relief. But their hatred for Mr. Rhodes led them to sacrifice everything to his capture; at a very critical moment Kimberley and Mafeking were the conductors which attracted the Boer lightning and transmitted it harmlessly to earth, thus preventing the storm in its full fury from wrecking the defenceless Cape Colony. Mr. Rhodes, perhaps, did not at the time realise the value of the service he was rendering by thus acting as a bait to the enemy; but it is now manifest and indisputable—recognised by the Boers themselves. His arrival at Kimberley was one more instance of that miraculous good fortune which the history of the war shows to have been always on our side. Though great friction arose between him and Colonel Kekewich, and though notoriously his criticisms did not help to the maintenance of discipline, his presence and his energy made themselves strongly felt. Without him the De Beers Company would scarcely have co-operated in the way it did. Except in his quarrels with the military, he set a fine example, riding out boldly round Kimberley, in defiance of the Boer sharpshooters. He equipped regiments, started relief works, made soup for the poor, and in a hundred ways rendered assistance to the defence. He telegraphed home that he felt as safe as in Piccadilly, and when a correspondent asked him what he would have done had the Dutch captured him on his way up, he answered, characteristically: " Oh, I should have asked them to give me a horse; it is not at all the weather for walking."

October wore away in trifling skirmishes, in one of which a Boer commandant from Boshof was killed. He had been in Kimberley just before the siege began, and had sneered at the small defence force, remarking that it would be a nice mouthful for the Boers to swallow. So far, though the enemy was slowly closing in upon the town, the population suffered little except from the absence of letters and news. But on November 1 great alarm was caused by a terrific explosion near Dronfield. The Boers had blown up the De Beers' stores of dynamite, which, at the demand of the Town Council, had been moved out of Kimberley. It is probable that the explosion was accidentally caused, as the enemy is not likely to have wasted so much valuable war material. Next day a smaller magazine of dynamite blew up in the same direction. On the 3rd the Boers attempted to carry off the De Beers' cattle, and, though driven back, managed to secure a few head of oxen.

On November 4 Commandant Wessels sent in a demand for the surrender of Kimberley. "In case your Honour should determine not to comply with this demand," proceeded his summons, "I

Surrender demanded. hereby request your Honour to allow all women and children to leave Kimberley, so that they may be placed out of danger, and for this purpose your Honour is granted time from noon on Saturday, November 4, 1899, to six a.m. on Monday, November 6, 1899.

TOWN HALL, KIMBERLEY.
Refugees from the suburbs congregated in the space in front of this building.

I further give notice that during that time I shall be ready to receive all Afrikander families who wish to remove from Kimberley, and also to offer liberty to depart to all women and children of other nations desirous of leaving."

The terms of this proclamation were not made public. Instead, a garbled version was published, running as follows:—"Head Commandant Wessels, of the Western Division

Boer proclamation garbled by the military authorities. Burgher Force, O F.S., having made known to the Commandant, Kimberley, that he is willing to receive into his camp any Afrikanders who are desirous of leaving Kimberley, the Commandant hereby gives notice that any persons accepting this invitation will not be allowed to enter Kimberley on any pretext whatever as long as the siege lasts."

It was obviously, both on military and humanitarian grounds, important that as many of the useless mouths as possible should be cleared out of the town. Already the disaster at Nicholson's Nek was known in Kimberley, so that it was evident that the war would not be the short and easy business which most men had at first anticipated. Yet the message of the Boer commander, thus distorted, offered no safe conduct for British women and children, and naturally its terms were not accepted by them. Moreover, suppression of the fact that an opportunity of removing the non-combatants had been given led to unjust and unmerited attacks at home upon the Boers for their inhumanity in pouring shells upon women and children. If fault is to be found with anyone, it must be found with the military authorities at Kimberley. On November 6, the period of grace having expired, the Boers opened fire, but merely pitched two shells into the town. Probably these were intended as a further warning of what was to come, since, on the 7th, the enemy began a much heavier fire, directing their projectiles, which were of 9-pounder calibre, at the Premier Mine. Here they did no damage whatever. Two or three shells fell in the town, but with so little effect that an Irish policeman, close to whom one exploded, took no more notice of the thing than to ask:

[Photo by Deale, Bloemfontein.

FREE STATE COMMANDANTS.

Upper row (reading from left).—Dickson (State Attorney), Snawpoel, Steenkamp, Ferreira, Fick, Potgieter, Wessels, Du Toit, Van der Merwe.
Middle row.—Major Albrecht, Du Plessis, Nel, President Steyn. Olivier, Prinsloo, De Villiers.
Lower row.—Prinsloo, Van Zyl, Du Plooy, Lubbe, Naudi.

"Begod, fwhat will they be playing at next?" On the 11th the enemy began to give more attention to the town, and their shells fell in it right and left, but, fired at extreme range from small guns, did little damage. One Kaffir woman was struck in the streets by a splinter and killed; a Dutch woman died of terror when a projectile landed near her house, and a Dutch cab-driver had his arm broken and one of his horses killed. It was noted with curious interest that in these early days of the bombardment the Dutch and the Boer sympathisers suffered most, in injury both to property and to life. All the week the bombardment continued with much the same result. There were some almost miraculous escapes; for example, a shell fell into the Queen's Hotel, just missing the dining room where thirty people were at dinner, and exploded in the pantry, killing only two cats. Again, the shells were falling about a house, when its inmates left the room in which they had been sitting and went to the door to look out. Hardly had they done so before a shell burst in the room, wrecking it. A woman lying ill was not hurt by a projectile which burst in her bedroom.

THE BOERS FIRING THE FIRST SHELL AT KIMBERLEY.

"Our men," writes Dr. Ashe, from whose deeply interesting diary of the siege most of these facts are taken, "got quite expert in dodging the shells. You heard the gun boom, and a few

Dodging the shells.　　seconds after the 'whiz' of the shell came, and you ducked close under a wall, or earth-bank, or shelter of any sort that was handy, and then the shell burst; immediately everyone in the neighbourhood tore frantically towards it to pick up the pieces, for which there was a ready sale." The moral effect was by no means great. The correspondent of the *Daily Telegraph* tells us: "No doubt there was secret terror and alarm in many a household, but out of doors the people behaved exactly as I have read of their doing during the bombardment of Paris. When they had got over their first shock of surprise and trepidation they looked upon the Boer shelling

much as they would have done upon an exhibition of fireworks. They gathered on the *débris* heaps and on the housetops of double-storyed buildings, and, oblivious of any personal risk, watched with curious interest for every flash and explosion; then, when a bomb burst anywhere near them, they rushed to the spot to pick up fragments. In vain was the danger thus incurred pointed out by the military authorities; the recklessness of the Kimberley gamins, and even of many adults, in their desire to obtain gratuitous supplies of an easily-marketable commodity, knew no bounds. The price of a complete shell, of which there were several in the market, was £5, the base of a shell sold for about a sovereign,

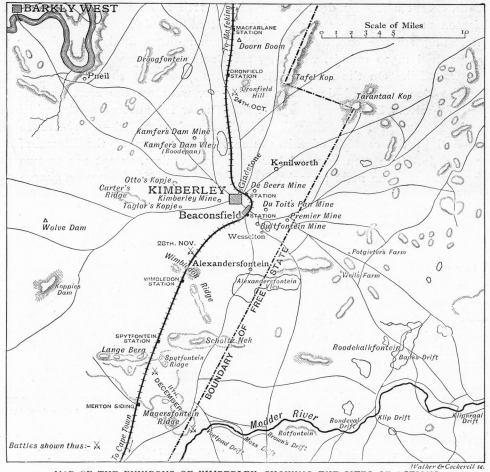

MAP OF THE ENVIRONS OF KIMBERLEY, SHOWING THE SITES OF ACTIONS.

and smaller pieces fetched anything from 2s. 6d. to 15s." To the Boer weapons the wretched little British 7-pounders could make no effective reply. Their range was too short to do any execution.

Sorties. All through November at intervals British sorties were made. Colonel Kekewich has explained that his plan was always to keep the enemy on the alert and in constant fear of attack from

THE BOER REDOUBT AT KAMFER'S DAM,
Whence they fired into Kimberley.

KAMFER'S DAM AFTER ITS EVACUATION BY THE BOERS.

an unexpected quarter, and thus to detain as many Boers as possible to watch the town. Had the garrison remained perfectly inactive, opposing only a passive defence, the Boers could have moved all their force

south, except a few hundred men. On the 11th 250 mounted men, under Major—who was now acting Lieutenant-Colonel—Scott-Turner, reconnoitred towards Kamfer's Dam, and had a sharp skirmish, chiefly interesting for the enormous amount of ammunition fired on each side without result. The British troops fired 2,500 rounds, wounding six Boers; the Boers 7,500 rounds, with a bag of one killed and one wounded. On the 16th an attempt was made to rush a Boer redoubt to the south of Kimberley, but the Boers, warned doubtless by traitors, were on the alert and repulsed the attack, inflicting a loss of twelve. Early on the 25th Scott-Turner led another sortie, which, like the others, was almost resultless, except in its long list of killed and wounded—thirty-five in all—and in the capture of thirty three Boer prisoners of the Bloemhof commando. The men were all low-class Transvaalers, except one or two Cape rebels. The most remarkable feature of the skirmish was a charge executed by the Kimberley Light Horse and Cape Police upon a Boer redoubt. The men had never before used bayonets or even held them in their hands, and, at the very moment when the assault was ordered, a sergeant was giving them instructions in the rudiments of their employment. Several of the troopers actually attacked with their rifle in one hand and bayonet in the other, displaying the most magnificent courage. In this affair Scott-Turner had his horse shot under him, and himself sustained

[Photo by Bennett.

BOER SHELLS FIRED INTO KIMBERLEY.
Above the shell on the right is a time-fuze.

a slight wound. He had already acquired a reputation for great bravery among his men, but, though the Colonials were ready to follow him, they thought him rash. Rightly or wrongly, it was said that

THE CHARGE OF THE KIMBERLEY LIGHT HORSE AND THE CAPE POLICE OUTSIDE KIMBERLEY, November 25, 1899

The men were using the bayonet for the first time, and without any experience of it as a weapon.

he neglected scouting and reconnaissance, as did most of our officers throughout the war, and to this he probably owed the subsequent loss of his life. Still he was so gallant, so kindly, so popular an officer that none would criticise him.

On the night of November 27 the search-lights, which had night after night called into the darkness to the south for news, with their signal ceaselessly repeated, "M D," "M D," at last elicited **Red tape absurdities.** an answer. Out of the darkness flashed "K B," "K B," the call for Kimberley, and touch was established. All waited breathlessly for news, after which the town hungered with a desire born of more than a month's severance from the outside world. Yet it was not till two or three days later that this flippant message, the first transmitted, came through:

[*Photo by Hancox, Kimberley.*

FOUR LEADING DEFENDERS OF KIMBERLEY.
Colonel Kekewich (seated on left), Lieut.-Colonel Scott-Turner (seated on right), Captain O'Meara (Intelligence Officer, standing in the centre), and Lieutenant Mac Innes (Staff Officer).

" Ascertain number on forefoot of mule omitted in Capetown return." Comment is superfluous, but the incident was most unfortunate. Respect for the British Army had been steadily declining among the Colonials, and this want of imagination—for such we must suppose it was —caused genuine bitterness, succeeded, as it was, by a solemn announcement in the garrison orders to the effect that "owing to the loss through death of one mule attached to the 23rd Company W.D.R.A. this animal is struck off the strength of the Company." The same orders contained no mention of the brave citizens who had suffered death or wounds in presence of the enemy. It is quite characteristic that Ladysmith made the same complaint of ridiculous and trivial messages, and that there, too, as at Kimberley, news was systematically withheld. It is also characteristic that when Lord Roberts reached South Africa he changed all this.

To divert the Boers' attention from the attacking force, a great sortie was **Death of Scott-Turner.** planned for the 28th. Fifteen hundred men issued from Kimberley in three columns, each 500 strong, under the supreme command of Colonel Turner. The advance was made towards Carter's Ridge, and Wimbledon to the south of the town. The centre column attacked three Boer redoubts without any adequate artillery preparation. The first and nearest redoubt was rushed without serious difficulty, and a quantity of gunpowder, a waggon-load of shells, and a large amount of clothing captured. Then, in the face of a tremendous fire, the second and third works were stormed, but only with heavy loss. Inside the third work it was seen that a fourth redoubt remained, in which the Boers had a gun. Turning to the devoted handful of men that he had so gallantly led, Colonel Turner cried: "My men, I want to take the next fort and to get the gun. Will you follow me?" They said they would; but at this very instant he was shot dead, and the force left without a leader. Complete demoralisation resulted; by some mischance the appeal for reinforcements of the officer who succeeded Turner never reached Colonel Kekewich, so that the British force had to retire as best it could. Luckily the Boers did not attack, but twenty-two British were killed and two more died of their wounds.   Many of those killed were simply riddled with bullets, and it was said, with what truth only the Boers know, that the enemy killed off those of the wounded who remained alive after the battle.   The death of Scott-Turner cast a deep gloom over the town.   He was buried on the following day, the 29th, amidst universal demonstrations of sorrow.

Meantime, late November and early December passed in anxiety and growing privation.   The military authorities, as was reasonable and necessary, took over the food supply and placed the city on an allowance of meat.   This caused some grumbling among the civilians, whose attitude of criticism had been encouraged by the incidents already mentioned.   No news was given out till it was weeks old; thus the townsmen did not know the result of the Modder River battle till sixteen days after it had been fought.   They heard the roar of the guns bombarding Magersfontein on the eve of the Highlanders' fatal assault; they heard the still louder thunder of the battle all the 11th, and made ready to welcome the troops.   But no troops came; instead, there arrived the painful intelligence that if Kimberley were relieved, the non-combatants must be ready to depart in what they stood in.

Non-combatants ordered to be ready to leave their homes.

They were to abandon everything —houses, property, and clothing —and to go they knew not where. No order provoked such a storm of indignant resentment.   It may have been necessary from the military standpoint, but the friction between the military authorities and the public of the town was thereby greatly increased. Mr. Rhodes, who had pressed the home authorities anxiously for relief, at the time when it was not really needed, remonstrated strongly against the order.   Had attempts been made to carry it out, the consequences might have been grave.   A civil population must always suffer terribly with

THE SEARCHLIGHT AT WESSELTON MINE

With which communication was established between the besieged and the relief force.   During the later stages of the siege the searchlight was surrounded by an armour plated shield, within which the signallers worked.

war in its midst; but here the people of the town could have no refuge, since Capetown and the villages of the Cape Colony seaboard were already overcrowded with penniless refugees from Johannesburg.

The first news of the Magersfontein defeat came to the garrison from the Boer signals, which flashed on the very afternoon of the battle the exultant message—" We have smashed up your fine column."   When the tidings reached the people of Kimberley, which was not till days later, it convinced them that the siege would be a longer, more serious affair than they had thought at first.   There were no more sorties—on

News of Magersfontein defeat.

December 9 there had been a brush with the enemy at Kamfer's Dam, which was the last skirmish fought till the very end of the siege—and there was a dearth of news and of incident. The military regulated the allowance of vegetables as well as of meat; the ration of the latter was now a quarter of a pound a day for adults and half as much for children under twelve. The supply of all such luxuries as milk, condensed milk, and butter was governed by severe restrictions; they could only be issued to invalids on a doctor's order. Consequently there was a sudden and surprising increase in the number of invalids. Vegetables were running very short; a shilling only purchased "five carrots, none of them big, four small parsnips, and nine beetroots, none of them as big as a big radish"—a three days' allowance for four people. The military authorities from an early date in the siege had regulated all prices; they now "commandeered" supplies and retailed them themselves—sometimes making an exorbitant profit, which was neither just to the merchants, who had been paid much less, nor generous to the citizens. Early in the new year horseflesh was issued for the first time, and though no one went into raptures over it, it was soon found to be palatable. A good story is told of Colonel Peakman, the commander of the Kimberley mounted forces, in connection with its first appearance. That day at the officers' mess he said: "Gentlemen, I am sorry that we were unable to get all our ration in beef to-day, and had to take part of it in horseflesh. This, which I am carving, is beef, the horse is at the other end, and anyone who prefers it can help himself." All chose the supposed beef, but when they had made an excellent dinner, the Colonel suddenly exclaimed: "By Jove! gentlemen, I find I have made a mistake in the joints; this is the horseflesh, and the other is the beef."

According to Dr. Ashe, if he had not known what his ration was, he could not have distinguished it from beef. It had a slightly different taste, and was darker in colour, but was "tender and good enough for anything."

Grave difficulties arose as to the feeding of the natives in the town. At the outset there were from 12,000 to 15,000 of them, and though there was plenty of corn stuffs for them, such a diet without any vegetables was found to cause terrible outbreaks of scurvy. As vegetables were essential, Dr. Ashe set to work to find a remedy. It occurred to him that the leaves of the thorny aloes round the town, when boiled and fermented, would make an excellent anti-scorbutic drink. The experiment was made, with the

Food supply restricted.

[*Photo by Bennett.*

FUNERALS OF LIEUT.-COLONEL SCOTT-TURNER AND NINETEEN MEN KILLED IN ACTION, KIMBERLEY, November 28, 1899.

best results; later still the green shoots from the vines at Kenilworth were issued as a kind of salad. But about this date the native trouble was greatly alleviated by Mr. Rhodes, who found means to get 8,000 "Kaffirs" out of the town and through the Boer lines. Apparently the Boers wanted them to work on the fortifications at Magersfontein and elsewhere, as previously they had turned back all who attempted to get out of the town. Another step taken by Mr. Rhodes was the starting of great relief works for the poor of the place.

During the weeks of dull and listless monotony, Mr. Rhodes and the De Beers Company in other ways came to the assistance of the defence.

"Long Cecil."

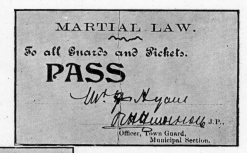

The head of the De Beers engineering works was an American named Labram, a man of great distinction and resource in his profession. In November he constructed a large cold storage room, and started making shells for the British 7-pounders, which projectiles were stamped "with C. J. R's. compliments," as a kindly

reminder from Mr. Rhodes to the enemy. Even earlier, he had been anxious to manufacture a powerful gun so as to annoy the Boers effectually, but the military doubted either his capacity or the practicability of carrying out the offer, and so did not encourage him. However, none the less he set to work in December, studied all the books he could get on gunnery and a file of *Engineering*, and prepared drawings. His rough material was an ingot of steel, 10½ feet long and 10½ inches in diameter. From this he calculated he could make a 4·1-inch gun firing 28-lb. shells. Special tools were constructed for the rifling of the gun, and finally "Long Cecil," a breech-loading weapon of original design, mounted upon a carriage made under his orders, emerged from the De Beers shops, after twenty-four days of unremitting work. During the making of the weapon the workshops were constantly under fire. "It was very trying," writes a Kimberley engineer, "for a man to stay at work at a lathe or other machine, hearing shells bursting all around and not knowing in the least whether the next would come inside or not." On January 19, at last, the gun was ready for trial, when its extreme range, to the delight of all, was found to be 8,000 yards. On the 23rd it was handed over to the military; it fired from first to last 255 shells in action. Its appearance astounded the Boers and was an extraordinary monument to the skill and fertility of resource of the distinguished De Beers engineer.

Meantime, the Boer artillery had increased in number and in power. On January 24 began a second and far **Second bombardment.** more serious bombardment with nine 12- and 15-pounders, stationed all round the town. On this and the two following days no less than 900 shells were thrown into the place, but without

From "The Sphere."

A SIEGE BABY
(Miss Agatha Oliver, born in Kimberley during the siege).

causing any serious loss of life. The daughter of the first man killed in the Rhodesian rebellion was among the victims; in another house the wife of a volunteer and two small children were badly wounded. There were some very narrow escapes. A shell burst close to a native working at one of the mine heaps, riddled his hat and left him unharmed. Another burst under the bed of an Indian woman who had just been confined and set the bedding smouldering, but did not harm her. Another dropped down the chimney of a house and burst on the hearth, but with so little effect that a woman in another room did not know what had happened. "No one can imagine the relief it was when the shelling ceased," writes Dr. Ashe. "It was not altogether a question of fear; but the knowledge that wherever you are, a shell may drop on you at any moment, and that you have to do your work all the same, does not much exhilarate you." Yet all went bravely about their work, and few gave way to panic. Bomb-proofs were in a few instances constructed for the women and children, though not systematically or at the order of the military authorities.

DIVINE SERVICE IN THE NATIVE QUARTERS.
The negroes in their native land, as in America, throw themselves with great fervour into their devotions. The Sunday rest from labour and from bombardment left them at liberty to worship in peace.

Meantime, alarming reports were current in the town to the effect that its relief would not be attempted in the immediate future. Lord Roberts had already telegraphed this message— "Hope I shall not be compelled to leave you in the lurch"—for so dark was the situation that it seemed more troops might be needed in Natal. The favourite scheme, too, of an invasion of the Free State from the south was again engrossing military attention. It was supposed that this must infallibly draw off the Boers from Kimberley. Such was not Mr. Rhodes'

"LONG CECIL," THE 4.1-IN. GUN MANUFACTURED AT THE DE BEERS COMPANY'S WORKSHOPS.
Mr. George Labram, engineer to the Company and designer of the gun, stands with his arm on the wheel. Mr. Labram was subsequently killed by a hundred-pounder shell in a room of the Grand Hotel.

belief, and with the instance of Mafeking as a touchstone, it is now certain that he was right. Many hard things have been said of him for emphasizing his conclusion and for the appeals which he made to Lord Roberts to effect an early relief. But there has always been a not unnatural tendency for men to clamour for special attention to be shown to the particular field of war in which they are present, and it cannot be denied that the loss of Kimberley would have been a terrible blow to the British cause.

After the second bombardment, there were rumours that another and fiercer one, with heavier weapons, would be tried, and the rumours proved to be well founded. On February 7 the roar of a big gun was heard in the town. "There was a big boom," says Dr. Ashe,

Boer artillery greatly strengthened.

"then a tremendous whiz somewhere over or near the house I was in, and then, by and by, a good big boom when the shell burst." For some days the Boers had been busy mounting a 6-in. Creusot, which with ease threw shells just under 100 lb. in weight, charged with melinite, into every part of the town. This terrible weapon shook the earth so that the

CASTING SHELLS AT THE DE BEERS WORKSHOPS.

seismograph, five miles distant and five feet under ground, clearly indicated when it was fired. No shelter had been prepared against its prodigious bolts, which tore through walls and houses, spreading terror and destruction. "All day long," says the correspondent of the *Daily Telegraph*, "the inhabitants were kept in a perfect agony of nervousness, for the shells came at such uncertain intervals that it was not safe to leave the shelters for five minutes. I myself while at the club had a rather alarming experience. About three o'clock in the afternoon a big shell pierced the side wall of the entrance lobby of a photographic studio, smashing a portrait of Mr. Rhodes, and toppling over some specimens of our locally-manufactured 28-pounder and 7-pounder shells which were on exhibition in a glass case. The projectile, encountering no further resistance, made its way into the street, and burst into many pieces in the roadway. One of these fragments, weighing $13\frac{1}{2}$ lb., crashed into the verandah of the club opposite, considerably splintering the woodwork, and a smaller piece hit one of the members in the leg. So tremendous was the shock of the explosion that all who were in the club at the time believed for the moment that the shell had burst against the building. I made my way out through the blinding smoke, and found the street full of people, who had escaped in the most marvellous manner with their lives, and were now scrambling as eagerly as children for the fragments of shell.

A scared mother came elbowing her way through the crowd holding in her arms a little baby bleeding at the neck. The poor woman was half demented with anxiety and terror, but the little one was happily more frightened than hurt. A local barman was in his bedroom in the upper story of an hotel, when he heard a shell whistling overhead. He put his head out of the window to see where the shell was going, and was almost instantly decapitated. Two iron buildings occupied by Chinamen were completely telescoped, and how the occupants managed to get out is a mystery, but the affrighted Celestials, white as a sheet, scuttled away somehow like rats leaving a sinking ship, and,

[*Photo by Bennett.*

WHAT A HUNDRED-POUNDER SHELL DID.
Effects of its explosion in Market Square, Kimberley.

strange to say, they were perfectly uninjured." The shells played strange, ironical tricks. A patient of Dr. Ashe's jestingly asked him to prescribe a draught which would make his knees feel stronger when the gun went off. The next instant there was a heavy boom and a shell landed in the shop next to the patient, all but destroying it.

On February 8 shelters were made by most people. They were holes dug in the ground with an opening away from the gun, covered over with balks of timber, iron, and earth. But the intense heat of Kimberley in the summer made these refuges almost unbearable, and tortured the women and children beyond endurance. A sys-

Shell-proof shelters.

tem of signalling was devised by Colonel Kekewich to tell the inhabitants when to run to earth. On the conning tower a bugler watched the gun, and directly he saw the puff of smoke sounded the alarm and waved a red flag. From the time of the smoke being seen to the arrival of the shell there was a period of fifteen seconds, if a sharp lookout was kept. Other watchers were stationed in other places to sound whistles and hammer iron bars which were suspended

THE SEVENTH AND EIGHTH REDOUBTS AT KIMBERLEY.
Partly made of inverted trucks from the mines.

as a cheap kind of bell, and the noise of which could be heard for a long distance. The Boers fired chiefly at the conning tower on the De Beers shaft, at the Town Hall, and at the Sanatorium, where Mr. Rhodes had taken up his quarters. But their marksmanship was so bad that they never hit their target; they did, however, succeed in producing a state of great alarm amongst the civilian population.

On the 9th the town had one of its worst shellings. The Boer method was to point the gun at some particular target—for instance, the conning tower—and fire six or eight shots as rapidly as was possible. Then while the big weapon was cooling down, they slewed it round and would fire in another direction. There were again some amazing escapes. One of the 94-lb. shells fell into a room where a lady was in bed, bruised her slightly, broke the bedstead, and buried itself in the foundations of the house without exploding. Had it exploded it would have wrecked the house and blown her to bits. The last shell of the day inflicted an irreparable loss upon the defence. It entered a bedroom of the Grand Hotel where Mr. Labram, the De Beers engineer, was dressing, exploded and mangled him most terribly, killing him instantly, but without scratching a native servant who was in the room. Death seemed to have marked him as its own, for before the day on which he was killed he had had several of the narrowest escapes.

Death of Mr. Labram.

[Photo by Bennett.

HOW THEY LIVED IN KIMBERLEY DURING THE BOMBARDMENT.
Families sheltering in bomb-proof dug-outs. The lower photograph shows a "model village" on the property of the De Beers Company.

On the morning of the 10th the bombardment continued, but very languidly. The reason was that picked marksmen had been placed as near as possible to the gun, and whenever the Boer artillerymen showed themselves even for a moment, they found themselves the target of a dozen rifles. Several artillerymen were killed, and M. Leon, the French engineer of the Creusot Company, who in defiance of France's outward neutrality was directing the bombardment, was severely wounded. What would Frenchmen have said, we wonder, had Lord Armstrong, in the Madagascar war, despatched a trained expert to direct the Malagasy artillery? In the evening, however, just as Mr. Labram's funeral was leaving the hospital, a rocket went up from one of the houses in Kimberley, and instantly the big gun started a most rapid fire. Several shells fell close to the procession; others crashed in and round the hospital where lay the sick and wounded, expecting each moment to be their last. "I felt so ill," said one of the patients, "that my heart stopped beating each time, from the bugle call till the crash, and then it went on with a leap that nearly suffocated me. I think that dreadful night took ten years off

THE SOUP KITCHEN AT THE DE BEERS CONVICT STATION.

[*Photo by Hancox, Kimberley.*

The siege soup was made from ox meat with vegetables supplied from the De Beers gardens at Kenilworth, and retailed at cost price, 3*d.* per quart. The group on the left of the photograph consists of Mr. and Mrs. Rochefort Maguire and Mr. Rhodes, who, with Captain Tyson and Dr. Smartt, organised the kitchen. The soup was carried round on the trolley shown in the background.

my life." And thus the burial service was said in the darkness over one who had stood bravely to his post in the hour of danger, with death and destruction on every side—to the accompaniment of the boom of the gun and the whiz of the shell, the crash and flare of its explosion, and the heavy metallic clatter of its splinters as they fell all around.

So great was the alarm caused by the gun that on the morning of the 10th Mr. Rhodes and the Mayor of Kimberley had addressed one more appeal to Lord Roberts, which, however, the military authorities refused to transmit lest it should bring to bear upon the Field-Marshal pressure which he—a man of cool and deliberate judgment—would be unable to resist. The message was in this wise:—

"Kimberley, February 10.—On behalf of the inhabitants of this town we respectfully desire to be informed whether there is an intention on your part to make an immediate effort for our relief. Your troops have been for more than two months within a distance of little over twenty miles from Kimberley, and if the Spytfontein hills are too strong for them there is an easy approach over a level flat. This town, with a population of over 45,000 people, has been besieged for 120 days, and a large portion of the inhabitants has been enduring great hardships. Scurvy is rampant among the natives; children, owing to lack of proper food, are dying in great numbers, and dysentery and typhoid are very prevalent. The chief foods of the whites have been bread and horse-flesh for a long time past, and of the blacks meal and malt only. These

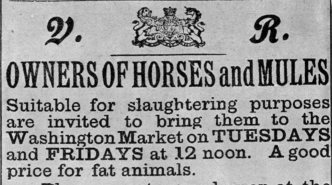
[*Photo by P. Pope, Kimberley.*
PREPARING MR. RHODES' CHRISTMAS PUDDINGS FOR THE TROOPS.

Mr. Rhodes' abortive appeal for relief.

hardships, we think you will agree, have been borne patiently and without complaint by the people. During the last few days the enemy have brought into action, from a position within three miles of us, a 6-in. gun, throwing a 100 lb. shell, which is setting fire to our buildings, and is daily causing death among the population. As you are aware, the military guns here are totally inadequate to cope with this new gun. The only weapon which gives any help is one of local manufacture. Under these circumstances, as representing this community, we feel that we are justified in asking whether you have any immediate intention of instructing your troops to advance to our relief. We understand large reinforcements have recently arrived in Cape Town, and we feel sure that your men at Modder River have at the outside 10,000 Boers opposed to them. You must be the judge as to what number of British troops would be required to deal with this body of men, but it is absolutely necessary that relief should be afforded to this place." Instead of this, it was intimated to Lord Roberts by the military authorities that Mr. Rhodes was anxious to surrender, if the town could not be at once relieved. This was scarcely a fair construction to place upon his representations, but his quarrels with Colonel Kekewich were such that now neither was on speaking terms with the other. The friction between the military and civil elements was daily increasing.

Lord Roberts replied to the distorted version of Mr. Rhodes' message in these terms :—" I beg you to represent to the Mayor and to Mr. Rhodes as strongly as you possibly can the disastrous and humiliating effect of surrender after so prolonged and glorious a defence. Many days cannot possibly pass before Kimberley will be relieved, as we commence active operations to-morrow. Future military operations depend in a large measure on your maintaining your position a very short time longer."

FACSIMILE OF AN OFFICIAL ADVERTISEMENT.

SERVING RATIONS TO THE LANCASHIRES DURING THE SIEGE OF KIMBERLEY.

The latter part of this message, at Mr. Rhodes' instigation, was published to the inhabitants, to console them and nerve them to the sternest endurance under the hail of shells from the 6-inch

Seeking safety in the mines.

gun. Meantime, Mr. Rhodes took steps, in view of a more terrible bombardment on the 12th—Sunday, the 11th, being, as was customary with the Boers, a day of truce—to place the women and children in security. A notice was issued advising them to proceed to the shafts of the Kimberley and De Beers mines, when they would be lowered into the mines. 2,500 people availed themselves of this offer, and the work of lowering was accomplished rapidly and without misadventure.

On the 12th, 13th, and 14th the shelling continued languidly. All these days curious clouds of smoke were seen in movement to the south, and from time to time firing was heard in that direction. Intense excitement prevailed, as no one could gather exactly what this portended, and hope long deferred had been succeeded by the resignation of despair. Anxiously these mysterious clouds were watched and their cause debated. No one in Kimberley had ever before seen a great army on the march, or known that a pillar of dust is the first indication of its approach. In that clear atmosphere the dust raised by the hurried march of the tens of thousands of British troops could be seen at a vast distance. The pillar of cloud moved always northwards—towards Kimberley—and in this fact there was reason for bright anticipations of rescue. On the 14th there were other signs that

something of great importance was happening to the south. For on that day it was found that the Boers had abandoned their strong position at Alexandersfontein, four miles from Beaconsfield. The place was at once occupied, and a few hours later four Boer waggon loads of stores walked into it and were captured. A large amount of welcome loot, in the shape of butter, vegetables, meat, and poultry, was captured, but the Army Service Corps promptly impounded all it could get—and rightly, as the siege might still be much prolonged. One man, however, carried away two pounds by tying it on his arm, and bandaging the arm in a sling, as though he had been wounded.

Alexandersfontein was reinforced, as it was feared that the Boers would attempt its recapture. On the afternoon of the 14th the columns of smoke to the

PLACARD SENT ROUND THE TOWN BY MR. RHODES.
Some 2,500 persons availed themselves of the invitation.

[*Photo oy Knight, Aldershot.*

LIEUTENANT-GENERAL KELLY-KENNY, C.B.

Major-General Thomas Kelly-Kenny, who commands the Sixth Division in South Africa, with the local rank of Lieutenant-General, was born in 1840; entered the Army as Ensign in the 2nd Foot, 1858; he served as orderly officer to Brigadier Jephson in the Chinese War of 1860, and was present at the taking of the Taku Forts; and he commanded a division of the Transport Train in the campaign in Abyssinia in 1867-8. Major-General, 1897; Inspector-General of Auxiliary Forces and Recruiting, 1897; appointed to his command under Lord Roberts in December, 1899.

17

[*Photo by Wilson, Aberdeen.*

VIEW OF KIMBERLEY FROM ROCK SHAFT.

south were much nearer, and seemed to be all round the left flank of Magersfontein. Hope revived, but was not yet very confident.

The pillar of cloud approaches.

With the morning of the 15th the Boers vigorously attacked Alexandersfontein. The Boer small guns poured in a heavy fire, and on the right the British were hard pressed. Then, in a moment, miles away a cloud of horsemen was seen upon the veldt. If they were Boers the situation was hopeless; Alexandersfontein must be rushed and captured. The little 7-pounders were trained on them as they galloped forward; the Union Jack was run up; all made ready to do and die. But looking, it grew clearer and clearer that they were uniformed and khaki-clad. The air rang with cheering; the Boers took to headlong flight, and Rimington's Scouts came dashing into Kimberley at the head of General French's advance. In a moment, almost without notice, Kimberley was relieved. The great news spread rapidly. From the De Beers and Kimberley mines emerged hundreds of women and children, "like rabbits from their burrows," and Kimberley spent a night of intoxicating joy, for ever freed from the terror of the great 6-inch shells.

Relief force arrives.

The town had not suffered in loss of life so much as might have been expected during its 124 days' siege. As officially returned, the casualties among the combatants were 38 killed,

ALEXANDERSFONTEIN.

133 wounded, and 4 missing. Disease made greater ravages. The deaths among the civilians averaged 200 a week during the last period of the siege. The mortality was greatest among the natives

Losses in the siege.

and among babies and children, the first suffering from scurvy and the last from the want of fresh milk. In all, the deaths were 1,694, of whom 161 were European adults. Typhoid, dysentery, and scurvy steadily increased as the food supply was more and more restricted. Most distressing, perhaps, of the casualties, though making no appearance upon paper, were the cases where women and children lost

Mr. H. A. OLIVER,
Mayor of Kimberley at the time of its relief.

their reason from sheer fright. The death rate among the small children mounted with alarming rapidity when the real stringency of the siege began to be felt—in December. In October, the rate for children under one year was 302 per thousand; in November, 330; and in December, 844.

For his valiant and skilful defence of the town, Lieutenant-Colonel Kekewich was most

Results of the relief.

deservedly promoted a full Colonel. His position was an awkward and difficult one; but the difficulties were as much within as without the town. The management of a large civil population in a fortress — and such Kimberley had unexpectedly become—is never an easy task. The Colonel made his dispositions admirably; with a caution which events amply justified he avoided all dangerous

LIEUT.-COLONEL CHAMIER, R.A.,
Second in command under Colonel Kekewich.

adventures, and it is possible that the casualties in the sortie in which Scott-Turner and so many

---

V R

PROCLAMATION NO. 12.

Whereas

It is deemed necessary to regulate the sale and supply of **Foodstuffs and Necessaries,**

Now, Therefore,

I, ROBERT GEORGE KEKEWICH, Lieutenant-Colonel Commanding Griqualand West and Bechuanaland do hereby proclaim and make known:—

1. That from and after Thursday, the 28th December, 1899, the allowances to Consumers per head per day shall be as follows:

	SUPPLIES.		EUROPEANS AND COLOURED COLONIALS.	ASIATICS.	NATIVES.
(a)	BOER MEAL	...	6ozs.	Nil.	Nil.
(b)	FLOUR	...	4ozs.		
	or BREAD	...	14ozs.	,,	,,
	MEALIE MEAL				6ozs.
	KAFIR CORN MEAL	}	2ozs of either	2ozs of either	4 ,,
	SAMP				2 ,,
	RICE	...	2ozs	8ozs	Nil.
	SUGAR	...	2 ,,	2 ,,	2ozs.
	TEA	...	½ ,,	½ ,, Tea, or	½ ,, Tea, or
	COFFEE	...	½ ,,	½ ,, Coffee	½ ,, Coffee

2. Any European or Coloured Colonist desiring to obtain Food Supplies shall, not later than 3 p.m. on the day prior to that on which such supplies are required, make and forward to the Office of the Issuer of Food Supply Permits regulating the Supplies for the Ward in which such person resides a declaration, in writing, giving full, accurate, and detailed particulars of all or any Supplies in his or her possession or control of any of the Foodstuffs or Necessaries enumerated in Section 1 of this Proclamation.

3. Every such person shall be bound to make and forward to the place and at the time mentioned in the last preceding Section a declaration showing the number of the members of the household of such person, and giving such other information as the Declaration Forms to be issued shall provide.

4. Any duly authorised Issuer of Food Supply Permits may issue a permit for such of the Foodstuffs and Necessaries hereinbefore enumerated and he shall be satisfied is necessary for the requirements of any applicant, but he may refuse to issue any permit should he deem it advisable to do so. In all cases of refusal to issue a permit the Issuer shall make an entry of the grounds of such refusal in a book to be kept for that purpose.

5. Any person applying for Supplies shall make application for a week's Supplies, and such person shall not be entitled to again apply for Supplies until the same day in the following week.

6. The person to whom any Food Supply Permit is issued may purchase and obtain the Foodstuffs or Necessaries mentioned in such permit, on production and handing over of such permit, at any Retail Store or Shop where the same are kept.

7. Every Retail Storekeeper Dealer or Salesman who owns, possesses, or controls any of the Foodstuffs or Necessaries enumerated in Section 1 of this Proclamation shall be bound on presentation, during business hours, of any Food Supply Permit to sell, supply, and deliver to the holder of such permit the Foodstuffs and Necessaries mentioned therein on payment being made therefor in cash, at the prices already or which may be hereafter fixed in respect thereof by Proclamation or Notice duly published.

8. No Storekeeper, Dealer, Salesman, or other Person shall sell, supply, or deliver any of the Foodstuffs or Necessaries mentioned in Section 1 of this Proclamation to any person other than the holder of a Food Supply Permit.

9. That all Food Supply Permits in respect of which Foodstuffs or Necessaries shall have been supplied by any Storekeeper or Dealer shall be forwarded to the Supply Office Lennox Street, Kimberley, when such Storekeeper or Dealer sends in his weekly requisition for further supplies.

10. Proprietors, Managers or Keepers of Hotels, Clubs, Cafes, Restaurants, Boarding Houses, or Eating Houses shall only be entitled to obtain supplies for their regular boarders.

11. Asiatics shall only be supplied at the Food Supply Depots specially appointed for the supply of Foodstuffs and Necessaries to Asiatics, and all Asiatics applying for supplies shall be bound to observe and comply with all rules and regulations from time to time exhibited in the Food Supply Depots for Asiatics.

12. Natives shall only be supplied at the Food Supply Depots specially appointed for the supply of Foodstuffs and Necessaries to Natives, and all Natives applying for supplies shall be bound to observe and comply with all rules and regulations from time to time exhibited in the Food Supply Depots for Natives.

13. Notice will be given by advertisement of the offices where Food Supply Permits may be obtained and of the places where Food Supply Depots are established for the supply of Asiatics and Natives.

14. Any Storekeeper, Dealer, Salesman, or other person whosoever who shall fail, neglect, or refuse to observe or comply with any of the provisions of this Proclamation, or who shall make an incorrect or false declaration, or who shall act in any way whatsoever contrary to the terms of this Proclamation, shall be liable to summary arrest, and to such penalties or punishment (including confiscation of goods) as to the Special Court of Summary Jurisdiction shall seem meet.

15. Every Storekeeper or Dealer shall be held liable and responsible for any act of his agent, assistant, or servant in contravention of any of the provisions of this Proclamation, and shall be punishable for the same, as well as such agent, assistant, or servant.

16. Notice No. 3, dated the 3rd day of December, 1899, signed by Major Gorle, is repealed as from the date of the publication of this Proclamation.

17. This Proclamation shall apply to the Districts of Kimberley and Beaconsfield (including Wesselton).

Given under my hand at Kimberley this 26th day of December, 1899.

GOD SAVE THE QUEEN.

R. G. KEKEWICH.

Lieutenant-Colonel, Commanding Griqualand West and Bechuanaland.

NOTICE NO. 8.

PUBLISHED IN TERMS OF PROCLAMATION No. 12.

It is hereby notified that the undermentioned are the Offices for issue of Food Supply Permits to Europeans and Coloured Colonists:

KIMBERLEY: Town Hall.   BEACONSFIELD: Town Hall.

2. Food Supply Depots where food may be obtained by Asiatics and Natives:

KIMBERLEY:—

ASIATICS: No. 6, The Crescent, Malay Camp.

NATIVES: No. 1 Location, Railway Crossing, Transvaal Road; No. 2, Barkly Road; Meyer's Location, No. 3 Halkett Road; Malay Camp, No. 2, The Crescent.

BEACONSFIELD:—

NATIVES and ASIATICS: Dutoitspan and Wesselton, Gregory's Store, Castle Street.

NATIVES: Green Point and Race Course Locations, Capetown Barrier Store, Maikoroane's Location, Boshof Road Crossing Store.

By Order.

Kimberley, December 26, 1899.   H. V. GORLE, Major, A.S.C.

REDUCED FACSIMILE OF THE PROCLAMATION OF December 26, 1899,
Regulating the supply of food in the beleaguered town, as published in the *Diamond Fields Advertiser.*

of the garrison lost their lives, were incurred because his orders were not obeyed to the letter.

Though he may have seemed cold and stern, and though his staff did unquestionably make mistakes in matters of tact, his services were great and undeniable, and he had the infinite satisfaction of keeping the flag flying. For the Boers the siege brought nothing but chagrin and disappointment. They sacrificed very much to take the town, and they did not take it. It was said that there was no time when they could not have rushed it; but, with the light which the war has shed upon the stopping power of the modern magazine rifle, this is at least

[*Photo by Shelley.*

BRITISH MAXIM AT OTTO'S KOPJE, NEAR KIMBERLEY.

doubtful. The younger Boers are known to have importuned Cronje to permit them to make the attempt; his answer invariably was that the republics could not afford to lose men, fathers and heads of families, in such an assault. In arriving at this decision he was, with-

WATCHING THE RELIEF FORCE.
7-pounders trained on the approaching horsemen.

out doubt, greatly affected by his knowledge of the complete failure of the attempt to carry Lady-

smith on January 6. Colonel Villebois Mareuil, the French filibuster, however, had matured and was preparing to carry out a plan for storming Kimberley, at the very moment when Lord Roberts began his operations for its relief. Naturally the Boers could not execute this plan, but if they had made the attempt, and even if by chance they had succeeded, their

KENILWORTH BARRICADE, FORMED OF THE TRUCKS USED IN THE MINES.

losses must have been enormous, since the magazine rifle has given to a small force of men behind well-designed earthworks the power of stopping almost any assault. The enemy might have had a better chance of compelling the surrender of the city had they begun their bombardment with the 6-inch gun earlier and concentrated every available heavy weapon

DU TOITS PAN ROAD, KIMBERLEY.
Du Toits Pan Road is the main street of Kimberley, in which are the principal shops, St. Cyprian's Church, the Public Library, the Club, the Masonic Hall, and many other buildings. To the left of the picture is Jones Street, which leads to the Market Place and to the Diamond Market and the local Stock Exchange.

against the place. A month's vigorous shelling might quite conceivably have accomplished that which a week's languid shelling failed to effect. But the truth is that they never credited Kimberley with the ability to resist either a prolonged siege or a short bombardment; they reckoned, in fact, without Colonel Kekewich, for whose singular capacity they did not make due allowance. When week after week passed, and month after month, and the town still held out, rage succeeded confidence, and blinded the Boers to the expediency of a prompt retreat from their positions to the south of the town. Indeed, not the least of the many services which Kimberley rendered to British interests, was that it was the direct cause of the presence of Cronje at Magersfontein, and the indirect one of his defeat at Paardeberg.

As a military achievement, the defence of Kimberley will always occupy an honourable place in history. Without any adequate assistance from the Governments responsible for the safety of the town, with only a handful of trained soldiers to protect it from attack, its defenders improvised a

[Photo by Hancox, Kimberley.

NATIVES AT WORK ON "SIEGE AVENUE."
Mr Rhodes's "relief work" for the unemployed, consisting of an avenue of vines a mile long, will remain as a lasting memorial of the siege.

garrison, and its inhabitants contrived to procure food sufficient to carry them through a four months' siege. The difficulty of the defence was increased by the perfect intelligence which the enemy could always obtain of all that was happening within the town, from traitors and Dutch spies.

[Photo by Hancox, Kimberley.

CARNARVON HOSPITAL, KIMBERLEY, WITH THE MEN WOUNDED IN THE SORTIES.

ON THE HEELS OF THE BOERS
Mounted infantry attacking a waggon train.

HIGHLANDERS FROM MAGERSFONTEIN ARRIVE AT WATERVAL.

The British prisoners in the hands of the Boers were originally accommodated on the racecourse outside Pretoria. About the end of the year 1899 a fresh
enclosure was prepared for them at Waterval, a short distance away from the town.

CHAPTER XVIII.

THE TRAPPING OF CRONJE.

Importance of capturing Cronje's force—The Boers evacuate Magersfontein—The British Army moves in a new direction—The
Sixth Division gives chase—Fight at Klip Kraal—Converging movements—Cronje's retreat intercepted—His fatal choice
—He entrenches himself at Paardeberg—British positions—Who commanded?—Preparations for battle—A frontal
attack inevitable—The enemy tries to break out—Attempts to rush the Boer position—Loss of Kitchener's Hill—British
casualties—The battle a mistake—An armistice demanded and refused—Lord Roberts arrives—The circle closed—The
Boer shelter-pits.

WITH the relief of Kimberley the first of the Grand Army's tasks was accomplished;
but the second, the more difficult and infinitely more important work of capturing
General Cronje's army yet remained to be achieved. Probably Lord Roberts had
calculated that his turning movement, from its excessive wideness, would at first
escape the notice of
the enemy, and thus
avoid the risk of pre-
maturely alarming the Boers. But what
would happen when
Importance of captur- General French with
ing Cronje's force. his cavalry reached
Kimberley, and the infantry divisions
occupied the line from Waterval Drift
to Klip Drift, could not be accurately
foreseen. If Cronje were wise, if he displayed the insight of a great general, abandoned his baggage, and marched post-
haste along the north bank of the Modder
to Bloemfontein, he could scarcely be
stopped. If, however, he clung to his
waggons, there was hope of surrounding
him, since the ox and mule waggons
used in South Africa are not capable of
travelling as fast as good infantry upon
veldt roads. And the well-known reluct-
ance of the Boer to part with such valuable assets as waggons and their teams was
a point in favour of the British general.

[Copyright 1900 by Underwood & Underwood.

A DRINK BY THE WAY.
Hurrying horses to the front for the R.H.A.

THE BOER POSITIONS AT MAGERSFONTEIN AFTER
THEIR EVACUATION.

When dawn of February 16 broke, Cronje's army was beginning its retreat upon Bloemfontein from the Magersfontein position, General French and his horsemen were resting round Kimberley or chasing the Boers to the north of the town, and the Sixth Division, under Generals Kelly-Kenny and Lord Kitchener, was holding

Boers evacuate Magersfontein.

Klip Drift, where skirmishing had been proceeding all the 15th with small parties of the Boers flying from Magersfontein or left behind by General French's rapid and daring movements. As the day rose over the limitless brown plain, all eyes in the British camp at Klip Drift were turned towards the west and north—towards Magersfontein, whose kopjes loomed up in the grey light, and towards Kimberley, in which direction General French had vanished. Then out of the twilight came the first clear sign of an army on the march. To the north a great cloud of dust was seen moving slowly over the plain. It headed north-eastwards, so that it could not be from General French. It was, in fact, the dust raised by Cronje's 4,000 men and 400 waggons.

As yet the precise direction of his retreat could not be ascertained, but all probabilities pointed to the fact that he was moving towards the main road from Kimberley to Bloemfontein, which crosses the Modder a short distance above Klip Drift, at Klip Kraal Drift. If so, he would strike into it at Klip Kraal. Another possibility was that he might follow the river as far as Koodoesrand Drift, still higher up, and then turn north to Boshof. But such a move was unlikely, as it would uncover Bloemfontein in the presence of a powerful British army, and expose it to easy capture.

The moment it was realised that Cronje was in retreat, the most vigorous measures were taken to arrest

The British Army moves in a new direction.

him. Lord Kitchener telegraphed the all-important news to Lord Roberts, and despatched messengers to General French, summoning his cavalry to the work of heading off the enemy. The Seventh Division was ordered to push one of its two brigades to Klip Drift and support the Sixth, the other

BILLY MUFFIT'S GOAT.
Pet goat of the Scots Guards taken from the Boer trenches at
Magersfontein.

with Lord Roberts' headquarters would follow later from Jacobsdal; the Ninth Division was to concentrate at Wegdraai, to be ready to advance in whatever direction might be ordered. No more could be done till the exact course of Cronje's retreat had been ascertained, for it was not yet certain that the column of dust veiled his whole force. The army was thus to effect a rapid wheel to the right, instead of continuing its northward advance. But not only had the divisions and brigades at an hour's notice to change the order and direction of their movements; the transport columns also, without which in that barren melancholy land men and horses must have been starved, had to alter all their arrangements. It is said that Lord Roberts, before he ordered the new dispositions, sent for the indefatigable head of the Army Service department with his force, and asked whether he could guarantee full supplies during the movement. " I cannot, sir," was the answer. " Three-quarter rations ? " " No, sir." " Half ? " " I cannot answer for it." " Quarter-rations ? " " Yes, sir." " Well," said Lord Roberts, " I think they will do it for me," and he was right. But a less determined, a less beloved general might well have shrunk from running so immense a risk or from laying so terrible a burden upon the physique and endurance of his men. For what if the move failed—if, as was quite possible, heavy reinforcements reached the Boers from Colesberg and from Ladysmith— and Lord Roberts' force was severely handled, as all the British armies had been in the previous weeks of war ? And what if the horrors of

CRONJE ON HORSEBACK.

starvation were piled upon the agony of defeat ? The loss of the immense convoy on the Riet, with its 200,000 rations of beef, and biscuit, and forage, was one which, at this juncture, only the most desperate exertions could make good. It meant short commons for every one of the officers and men during a most trying and arduous week.

Meantime, Lord Kitchener with the Sixth Division took immediate steps to

The Sixth Division gives chase.

harry and delay the Boer retreat. The mounted infantry were despatched at their best pace to get into touch with Cronje's column and work to the north of it, cutting it off from Boshof. The Thirteenth Brigade under General Knox marched rapidly along the north bank of the Modder—which river, to the east of Klip Drift and between that point and Klip Kraal Drift, bends sharply to the north—with the object of getting between the enemy and the important series of fords in the neighbourhood of Paardeberg. The Eighteenth Brigade under

A DUTCH AUCTION.
Selling the clothes and belongings of a comrade killed in action.

General Stephenson advanced behind the Thirteenth. On their part the Boers made counter-preparations to delay the British attack. A strong rearguard strove by vigorous skirmishing to compel the continual deployment of our men, always retiring before it could be closely engaged. There were few casualties incurred in this irritating work, but time was gained by the enemy.

Towards 11 a.m. on February 16, the Boers were compelled by the weariness of their waggon teams, exhausted by the prolonged march in a suffocating cloud of dust under a broiling sun, to halt at Drieput Farm, which lay half-way between Klip Drift and Klip Kraal Drift. Their rearguard seized a position on some kopjes two miles further to the east, from which, after prolonged shelling by the 81st Battery,

it was driven back to Drieput. Here was a yet stronger line running along a series of kopjes north-westward from the river. Already signs of Boer distress were manifest. Here and there waggons had dropped behind and had fallen into the hands of the Sixth Division, the men of which pressed forward with all the more ardour and eagerness as they realised what a splendid prize was slipping from their grasp. Perspiring under a sun whose rays beat down upon their heads with all the fierceness of the tropics, gasping for breath in the dense red cloud of dust which choked mouth and nostrils and caused a torturing thirst, not to be assuaged by the few drops of the tepid muddy fluid, called water in the Free State, that remained in the water bottles, the men of General Knox's splendid brigade of infantry marched magnificently in pursuit. It was the sorest and sternest trial of British endurance that had yet been inflicted in this war, though it was as nothing to the efforts which were to follow. So fearful was the fœtor and the heat in the long column, so extreme the want of air in that burning simoom, tossed up by the trampling feet of thousands, that for all their pluck and zeal men every moment dropped overcome to the rear. And close upon the march, merging into it without intermission of time, came battle, fierce determined battle

[*Photo by Elliott & Fry.*

MAJOR-GENERAL CHARLES E. KNOX,

Commanding the 13th Brigade of the 6th Division of the South African Field Force, was born in 1846. Entered the army in 1865; Major, 1883; served under Sir Charles Warren in the Bechuanaland Expedition in 1884-5, when he raised and commanded the 4th Pioneer Regiment; Lieut.-Colonel, 1885; Colonel, 1889; appointed to his command in South Africa with local rank of Major-General, 1899.

with a redoubtable enemy, superior in force, but to be held fast at all cost. Men dying with thirst passed into the firing line to die of bullet and shell wounds. In the memory of those who fought through this and the following days, the scene dwelt with but the shadowy indistinctness of some awful nightmare; heat and dust, and hunger and thirst, and showers of bullets, combining to torture and madden suffering men till it seemed that there was no limit to human agony.

Against the Drieput position the British troops deployed in very open formation. On the right were the Oxfordshires, in the centre the West Riding battalion—keen, valiant

Fight at Klip Kraal.

Yorkshiremen from the moors and looms of that far-off county, which has ever prided itself upon the bravery of its sons—and on the left the Gloucesters. The East Kents feinted on the right, to cut the Boers off from the river; the 81st Battery plied the southern end of the enemy's position with shrapnel; and the mounted infantry in the river bed and on its banks endeavoured to turn the Boer flank and to get in between the Boer rearguard and the convoy, which was now, after its rest, resuming its retreat. The enemy had good cover; the British force was not markedly superior in numbers and was particularly weak in mounted men and guns, without which little could be accomplished. Frontal assaults under such circumstances had been strictly forbidden by Lord Roberts, with an eye to what had happened at Belmont, Enslin, and Modder River. All that resulted from the British attempts to work round the flanks was a persistent interchange of fire—a featureless battle, destitute

BRIGADIER-GENERAL THEODORE EDWARD STEPHENSON,

Commanding the 18th Brigade in South Africa; Captain, 1881; Major, 1883; Lieut.-Colonel, 1895; Colonel, 1899; left for South Africa in November in command of the 1st Essex Regiment; distinguished himself at Paardeberg, and was promoted to the command of the 18th Brigade, Sixth Division, on the march to Bloemfontein. This Brigade, including the 1st Yorks, 1st Essex, 1st Welsh, and 2nd Royal Warwicks, was transferred to the Eleventh Division, and was led by Lord Roberts into Pretoria.

of episode and incident. As the afternoon went on a naval gun joined in from the south bank of the river, firing at long range upon the enemy. The East Kents were now moved across the rear of the British line to its other flank, and directed to feint against the Boer right, as no impression could be made on the enemy's left. In this quarter the mounted infantry were checked and driven back by the Boer fire, the acting colonel of Kitchener's Horse, Captain Vaughan, receiving a severe wound, notwithstanding which he kept his place in the field. Colonel Macdonald, in command of the British artillery, was also severely wounded. Night fell upon an indecisive field, and the British had won no apparent advantage. But already General Stephenson with the other brigade of the Sixth Division had crossed the river at Klip Drift and had made all preparations for a forced march at earliest break of day along the south bank of the Modder towards Paardeberg. His advance would place him astride of Cronje's line of retreat to Bloemfontein. The fight at Drieput—or Klip Kraal, to call it by its official name—had given the Boers, it may be, time to withdraw some of their waggons, but it had also given the British time to call up reinforcements from all quarters, now that it was certain Cronje's main force was speeding eastward along the Modder.

The British losses in this skirmish were not serious: 11 men were killed, 107 wounded, and 7 missing. It is impossible to say what the Boer casualties were, but there is excellent reason for thinking that they were quite as heavy, though they were returned at 8 killed and 12 wounded—the usual fiction. Cronje maintained his position until late into the night; then, perhaps hearing the tramp of General Stephenson's Brigade marching along the south bank to cut him off, held a council of war. Many commandants are said to have been for an immediate surrender, supposing that the British cavalry would already have worked to their rear. But when morning dawned and no cavalry were in sight they plucked up heart. Seventy-eight waggons, the teams of which were unable to bear the strain of further marching, were abandoned, and the whole force struck east for the Paardeberg and Koodoesrand Drifts.

Already other troops than those of the Sixth Division were moving impetuously to intercept them. From Wegdraai and Jacobsdal one brigade of the Seventh and the whole Ninth Division were marching on the morning of the 17th at their best speed—a long and

Converging movements.

terrible march—towards the Paardeberg Drifts. The morning cool gave place to the sweltering heat of noon; noon in turn yielded to night, and still the column of dust raised by 10,000 men moved slowly and steadily to the strategic point. It was a march which put in the shade even the achievements of the Sixth Division. "The track was very heavy, there often being from two to three inches of sand," says a medical officer with the troops; . . . . "We had regular halts every half-hour for a few minutes, and I, along with many others, went absolutely to sleep during these short intervals. Our course was north-east, making for Klip Drift, on the Modder; this we—the baggage guard —reached at 7.30, having travelled sixteen miles. Our men were greatly fatigued, and many fell out. We tried to induce them to struggle on, which they did, telling them that as we were the rearguard they would simply be left on the veldt at the mercy of the enemy. . . . On

PLAYED OUT.
A burst gun at Modder River Camp.

halting at Klip Drift, we immediately got down our dizies and made tea for all; without it we were too parched to swallow the biscuits. . . . At 9.15 we got orders to march again at once, and heard that the baggage was to follow us at 2. With a weary heart we started to jog on again, and as the heat increased it tried our pluck and endurance to the utmost. On and on we marched. We saw a kopje a few miles in front of us, and then we cheered up, saying our halting-place must be just over on the other side. But no, it was not, and still we jogged on. Soon the jog became a stagger, and you would have thought all our troops were composed of old men, with their chins on their chests. My pony was also done up, hanging down her head, even though I had spared her by walking as much as possible. The officers on foot were in as helpless a state as the men.

"When we had gone fourteen miles (how, I know not) we came to a few huts and to a pond. To the latter we all rushed. The water was too filthy to drink — even our horses refused it; anyhow, this was our

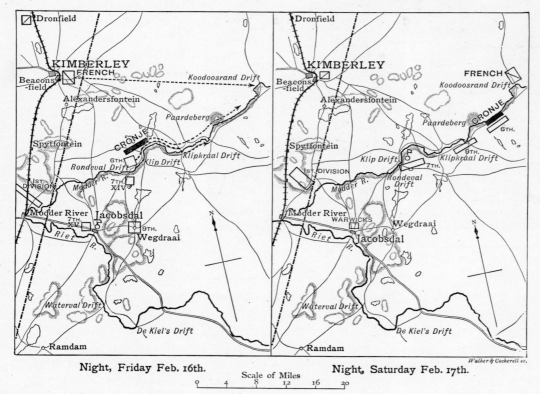

Night, Friday Feb. 16th.

Scale of Miles

Night, Saturday Feb. 17th.

Walker & Cockerell sc.

These maps, in conjunction with those on pp. 348, 352, give a complete view of the operations which resulted in the relief of Kimberley and the capture of Cronje.

halting-place, we thought, and the men lay down exhausted, with their helmets covering their faces. In ten minutes an order came to resume marching, and a few of us found out that we had four more miles to cover. With the greatest difficulty we got our troops up, by means of a mixture of discipline and encouragement. How could we march for twenty-one hours with only three biscuits in our stomachs? But we did it. The stragglers increased, but as a whole our companies staggered steadily on."

And from another quarter yet a fresh converging movement was proceeding. As the 17th broke, General French's men — or rather such of them as were in condition to march — were riding out of Kimberley. 1,200 horsemen of Broadwood's Brigade, the only one of the three whose horses were fit for work, and three out of the seven Horse Artillery Batteries left at 3.30 a.m., with orders to push on at their very best speed for Koodoesrand Drift, where Cronje was to be met and headed. General French himself left Kimberley an hour later, after giving instructions to his other brigades and batteries to follow as soon as they could. Even General Broadwood, noted though he was for his care of his horses, could not have made the required move had he not been able to borrow a large number of remounts from the Diamond Fields Horse and from the De Beers Company. All the morning the horsemen rode as hard as they could; about 7 a.m. a short halt was ordered, but not for very long. As the brigade sped over the veldt, herds of game — buck, hares, and birds, strange to English eyes — fled before it, until about 10 a.m. the green trees on the banks of the Modder came into sight. "The excitement," writes the gallant Captain Boyle, who rode with General French, "was intense. On our left we saw a fairly large body

Allan Stewart.]   [*After photographs.*

LORD ROBERTS WITH HIS STAFF AT LUNCH ON THE MARCH.

of men moving eastward. Was this Cronje's force? At 11.15 we debouched into the plain from behind a long range of kopjes, and the fact of surprising the farm of Kameelfontein, with its Boer inhabitants and taking some Boer waggons, increased our hope that Cronje would be taken by surprise."

Immediately the horses were ordered to be watered at the farm, which lay just six miles north of Wolveskraal Drift, which is one of four drifts crossing the Modder between Paardeberg and Koodoesrand Kopjes. The westernmost of the four is Paardeberg Drift, just under the lofty flat-topped kopje, 300 ft. high, from which it takes its name; then come Wolveskraal and Banks Drifts, in order from west to east, and last of all Koodoesrand Drift. The river Modder here, as elsewhere, flows in a broad bed, which it only fills in times of heavy rains; its banks are high and much intersected by dongas or small water courses.　Along these banks grow almost the only vestiges of trees to be found in the dreary, brown desert of the veldt; mimosas and willows break the arid expanse of plain and rest the eye with their greenery.　Towards the river General French rode forth a little way to reconnoitre, and to his joy saw that his prize was there.

Three miles away a long line of dust rose over the plain, and through it journeyed in unending procession the 300 waggons and

Cronje's retreat. 4,000 odd horsemen of General Cronje.　As the British cavalry leader looked, he saw the head of the great procession peacefully descending to the river bed at Wolveskraal Drift, all ignorant that a determined and powerful force watched upon the flank of its line of retreat to Bloemfontein.　The movements of the British cavalry had been hidden by the kopjes from the Boers, so that what followed was to them a terrible surprise. An orderly was sent back at full gallop by General French to bring up the guns at a walk.　A walk

A WORK OF MERCY:
Giving a cup of water to a dying foal.

[*Photo by H. C. Shelley.*]

was necessary if the inevitable dust was not to announce their coming to the unsuspicious enemy.　The guns were to take post upon the gently rising ground, afterwards known as Artillery Hill, 4,000 yards north of Wolveskraal Drift.　Just behind the ridge and out of sight of the enemy the eighteen 12-pounders unlimbered; at 12.15 p.m. a shrapnel crashed into the waggons near the drift and told Cronje that his retreat was intercepted.

The moment must have been a terrible one for the Boer leader.　What his feelings were we do not know, for he was not a communicative man.　But he must in an instant have realised his extreme peril. Here on the road to Bloemfontein were the ubiquitous British cavalry, who had already taught him one lesson by bursting through his lines into Kimberley.　He could not know their precise strength and disposition; it was at least probable that the whole 4,000 odd horsemen and forty-two guns were there upon his line of retreat—a force with which his four or five guns and 4,000 weary burghers could

NATURE'S SCAVENGERS.
Clouds of vultures awaited the last struggles of the dying animals which lay dotted along the line of march.

not hope to contend on equal terms.　Behind him, too, were the ominous pillars of cloud that marked the coming of the British infantry.　What hope could he have if he delayed?　The moment had come—the psychological moment—when the presence or want of good generalship is manifested in the leader.　Cronje had to make his fateful choice.　He might abandon his 300 waggons, his ammunition, and his cannon, and beat the hastiest of hasty retreats with such of his mounted men as could run the gauntlet of General French's fire.　Or he might cling to waggons and guns and trust to the stupidity of British generals,— who from his experience were only too ready to run their heads against a brick wall,—to extricate him from his entanglement. Perhaps for a moment he lost his coolness of judgment in this terrible situation, else he should have seen that even a new Modder River or Magersfontein battle could not save him. The disturbing element was the presence of General French's large mounted force. However the British infantry might be cut up, this force would still remain to strike him the minute he harnessed his teams and resumed the retreat.

He made his choice. It was to cling to his waggons. Forthwith a small party of Boers dashed out to seize a kopje on the British right, known thereafter as Roberts' Hill, but the British cavalry **His fatal choice.** raced and beat them. The Hussars were first, seized the hill, and drove off the enemy in confusion. Down by the river the Boer waggons were gathering in a laager, and presently two Boer guns pushed out and opened fire on the Horse Batteries. But two guns against eighteen could effect nothing, and were speedily silenced; then the bulk of the British weapons turned their attention to raining shell upon the laager, while one battery devoted its efforts to a kopje held by the Boers who had been driven back from Roberts' Hill. No response was made

F. Dadd, R.I., & S. T. Dadd]   [After a sketch by G. D. Giles.

THE 10TH HUSSARS FOIL THE BOER ATTEMPT TO SEIZE ROBERTS' HILL.

to the fire; that it was effective was proved when half-a-dozen waggons burst into flame and ammunition began to explode right and left. The Boers around the laager had already fallen to digging trenches; they could be made out in scattered parties working like ants with their spades, to win shelter from the showers of shrapnel. They had reason for their frantic efforts. Gazing over the plain the British cavalry could discern far away to the south-east the dust of the advance of General Kelly-Kenny's Sixth Division. But it approached the scene of action with appalling slowness, or so it seemed to the anxious watchers. The sun set and yet it had not arrived. To guide it upon its way, as the day went down, the Horse Batteries opened a heavy fire, and the glare and crash of their shells served as a beacon through the darkness of a pitch black night to the weary, thirsty infantry.

General French's horsemen had to bivouac as best they could, with no shelter and only what they could loot at Kameelfontein to eat. The three days' rations with which the troopers had left Klip Drift on the morning of the 15th, where they had not been judiciously eaten at once by those who thought it best to carry their food in their stomachs rather than in their haversacks, had for the most part been lost in the fierce charge which preceded the relief of Kimberley. At Kameelfontein little was to be found except sheep and cattle, but some of these were rounded up, and on them the troopers fared passably. The horses were in worse plight. There was no corn for them to eat, and they had to do the best they could for food, grazing on the veldt. The losses of horses were naturally heavy; they had started in bad condition, their strength had been taxed to the utmost, and they felt the heat, the hard work, the want of water, and the short commons far more than the men; 990 out of 4,800 in the division had already fallen, though the casualties among the troopers did not as yet number 50.

SCOTS GUARDS WITH LOOT FROM THE TRENCHES
AT MAGERSFONTEIN.

The Guards remained with Lord Methuen at Modder River, watching Cronje, during the turning movement. As soon as the Magersfontein trenches were found to be empty they were examined and looted, and the photograph represents some of the odd articles appropriated by the Scots Guards; umbrellas, an accordion, &c.

Meanwhile, Stephenson's Brigade of the Sixth Division had crossed the Modder at Klip Drift, and thence marched in the very early morning of the 17th to Klip Kraal Drift, along the southern bank of the river, while Knox's Brigade had marched along the north bank, skirmishing with the enemy. At Klip Kraal, after a long halt during the heat of the day to rest the men, Knox's Brigade crossed to the south, and the whole division continued its advance towards Paardeberg. The mounted infantry were sent on ahead and directed to occupy the ground to the south of the point where the Boers were found. The infantry followed painfully in an unending line, along the awful tracks which in that country do duty for, and go by the name of, roads. Behind the Sixth Division marched the Ninth with the 65th Howitzer Battery

OFFICERS WATCHING AN ENGAGEMENT NEAR JACOBSDAL.

in its charge. The veldt was shrouded in night long before either of these two divisions reached their appointed bivouacs. By a fortunate accident part of the mounted infantry overshot the mark and marched well beyond and to the south-east of Wolveskraal Drift. This placed them between Cronje and Bloemfontein, thus completely barring the enemy's retreat. But the gap was not closed till far into the night. During the early hours of darkness Cronje had a chance, his last chance, of escape. Had he stealthily drawn off his 4,000 combatants, abandoning the waggons and baggage, he could still have got away. De Wet and many other of the Boer leaders in his place would have nerved themselves to the sacrifice.   No efforts of the British cavalry in the pitchy blackness could

He entrenches himself at Paardeberg.

have availed to stop him.   But once more Cronje allowed his contempt for his enemy and the extraordinary fondness of the veldt Boer for waggons and cattle to detain him.   He spent the night in entrenching himself against the attack, which he divined, with true Boer instinct, would come with day.

In the British bivouacs the weary infantry cooked as best they could the miserable half rations, which were all that the supply trains could

British positions.

afford them.   The Sixth Division was near the Paarde-berg drift ; the Ninth some little distance behind. Some of the men had the emergency ration, but not all ; fortunate, indeed, were its possessors. The night, as always on the veldt, was icy cold after the fierce heat of day, so that there was no intermission in the suffering of the soldiers. Yet so exhausted were the men that they fell asleep in spite of cold and empty stomachs. But the sleep was not for long.   With the peep of day of the 18th the Boers opened a sharp rifle fire upon the mounted infantry.   And thus began the battle of Paardeberg, the fiercest and most terrible of the war after Spion Kop.

The absence of official reports and des-patches renders it extremely difficult from this point onwards to give an even approximately

GORDON HIGHLANDERS GETTING THEIR BREAKFAST.

FIXING UP THE CAMP KITCHEN OF THE GORDON HIGHLANDERS.

accurate account of what happened. The battlefields of this war, under the

Who commanded?

new conditions in-troduced by smoke-less powder, long range weapons, and magazine fire, covered such an extent of ground that no one correspondent could give a coherent version of the whole action.   Individual officers and soldiers, except when they were with the staff with means of knowing the orders issued, would have even less op-portunity of ascertaining what was hap-pening.   In battle the soldier's attention is concentrated upon his immediate surroundings ; of necessity he is unaware what is transpiring at a distance.   So complete is our ignorance at home of events that it is not yet known definitely and certainly who was in command of the British Army—whether General Kelly-Kenny or Lord Kitchener.   The fact must be recorded as one of the most extraordinary things in history ; but it is not so extraordinary as other facts which are to follow in the later course of the war. The remarkable system of promotion devised by our War Office, and based on seniority, left Lord Kitchener, though Chief of Lord Roberts' Staff, inferior in nominal rank to one of the division commanders of the Army. Whether in virtue of his office as Lord Roberts' representative, Lord Kitchener took precedence, may be debated. It is probable that he did, but there is nothing definitely to prove it, and the correspondents contradict one another on this subject.

With the coming of morning and the beginning of the sputtering fire from the Boer trenches, the Boer position was anxiously examined by General French on the north bank of the river and Lord Kitchener on the south. Each looked eagerly to see if the enemy was still in the river bed, or if he had snatched his last opportunity and escaped in the night. But to the vigilant eye of General French it was clear that the waggons were just as they had been the evening before; there was no dust cloud on the horizon, and no indication whatever of a hurried flight. The Boers, as always, were invisible, but that they were there few now doubted. From the south Lord Kitchener could see the great cluster of waggons, the smoke of the camp fires, and the signs of human life in the line of greenery that parted the desolate expanse of the veldt. The infantry realised with fierce exultation that another task had been successfully performed, and that at last the redoubtable Boer leader had been run to earth. "We've got him at last," ran along the line of expectant men. But to drag the fox from his earth, how was this to be accomplished? By main force, or by waiting till hunger did its inevitable work? Only in the last case there was danger of the other Boer armies, with the interior lines in their favour, hurrying to the spot and interfering with the progress of the

GENERAL KELLY-KENNY, COMMANDING THE 6TH DIVISION, AND STAFF.

investment—perhaps of their effecting a rescue and snatching the prey at the last moment from the mouths of the hounds.

It is not probable that what followed was intended to be more than a reconnaissance in force. But, whatever the intentions, it speedily developed into a first-class battle, as when the troops were once

Preparations for battle.

engaged it was impossible to extricate them, and more and more men were drawn into the conflict. Between the British camp and the Boer position stretched a level plain absolutely devoid of shelter, and shelving gently to the river. Not an ant hill, not a heap of stones, not even a mimosa bush, broke its monotonous surface. None the less, while the mounted infantry returned the enemy's fire and skirmished in the river bed to the west of the Boer laager, the Sixth Division marched down the gentle slope, first in the direction of Paardeberg Drift; then, when it was seen that the Boers were farther to the east, towards Wolves-kraal Drift. On the right was General Stephenson; on the left General Knox. They deployed to the south of the Boer laager, while simultaneously fire was opened by the artillery; General French's horse 12-pounders shelling the Boers from the north bank; the 76th, 81st, and 82nd Field Batteries, the naval guns and the 5-inch howitzers pouring in projectiles from the south. But though the laager could be seen and its waggons bombarded with effect, the Boers themselves were out of view, and this shelling caused them small harm.

As the Sixth Division deployed for battle, the Ninth Division began to arrive on the British left. The Highland Brigade under General Hector Macdonald marched in, full of fight, notwithstanding the sufferings of the past day and night, and relieved a detachment of mounted infantry in the river bed to the west of the laager, whereupon the mounted infantry moved round across the rear of the British line and came into action on the left of the cavalry and to the east of Wolveskraal Drift. The envelopment of Cronje on the northeast, east, and south, was now complete; it remained only to close up the north-west, which still lay open. General Smith-Dorrien with the Nineteenth Brigade of the Ninth Division was directed to cross the river to the north bank, and attack from this side. On the northeast reinforcements were on their way to General French. General Gordon with the sorry remnant of a brigade, 160 out of some 1,200 mounted men with whom he had begun the campaign, was riding from Kimberley. Even of this 160, 120 had been

W. Hatherell, R.I.] [After a photo by Reinhold Thiele.
THE CANADIANS (OF THE NINTH DIVISION) CROSSING PAARDEBERG DRIFT, February 18, 1900

horsed by the Diamond Fields Horse. So terrible was the plight of the surviving horses, that the 9th Lancers could only muster twenty-eight fit for duty, and only three Horse Artillery batteries could be utilized.

The British infantry, a long line of khaki-clad men, now entered the zone of fire. On the right, to the south of the river, were the 1st Welsh and 1st Essex; in the centre the East Kents, Oxfordshires, West Ridings, and Gloucesters; on the left the Argylls, Royal Highlanders, and Seaforths. As the line was prolonged to the north of the river by the successive arrival of General Smith-Dorrien's battalions, the Shropshires, Canadians, and Gordons came into action in this quarter. The important kopje, known as Kitchener's Hill, directly south of the Boer laager and to the rear of the Sixth Division, was held by three companies of Gloucesters. Just under it were the two farms known as Osfontein and Stinkfontein, the latter, with its pond of filthy, stagnant water, richly deserving its name.

A NIGHT ATTACK ON A KOPJE.
The picture records an incident in the pursuit of Cronje, when the Gloucesters engaged a party of the enemy until nightfall, and then captured the kopje at the point of the bayonet.

As was their custom the Boers held their fire, allowing the British infantry to close to within about 1,000 yards. Then here, exactly as at the Modder River battle, which in most of its details this new fight upon the banks of the self-same stream closely resembled, they poured in a vehement magazine fire. Once more the British infantry found itself committed to a frontal attack upon an entrenched position under precisely those circumstances which the futile and indecisive actions fought by Lord Methuen's division in the past had made so painfully familiar. To rush the Boer camp, held by 4,000 determined men armed with the finest modern rifles, was impossible. Yet from hour to hour ground was gained. To the east the Welsh and Essex battalions succeeded in pushing back the Boers; to the west, on the north bank, the Canadians and Shropshires pressed forward with impetuous valour. Splendid indeed was the conduct of the Canadians, and such as to make the mother country proud of her children.

A frontal attack inevitable.

Over all the tumult and carnage of the confused battlefield, the burning rays of the pitiless sun beat down upon the living and the dead, till men went mad for want of water. So desperate

S. Paget.]

[*After a sketch on the spot by W. B. Wollen, R.I.*

THE BATTLE OF PAARDEBERG, Sunday, February 18, 1900.   French's cavalry are in the plain below, and Cronje's laager is seen towards the left where the clouds of smoke and dust from the lyddite shells
The picture is taken from the position of the Sixth Division.   are rising.   Our guns are posted on the left in the far distance.   The line of bushes indicates the course of the Modder River.

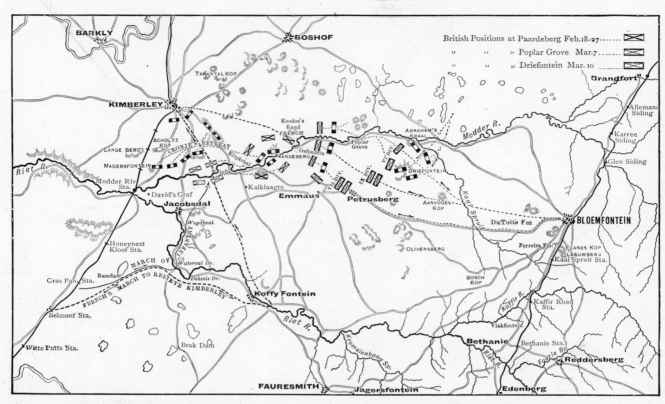

GENERAL MAP OF THE MOVEMENTS OF THE GRAND ARMY BETWEEN MAGERSFONTEIN AND BLOEMFONTEIN.

was the desire that men would boldly expose themselves to the Boer sharpshooters in the river, if only they could drink, preferring death or wounds to the anguish caused by the suffocating heat and the parched throats choked with dust. The roar of artillery, the ceaseless crackle and sputter of the rifle filled the baking air, and from the ground the heat waves danced, unsettling the aim of the prone infantrymen. At times the Horse Artillery guns to the north-east of the laager, while playing upon it and enfilading it, sent their shrapnel dangerously near the British attack from the west. The Highlanders in particular seem to have suffered actual loss from the fire of our own guns. Such incidents are probably inevitable, with the very finest management, on a field of battle of immense extent, and with the invisibility which has come since smokeless powder was adopted.

HARD MARCHING.
Bandaging a sore foot.

To strengthen the firing line the Gloucesters were withdrawn from Kitchener's Hill and replaced with a squadron of Kitchener's Horse. At

The enemy tries to break out.

this point a new force of Boers moving from the south and southeast—commandos hurriedly called up from Bloemfontein and Colesberg to succour Cronje—began to attack, and the British infantry and artillery found itself between two fires. At the same time the Boers in the laager made a determined attempt to break out towards the east, but were met and held in check with the most superb coolness by the Welshmen. Bullets came, or seemed to come, from all sides, and added to the perplexities and embarrassments of the terrific struggle.

Noon passed and the sky suddenly darkened. Thunder clouds gathered and a tremendous storm raged over the heads of the combatants. The rain descended in sheets—a boon to the thirst-tortured men—the roar of the thunder peals dominated even the crash of the artillery, and the lightning played with dazzling radiance over the veldt, adding to the terror and grandeur of the spectacle. On all sides the attack on the Boer position was being pressed. A crackling circle of jets of flame from the British rifles encompassed it, while the intensely bright flashes of fire from the forty guns in action showed up vividly in the momentary gloom, and the whizz and dull boom of the shells, alternating with the horrible clangor of the two Boer "Pom-Poms," held the attention in the intervals between the claps of thunder. From the west General Smith-Dorrien's men broke forward in a determined rush, Canadians, Gordons, and Shropshires commingled. Yet they failed

Attempts to rush the Boer position. to reach the Boers, though they steadily drove them back. Now it was that Colonel Aldous led his Cornishmen upon the enemy's trenches with the cry, "Let us make the name of the Cornwalls ring throughout the world!" He was splendidly supported; furiously opposed. But no living thing could win through the hail of bullets that was poured in upon him and his men. He fell; his adjutant fell; and more than ninety of the splendid battalion that he led bit the dust. The 81st Field Battery, which was supporting their rush, was severely handled by the Boers, and only the constancy of its escort of Gordons saved it from capture.

On the west, led by General Hector Macdonald, the Highlanders rushed at their enemy, burning to avenge the defeat of Magersfontein and to show their mettle. The General was wounded in the foot by a Mauser bullet, and his horse killed beside him as the wound was being dressed. The

Seaforths charged with the bayonet and forced back the Boers, many of whom hid themselves in the trees on the river banks, and thence directed a deadly fire upon the British infantry. The British, however, were not to be denied. They reached the river, and pouring down to it drank eagerly of the turbid liquid which it afforded. A number of the Highlanders crossed the stream and joined in the attack

O. Eckhardt.]   [After a sketch by W. B. Wollen, R.I.

THE CORNWALLS DRIVING THE BOERS FROM THE RIVER BANK.

of Smith-Dorrien's Brigade, while in exchange a wing of the Cornwalls from this same Brigade aided the Highlanders. Here, as elsewhere, there was the same splendid bravery on the part of the men, and the same complete failure to secure a decisive advantage. When ammunition ran short in the firing line, one private displayed conspicuous courage, rising on more than one occasion, walking coolly back for cartridges, and distributing them among his comrades. But the Boer sharpshooters marked him and he fell dead.

To the south the Sixth Division were busy all along the line, advancing with invincible bravery or beating back the attempts of the enemy to break out. "There was a continual flight of bullets about us," writes a soldier of the Oxfordshires. "I dreamed of a battle the night before, but I never thought it could be as terrible as this. We were mad with thirst, and our officers flopped down like ninepins." General Knox was wounded on the left; on the right the West Riding men, in a fierce onfall, had occasion to use the bayonet, but, though they inflicted some loss upon the enemy, they suffered heavily themselves. Nor could anything excel the impetuosity of the Welshmen, who strove to storm their way down the river bed on the east. They advanced with such fury and resolution that, in one party of twenty-five who essayed to enter the Boer laager, all but one were killed or wounded. It was a fight to the death. On the north of the stream, in the wild intoxication of battle, Colonel Hannay led the most extraordinary manœuvre that has ever been attempted in war. He rode his mounted infantry at a gallop upon the laager, but was killed with many of his men before he could close. There were some signs in this quarter of an effort on the part of scattered Boer parties to escape; these were defeated, however, by the fire of the mounted infantry and the demonstrations of General French's horsemen.

Yet further to the south the party of Kitchener's Horse, which had been detailed to guard Kitchener's Hill, was for some unexplained reason at Osfontein Farm, watering the horses and cooking a meal. A man in khaki, who looked like a British officer, but was more

Loss of Kitchener's Hill. probably a Boer scout, had told them that British troops occupied all the points near. The Gloucesters, it will be remembered, had for a time occupied Kitchener's Hill, so that it is just possible that he spoke in good faith. Be this as it may, the British horsemen had off-saddled and were off their guard, when suddenly the alarm was given that the enemy was upon them. The Boers surrounded the farm and shot down the soldiers or made them prisoners. Only one or two escaped. Lieutenant Watermeyer ran, on the instant when the alarm was given, to his horse, and was mounting it when a Boer a few yards off fired at him. The bullet wounded the British officer slightly in the left shoulder, whereupon he raised his rifle and shot the Boer dead, escaping himself by leaping the garden wall. But not less than forty-three officers and men were killed, wounded, or captured. The fight raging in front of the Sixth Division occupied all attention, else it should not have been difficult to send reinforcements and obviate this mishap. The loss of

[Photo by Heath, Plymouth.
GENERAL HECTOR MACDONALD.
Wounded at Paardeberg. (See the biographical note on page 197.)

Kitchener's Hill was a serious matter, as the hill dominated all the ground south of the Boer laager at Wolveskraal. It was strongly held by the enemy, who now placed 400 or 500 men upon it, and from it poured in a tremendous fire upon the 76th Field Battery, which was stationed on the right. Four guns of this battery fired to the south, at the hill; the other two played upon the Boer laager, receiving in return a terrible fire from one of the enemy's "Pom-Poms." At one gun every man was put out of action except one; he continued laying, and loading, and firing as coolly as if he were on parade, a proud and splendid sight to the armies which gazed upon his consummate bravery. "These English," said a foreign observer, "are so enduring." Yet this deed has passed without its due tribute; the devoted gunner's name is unknown.

Evening was now drawing on after a prolonged and furious action. On either flank the British troops had secured the river bed up to about a mile of the Boer laager, but could get no farther. As darkness fell the artillery increased its fire upon the waggons in the laager, and once more flames and explosions proved that the shells took effect. "The whole scene towards nightfall," writes a correspondent with the army, "was terribly picturesque; waggons were blazing, and the roar of artillery was mingled with the crackle of the infantry fire." "Waggon after waggon of ammunition," writes Captain Boyle, "exploded like a terrific fusillade. . . . It seemed as if no living thing could come out of that laager. . . . One prisoner, who walked quietly up Roberts' Hill with his rifle slung, raised his hat and gave himself up. On being questioned he said Cronje was still there, sitting disconsolate but defiant, 'holding Mrs. Cronje's hand and comforting her in the river bed.'" Yet terrible though it was, this bombardment was as nothing to that which was to follow.

Soon after night came on the bombard-

British casualties. ment ceased, more from the utter exhaustion of the gunners than from any other reason. All the day the Boer guns, with the exception of two "Pom-Poms" had done little. Either from want of ammunition or because they were so heavily outnumbered, they had been quite unable to effect anything against the British artillery. The casualties in the British army were very heavy. Out of a total strength of about 15,000 engaged, 1,250 or more had been killed, wounded, or taken prisoners. The losses were distributed with singular evenness among the various battalions taking part in the battle, though the exact numbers cannot be

Copied, by special permission, from a portrait at Haresfoot Park.]   *[Photo by Newman, Berkhamsted.*

MAJOR-GENERAL SMITH-DORRIEN, D.S.O.

Horace Lockwood Smith-Dorrien is a son of the late Colonel Smith-Dorrien, of Haresfoot Park, and a brother to Mr. T. A. Dorrien-Smith, the "King of Scilly" (the brothers using the compound name differently). He entered the Army in 1876; Captain, 1882; Major, 1892; Lieut.-Colonel, 1899; Brevet-Colonel, 1898; served in the Zulu War in 1879, and raised and commanded the Mounted Infantry of Sir Evelyn Wood's Brigade in the Egyptian War of 1882; served in the Sudan Campaign of 1885; with the Sudan Frontier Field Force in 1885-6, when he was awarded the D.S.O.; and under Sir W. Lockhart in the Tirah Campaign of 1897-8. Colonel Smith-Dorrien commands the Derbyshire Regiment, and was promoted to the local rank of Major-General and the command of the 19th Brigade in February, 1900.

given, as in the official returns the casualties of the days from the 18th to 27th are lumped together. What was most serious was that no preparations had been made to deal with the great mass of wounded men. The ambulances and field hospitals had been for the most part left behind in the hurried march to save Kimberley and cut off Cronje. Of course, this was due to the need of cutting down the impedimenta of the army to the utmost, and to the immense difficulty of negotiating the drifts over the Riet, and not, as has been insinuated, to the callousness of Lord Roberts' staff. In consequence,

the sufferings of those who had been maimed and injured were appalling. They were jolted for
days in slow-going ox-waggons, and taken to
Kimberley, where only too many of the barest
hospital necessities were wanting. But for the
generosity of the De Beers Company, which
supplied food, surgical requisites, and bedding,
the men would have fared even worse than
they actually did. The estimates of the Boer
casualties varied between the wholly preposterous figure of 900, given by prisoners, and
the equally preposterous figure of "fourteen
killed and wounded," which a Boer official
report declared to have been received from
Cronje. It is probable that the actual Boer
loss was about 100, the majority killed by
artillery fire. The disproportion between the
British and Boer loss is here, as in other battles
of the war, startling and almost inexplicable.
Even when allowance is made for the fact that
our men were attacking and the enemy perfectly
concealed with excellent cover—so perfectly
concealed that, as a Scotch soldier said to

GENERAL AND MRS. CRONJE.
From a photograph taken at St. Helena.

Mr. Hands, the *Daily Mail* correspondent, "Man, the guns would be better sighted wi' ear trumpets"
—we should yet have expected heavier loss to have been inflicted on the Boers, especially as at times
the combatants were only 400 yards apart. Yet the number of wounded found in the laager upon its
capture, nine days later, shows that the total loss could not have much exceeded the figure given.

Those who are wise after the event, will naturally recognise that the battle was a great mistake.
Results were purchased at the cost of 1,250 casualties, which might, perhaps, with greater patience, have
been secured for one tenth that terrible price. It was, we believe, honestly confessed by the British
generals that the action should not have been fought. Yet

The battle a mistake.

those who care for justice
will admit that there were
sound arguments on the
morning of the 18th to
counsel an attack. If it
was physically possible to
rush the laager, it would
be well to rush it at once,
even though heavy losses
were thereby incurred. The
siege of such a position
in a fever-contaminated
country might be even
more costly in ultimate
loss of life than the plan
of resolutely storming the
camp at whatever sacrifice.
Moreover, in the end, the
siege did lay the seeds

SOME OF THE WOUNDED FROM THE BATTLE OF PAARDEBERG, February 18, 1900.
The photograph was taken at one of the dressing-stations where the wounded had to wait their turn to be taken to hospital.

of a fearful outburst of enteric. A second motive for haste and immediate action lay in the certainty that Cronje's men would be wearied with marching. If they were given time, they would be able to recruit their strength and to improve their earthworks. Lastly, the plight of Ladysmith rendered it important to hasten forward the campaign and reach Bloemfontein as speedily as possible. All these were motives the reasonableness of which must be acknowledged. In somewhat similar circumstances Wellington was quite ready to face the risks and awful bloodshed of the assaults upon Ciudad Rodrigo and Badajoz. And though he succeeded, while at Paardeberg the British generals failed, it does not follow that the latter are to be wholly condemned. One great result the battle undoubtedly had: though the mortality among the Boer men, due to the British fire, was small, the mortality among their horses and oxen was most severe. The force was deprived of all its mobility;

H. C. *Seppings Wright.*]   [*After a sketch on the spot by Fred. Villiers.*

CRONJE'S STRONGHOLD IN THE BANKS OF THE MODDER AT PAARDEBERG.

moreover, the fierce determination with which the British attacks had been made cowed the enemy and deprived the few, who still had mounts, of any inclination to attempt to cut their way out. It is at least open to question whether if the fight had not been fought, Cronje would not, on the night of the 18th–19th, have made one more effort to escape—perhaps with success. On the whole it is probable that the verdict of posterity will be lenient to the British generals, whatever the hasty criticisms of the passing moment.

At nightfall the ground actually held by the Boers round the laager was a square about two miles long and two miles broad, intersected by the river Modder. Outside the laager and parted from it by the intervening positions of the British troops, were the 500 men on Kitchener's Hill. The headquarters of the Sixth Division were to the south of the river, under a low eminence known as Signal Hill, about four miles from Wolveskraal Drift; those of the Ninth Division opposite, on the north bank.

With dawn of February 19, Cronje demanded an armistice for the burial of his dead, whereupon Lord Kitchener replied that he had no power to grant it, but that Lord Roberts would shortly arrive and

An armistice demanded and refused.

the request should be referred to him. The truth was that the Boers wanted to get rid of their dead horses, the taint of which poisoned the air and rendered life inside the laager horrible; moreover, they had everything to gain by delay, as reinforcements might arrive to extricate them, while in any case they could strengthen their trenches and provide shelter against shell fire. With Lord Roberts the whole of the Seventh Division and four

more batteries of Field Artillery were marching to Paardeberg, while the remainder of the cavalry, with the rest of the Horse Artillery, were summoned in the same direction from Kimberley, though, owing to telegraphic breakdowns, they did not all arrive before the 21st or 22nd.

During the morning the British guns refrained from shelling the laager, but there was some fighting to the south of Kitchener's Hill between the Boers, who held that

THE REMAINS OF THE BOER WAGGONS SET ON FIRE BY THE BRITISH ARTILLERY.
From a photograph taken after the surrender.

eminence, and the mounted infantry. In the afternoon Lord Roberts arrived,

Lord Roberts arrives.

and was received by his men with extreme enthusiasm. "Without any sign or badge, wearing a plain khaki coat with ordinary shoulder straps, cord breeches and putti gaiters, and helmet, and a pair of glasses hung over his shoulders, Lord Roberts has the appearance more of a private individual than the Commander-in-Chief in whom England has put its trust," writes a correspondent who witnessed his coming. "Yet everyone knows him and he is recognised when still afar off. He is universally loved by all. If 'Bobs' is there all have confidence—nothing can go wrong."

BOER TRENCHES AT PAARDEBERG.
These trenches were roomy beneath, with narrow openings, as indicated in the accompanying diagram, and were from five to six feet deep. In them the Boers lived day and night, with results which even a seasoned sanitary inspector would not care to contemplate.

Notwithstanding the suspension of the bombardment, and possibly through some accident, the Boers, while constructing earthworks for the defence of their laager, suddenly opened fire on the British troops. The result of this breach of the informal truce was the prompt renewal of the bombardment by such guns as were ready.

In the afternoon and evening of the 19th the Seventh Division marched in and took up its position to the east of Cronje's laager, holding both banks of the river, and thus setting free the

cavalry and mounted infantry for operations against any relief force that might approach.   Its batteries were placed in position to join in the bombardment, the 18th, 62nd, and 75th Field Batteries, sup-
The circle closed.   porting the 65th Howitzer Battery, and directing their fire upon the laager and the river bed.   But the ground was soft, and the Boer trenches were so contrived as to give almost complete shelter against artillery fire.   They consisted of deep, narrow pits dug in

LORD AND LADY ROBERTS, WITH THEIR ELDER DAUGHTER AND THEIR SON (THE LATE LIEUT. ROBERTS, V.C.).

the earth ; only a few inches wide at the top, they broadened out below and gave room for their occupants to sit or lie down, secure unless a shell actually entered the trench.   Other shelters were made
The Boer shelter pits.   by tunnelling horizontally into the high river banks.   And thus it came about that, while the British army watched with bated breath the hail of projectiles descending upon the Boer lines, and speculated upon the ghastly possibility of Cronje's whole force being blown to pieces, Cronje's men lay safely in their lairs.   What was more serious was the steady depletion of their food supplies.   They had started with provisions only for a week, and these were being rapidly consumed.

SOME OF THE BOER PRISONERS IN OUR CAMP AT PAARDEBERG.

CHAPTER XIX.

THE CAPTURE OF CRONJE.

Investing lines drawn closer—Renewed bombardment—Ineffective lyddite—Second demand of an armistice refused—Cronje's indignant repudiation of surrender—Botha dislodged from Kitchener's Hill—Driven from point to point—Casualties—Desultory shelling—Relief force everywhere repulsed—Cronje's stubborn resistance—The chain drawn tighter—Lord Roberts besought to avenge Majuba—Final attack planned—Brave advance of the Canadians—Cronje's surrender—Lord Roberts' reception of Cronje—Appearance of the prisoners—Boer losses slight—Structure of the trenches—Condition of the laager—Severe British casualties—Moral effect of the victory.

Investing lines drawn closer.

N the night of the 19th the troops both to east and west of the laager trenched forward in the river bed. In this way henceforth a few yards were gained night after night, each diminution of the intervening space rivetting the more tightly their inexorable fetters upon the Boers. A handful of deserters came in to the British outposts with thrilling tales of the hardships endured within the laager, and a very few more Boers succeeded in stealing through the British lines. But Major Burnham, the famous American scout, who night after night, with the most magnificent daring, crept up to the enemy's lines, was convinced that only an insignificant handful got away. With daylight of Tuesday, February 20, skirmishing began in the river bed: as the day grew clearer the Boers could be seen working like busy ants on their trenches, till the sudden boom of the British guns and the whiz of the British shrapnel sent them scuttling like frightened insects to their holes. But when once they had been driven back, the bombardment was not

Renewed bombardment.

pressed. Anxious to spare bloodshed, and hoping that Cronje would realise the desperate nature of his position, Lord Roberts deliberately refrained from shelling him all the morning. Only in the afternoon, when no sign of surrender was noticed, was the bombardment resumed. On the south bank, the 18th, 62nd, and 75th Field Batteries, with two naval 12-pounders, opened fire; on the north bank, enfilading the river bed, the 76th, 81st, and 82nd Field Batteries, with the 5-in. howitzers and three 4·7 naval guns, came into action. These forty-seven weapons concentrated their terrible fire upon a space a mile square. Says a correspondent:—" The lyddite shells raised great clouds of green smoke, which filled the bed of the river, while shrapnel burst along the edge of each bank, except

MAJOR BURNHAM, THE SCOUT.

F. R. Burnham is a Canadian by birth, and spent many years in close contact with the Red Indians, from whom he learned many of the mysteries of woodcraft, tracking, and scouting, or, as it is called in South Africa, "spooring." He was one of the first men to explore British Columbia, and he has practically spent the whole of his life in the wilds. In the Matabele War he was of the greatest service to the pioneers, and later on he succeeded in tracking and killing the famous witch-doctor Milinio. During the present war Lord Roberts cabled for him to join the Intelligence Staff. He has since been captured, but made his escape.

for a small space where the proximity of our infantry would have made the artillery fire dangerous to them. Our shells searched every bush and every ravine on the river banks. The enfilading guns must have done terrible execution, yet, in a spirit of desperate madness, now and again a Boer would attempt a 'sniping' shot at one of the naval guns, which were firing at a range of only 1,000 yards. On each side of the river lay two battalions, the whirring of whose Maxim fire sounded petty by the side of the deafening roar of the big guns." This was by far the severest bombardment that had as yet been directed against the Boer force. Its results were as lamentably inconclusive as those of the former shellings, and the net issue, in the light of our after-knowledge, has been to establish the belief that artillery is all but powerless against skilfully devised entrenchments held by determined men. Still, the Boers were kept crouching in their trenches, and were condemned to watch their waggons one by one catching fire and burning to ashes. What horses and cattle in the laager had not been killed in the previous bombardments perished in this, and the interior of the laager became a horrible

F. de Haenen.]   [After a photo by C. Knight.

TAKING A 4·7 GUN ACROSS PAARDEBERG DRIFT.

mass of putrefying carcases, the stench of which poisoned the air for miles. The water in the river was so low that it would not carry off the bodies, and there was nowhere to bury them. So foul was the horrible fluid which the river yielded that it came to be known among our men as "Dead horse soup."

Here, as before in the war upon many occasions, the effects of lyddite were most disappointing. "A charge of lyddite from the 4·7 bursting in the midst of a dozen cattle feeding loosely together

Ineffective lyddite.   might, perhaps, knock one or two over, but the rest would go on with their meal," says Mr. Battersby. Major Albrecht, the Boer gunner, when questioned as to his experiences with these shells, stated that one burst only a few yards from him, covering him with dirt and leaving an evil taste in his mouth, but not otherwise injuring him, and even failing to throw him down. Without doubt the softness of the ground was in a great degree the cause of this singular harmlessness. The Boer guns throughout the bombardment remained all but inactive. Two of them had been placed in a strong work to the north of the river, but from shortness of ammunition they were rarely or never fired.

On the early morning of the 21st the Boers suddenly opened a tremendous **Second demand for an armistice refused.** rifle fire upon the Essex and Gloucestershire battalions, which, through some mistake, had bivouacked far too close to the Boer lines on the north of the river; but as a matter of fact they inflicted only the most trivial losses. There was the usual "sniping" interchange of shots all day as the British troops on all sides of the laager gradually encroached. It was now that Cronje reiterated his demand for a day's armistice, in order to attend to his wounded and bury his dead. Lord Roberts, suspecting that his object was only to gain time, was compelled, although reluctantly, to refuse the request. He offered to send doctors into the laager, however, and to permit them to attend to the wounded.

MAP OF THE BOER POSITION AT PAARDEBERG.
Showing also the positions of the entrenched British forces immediately before the surrender.
(See also map on page 425.)

This Cronje refused, insisting that if they came into his lines they must stay there, and denouncing Lord Roberts for inhumanity. He wound up his letter with **Cronje's indignant repudiation of surrender.** the words, "Under the circumstances I have no other choice." This ambiguous phrase was at first understood in the British lines to mean that he surrendered, and there was great cheering when rumours to that effect reached the men. But when an answer was sent by an aide-de-camp, giving certain directions with regard to the surrender, Cronje indignantly repudiated the construction placed on his letter, and declared that far from laying down his arms, he was determined to fight to the death. Eventually it was arranged that he should hand over some of his wounded to the British, who would treat them as their own men and release them when recovered. The extraordinary generosity

THE GUNS USED BY CRONJE AT PAARDEBERG.
The photograph was taken at Capetown, whither they were removed after Cronje's surrender. The old muzzle-loader on the right was not, of course, one of the number.

of this concession seems to have made little impression upon the Boers.   Still, it is only fair to them to say that they treated two British officers, whom they had with them as prisoners, with the greatest kindness, placing them in a secure burrow, where these officers could perfectly observe the bombardment without suffering from it.   Lord Roberts further offered a safe-conduct for all the women and children in the laager, but this also was declined most ungraciously by the enemy.

Yet although the Field-Marshal would not grant a formal armistice, he conceded what was virtually an informal one.   The guns did not resume the pitiless bombardment, as Lord Roberts had determined to turn the attention of his troops for the nonce towards ridding himself of the Boer relief force, now about 2,000 strong, under

Botha dislodged from Kitchener's Hill.

General Louis Botha, which had seized and held Kitchener's Hill.   From this point the enemy caused great annoyance by their "sniping" of officers and men, and might, if strongly reinforced, have had some chance of breaking through the British lines ; while if Cronje attempted a sortie they could effectively co-operate with him.   The kopje they held was completely isolated on the plain. Another detached kopje to the north-east of it, during the night before, had been occupied by some squadrons of Roberts' Horse.   Two brigades of cavalry, Gordon's and Broadwood's, under General French, had also

Lt.-Col. Schiel, taken at Elandslaagte.   Baron Van Dewitz (Height, 6 ft. 7 in.).   Major Albrecht, F. S. Artillery.   Lt. Van Heister, F. S. Artillery.   Lt. Müller, F. S. Artillery.

[Photographed on board the SS. "Mongolian," en route for St. Helena.

MAJOR ALBRECHT AND OTHER CAPTURED OFFICERS.
The three officers standing in the front row are all old South Africans, although Germans by birth.   Lt.-Col. Schiel was in the Transvaal service, and the other two in that of the Free State.   Lt.-Col. Schiel was taken prisoner at Elandslaagte ; Major Albrecht, Van Dewitz, and Van Heister at Paardeberg.

started with the Horse Artillery from the cavalry camp at daylight.   Broadwood approached the kopje from the south-east, and Gordon from the north-east ; while the Field Batteries searched its face from the north-west and west.   The artillery fire speedily took effect.   The Boers hastily fell back, leaving the kopje and taking with them two "Pom-Poms."   They first of all attempted

Driven from point to point.

to retire upon the hill held by Roberts' Horse, but were received with so hot a fire that they had to retreat in a fresh direction.   Here they came into collision with Broadwood's brigade of cavalry, which all but cut them off, and compelled them once more to turn tail, under a sharp fire from the Horse Artillery.   Had the British horses been in better condition, the whole force of the enemy would have been captured.   Taking to flight in a fresh direction, the Boers were charged by the 16th Lancers, and a good number of them killed or made prisoners.   One waggon was captured, the pole of which had been broken by a splendid shot from one of the Horse Artillery guns, but the Boer guns got away.   At this juncture some confusion prevailed.   It was not possible accurately to distinguish British and Boers at a distance, and, owing to this fact, a force of about 500 Boers was able to close suddenly upon General French's Staff, Gordon's Brigade, and a battery of Horse Artillery.   A storm of bullets was poured in upon the British horsemen as they rode forward.   Just at this moment matters were further complicated by the

18*

Horse Artillery getting mixed up in an elaborate wire entanglement. The cavalry rode at full speed to clear the front of the guns, and there was a scene of great disorder, which looked as if it might issue in something worse. Fortunately, the gunners kept perfectly cool and opened a deadly fire, while the cavalry rallied, dismounted, and poured in volleys from their futile little carbines. The Boers recoiled and retired once more, losing heavily in killed and prisoners. Their main body finally escaped, simply because the British horses were too tired and worn out by hard work and bad food to pursue. Yet General Botha only eluded capture by the skin of his teeth. His waggon was taken with a great quantity of important papers.

Casualties. The casualties in this affair were extraordinarily small on the British side, and proved that the Boers were contemptible in attack, when faced by a superior force. Only six men were wounded, whereas the enemy lost thirty or forty in killed alone, and some fifty prisoners, who stated that they had come direct from Natal to the succour of Cronje. The total of prisoners was

[*Photo by R. Thiele.*

HOLES IN THE RIVER BANK
Where Captain Faussett (1st Essex) and Lieut. G. W. Herbert (1st Welsh Regiment) were confined by the Boers. They had been captured while carrying despatches to Lord Kitchener (page 421).

now fast mounting up; what with desertions from Cronje's laager, men attempting to escape through the British line of investment, and those who fell into our hands from the various forces attempting relief, 460 Boers had already been captured by Lord Roberts' army.

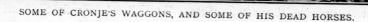

SOME OF CRONJE'S WAGGONS, AND SOME OF HIS DEAD HORSES.

Kitchener's Hill taken, it was at once strongly garrisoned. It afforded an excellent position from which to meet and beat off attempts at relief from the south, while so long as it remained in British hands, the artillery bombarding the Boer laager from the slopes just under it could not be annoyed by **Desultory shelling.** sharpshooters. In the evening of the 21st the guns resumed their fire, but there was no attempt to direct such a storm of shrapnel upon the laager as had been poured into it during the bombardment of the 20th. A minor catastrophe happened during the languid shelling. The mules of the 82nd Battery bolted with the ammunition waggons, and one waggon is believed to have been captured by the Boers. As the artillery fired its last shots for the night, the Shropshires, who held the river bed to the west of the laager, gallantly dashed forward and won about 200 yards of ground before the startled Boers discovered what they were about. The point thus gained was immediately entrenched, and early in the morning of the 22nd the place of the Shropshires, after they had been

COMMANDO OF JOHANNESBURG POLICE.   [*Photo by Barnett.*
These are some of the men brought from Natal to endeavour to relieve Cronje.

almost continuously under fire for three days, was taken by the Gordons. On this day the shelling continued languidly as before, and a German ambulance from Jacobsdal was permitted to pass through the lines and enter the laager. The Boer cattle had strayed from the laager where they had not been killed by shell fire; deserters complained bitterly that Cronje was simply murdering his men, and the horrible stench of rotting animals poisoned the air for miles around. On the afternoon of the 22nd, however, a terrific thunderstorm broke over the laager; the Modder rose, and some of the dead animals were carried down in its chocolate-coloured turbid flood. During the night the Gordons gained another 200 yards to the west of the laager.

On the 23rd the Boer relief force made its last desperate effort to reach the hard-pressed Cronje. Under De Wet and Botha some 2,000 of the enemy essayed to break the British line of investment, but

[*Photo by Wrypes Bros.*
HOW THE JOHANNESBURG COMMANDO WAS HORSED.
Horses "commandeered" from the townspeople.

FARM AT OSFONTEIN, FLYING THE WHITE FLAG.
The Boers hoisted the white flag on their farms to prevent looting.   The "Cape cart" with six horses is that of the correspondent of the *Daily Mail.*

found Lord Roberts perfectly ready for them.   Every height which they endeavoured to seize was occupied.   First of all they rode towards a kopje which did not seem to be held, on the British left front.

Relief force everywhere repulsed.   But as they neared it the Scottish Borderers, who were under cover upon it, opened a vigorous fire and emptied many saddles.   Two more kopjes were tried, but at each the reception was precisely the same.   For the possession of a fourth the Borderers raced the Boers and won by a neck.   Completely foiled on the left the enemy now attempted a dash at Kitchener's Hill, but this was garrisoned by the 1st Yorkshires, who greeted their assailants with a steady fire.   The East Kents were thrown forward, supported by the 75th Battery on the right, while on the left, from near Osfontein, the 62nd Battery opened fire and the Scottish Borderers advanced.   The Boers fell back on a kopje and made no answer.   Accordingly, a company of Yorkshires was directed to assault the kopje, whereupon the Boer rifles got to work immediately.   In face of their heavy fire the attempt to storm the hill was not persisted in, but instead the turning movements were allowed to make progress.   It was not long before the Boers, alarmed at the flanking advance, tried to break out.   They were met, however, by a fearful rifle and Maxim fire, and at last the East Kents succeeded in cutting off the retreat of a large party about 10.30 a.m., compelling their surrender.   They numbered eighty-seven, including two field cornets and a commandant, and were of the Johannesburg and Heidelburg commandos, but newly come from Ladysmith.   Nearly all had expanding bullets upon them, and, characteristically, they complained of their leaders for landing them in such a position.

Simultaneously with this movement, a party of the 9th Lancers to the east of the laager was attacked

HOW THE HORSES OF THE 9TH LANCERS WERE TAKEN TO AFRICA.

by 500 Boers with a " Pom-Pom." The cavalry, however, supported by a battery of Horse Artillery and a squadron of the 12th Lancers, quite held their own.   In the afternoon the balloon, which had just arrived, was sent up to the west of the laager. From it, on the 24th, the fire of the bombarding guns was directed upon four ammunition waggons in the river bed.   These were speedily exploded, and then the British shrapnel was turned to the last remnant of the Boer horses, near the waggons.   On this day the fire upon the laager was renewed with all the severity of the 20th, but with more guns.   The sufferings of the enemy from hunger, from the stench, and from the ceaseless nerve-torment of the shell-fire were extreme, and Cronje was hard put to it to persuade his men to continue their desperate and stubborn resistance.   He was

Cronje's stubborn resistance.

especially anxious not to surrender before Majuba Day had passed, and finally he induced his commandants and field cornets to promise a continuance of the defence until the 28th, when, if no reinforcements reached him, he said that he would bow to the inevitable. Perpetual rain converted his trenches into pits of slimy mud and aggravated the torments of the siege. Almost as great were the trials of the British infantry, who had to endure wet and cold by night, and torrential rain and broiling heat by day.   But at least they were

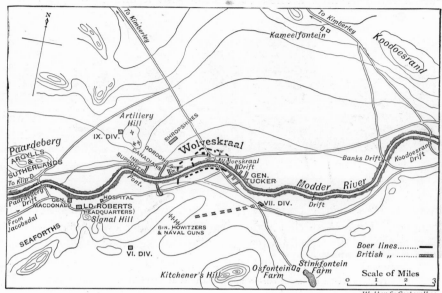

[*Based, by permission, on the map published in "The Times."*
MAP OF PAARDEBERG AND ITS SURROUNDINGS.

relieved regularly in the trenches, so that they were not continuously under fire, while the provision trains had arrived and full rations could be issued to all—a welcome change from the slow starvation of half-rations.   To the credit of the men be it said that their conduct was splendid.   They did not complain, and, as they grew in confidence that their prey could not escape them, were in an excellent mood.

Night after night the jaws of the vice tightened upon the Boer laager.   To the east and west the

The chain drawn tighter.

infantry worked their way in, crawling forward with obstinate bravery under the hail of Boer bullets, and constantly gaining ground.   The bombardment, too, was pressed more sternly.   A perpetual rain of shells descended upon the enemy's trenches, and on the 26th, in addition to three "Pom-Poms," whose first appearance this was in the British artillery,

[*Photo by Russell & Sons, Southsea.*
SERGEANTS OF THE 15TH COMPANY ROYAL ARTILLERY, IN CHARGE OF THE SIEGE TRAIN WITH LORD ROBERTS.

the great 6-in. howitzers of the siege train arrived to join in the attack. These terrible weapons, four in number, fired a shell of 118 lb. with a charge of 46 lb. of lyddite inside it. They opened on

A BRITISH "POM-POM"
(Vickers-Maxim automatic one-pounder), first used at Paardeberg.

a red house to the north of the river where Cronje had his headquarters. At the explosion of their immense projectiles the laager was filled with green smoke. Yet, as before, the actual effects of this bombardment appear to have been small. It was appalling to watch; utterly disappointing in its execution. "As each shot reached its target," writes a correspondent, "there rose from the river side huge masses of smoke, which took on the form of rows of magic trees springing suddenly into life. It was picturesque to watch, but must have been far from picturesque to the poor burghers in whose midst the magic trees were growing." From north, and south, and east the boom of big guns and field pieces was unremittent all the morning and afternoon. It was the last effort of the British artillery to shake the nerves of Cronje and force him to surrender when the fateful anniversary should dawn.

Already strong pressure had been brought to bear upon Lord Roberts to assault that night of the 26th–27th, and thus pass a clean sponge over the record of dishonour. From his bed of pain General Macdonald sent a note of reminder, as he had the right to do, considering the noble **Lord Roberts besought to avenge Majuba.** part which he had played upon that disastrous day nineteen years before. His fiery spirit chafed at such an opportunity of wiping out the past being allowed to go by. General Colvile, too, was eager for attack—attack at all costs. But Lord Roberts, calm and even-balanced in mind, was not ready to risk hundreds of men's lives for reasons of sentiment, to win what was already as good as his. It was only the earnest entreaty of the Canadians, as the most honoured and oldest of British colonists, to be permitted to avenge the stain upon British renown, that finally moved the resolute humanity of the Field-Marshal. Reluctantly he gave way; in the early hours of

the morning the Canadians were to make the attempt.

Great fear was felt that the Boers under cover of darkness might make a last despairing effort to break through, and perhaps succeed, for desperate men are always most dangerous. As night came on the batteries were trained on Wolveskraal Drift and occasionally fired a shot to prevent such an attempt and show that the British were on the alert. The spectacle of the discharge of the big guns in the darkness was wonderfully picturesque. At each shot they created, says a correspondent, "an effect comparable to the momentary appearance of a huge and brilliant arc-lamp."

6-IN. HOWITZER OF THE SIEGE TRAIN,
With some members of its double howitzer company of the Royal Artillery.

The charge was shrapnel, and as the shell burst over the river banks "a secondary arc-lamp flashed into a brief existence." But no sign of sortie could be detected. Evening passed into night, night drew near to dawn, and silence, excepting for the sniping shots of outposts, held the weapons of the Boers. The time had come for the Canadians to fall to their business.

Five hundred and fifty yards from the outermost Boer works, on the northern bank of the Modder, and at the western end of the laager, ran a long trench, which was held at the river end by **Final attack planned.** the Canadians, at the other end by the Gordons. The orders given to the Canadians were these:—At a given signal they were to advance in perfect silence in two lines, and, if they could surprise the Boers, to carry the position with the bayonet. If they failed in surprising the enemy, at the first shot they were to fling themselves down and retire under cover of the fire of their supports. No orders were to be given aloud; everything was to be done by the pressure of hand upon hand. Close behind them was to follow a detachment of Engineers with entrenching tools, to secure any ground that might be won. The attempt was bold and hazardous; through the brushwood were the Boers within easy range, and, had they been upon the alert,

COLONIALS INVALIDED FROM LORD ROBERTS' ARMY.

[*Russell & Sons, Windsor.*

This group includes forty-three non-commissioned officers and men of the New South Wales, Queensland, South and West Australian, New Zealand, Roberts' Horse, and South African Light Horse contingents, and Royal Canadian contingent of Mounted Rifles, invalided from South Africa. Under the command of Captain A. Stourton they visited Windsor on September 3, 1900, and were entertained at the Guildhall by the Mayor and several members of the corporation. They had an enthusiastic reception, and visited St. George's Chapel, the Albert Memorial Chapel, the State Apartments, &c. Many of these men had served at Paardeberg and in the dash on Bloemfontein.

they ought to have detected the movement directly it began. The night was not unfavourable; only a faint glow shone from the failing moon. About a quarter to three all was ready, and four companies of the gallant Colonials deployed in absolute silence for the perilous advance. On their left the Gordons were watching in breathless eagerness, and beyond them again were drawn up the fighting Shropshires in such a position that they would be able to enfilade the Boer advanced works.

Nearly 500 yards the Canadians stole forward in the darkness with fast-beating hearts, each man wondering when the enemy would see what was happening and open fire. Though ground **Brave advance of the** was rapidly gained, minutes seemed like hours in the dreadful suspense, when the **Canadians.** nerves of all were at the utmost tension. But now, as the low earthworks of the enemy came into view, a short stone-throw away, the trampling of the men upon the undergrowth at last gave the alarm. The face of the trench before them broke into a sheet of flame, and the hiss of bullets and the cries of the dying and wounded told that the Boers shot true. Under this fire the Canadians behaved with the most magnificent steadiness, the French company of Major Pelletier especially distinguishing itself by its coolness and valour. The front rank, strictly obeying its orders, fell prone to the ground, and crawled back to the supports, who immediately opened a steady and rapid fire on the Boers. Behind the supports the Engineers dug like demons, frantically throwing up cover against daylight, and paying not the slightest attention to the bullets which whistled around them. On the left the Gordons and Shropshires had opened a heavy fire, and the Boer work was steadily deluged with a stream of lead. The Canadians, only eighty yards off it, shot with such deadly accuracy that the Boers no longer dared to show their heads above its crest. They were content to hold their rifles above their heads and pull their triggers at random, a fact which accounts for the complete ineffectiveness of their fire. From 2.55 to 3.10 a.m. continued this furious fusillade, and then the Canadians retired behind the cover of the frail rampart, hastily dug for them, and waited till dawn. The position they had gained, at the small cost of thirteen killed and thirty wounded, completely commanded the interior of the laager and enfiladed the whole river bed.

Edward Read.]

THE ATTACK BY THE CANADIANS ON THE BOER POSITION AT PAARDEBERG.

It was so near to the enemy that now an assault had become perfectly feasible; only, for such an assault it was necessary to wait for day. In reporting this advance of the Canadians, Lord Roberts speaks of it with soldierly appreciation as "a gallant deed, worthy of our Colonial comrades," which "appeared to have clinched the matter." Cronje's surrender had now become a question, not of days, but of hours, almost of minutes.

The heavy crackle of the firing was heard all over the British camp, though few knew its explanation, and most men supposed that it was the first sign of a Boer sortie. Once more, however, silence fell, and all waited eagerly for the grey light of dawn. As day began to break signs of complete disorganisation within the laager multiplied. Shots were, indeed, exchanged to the north and east, but every now and then small parties of the enemy would break from their defences opposite the Canadian trenches, throw up their hands, and bolt towards the British lines. Here and there white flags were revealed flying, yet the British infantry knew how these emblems had been abused by the foe, and refrained from showing themselves until General Colvile rode down to the advanced positions of his men with the news that at last the signal of surrender was up, and that a Boer parlementaire was on its way into the British lines. It was 6 a.m. of the 27th, the morning of Majuba Day, and, as the full significance of the victory that had been won dawned on the British soldiers, the sound of exultant cheering rang over the veldt.

First word of Cronje's surrender was brought in by two Boer officers, riding horses that had been slightly wounded by the British shrapnel fire, almost the last horses left in the laager. Cronje, **Cronje's surrender.** the determined, the indomitable, had been compelled to yield before the clamour of his men, who dreaded the awful slaughter of the bayonet assault, which they saw impending. A message was sent back from the British Commander-in-Chief requesting the Boer general to make his surrender in person to Lord Roberts. It has been pretended by American and Continental critics that such an act was cruel and ungenerous on Lord Roberts' part. But it was peculiarly necessary to take every precaution against mistakes and trickery, and it has always been customary in war for a beaten general himself to hand over his sword to the victor. Lord Roberts was the last man to press hardly upon a defeated foe, whom, indeed, he rather honoured than humiliated by a formal and ceremonious reception.

General Pretyman with a small escort **Lord Roberts' reception of Cronje.** rode out to meet the stubborn soldier of Modder River and Magersfontein. The momentous scene at

COMMANDANT GENERAL CRONJE.
The photograph was taken immediately after his surrender, when he was under the care of Capt. Watermeyer (Capetown Highlanders), Aide-de-Camp to Lord Roberts.

Lord Roberts' headquarters is thus described by a brilliant eye-witness, Mr. Hands:—"The trim figure of the Chief caught my eye first. He was alone in front of the little lean-to tent fixed to the side of a travelling waggon in which he works and sleeps. His grey face, grave and thoughtful, showed no sign of elation. He looked around, gave an order to one of his Staff, and a table and two chairs were brought out of his tent and placed under the shade of a tree at the edge of the river bank.

"He gave another order, and half a company of Highlanders formed up in three sides of a square about the spot.

"The Chief looked carefully around, saw that everything was in order, then walked to his tent. When he came out again he was wearing his sword—a heavy sword with a jewelled hilt. It was the first time I had seen him wearing it since the column started. But he forgets nothing, overlooks nothing, considers everything. And he had donned his sword now as a mark of respect for his fallen foe.

"Presently the body of horsemen came past the hospital tents into the camp. Major-General Pretyman was one of the leading horsemen, his compact figure lightly swinging with the movement of his charger. By his side a great heavy bundle of a man was lumped atop of a wretched little grey bony Boer pony.

"And this was the terrible Cronje.

"Was it possible that this was the man who had held back the British army

LORD ROBERTS' HEAD-QUARTERS NEAR PAARDEBERG.

We have already given a portrait of Lord Roberts in his travelling head-quarters (page 340). The present picture represents the same waggon, with a lean-to tent attached, beneath which the Commander-in-Chief sits writing at a table, while an officer awaits his orders. It was before the tent thus arranged that Lord Roberts received Commandant-General Cronje.

at Magersfontein? Great square shoulders, from which the heavy head was thrust forward so that he seemed almost humped; a heavy face, shapeless with unkempt, grey-tinged, black hair; lowering heavy brows, from under which small, cunning, foxy eyes peered shiftily. A broad-brimmed grey Boer felt hat was pulled down low, a loose brown overcoat, ordinary dark trousers; nothing military, not even spurs on his brown veldt boots. The only thing he carried that seemed to speak authority was his sjambok, a thick, heavy stocked whip of hide, which he grasped and swung as one accustomed to use it."

With Cronje rode a lean and spectacled interpreter; for though the Boer general spoke English perfectly, it suited him to pretend that he knew only Dutch. Lord Roberts stepped forward, saluted, shook hands, and handed his fallen enemy a chair. The two sat down and fell to quiet, unemotional talk. "I am glad to see you; I am glad to meet so brave a man," was Lord Roberts' welcome to his foe.

Cronje's face was set and sullen. Few, perhaps, of the correspondents and officers who stood watching that historic meeting realised the agony of heart which this moment of surrender meant for the Boer. His shabby attire suggested the tramp rather than the soldier, yet in its very uncouth simplicity there was pathos. As a soldier and a patriot the Boer general recognised in that hour that his country was doomed. The loss of his army, the capture of the Potchefstroomers, who were as the Old Guard of the Transvaal, meant the bringing to naught of all the proud Boer hopes. The leadership that had overcome him could not be withstood by his brother commanders. As he looked forth beyond the guard of motionless Highlanders, he saw the thousands upon thousands of British soldiers, their cannon,

BOER FIELD HOSPITAL AT BOTHA'S HOEK.

The photograph was taken when French's Cavalry passed Botha's Hoek on the way from Kimberley to Paardeberg.

R. Caton Woodville.

THE SURRENDER OF CRONJE, February 27, 1900.

their countless transport waggons, and all their elaborate apparatus of war. He knew that this was the first occasion in the campaign upon which a perfectly equipped force had entered the field under a leader of genius. Behind the tragedy of his per-

[Photo by Surgeon-Major Beevor.

CRONJE'S CAVALRY, AFTER THE SURRENDER.

sonal defeat, and overshadowing it, was the yet greater tragedy of his country's downfall. He averted his eyes steadily from his conqueror until at last the painful meeting terminated. Lord Roberts rose, bowed, and retired, and Cronje was left to the staff.

He had already asked and obtained that his wife, grandson, private secretary, and one or two of his staff should not be parted from him in his captivity. And now as the passion of hunger asserted itself,

HEAP OF MAUSERS AND MARTINI RIFLES SURRENDERED BY CRONJE'S ARMY.

he fell to breakfast upon the last ham which the British staff could muster and smoked the staff's last cigar. Meantime, the force he had led paraded in the laager, the various commandos sorting themselves and piling their Mausers in an enormous stack by the river bank. The total number of unwounded prisoners was 3,997, of whom 2,847 were Trans-

vaalers and 1,150 Free Staters. Among the captured officers were many Boers of note; Chief-Commandant Wolmarans, nine commandants, two assistant commandants, one camp commandant, eighteen field cornets, Major Albrecht, chief of the Free State Artillery, and many adjutants and lieutenants. The guns captured were six in number, three Krupp field pieces and one "Pom-Pom," belonging to the Transvaal; and one Krupp and one "Pom-Pom," the property of the Free State. The

breech blocks of the guns had been removed and thrown into the river, so that the weapons were useless; their ammunition had been all fired away. If there were more guns with Cronje they must have been either buried or thrown into the river.

CRONJE'S INFANTRY ON THE MARCH TO KLIP DRIFT UNDER ESCORT OF A BATTALION OF
THE GLOUCESTERS.

A SCANDINAVIAN OFFICER OF THE ORANGE FREE STATE
ARTILLERY WITH CRONJE.

Undoubtedly the greatest surprise to the British army was the appearance of the prisoners.

Appearance of the prisoners. They were a shabby, dirty, dilapidated lot of men with not a touch of soldierly smartness about them. As they came forth from their lairs, clad in ill-fitting garments of extraordinary incongruity, laden with parcels, bundles, teapots, and bottles; many with umbrellas and many with goloshes, those last refuges of the effeminate; in appearance a mob of frowsy vagrants; officers and men wondered that such a force had been able to hold back a splendidly disciplined British division for a whole day at Modder River, to repel at Magersfontein the desperate valour of the Highlanders, and at Paardeberg to endure nine days of battle and terrible bombardment. Some dozens of women and children were with them weeping piteously; among them was Mrs. Cronje, " a thin, decrepit old woman, and in rough straw hat and dirty old black dress, without cloak or shawl of any sort, presenting a hopelessly miserable, draggled, and woebegone appearance." Bystanders noted with some amusement that she carried over her arm a smart dress, " commandeered " from Lady Sarah Wilson's belongings, with the name of its Bond Street maker showing. Nor was it only that the enemy were ill-dressed and unclean; men who had lived for days in the trenches under an appalling fire might well be pardoned for that. " There was," says Mr. Hands, " a mean, underhand, shifty-eyed look about the most of them, that would have set the most complaisant house dog barking." " They are the worst-looking men I have ever seen," said the American, Mr. Ralph. " They are wild-eyed, savage, dull witted, misshapen. Those who show symptoms of a brain appear to be unbalanced. . . The different parts of their bodies do not fit together. This one's legs do not match his trunk. The next one has a head like a button on the shoulders of an ox. A fourth has the long arms of an orang-outang." All who saw the prisoners carried away with them a vivid impression of their sullen ferocity.

But not less surprising than the appearance of the captives, was the discovery that their losses had really

[*Photo by Lieut. W. O. Lynne.*

CHIEF-COMMANDANT WOLMARANS (BROTHER-IN-LAW OF PRESIDENT KRUGER),
Captured at Paardeberg.

been insignificant.   The terrific bombardment had caused discomfort rather than destruction, so far as the life of human beings was concerned.   Instead of the thousands of killed and wounded that the

Boer losses slight.   awe-stricken witnesses of the British shell-fire had expected, there proved to be but 170 wounded men inside the laager.   Many of these were in a shocking condition from neglect, and had evidently received their hurt as far back as the battle of the 18th, or

even the rearguard action of the 16th.   The number of dead, of course, could not be ascertained, but since experience shows that the ratio of dead to wounded is usually as one to three or four, or, with small-bore bullets, is even lower, the killed are not at all likely to have exceeded 100, even when allowance is made for the heavy mortality caused by artillery fire.   The Boers put it far lower, but little value can be attached to their statements when these have to do with figures, since on such a point as the number of men he commanded, Cronje either was, or professed to be, ignorant. He told Lord Roberts

[Copyright 1900 by
Underwood & Underwood.

A REST ON THE WAY.
The long line of prisoners is dimly seen stretching away in the distance on the right.

that his force was about 3,000, when it was actually 1,000 stronger.

The careful construction of the Boer trenches

Structure of the trenches.   was the real explanation

of these small losses. They are thus described by Mr. Battersby, a correspondent with Lord Roberts :—
" The trenches, which had proved so impervious to

[Stereoscopic photo by Underwood & Underwood.

THE PAARDEBERG PRISONERS ENTRAINING AT MODDER RIVER.

our fire, were very interesting.   It was difficult to trace in their outline any military design, or even a wilful divergence from, and improvement on, the accepted patterns.   Nor did there seem to be any systematic attempt to provide a cross or flanking fire to cover dead angles.   They might have been drawn by a man with no military knowledge, but they could only have been dug by experts in war.

Very narrow, in some of them a broad man could scarcely have turned his shoulders; very short and very deep, they offered the meagrest opportunities to shell fire that can be conceived. They were burrows rather than trenches, cut with extraordinary squareness to a depth sometimes of over six feet, and with shelves scooped out three and four feet below the surface in which a man could lie, secure from anything which did not burst inside his burrow. Long dead-heads of earth broke the lines of the trenches, and through these tunnels were carried, by which a man might creep from one end to the other. The earth was thrown up equally on either side, and an occasional sort of private box trench, holding two or three, was dug here and there immediately behind the first, the object of which was not apparent. A domestic air was given to the whole by the portmanteaus and tin boxes, sunk in small square pits behind the trenches with the cover flush with the ground."

[*Copyright* 1900 *by Underwood & Underwood.*

MR. AND MRS. CRONJE ENTERING THE TRAIN AFTER THE SURRENDER.
Each of them carries a bundle of belongings under the arm.

No words could sufficiently express the filth, disorder, and confusion of the interior of the laager. Here lay 300 waggons and carts, scattered over an area of half a mile, and for the most part wrecked and burned by the British shells. Here amongst them lay the putre-

Condition of the laager.

fying carcases of oxen and horses, in terrible heaps of mouldering red flesh; all about were mattresses, odds and ends of furniture, cooking utensils, bowls, collars, clothing, Bibles, and boots, an assemblage of strange, incongruous things, which yet showed that the Boer knew the art of making himself comfortable upon the battlefield. The stench was so sickening and terrible that only the strongest nerves could

BOER PRISONERS ON THE WAY TO
CAPETOWN.

endure it. For the most part the prisoners seemed to be glad to have done with living under such horrible conditions, and one and all asserted that they were weary of the war. "But you," they said, turning to the British soldiers about them, "will have to go back and fight." They were sent down under escort of the City Imperial Volunteers to Modder River, thence to be entrained for Capetown. Cronje was treated throughout with the utmost deference, and was given a cart drawn by six artillery horses in which to make the journey. His demeanour continued sullen and forbidding throughout. At Capetown he was placed upon the British cruiser *Doris*, and given, by Admiral Harris,

AN ERRAND OF MERCY.

British stretcher-bearers crossing the Modder at Paardeberg to assist the Boer wounded remaining in the trenches after the surrender.

[*Photo by R. Faulkner & Co.*

MAJOR-GENERAL LORD DUNDONALD.

Douglas Mackinnon Baillie Hamilton Cochrane, Earl of Dundonald, C.B., M.V.O. (see page 214), was born in 1852; educated at Eton, and entered the 2nd Life Guards in 1870; Captain, 1878; Major, 1885; Lieut.-Colonel, 1885; Colonel, 1889. He served with the Nile Expedition, 1884-5, in command of the 2nd Life Guards detachment of the Camel Corps; carried despatches to Korti; commanded the transport and baggage of the Desert Column under Sir Herbert Stewart in the advance on Metammeh, and acted as guide to the reinforcements for Abu Klea; carried despatches from Gubat announcing the fall of Khartoum. He was in command of the 2nd Life Guards from 1895 to 1899, and at present commands the 3rd Cavalry Brigade, South Africa Field Force, with rank of Major-General.

MR. AND MRS. CRONJE BREAK THEIR JOURNEY TO CAPETOWN.

the flag officer's state cabins. It was, however, thought unwise to keep him and his men so near thousands of sympathisers in Cape Colony. Many attempts at escape were detected, and at last it was decided to send the prisoners to the island of St. Helena, which derived fame from the fact of having been Napoleon's prison. There they all safely arrived, notwithstanding a daring attempt of Colonel Schiel to get away, and there Cronje with them spent his captivity.

On the British side the casualties in the whole series of actions round Paardeberg reached the heavy total of 1,534. Of these 255 were killed, 1,209 wounded, and 70 captured by the enemy or missing. The vast majority of these casualties were, of course, incurred in the great

Severe British casualties. battle of the 18th. But from first to last, counting in Lord Methuen's battles, the operations against Cronje and the Boer western army cost the British the terrible total of 3,481 men.

The victory of Paardeberg was the turning **Moral effect of the victory.** point of the war—the one decisive action that was fought from beginning to end. It was the first real victory accompanied by solid results in the

[Photo by L. Jenks, Simon's Town.

CAMP OF BOER PRISONERS AT SIMON'S TOWN.

This camp was originally formed to accommodate the prisoners taken at Elandslaagte and the other early actions of the campaign; some of Cronje's men, also, were quartered here. H.M.SS. *Powerful* and *Terrible* are seen in the Bay.

shape of the capture of the enemy's troops and artillery. It broke a long series of defeats—Stormberg, Magersfontein, Colenso, Spion Kop, and Vaal Krantz—and substituted success for disaster.

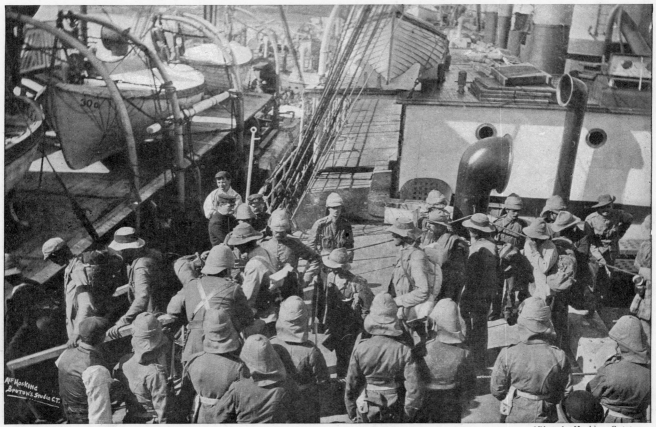

It deprived the enemy of the man who was their best, or almost their best, general, of a large amount of war material, in the shape of the hundreds of waggons captured or destroyed, and of a powerful army. Short of men as the republics were, the loss of the 4,500 burghers and merce-

SIGNATURES OF COMMANDANT-GENERAL AND MRS. CRONJE, THEIR GRANDSON, AND STAFF.
From the passenger list of the *Milwaukee.*

naries, who were captured from first to last in the fighting around Paardeberg, was an irreparable blow, infinitely more serious than the loss to England of 3,500 men. Moreover, the defeat produced a great moral effect throughout the Boer territories. Superstitious as they were by nature, their run of victories had encouraged in the burghers the firm belief that God was upon their side, and that He had doomed the British to defeat and overthrow. It now seemed to them that He frowned upon their cause. Disheartened, doubting their own strength, and above all fearing the enveloping tactics of Lord Roberts, they prepared in no joyful mood to meet his threatened advance to Bloemfontein. Their strategy had in a moment collapsed. Already they had had to draw heavily upon their forces in Natal for men to come to the relief of Cronje, with the result that General Buller had at last been

[Photo by Hosking, Capetown.

BOER PRISONERS OF CRONJE'S COMMAND GOING ON BOARD THE "MANILA."

THE GRAVE OF NAPOLEON
AT ST. HELENA,
Where his body was laid
before its removal to
the Hôtel des In-
valides, Paris.

VIEW IN
SANDY BAY,
ST. HELENA,
Showing the character
of the country where the
Boer prisoners were accom-
modated.

able to make headway northwards to Ladysmith. They had no other army to meet Lord Roberts, and at the very moment when they needed every burgher, many of their men were deserting the commandos under various pretexts, anxious only for an end of their sufferings.

The credit of Cronje's capture belongs in equal degree to Lord Roberts and the officers and men he led. The work of General French and of the Sixth Division in forcing Cronje to halt was particularly meritorious; nothing could surpass the marching and endurance of the British infantry. In the actual fighting the Cornwalls and Canadians especially covered themselves with glory, but all arms and all ranks displayed a spirit truly heroic.

JAMESTOWN, THE CAPITAL OF ST. HELENA, WHERE THE BOER PRISONERS WERE LANDED.

[Photo by Caney.

BOER FOOTBRIDGE ACROSS
THE TUGELA

On the rocks forming the rapids
below Pieters Station.

The railway line can be distinguished running along the bank on the right. The bridge is built of sleepers held together by "metals" from the railway lines and supported by heaps of sleepers resting on rocks, and does credit to Boer engineering.

CHAPTER XX.

THE RELIEF OF LADYSMITH.

Buller's troops confident in spite of defeat—Arrangements for an eastward flanking movement—Monte Cristo the key to Ladysmith—Disposition of the Boer forces—Expedition into Zululand—Buller reconnoitres—Disposition of the British forces—Hussar Hill seized—Scarcity of water—Attack on Cingolo—Monte Cristo seized—Hlangwane evacuated by the Boers—Capture of the enemy's camp—Heavy guns on Green Hill—Colenso occupied—The river crossed—Reconnaissance by Coke's Brigade—The advance commences—Deadly experience of the King's Royal Rifles—Attack on Railway and Inniskilling Hills—Furious fighting—Hildyard's Brigade relieves the Irish—Change of front—A Sunday truce—Renewal of hostilities—"Remember Majuba!"—Storming of Railway Hill—Victory at Last—Pieters Hill evacuated by the Boers—Ladysmith relieved—British losses—Boer losses—State entry into the town—Honours for the Irish.

Buller's troops confident in spite of defeat.

FROM Spion Kop and Vaal Krantz, after a month of marches and unsuccessful battles, the heroic army of Natal fared back to Chieveley with the bitterness of defeat at heart. Yet neither general nor soldiers lost confidence in themselves. Checked they had been, compelled to retreat, but they ascribed this rather to natural obstacles and the malice of circumstances than to any prowess of the Boers. One and all the men asked, not for a month's repose in camp, but to be led again towards the gloomy mountains and the green banks of the swift-flowing Tugela, to succour and save their valiant comrades in Ladysmith. In no respect had General Buller's popularity suffered by his reverses. He was still the idol of his men, to whom his care and consideration for their well-being had endeared him not less than an implicit belief in his bravery and obstinate resolution. Unfortunate in his command he might be; unsuccessful he was hitherto; but Thomas Atkins trusted him and felt sure of his ultimate victory. By February 11 his whole command was concentrated at Chieveley, with the exception of Colonel Burn-Murdoch's brigade of cavalry, the York and Lancasters, and the Lancashire Fusiliers, who were left to guard the line of the Little Tugela. Springfield Bridge

[Photo by H. W. Barnett.

COLONEL BURN-MURDOCH.

Lieut.-Colonel John Francis Burn-Murdoch, J.P., was born at Cambridge in 1859, and is the son of the Rev. Canon Burn-Murdoch. He was educated at Eton; joined the Royal Dragoons in 1878; Captain, 1885; Major, 1892; Lieut.-Colonel, 1896; served in the Nile Expedition, 1884–5 with the Royal Dragoons' detachment of the Camel Corps; took part in the actions of Abu Klea, El Gubat, Akasheh, and Firket, and in the capture of Suarda and Dongola.

was destroyed the better to protect the British flank. Fresh from one defeat the British army had returned to the scene of another. It had learnt at last, after days and weeks of groping amid the intricacies of the unmapped mountain-land of the Upper Tugela, that there was no way round by the west. It had discovered that the Colenso position was impregnable to frontal attack. There remained only, as a last resource, to find a route round the enemy's left. If that should fail—but the thing was unimaginable. This time the army must fight its way through at all costs. Honour, duty, and—when the advance in the west began—the desire to emulate the deeds of Lord Roberts' army, tuned the strings of men's hearts to the highest pitch.

For the supreme effort General Barton's Brigade, hitherto in garrison at Chieveley, containing the Colenso Boers, would be available. It was a noteworthy rein-

Arrangements for an eastward flanking movement.

forcement, fully making good the losses of Spion Kop and the flank movement. Two changes were made in the higher commands before the last attempt to break through to Ladysmith began. General Clery had been temporarily disabled by an injury to his leg: he was replaced in command of his division by General Lyttelton, who had particularly distinguished himself in the attempts to turn the Boer positions at and near Spion Kop. As his promotion left vacant the command of the Rifle Brigade, Colonel Norcott was appointed to that position.

To the east of Colenso the ground is broken, mountainous, much intersected by watercourses, and covered with dense, almost impenetrable bush. At Colenso the Tugela bends sharply north and, after pursuing a generally northward course for three miles, turns once more east. Thus a flanking movement in this direction would, without crossing the Tugela, bring the British army almost to Pieters, which lay only nine miles from Ladysmith. The obstacles to a turning move-ment were the mountains and bush. Just to the east of Colenso stands the knob of rock know as Hlangwane, upon which an attempt had been made in the battle of Co-lenso. This emi-nence was now strongly held by the Boers, and its whole front had been seamed with innumerable trenches till it had

OFFICERS OF THE LANCASHIRE FUSILIERS AT MESS IN CHIEVELEY CAMP.

become a perfect fortress, impossible of direct attack. The Hlangwane ridge is prolonged by a round green hill, known from its appearance as Green Hill, which runs eastwards, till it meets the long ridge of Monte Cristo. This ridge is broken about its centre by a nek or pass. There is a second nek at its southern end, and then succeeds another long ridge known as Cingolo. The three ranges, Monte Cristo, Hlangwane, and Cingolo, may be likened to a Y laid aslant. The left arm is formed

[*Photo by Bassano.*

MAJOR-GENERAL BARTON, C.B.

Major-General Geoffry Barton is the younger son of the late C. C. Barton, of Rownhams, Hants. Born in 1844, he was educated at Eton, and entered the Army as Ensign in the 7th Foot (now the Royal Fusiliers) in October, 1862; Lieutenant, 1865; he was Adjutant of his regiment from 1869 to 1874; was employed in the transport service in Ashanti in 1874; Aide-de-camp at Aldershot, 1874-7; on special service in South Africa in 1878-9, and served throughout the Zulu War; D.A.Q.M.G. with the Expeditionary Force in Egypt, 1882; served in China, 1884-5; and the Sudan, 1885; Colonel, 1886; Acting Adjutant-General of the Thames District, 1895-7; and of the North-West District, 1897-8; C.B., 1889; Major-General, 1898; appointed to the command of the 6th Brigade of the Third Division, October, 1899.

by Hlangwane and Green Hill, the right by Monte Cristo, and the stem by Cingolo. Monte Cristo

Monte Cristo the key to Ladysmith. towered to a height of 2,500 ft. from the Tugela River, upon which its northern extremity looked down at a point far to the north-east of Colenso; it commanded the whole country round as far as Grobler's Kloof and Bulwana. On this side it was emphatically the key to Ladysmith. Cingolo was slightly lower than Monte Cristo, but was

COLENSO.

The photograph shows the village and the road-bridge across the Tugela. The sugar-loaf shaped hill in the distance is Spitz Kop, where the Klip River (which runs through Ladysmith) joins the Tugela. The flat hill on the left is Bulwana. Directly over the bridge is seen the spur of the Biggarsberg, around which the troops marched on the memorable retreat from Dundee.

very rough and precipitous. Opposite the junction of the stem and arms of the Y rose yet another height, named Hussar Hill, which lay between Cingolo and the British camp at Chieveley. A deep valley, densely covered with bush, parted Hussar Hill from the Hlangwane and Cingolo ridges; through the valley, amidst a garden of sweet-scented mimosas and odorous oleanders, brawled the mountain torrent known as the Gomba, which in turn poured its crystal water into the turbid Blaauwkrantz, a stream which rose beyond Frere, and flowing north-east into the Tugela shut in on the south the mountain-land upon the left of the Boer position.

General Buller's new plan was this: First of all to seize Hussar Hill and place his heavy artillery upon it, so as to sweep Cingolo with its fire. Then Cingolo was to be stormed by the infantry, attacking it at its southern end. This height in his possession, he meant to go forward to Monte Cristo, which, once captured, would enfilade and render untenable Hlangwane and Colenso. The plan gave every promise of success; it had, indeed, been under consideration weeks before, but was then abandoned in favour of the westward flanking attack which resulted so disastrously. The weak point about the Boer left was that it could not be indefinitely prolonged. Here it had no insurmountable obstacle, such as the Drakensberg, upon which to rest. Sooner or later the superior British army must be able, by steadily working to the east, to turn it. The plight of Ladysmith, which was now so serious as to cause general anxiety, however, prevented slow and deliberate movements such as had characterised the Spion Kop operations; there was reason to fear that the garrison might be overwhelmed or compelled by hunger to surrender before the British army could get round the Boer left. Still, despite the importance of time, there was no undue haste on General Buller's part. Knowing what terrible issues hung upon success or failure, he seemed determined to omit no preparation or precaution, and to run no unnecessary risks.

ON THE WAY TO LADYSMITH: AN OFFICER ISSUING INSTRUCTIONS TO HIS REGIMENT.

The Intelligence Department with the army had been reorganised and now worked with a refreshing efficiency. Accurate information as to the location and strength of the Boer forces in General Buller's

Disposition of the Boer forces.

front had been obtained as the first preliminary of success. It was known that they held Hussar Hill at night and the bed of the Gomba by day, that they had camps on Hlangwane and Cingolo, and that the western slopes of this last mountain had been entrenched. A Creusot field gun and a " Pom-Pom " were reported on Hlangwane ; one gun was detected near Green Hill ; and just north of Colenso, amidst the kopjes at the foot of Grobler's Kloof, were made

SCOUTS OF BETHUNE'S MOUNTED INFANTRY.

out six other guns or " Pom-Poms." The actual force of the enemy in the neighbourhood of Colenso about February 10 was probably between 10,000 and 12,000, but in the next few days the influence of Lord Roberts' movements in the Free State was distinctly felt, and 5,000 or more of the Free Staters and Transvaalers left to oppose the British Commander-in-Chief. Round Ladysmith there may have been from 5,000 to 8,000 Boers, so that their total strength in Natal, before the invasion of the Free State began, was from 15,000 to 20,000, all seasoned men, flushed with repeated victory.

PREPARATIONS FOR THE ADVANCE INTO ZULULAND :
Bethune's Mounted Infantry packing their kit.

Against them Sir George White had now not more than 6,000 men capable of lining his trenches, and of these scarcely one could be trusted to march a mile. Sir Redvers Buller, the " Red Bull " as the Boers called him, may have had 24,000 combatants fit for duty ; they, too, were well-tried veterans, trained in the bitter school of defeat ; and because of that very fact, perhaps, more to be trusted than any other army of their strength. They were eager for a fresh impetuous assault upon the frowning heights, though they well knew that success could only be purchased by terrible sacrifices.

On February 12, as a preliminary to the advance by Monte Cristo and Pieters, Hussar Hill was reconnoitred. On the previous day Bethune's Mounted Infantry had been despatched to the Zululand

Expedition into Zululand. frontier with two objects in view—to protect eastern Natal from raiding parties of Boers, and at the same time to menace the extreme Boer left. This weakened Lord Dundonald's Cavalry Brigade and left him with only the South African Light Horse, Thorneycroft's Mounted Infantry, the Composite Regiment of Mounted Infantry, and the various Natal volunteer organisations. With these, one field battery and a single battalion of infantry, the Welsh Fusiliers, in support, General Buller and Lord Dundonald marched out in the morning. The day was intensely hot and the advance excessively trying to the troops, but the Boers offered practically no resistance. A sputtering fire, not a steady roar of musketry, came from the cover on the hill, and Colonel

Thorneycroft was able to push rapidly forward and seize it without loss of any kind. Then Gene-**Buller reconnoitres.** ral Buller rode up and with a powerful telescope scanned the face of the country before him—the green valley of the Gomba, the rock-ribbed barrier of Cingolo and

GROBLER'S KLOOF: KRAAL NEAR THE SUMMIT.

[Photo by Caney.

GROBLER'S KLOOF SPRUIT: JACK IN POSSESSION.

Note the sand-bag defences; they were placed there by the Boers, who used the bridge as a sniping station. The main road from the Tugela, at Colenso, to Ladysmith passes over this bridge.

Monte Cristo, and away to the left the glistening tin roofs of Colenso, which had witnessed his former reverse. To the north Bulwana stood up before him, and puffs of smoke from its summit showed that the Boer guns were still busy at their congenial work of bombarding Ladysmith. As he gazed upon the landscape the Boer skirmishers grew in audacity and had to be given a few rounds from the Colt guns and artillery. About noon the British force was ordered to retire, since General Buller was not as yet ready to begin his advance, and Hussar Hill was not by nature a defensible position. As the troops fell back, the Boers dashed forward, and opened a tremendous long-range fire upon the mounted infantry. The squadrons opened out and Lord Dundonald's Colt guns speedily replied, supported by the rifles of the mounted infantrymen. The fire was fierce, and yet the casualties were trivial in the extreme; Lieutenant J. Churchill, brother of the famous war correspondent, Mr. Garrard, an expert who was entrusted with the management of the Colt guns, and ten men were wounded, but not severely. The Boers, as usual, were quite invisible to the naked eye. The enemy were temporarily checked by the shower of bullets, and the retirement of the British proceeded without further incident.

The 13th passed in preparation for the advance. The troops rested and made ready for the desperate work before them. The great 6-inch naval gun was placed in position near Chieveley, side

J. Finnemore, R.I., R.B.A.]

AN ALARM IN CAMP.

Incidents of the kind here depicted were of frequent occurrence in Buller's camps. A patrol coming in touch with the enemy would call for supports, and immediately a detachment would be sent out to their assistance. On the occasion depicted it was the "Cockiolly Birds"—the South African Light Horse—who were thus called upon. These men distinguished themselves in the capture of Hussar Hill (page 448).

by side with two naval 4·7's, so that all three weapons could fire as required either upon Hussar Hill, Hlangwane, or Cingolo; three more 4·7's had reached Chieveley on trucks, but as they were upon

Disposition of the British forces.

ship-mountings could not as yet be employed. General Hart was detailed with his brigade to guard the camp, and two fresh 5-inch siege guns arrived and were added to General Buller's long-range artillery. Into the valley of the Blaauwkrantz marched General Lyttelton with the brigades of Hildyard and Norcott, and took post for the night two miles east of Chieveley. On the morning of the 14th the great advance, which was to end at Ladysmith, began. The troops knew that already in the west the invasion of the Free State was in progress, and that in every quarter the Boers were being vigorously pressed. Ladysmith, too, knew it, and the hearts of its starving garrison beat higher. Help was coming both from the west and south—indirectly from the west, directly from the south.

THE DASH INTO ZULULAND: BETHUNE'S MOUNTED INFANTRY CROSSING A DRIFT NEAR BOTHA'S CASTLE.

The Boers, as was their wont, had retired from Hussar Hill for the day; but when the South African Light Horse rode briskly forward towards that eminence they realised its importance. From the

Hussar Hill seized.

dongas of the Gomba they ran a neck-and-neck race with the Colonial troopers for the summit, but the Colonials won. Just in time the "Cockiolly birds," as they were called from their hats with feathered plumes, and, perhaps, also from the swagger with which they bore themselves, gained the summit. Once in possession they held fast to the hill, engaging in a vigorous rifle duel with their enemy. Behind them advanced in an endless line the British infantry, General Barton on the left, Generals Coke and Wynne in the centre, and Generals Hildyard and Norcott on the right. For the first time in this war the whole available strength of the Natal army was to be employed against the enemy. General Buller must have been a proud man, as that day he watched the spirited advance of his splendid soldiers and saw them straining at the leash to be let go against the Boers, as he realised that the twenty-five thousand men he commanded were prepared to face everything—bullets and shells and death—to wash out the stain of defeat which smirched his record and theirs. General Barton followed the Colonials on to Hussar Hill and began the construction of entrenchments there, while on his right General Lyttelton, and on his left General Warren, swept steadily forward.   Upon the height thus won General Buller planted his powerful artillery.   The naval 12-pounders were stationed behind sandbag defences, which enabled them to defy the enemy's projectiles; the 5-inch position guns, the 5-inch howitzers, and the field artillery were placed in the

[Photo by the Biograph Company.

SAILORS DRAGGING A NAVAL GUN INTO POSITION.

open. The Navy believed in cover, the Army did not. And then, from Hussar Hill, the troops looked out across the green valley of the Gomba, still full of Boer sharpshooters, upon the slopes of Cingolo and the flat-topped, boulder-covered Green Hill, which were to be the objectives of the next movements.

During the night which followed the capture of Hussar Hill the heavy guns at Chieveley maintained a desultory fire upon Hlangwane.   With dawn of the 15th the weapons on Hussar Hill began to shell Green Hill and Cingolo, while the troops in open formation cleared the eastern spurs of Hussar Hill and drove back the Boer "snipers," under cover of the artillery, which now mustered no less than four 5-inch, two 4·7-inch, six naval 12-pounder, six Horse Artillery 12-pounder, forty-two field 15-pounder, and six mountain 7-pounder guns, with six 5-inch howitzers, all in position on Hussar Hill.   The guns were better worked and more skilfully directed than upon any previous occasion in Natal; better means of communication had been arranged, so as to facilitate a concentrated fire upon the enemy.   The army, in short, had profited by defeat.   The Boers answered the British fire with two long-range guns and a "Pom-Pom," which, as usual, it was impossible to locate.   No clouds of dust and smoke disclosed their position.   Yet they burst shells in all directions about the British troops and British guns.   "Sometimes they fired at the guns for a few minutes," says Mr. Atkins, "then they would change to a group of battery horses, then to a firing line of infantry, then to a transport train.   And we!   Why, on those rare occasions when we see a gun or a few Boers we are only for the moment relieved from the constant puzzle of having nothing to fire at."

UNDER MARCHING ORDERS: OFFICERS INSPECTING THE RIFLES AND THE FEET OF THEIR MEN.

INOFFENSIVE ENTRENCHMENTS: THE CAMP KITCHEN OF THE DUBLIN FUSILIERS ON THE TUGELA.

The day was one of fierce heat, and water was exceedingly scarce. Iron tanks, mounted on waggons, brought up a small supply; nevertheless the sufferings of horses and men were severe.

Scarcity of water. Hussar Hill had no springs upon its summit; the nearest points from which the precious fluid could be obtained were the stream of the Gomba, brawling in the valley below, and farther away the stream of the Blaauwkrantz. Perhaps it was their thirst as much as their renowned valour that carried the West Surreys through the thick bush which covered the north-eastern slope of Hussar Hill, as far as the Gomba, but General Buller was not as yet ready to advance so far, and they were recalled. The fighting came to an end about 2 p.m., and had little result.

On the 16th the weather was again suffocatingly hot, and the general unprepared to force matters to a conclusion. Fighting began with day, but the Boers seemed to be in small force, and it was supposed that the British army had only to deal with a weak rearguard. There was, as before, a sharp artillery duel. "Shrapnel," says Mr. Bennet Burleigh, "burst around the batteries, and 'Pom-Poms' snapped and whipped up dust and rock, occasionally within a few yards of General Buller and his staff. . . . Until 11.20 a.m., time and again the enemy's artillery broke out anew, after being temporarily silenced, proving that neither our lyddite nor shrapnel had quite got home upon them." The infantry prepared to push forward and cross the Gomba—Barton's brigade towards Green Hill, Hildyard's and Norcott's towards Cingolo; but in the morning, owing to the intense heat, it was thought wiser to recall them after they had gained a good deal of ground. The day thus passed, as the 15th before it, resultlessly. As the British retired a small body of Boers pushed after them, and had the audacity to close in to a distance of less than 500 yards from the British outposts. The enemy were only driven back by a concentrated fire

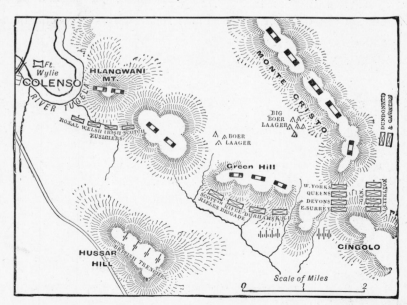

MAP OF THE ATTACKS ON GREEN HILL, MONTE CRISTO, AND HLANGWANE,
February 17-19, 1900.

from the British guns, which pitched lyddite shells and shrapnel liberally among them, causing them, it was afterwards known, heavy loss. They went back as quickly as they had come, and henceforward the British possession of the northern slopes of Hussar Hill was undisputed. New trenches were made to assure the ground won, and water was brought up to the thirsty men.

With sunset of the 16th came the end of inaction. Everything was now ready for the advance, and orders were issued for a general movement on the 17th. At dawn the artillery on Hussar Hill began a vigorous bombardment of Cingolo and Monte Cristo. With Hussar Hill as its pivot General Lyttelton's whole division was to extend and sweep round, enveloping Cingolo and getting beyond the Boer left. At the same time Lord Dundonald with the mounted infantry, making a yet wider circle, was to strike farther to the enemy's left, and to fall upon the north-eastern slopes of

| Capt. Reichman | Lieut. Thomson | Col. Gourko | Capt. Allum | Capt. Demange | Lieut. Duval. |
| (U.S. of America). | (Holland). | (Russia). | (Norway). | (France). | (France) |

Mr Fisher (Orange Free State).

FOREIGN ATTACHÉS WITH THE BOERS.

Cingolo. Thus, in order from left to right, the brigades in the British line, stretching from Chieveley to far south-eastwards of Cingolo, were Hart's, Coke's, Barton's, Norcott's, Hildyard's, and Dundonald's. The thick brushwood veiled their movements from the enemy and gave excellent cover, at the risk of their suddenly finding themselves in the midst of the foe. But, superior in numbers, and armed with the bayonet for hand-to-hand encounter, the British troops had little cause to dread such unexpected contact with the enemy.

Lord Dundonald first marched ten miles to the east, his men in single file, and then, swinging round, began to climb through trees and boulders up the rough, precipitous side of Cingolo. So

Attack on Cingolo. thick was the bush that a path had to be cut, and progress, in consequence, was slow. From dawn until the sun was high the troopers were hidden in the jungle, but about 11 a.m. a handful of men reached the summit at its southern extremity, and found it comparatively open ground, broken here and there by copses and strewn with boulders. As they debouched, a party of Boers opened fire. First came one shot, and then a heavy volley, while every man

BRITISH 5-IN. POSITION GUN.
This is the military gun, as distinguished from the 4·7 in. naval gun. It was drawn by oxen.
[Photo by Capt. Pilleau.

in the British force held his breath. If the enemy were in strength, they must with little trouble hurl back this small detachment, which, from the difficulty of the path up the mountain, could only be slowly reinforced. Fortunately, as it turned out, there were but a hundred Boers on that part of the ridge, acting as an outpost—for they had never expected the British to approach in this direction—and they fell back precipitately as our men returned their fire, suffering some loss. A footing upon the height had been won, and, seeing this, the rest of Dundonald's Brigade pushed northwards along its slope towards the nek which parts Cingolo from Monte Cristo, so as to threaten the retreat of the parties of the enemy holding the ridge of Cingolo.

From other quarters the attack was developing. While shrapnel searched the western face of Cingolo, and while the howitzers seared the summit of Green Hill with their rain of lyddite till the mountains reverberated the roar of the cannonade, the infantry advance made progress. "The noise was deafening," says a correspondent, "and expressions of pity could be heard in the ranks of the Irish Fusiliers, such as 'Poor beggars! Why don't they go home and look after their farms?' The swish of the heavy missiles from the howitzers was delightful to listen to as they sped over our heads, especially to me, who had been driven by the enemy's long-range guns from town to town. The sides of the hills began to assume a most peculiar appearance. The yellow smoke from the lyddite, and the brilliant white of the shrapnel, as they burst in the air together, mingled with the clouds of dust that the common shells raised up like so many variegated spread-out fans, presented a picture not yet represented on any wall. For a full hour our stream of fire continued, without disclosing the presence of a single Boer. The enemy took our pills of iron, as he always does at the outset of an engagement, with dogged silence. He sat tight. He was not to be drawn in such a

Alec Ball.]
ANNIHILATION OF A GUN'S CREW BY A BOER SHRAPNEL SHELL.

fashion." As the day went on, the Boers at last began to reply with a well-directed fire, and shrapnel and shell fell in unpleasantly close proximity to the British guns. Again and again their sandbag redoubts saved the naval 12-pounders; the regular artillery now suffered for its disregard of cover. A Boer shrapnel burst accurately among the crew of one of the 5-in. position guns, and killed or wounded all the six men in it. There were other narrow escapes, but the gunners never flinched or showed a trace of fear. Their work was done as coolly and correctly as if they had been at drill

on the parade-ground, and as if they had not had to fear the shrieking missiles of an invisible enemy. "No. 1 Gun, Fire! No. 2 Gun, Fire!" repeated the officer in charge with calm and monotonous precision, unmoved by the tumult about him. On either flank of the 5-in. weapons were the field guns, and behind, concealed by the ridge from the Boers, the dumpy howitzers. The hot morning air was suffocating with the smell of burnt wool—the characteristic scent of cordite— and greasy with its fine powdery ash.

Hildyard's and Norcott's Brigades, meantime, crossed the Gomba and closed upon Cingolo, opening a heavy rifle fire upon the Boers. Parties of the enemy could be made out from Hussar Hill, hurrying across the nek which divides Cingolo from Monte Cristo to reinforce their outposts on the summit, which they now saw was the object of attack. But as their whole attention was concentrated upon the repulse of the infantry climbing the western

J. Finnemore, R.I., R.B.A.]   *[After a sketch by Ernest Prater.*

THE SCOTS FUSILIERS ADVANCING THROUGH THE BRUSHWOOD TO THE CAPTURE
OF GREEN HILL.

slopes, the enemy overlooked the cavalry and mounted infantry threatening the southern and south-eastern approaches. It was for this reason that, covered by the rifle duel which was proceeding on the western slopes, Lord Dundonald's advance was so easy. The West Surreys were now detached from Hildyard's Brigade and climbed the hill from the south, joining hands, as the top of the ridge was reached, with Lord Dundonald. About noon, or soon after, a heliograph was seen winking on the summit, and it was generally known that success had crowned the assault. Then the mounted infantry were made out driving the Boers before them to the nek. Forthwith the infantry of Hildyard's, Norcott's, and Barton's Brigades pressed forward to co-operate with and support the mounted men. The Irish Fusiliers, indeed, or some of them, went too far. An officer and 20 or 30 men actually pushed on to the western end of the Green Hill ridge, and found that Green Hill was not occupied by the enemy. They attempted to signal back the fact to the rest of the brigade, but failed to

attract attention; yet none the less they were able to do good service by protecting the flank of the West Yorkshires, who were now swarming into the nek at the northern end of Cingolo; and though withdrawn at the close of the day, they were replaced by a company of West Yorkshires, so that the ground they had gained was not lost. As the afternoon wore on the last small parties of Boers were dislodged from Cingolo, and hold upon that height was secured by entrenchments. From the top Ladysmith could be seen fourteen miles off, and with it signals were at once exchanged. Guns were hurried up in readiness to open fire the following day upon Monte Cristo and Hlangwane, which were the next points marked ou: for capture. At nightfall the British infantry bivouacked in the nek, and prepared with rising spirits to renew the struggle. The casualties of the day's fight were low owing to the excellence of the cover, not much exceeding 50 killed and wounded. A distinct success had been gained at

Oscar Eckhardt, R.B.A.]   *[After a sketch by Ernest Prater.*

THE CAPTURE OF MONTE CRISTO.

The Surrey men advancing and firing from cover, "playing the Boer game, and beating them at it," as the artist and correspondent writes.

trivial cost. But the army of Natal had too often been baulked at the last moment, after initial victory, to build unreasonable expectations upon what it had attained.

Until darkness fell the outposts of the two armies continued to exchange shots, and far into the night the artillery maintained its bombardment of Monte Cristo and Hlangwane. With dawn of the 18th the fight recommenced. Again the long line of British guns showered projectiles upon Monte Cristo, while the infantry set to work to storm the mountain. The 64th Field Battery took up a position on the slopes of Cingolo, whence it could enfilade the Boer position; from the hollow between Green Hill and Cingolo the 7th Field Battery directed its projectiles alternately upon Green Hill and Monte Cristo.

Monte Cristo seized. The Boers on the latter height were in considerable force, but had expected the attack to come from Green Hill, and not from their flank and rear; they were greatly disheartened by the turn matters had taken, and seemed no longer to fight with their old spirit. Their guns, however, rained shells upon the top of Cingolo, which was held by the West Surreys, and, despite the excellence of the cover, inflicted some loss upon that battalion. Then towards 8 a.m., the infantry of Hildyard's

[Photo taken on the spot by R. Bicknell, Newmarket.
THE WEST YORKSHIRES ATTACKING MONTE CRISTO.

brigade began their climb up the steep slopes of Monte Cristo, the West Yorkshires leading, and the West and East Surreys supporting. Simultaneously Barton's Fusilier Brigade pushed on up the ridge of Green Hill, its tiers upon tiers of trenches now all asmoke with the shells from the British guns, bursting well in advance of the assaulting infantry. "The musketry," says Mr. Winston Churchill, "swelled into a constant crackle, like the noise of a good fire roaring up the chimney; but in spite of more than a hundred casualties the advance was never checked for an instant, and by half past ten o'clock the bayonets of the attacking infantry began to glitter among the trees of the summit." Before that dauntless, unflinching advance the courage of the commandos who held Monte Cristo evaporated, and the Boers leaped upon their little ponies and retired helter-skelter. A Boer 'Pom-Pom' at this moment all but fell into British hands, only making its escape by a stroke of good luck. It was afterwards found buried on Hlangwane. Then on the British skirmishers upon the summit descended a hail of

BOER CREUSOT GUN, SHOWING THE ACT OF LOADING

projectiles from the Boer guns—shrapnel from the big Creusots, strings of little steel bolts from the deadly 'Pom-Poms'—and in the turmoil and dust of lashing bullets our men could be seen from Hussar Hill frantically working at the construction of schanzes and entrenchments. For a moment or two it seemed that there might almost be a repetition of Spion Kop, and that for all their courage the British troops might be driven back by artillery fire from the heights they had so nobly won. But then to the anxious watchers came the sight of the rush of wave upon wave of reinforcements; of a fierce dash which carried the Fusilier Brigade and Norcott's Brigade to the top of Green Hill with the loss of no more than three men—so well had the guns done their work—and the sound of exultant cheer answering exultant cheer. Monte Cristo was won; Green Hill was won, and bright with flashing bayonets; a success greater than the army knew had crowned its

stubborn efforts. The Boers were in flight, and the fire of their artillery was not to cover and prepare a counter-attack on their part, but only to safeguard their retreat.

Norcott's men pushed rapidly over the hollow which parts Green Hill from Monte Cristo towards a Boer laager which now came into sight. They were upon the enemy's line of retreat, though they hardly knew it. Presently they made out a large body of mounted men, manœuvring in good order and apparently disposed in squadrons and regiments. For this reason they took it for Dundonald's Brigade and refrained from firing. The Boers, for Boer the force was, were thus enabled to escape without suffering complete disaster, as when the British troops detected their error it was too late for them to cause the enemy serious mischief. Yet the Boers did not get away scatheless. The gunners of the big naval 6-inch weapon at Chieveley caught sight of a large commando formed up, and dropped

W. D. Almond, R.I.]　　　　　　　　　[*After a sketch by Ernest Prater.*

THE MEETING OF LYTTELTON'S AND BARTON'S BRIGADES AFTER THE STORMING
OF GREEN HILL.

right into the midst of it a lyddite shell, which is said by the Boers themselves to have done the most terrible execution. It was, probably, the deadliest shot fired in the war. General Buller personally thanked the naval officer responsible for it.

The loss of Green Hill and Monte Cristo at once rendered Hlangwane untenable, and the Boers immediately evacuated the eminence. It was the key to the Colenso position. In such haste did the

Hlangwane evacuated by the Boers.

Capture of the enemy's camp.

Boers retreat that two of their camps with large quantities of stores and equipment fell into the hands of General Buller's men. "The deserted laager and entrenchments," says a correspondent of the *Daily Telegraph*, "formed excellent ground for exploration. Here I saw the dreadful effects of the heavy fire of our large ordnance.

Thousands, nay, tens of thousands of rounds of Mauser ammunition were found scattered over every trench, strewn over the roads, and in the tenantless tents. Cartridges for the

Maxim-Nordenfeldt were found by the dozen cases unopened. The Boers in their hurry had tried to trundle them away in wheel-barrows, but our swift advance spoiled this mode of transportation, and barrows and ammunition were abandoned. There were hundreds of blankets of every description, also overcoats, jackets, trousers, and mackintoshes. The enemy had been living, if not sumptuously, at least with enough and to spare of good foodstuffs. There were evidences of women having been in the camp from articles of female dress lying nearly everywhere about. Meals were disturbed during the interesting process of cooking, and potatoes ready for the pot were found here and there in the camp. From one laager to another we 'prospected' until we reached that under the command of Commandant Breytenbach. It was filthy and unsavoury, but Psalm books and Bibles were found in every tent." Among the papers found were letters asking for reinforcements, and a reply from headquarters before Ladysmith to the effect that 150 men should be sent, but that more could not be spared, as the besieging force was none too strong for its work. The enemy's trenches which seamed the southern face of Green Hill were of remarkable pattern, many of them blasted five or six feet deep in the rock, with well-designed bomb-proofs and carefully screened entrances and exits. The place was a fortress of such strength that all marvelled at its easy capture. Of the am-

R. Caton Woodville.] [*After a sketch by a Naval Officer.*

ONE OF THE 4'7 NAVAL GUNS SHELLING GROBLER'S KLOOF.

munition captured, a great quantity was found to be loaded with expanding bullets of Dum-Dum pattern, soft-nosed or split-nosed, the employment of which is contrary to the conventions of civilised war.

From Ladysmith men saw with bursting hearts the steady advance. Cingolo taken was a source of encouragement; much more so the appearance of British infantry in full view upon the summit of Monte Cristo. The garrison grew as jubilant as the force that marched steadfastly to its relief through bullets and shells. And from Monte Cristo in its turn the relief force looked down through the gap between Bulwana and Cæsar's Camp upon the tin roofs of the persecuted town, but a bare ten miles away.

The British casualty list for the day's fighting was but 179, and this time not a drop of blood had been shed in vain. The exchange of shots with the enemy's rearguard only ceased at nightfall, when heavy rain fell and the defeated Boers drew back across the Tugela, evacuating Colenso and the works which had two months before repulsed the onset of the British army. On the 19th the Fusilier Brigade of General Barton advanced and occupied Hlangwane without resistance. It is said by a correspondent with the Boers that this easy capture was due to the disobedience and cowardice of a commando which had been ordered to occupy the height and to relieve another commando. The commando on duty went quietly off, and the commando which should have relieved it calmly bivouacked some distance away from Hlangwane. Be this as it may, the hill could not have been held against the enfilading fire which

[Enlarged from
a snap-shot photo.

BUILDING THE TRESTLE BRIDGE OVER THE TUGELA AT COLENSO.

could have been directed upon it from Green Hill and Monte Cristo. The British heavy guns on this day pushed forward and took post upon Green Hill, whence they could shell Grobler's Kloof and

Heavy guns on Green Hill. the Boer lines south of Ladysmith. It was otherwise a day of rest for the majority of the British army, after the hard work of the 17th and 18th; the only incident of importance which marked it was the reappearance of a small force of Boers—possibly the missing commando—who crossed the Tugela once more and opened a sniping fire from the bush-covered, broken ground north of Hlangwane. They retired, however, in the evening;

Colenso occupied. in the afternoon the Rifle Composite Battalion entered the village of Colenso and occupied it. The place was found in a lamentable state of filth and disorder. "Every inside of every house," says a correspondent, "was wilfully wrecked, besides windows and doors, which were smashed beyond repair. The house of the stationmaster was in a disgusting state. The walls were written over in various languages. . . . I observed a few incriminating signatures, resembling those of Natal Dutchmen, which at a future time may serve as useful evidence, and the management

[*Photo by Allerston, Pietermaritzburg.*

COLENSO: THE BROKEN RAILWAY BRIDGE, THE TRESTLE BRIDGE, AND FORT WYLIE.
Fort Wylie (the hill here shown) played an important part in the first battle of Colenso (see pp. 90–91), and from positions on its slopes the artillery covered the advance of the infantry on February 22, 1900.

might do better than obliterate the 'writing on the wall.' The school furniture was demolished, as also the slates and copybooks of the scholars." For such wanton destruction there was no excuse; it was a grim commentary upon the sanctimonious professions of the Boers and their leaders. The construction of a new trestle bridge at Colenso, across which to carry the railway, was at once begun, while all the material for the repair of the original bridge was hurried to the spot. On the 20th the Boers were thoroughly cleared out of the ground south

The river crossed. of the river, and Colonel Thorneycroft and his men crossed the Tugela at Colenso, reconnoitred the kopjes immedi-

ately to the north of the town and came under a sharp fire from them. The news from the west, the relief of Kimberley, the fact that Cronje had been brought to a standstill and surrounded at Paardeberg, combined with the dispirited manner in which, during the past few days, the Boers had opposed the advance of the Natal army, all contributed to inspire the belief that the enemy was retreating, and that now little more remained but to march northwards to Ladysmith. The belief was erroneous; not thus easily was Ladysmith to be saved; but it led General Buller to abandon the line of advance direct-

ly northwards from Monte Cristo, round the left of the Boers— a line which had great advantages supposing that the advance was to be determinedly opposed. He decided to move by Colenso and the Boer centre, generally following the course of the railway. In England and Natal the news of his successes had caused general jubilation. It was thought that the relief of Ladysmith was now only a matter of hours, and reports that it had been already effected were current.

GENERAL HART SUPERINTENDING THE LAUNCHING OF A "PONT" ON THE TUGELA AT COLENSO.
The bridge shown in this photograph is the road-bridge.

The line now held by the enemy stretched from the high land to the north-west of Colenso, generally parallel to the course of the Tugela, and about a mile back from it, across Onderbrook Spruit, and through the hills known afterwards as Hedge Hill, Railway Hill, with its two eminences —Hart's or Inniskilling Hill, and Kitchener's Hill—and Pieter's or Barton's Hill, to the extreme Boer left, which curved northwards across the open ground to the southern end of Bulwana. Hedge, Hart's, Kitchener's, and Pieter's Hills lay just to the south of Pieters Station, where the open country, which stretched as far as Bulwana and Ladysmith, gradually rising all the way, began. Indisputably the weakest point in the Boer position was their left, for the gap between Pieter's Hill and Bulwana was wide, and practically indefensible. On their right the ground was wooded and much intersected by dongas and hollows, with the inevitable stone-covered kopjes at every turn, until the lofty mountains were reached. A pontoon bridge was built near Colenso by General Buller on the 21st, and General

GENERAL COKE'S BRIGADE CROSSING THE TUGELA NEAR COLENSO BY THE DRIFT AND THE PONTOON BRIDGE.

Coke's Brigade, with a field battery, and half General Wynne's Brigade, moved across. Their orders were to reconnoitre thoroughly the kopjes and broken ground beyond Fort Wylie, and then to advance in the direction of Onderbrook Spruit, to ascertain the strength of the Boers. They were not to deliver a 'serious attack. Already the Boers, noting that the British were not, after all, pressing the forward movement by way of Monte Cristo, had ceased to retreat. Their waggons had been seen trekking north and west, and their camps breaking up, on the previous day, but now they seemed to be returning; they had, in fact, plucked up heart as they felt that their position could be defended against attack coming from the direction of Colenso. They returned, therefore, in some strength, and occupied their entrenchments. Boer writers put their force at 2,500, and, knowing the Boer weakness for always looking at their own numbers through the wrong end of the field-glass, we may safely reckon it as 5,000 to 6,000 men, commanded by the best and youngest of their generals.

Reconnaissance by Coke's Brigade.

Covering the reconnaissance of Coke's Brigade, the British artillery shelled the supposed position of the Boers, and poured lyddite shells into Grobler's Kloof till the houses of Colenso shook under

the repeated explosions, and men turned out in alarm, believing that the British guns were by accident firing upon them. The Boers sullenly replied with their Creusots and field guns. Up to a certain point General Coke's men advanced with little loss. As usual, the Boers, invisible and under perfect cover, were holding their fire and waiting for the British. At dusk our troops were in open ground, the Somersetshires leading, when suddenly, at a range of little over 200 yards, the slope of the hill in front of them burst into flame. Immediate retreat was the only course, but before the brigade passed out of the zone of fire it had lost 200 men, nearly half this loss falling upon the devoted Somersets, whose first action this was. They behaved with the utmost courage under trying circumstances.

All the 21st, men and guns had been crossing the Tugela, and not till well on in the morning of the 22nd was the bulk of the army over. The artillery was in position to cover the

[*Photo by Knight, Aldershot.*

BRIGADIER-GENERAL FREDERICK W. KITCHENER.

General Kitchener is a younger brother of Lord Kitchener of Khartoum. He was born in 1858; entered the West Yorkshire Regiment, 1876; Captain, 1882; Major, 1892; Brevet Lieut.-Colonel, 1896; Brevet Colonel, 1898; Lieut.-Colonel, 1899. He served in the Afghan War of 1878-80, under Lord Roberts, as Transport Officer of the Cabul Field Force, and with the Dongola Expedition, under his brother, the Sirdar, in 1896, as Director of Transport; Governor of Khartoum, 1898. He was given the command of the 7th Brigade of the Fourth Division in 1900, with the local rank of Brigadier-General, in succession to General Wynne, wounded, who himself succeeded General Woodgate, mortally wounded at Spion Kop.

meditated attack—the howitzers disposed under Fort Wylie, the 19th and 63rd Field Batteries at the sharp angle of the River Tugela opposite Onderbrook Spruit railway bridge, and on Hlangwane or its slopes two 4·7's, four naval 12-pounders, and the 64th Field Battery; among the kopjes north of Fort

Wylie were the 73rd, 28th, and 78th Field Batteries. These guns poured shrapnel over the country, but whether the shrapnel struck anything is doubtful. The Boers were scattered over several square miles of ground covered with bush and boulder, giving perfect protection and concealment. Rarely or never was the enemy seen. Thus began a day of most desperate and difficult fighting, which proved once more to the full the indomitable valour and unflinching dash of the British infantry.

It was the afternoon before the real advance northwards along the railway line was in active progress. To the note of the booming of the guns battalions deployed, lines went forward, and the brushwood which hid the Boer sharpshooters began to crackle with the fire of

The advance commences.

multitudinous rifles. From the slopes of Grobler's Kloof, from Hedge Hill and Hart's Hill, came the swishing bullets. The men who had fought on Spion Kop —the admirable Lancashire Brigade that had been General Woodgate's, and now was under the orders of General Wynne—was in the vanguard, the South Lancashires and 1st Lancasters forming the firing line. Each yard of the advance was hotly contested. From the circumstances already recorded, the guns could give little help; it was an infantry fight, pure and simple, in which everything

MASSING THE TRANSPORT ON THE NORTH SIDE OF THE TUGELA, OPPOSITE COLENSO.
The little town is seen in the centre of the picture just above the piers of the broken bridge.

depended upon the bravery of the private soldier and his regimental officers. Once more the spectators were thrilled at the sight of the stolid valour which the men displayed. "The line of attack," says Mr. Atkins, "lay over a broken sea of country. It was, like all advances of British infantry, steady and unquestioning. I remember one deep trough in this frozen sea, where the shells fell again and again. The road lay through it, and guns and ammunition train must all pass that way. The shells seemed to come regularly, and you could almost calculate where the moving column would be punctuated with death." In support of the Lancashire Brigade marched the 3rd King's Rifles, the Composite Rifle Battalion, and Hildyard's Brigade. Twilight fell, and the advance still continued, while the fierce, disjointed fight raged on all sides. The necessity of clearing the lower slopes of Grobler's Kloof, which threatened for miles the left flank of the British Army, had compelled a change, or rather an extension, of front. The British firing line now ran almost parallel to the Tugela, facing westward, with its right on the river, close to Onderbrook Spruit, and its left in the air, to the north west of Colenso. Shrapnel and shell from the Boer guns fell everywhere—now amongst the roofs of Colenso, now amongst the waggons crossing the pontoon bridges, and now again amongst the British guns and limbers. At last, with the blackness of night, the artillery fire ceased, but the rifle fire swelled up in a furious roar, which told eloquently that the Boers were delivering a counter-attack. Among the casualties of the day's fight was General Wynne, the successor of General Woodgate, wounded. His command was taken over by General Kitchener, brother of the famous conqueror of the Sudan.

Many strange things happened in the darkness. The King's Royal Rifles, on the British left, advanced to place outposts for the night upon the crest

Deadly experience of the King's Royal Rifles. of a ridge which rose before them, when their leading companies received on a sudden a hot fire from a number of Boers who, unknown to the British, were holding the ridge. One company thereupon charged, drove back the Boers, and gained the ridge, but found itself alone, without support, close to a strongly manned Boer trench which lay on the flat summit. There this company fought and waited through the evening and night, without food or water, hearing all about it the agonised cries of the wounded, to whom no help could be given, praying for the reinforcements

[*Photo by Knight.*
LIEUT.-COLONEL HARRIS,
East Surrey Regiment.
Wounded February 23.

which could not come, because no one below knew what had happened, exposed to the bullets of the Boers in front and of the British behind. At last the order was given to retire. By twos and threes the King's Rifles began to fall back, though, as an officer on the spot records, "the movement of a finger, even in that half-light, brought a devastating fire from the Mausers in front, and, it is more than probable, from the Lee-Metfords in the rear." Each man had to jump up and race for safety, taking his chance, and as he showed the nickel-nosed bullets sped after him. Nerve-shaking was the experience of that instant when the turn came, and the gauntlet of death had to be run. It was strange to watch the varying demeanours of various characters: this one would bolt at his topmost pace; that one would refuse to hurry; and upon both alike, the slow and swift, impartially descended the hand of fate. At this juncture the plight of the Rifles was seen from below, and four companies of East Surreys sent to cover their retreat. They too suffered horribly under a terrible fire. As the last of the Rifles fell back in a disorganised crowd, the Boer rifles blazed up, and matters looked

MAP OF THE ATTACKS ON INNISKILLING AND
RAILWAY HILLS.

critical for the Surreys. To support them in their hour of distress the Devonshires pushed forward, took the place of the King's Rifles, and renewed the fierce struggle with an enemy little more than a long stone-throw away. Towards dawn of the 23rd so close had the enemy crept that Colonel Harris of the East Surreys led a bayonet charge to force back the Boers. In the charge he was wounded, and before he could be carried off the field, was hit again not less than ten times. In all, the battalion of East Surreys lost 140 men in the time that it was under fire. It was relieved at last by the Composite Rifle Battalion about mid-day.

While these things were happening in the grey light and growing day upon the British left, on the right a not less desperate action was about to

Attack on Railway and Inniskilling Hills. begin. Under General Hart the famous Irish Brigade marched out to storm Railway and Inniskilling Hills by a frontal attack. Railway Hill was an eminence, steep in its upper slopes, rising gently from the Tugela in its lower slopes, along which

[*Photo by Chancellor.*
LIEUT.-COLONEL THACKERAY,
Inniskilling Fusiliers.
Killed February 23.

the railway between Colenso and Pieters ran. It was boulder-covered, strongly entrenched, and afforded the Boers admirable shelter. The spur, known as Inniskilling Hill, which ran out to the south-west of it was virtually part of it, and in descriptions of the fight that followed is usually included with it under the one name of Railway Hill. To approach it, it was necessary for the British infantry to pass in single file under the fire of the Boer guns and rifles along the narrow iron railway-bridge which crosses Langverwacht Spruit. Here there was no cover of any kind against the storm of shells and bullets; each man had to run the gauntlet without the faintest opportunity of replying to the enemy's fire. The passage of the "bridge of death" by the Irishmen was an epic in itself, an epic of heroism and faithfulness unto the last. The men seemed one and all to be animated with a determination at all costs to fight their way through to Ladysmith, even though they left half their comrades on the

Ernest Prater.]   [*From a sketch on the spot by the artist, used for this illustration by kind permission of the proprietors of "The Sphere."*

THE GALLANT ATTEMPT OF THE INNISKILLING FUSILIERS TO CAPTURE INNISKILLING HILL, February 23, 1900.

road. The unending file of khaki-clad figures passed steadily over the bridge, while an equally unceasing train of "Pom-Pom" shells flecked the permanent way with puffs of smoke and dust. Now and again would come the deadlier shrapnel, leaving in its wake a group of recumbent figures. But the line never paused or checked; the recumbent figures grew in number, yet the living passed eagerly on and gathered on the farther side, under the shelter of an embankment, for the assault.

Meantime the British artillery fire upon Railway Hill was so terrible that men wondered anything could live under it. From the angle of the Tugela thirty guns, and from the hilly ground to the

Furious fighting.   north of Colenso forty more weapons, showered projectiles upon the slopes and ridge, where slouch-hatted men could be seen silhouetted against the sky-line. The hill was constantly hidden in the smoke and dust thrown up by the bursting shells and shrapnel;

Lance Thackeray.]   [*After a sketch by a British officer.*

THE BOERS REPELLING THE ATTACK OF THE INNISKILLINGS ON INNISKILLING HILL.
When the attack was seen to be failing, some of the bolder Boers leaped from cover, and came to close quarters with the Irishmen. The fighting on both sides was of a most desperate character.

the summit seemed aflame. Yet those who remembered the first battle of Colenso when Fort Wylie "smoked like a volcano" under the hail of lyddite, without the Boers losing heavily, might have been excused some misgivings. The Boers faced the artillery fire with a rare and devoted courage. They were worthy antagonists of the battalions now preparing to close with them in the death grapple, and their shooting never wavered or became unsteady, though the shells fell with swift and terrifying accuracy, tossing earth and men in the air.

In the roar of this bombardment, which drowned the sharp crackle of the ceaseless rifle fire, through an atmosphere reeking with the villainous fumes of cordite and powder, the Irish Brigade advanced to the assault. The Inniskillings led the way. Day was declining, but the evening was still and clear as the line of men moved over the open ground to the foot of Inniskilling Hill, under a fire from front and flank so terrible that men went down before it like the swathes of corn before the mower. The front was narrow; there was little space to deploy, and the troops were in consequence forced into unduly close formation. Yet they did not slacken or halt. They went forward swiftly through the hail of bullets, neared the first line of Boer works upon Inniskilling Hill, carried it, and then only came to a standstill before a second line. In a few moments the Inniskillings lost all their officers but four. Lieut.-Colonel Thackeray, a soldier of the most intrepid valour, and both the majors of the battalion, were slain; six of the officers were wounded, and men were brought down, in the expressive words

"GOOD SHOT!"
The large hole in the centre of the photograph is a Boer trench. Close beside is the circular hole made by a shell from a 4·7-in. naval gun.

of an eye-witness, "like rabbits." The fire was described by those who passed through the terrible ordeal of that day as worse than anything encountered at Colenso. Again and again the shaken remnants

[*Photo by Bartlett.*

LIEUT.-COLONEL SITWELL,
Dublin Fusiliers. Killed Feb. 24.

of the battalion sprang forward with fixed bayonets, and strove to storm their way across the few hundred yards of ground which parted them from the Boers; again and again as they did so the enemy could be seen through the thin blue haze of the cordite, and the clouds of smoke from bursting shells, standing boldly up and firing with furious rapidity, or pressing forward on the flanks of the Irishmen. The rain of projectiles from the British artillery could not shake their nerve, and through the stream of lead which poured from the muzzles of the Boer rifles no living thing could win its way. The Irishmen fought with equal determination; they died on the slopes of the hill, but they would not retreat. Once more night fell, and the Connaught Rangers and Dublin Fusiliers through the twilight made another determined effort to come to hand-grips with the foe, but fiercely though they went forward, their repulse was bloody. The Boers still held the summit of Railway and Inniskilling Hills. The Irishmen fell back a little in the night, and built themselves rough shelters on the lower slopes of Inniskilling Hill. There they took what rest they could, "amidst continuous sniping, pom-pomming, and occasional shelling, while the storm of bullets still whistled and wailed *pizzicato* over the plateau, across the railway." On the slopes above them lay the dead and dying— victims of the magnificent courage which had given a lustre to an undisguised repulse. Once more the relief of Ladysmith appeared almost beyond hope, and the task set the Natal army impossible of performance. Resolute, indeed, were the generals and men, who persevered through hours such as the night of the 23rd and did not despair.

Dawn of the 24th rose. Help had been promised by General Hart with daylight, but no help came. The Boers in their turn attacked the Irishmen, creeping round their flanks—it is said by our men, under cover of the white flag—and by firing into their trenches from flank and rear compelled them to retire yet further. There was a controversy as to what exactly happened, the Boers claiming that they came out of their shelter under the Red Cross flag to attend to the unhappy wounded who lay in crowds without food, water, or dressings, between the two firing lines, and whose miserable plight had stirred their pity. They asserted that while thus occupied the British had fired upon them. The other version of the story is, however, that the British withheld their fire so long as the Boers were

QUESTIONING BOER PRISONERS.

seen to be ministering to the sufferers, but that presently the enemy fell to robbing the dead and wounded, emptying their pockets and stripping them of their boots, while at the same time their sharpshooters moved forward, which so infuriated the Irishmen that they recommenced their fire and brought on the attack. So fierce were the passions provoked that the Boers behaved with the most savage cruelty to many of the wounded. No sooner was a man seen to be attempting to crawl away than they riddled him with bullets. From far away spectators watched with agonised attention the efforts of the injured to seek shelter and assistance; they would see a man, perhaps, come within a few feet of safety after a morning's arduous progress on hands and knees, and then ironical death would in the last moment of his pilgrimage claim him as its own. Watching this the rage of the army grew.

The guns had recommenced their monotonous fire, and on either side shells and shrapnel were falling among the combatants. It was now decided to withdraw the shattered Inniskillings and replace them with fresh troops — to wit, the Durham Light Infantry. The retirement was nobly accomplished, Lieut.-Colonel Sitwell, of the famous Dublin Fusiliers, falling in the course of it a victim to that proud spirit which dictated that the first in rank should be last in the ranks in the moment of retreat. Disdaining to quicken his pace, he was killed. Hildyard's Brigade at last

Hildyard's Brigade relieves the Irish.

arrived upon the scene to support the Irishmen, and its coming was greeted with prolonged and exultant cheers. Late in the day some of the ground lost was re-

J. Finnemore, R.I., R.B.A.]   [After a sketch by Ernest Prater.

THE PLIGHT OF THE WOUNDED ON INNISKILLING HILL.

The fighting lines were so close to one another that the British could not rescue the wounded, nor could the Boers capture them. The Boers called to Captain Foot, who was wounded in the head, to put up a white flag. "No," he replied; "I will die first!"

gained, and the British troops succeeded in reoccupying the schanzes and trenches on the side of Inniskilling Hill. These they held henceforward till the end of the fighting. On the British right some ground was gained, but not very much, while the battle on Railway Hill was at the height of its fury.

The Boer Artillery that day was more effective than it had been hitherto. Eight of the infantry were killed or wounded among the kopjes north of Colenso by a single well-timed shrapnel, seven men in the Howitzer Battery by another, and four by a third—all in the space of two minutes.

Fortunately the Boers could not see how successful their shooting was, and, after their almost invariable custom, changed the direction of their fire at the very moment when it was deadliest.

LAUNCHING A "PONT" ON THE TUGELA.

Change of front. The fierce opposition which General Buller had encountered on the 23rd, and the evident fact that the Boers were in great force in his front, now led him to reconsider his plans and once more to feel for the enemy's left. Leaving the Irish Brigade with Hildyard's men facing the defiant Boers on Inniskilling Hill, he began the transference of his infantry and guns from their left to their right, so that the Irishmen would henceforward be upon the extreme left, and not the extreme right of the British Army. The guns were massed along the northern slopes of Hlangwane and Monte Cristo—six Field Batteries, A Horse Artillery Battery, the Mountain Battery, the Howitzers, two 5-in., four 4·7-in., and eight naval 12-pounder guns —a total of 68 weapons. While this change of front was in progress, continued skirmishing went on under Inniskilling Hill, and towards evening the Boers made a vicious attack on Hart's Brigade, attempting to work round its right. The effort was foiled, and from a heavy roar the firing died down to an intermittent crackle.

Sunday, the 25th, was a day of peace. The plight of the British wounded lying out, untended, for thirty-six hours or more without food and water, upon the slopes of Inniskilling Hill, led General Buller, **A Sunday truce.** however reluctantly, to direct General Hart to sue for a day's armistice. Into that awful field of death, amongst the dying and the dead, Colonel Hamilton, of the West Surreys, went forward with a white flag, followed by a little knot of officers and men, who cast uneasy glances around upon the multitude of prostrate figures, fallen like waxworks in strange attitudes, from which under the heat and rain all semblance of humanity had faded. There they lay, distinguished and undistinguished, officers and privates, brave men all, who had offered their lives for their country, and this was the end of their story upon earth. Below and behind, the Tugela roared in flood, else there was a silence that sorted well with the dank odour of death and the

A BOER ARMSTRONG GUN AND CREW OUTSIDE LADYSMITH.

John Charlton.]

COLONIAL TROOPS CROSSING A SPRUIT NEAR PIETER'S HILL UNDER HEAVY FIRE.

[After a sketch by a British officer.

smothered feelings of the *parlementaire*. Presently the Boers saw the white flag, and themselves came forward; a suspension of hostilities was arranged, though neither side was prevented by stipulations from making military movements; and the soldiers and burghers exchanged small talk and tobacco, while the stretcher-bearers fell to the grim work of clearing the hill. "Three years, yes! three years we will stay out and fight," said one burgher to a British officer who questioned him whether he was not weary of the war. "As to three years," was the Englishman's reply, "why, *we* are prepared to fight you for thirty if necessary." "A rough time?" said General Lyttelton to another Boer; "Yes, I suppose so. But for us, of course, it is nothing. We are used to it and we are each paid for it. This is what we are paid for. This is the life we lead always—you understand?"

"Great God!" exclaimed the Boer.

The evening of the day of peace drew on. The waggons were rumbling back over the pontoon bridges; the last of the slain had been committed reverently to earth; the last of the wounded borne

Inniskilling Hill.   Railway Hill.

[*Photo by B. W Caney.*

ITS WORK ACCOMPLISHED: NAVAL GUN ON HLANGWANE, February 27, 1900.
Naval Brigade and Natal Naval Volunteers in charge of a 4·7-in. gun after the battle of Pieter's Hill.

from the hill to the ambulances; the informal truce was over. The enemies, who had for a brief day **Renewal of hostilities.** become friends, again became enemies, and made ready to kill each other; Briton and Boer parted, and rifles were loaded. In the darkness of night the roar of firing began again, the Boers opening an unaimed and very rapid fire upon the kopjes north-west of Colenso, and the British replying. Thenceforward there was never silence till the close of the terrific conflict which at last opened the way to Ladysmith.

Feeling in the British army was strained to the utmost that Sunday evening. The last effort was to be made after four successive repulses, and more than five weeks of almost continuous fighting. Its issue no man could foretell; there were many uneasy hearts in the British lines. Yet, as Mr. Atkins wrote, "when our soldiers have failed, and failed, and failed again, they are not further from success than they were at the beginning." In truth the tide was now at last to turn; the long discipline of misfortune which had assayed the Natal army and raised its temper to the truest was over. Both general and men were to reap the reward of that heroic patience which had carried them through the trials of three terrible months. The Boer guns on Bulwana might still pitch their shells into Ladysmith, but the end of the siege was coming more quickly than any expected or knew.

All the 26th the British artillery on the slopes of Hlangwane battered the Boer trenches on

F. Dadd, R.I.]　　　　　　　　　　　　　　　　　　　　　　　　　　　　　[*After a sketch by a British officer.*

THE ROYAL LANCASTERS CARRYING THE CREST OF PIETER'S HILL.

Inniskilling, Railway, and Pieter's Hill, while brigade after brigade moved from the British left to the right. Half Norcott's Brigade, all Kitchener's and Barton's, drew up under the guns, and preparations were completed for throwing a new pontoon bridge across the Tugela at a point just to the south of Inniskilling Hill. Every gun and man was to be used in the great final assault. The orders for the work of the next day were as follows: Barton was, at the critical moment in the afternoon, after a full and careful preparation by the artillery, to storm Pieter's Hill on the extreme Boer left; then Kitchener was to attack Railway Hill, and Norcott, on the left, Inniskilling Hill, while five battalions deluged the Boer trenches with lead by long-range fire from the slopes of Hlangwane, and Dundonald's cavalry protected the British right flank.

The anniversary of Majuba, February 27, broke cloudy, and with early morning the guns, battery after battery, got to work. Lyddite and shrapnel were poured upon the three heights marked down for attack. Maxims and rifles joined in till the hills echoed with the prolonged heavy roar of death. The spectacle from Hlangwane is thus described by Mr. Winston Churchill. "Deep in its gorge below our feet flowed the Tugela, with the new pontoon bridge visible to the left, just below a fine waterfall. Behind us, on a rounded spur of Monte Cristo, one of the long-range batteries was firing away busily. Before us, across the river, there rose from the water's edge first a yellow strip of sandy foreshore, then steep, scrub-cover-

"Remember Majuba!"

H. C. Seppings Wright.]   [After a sketch by F. A. Stewart.

PARTING SHOTS: THE WEST YORKSHIRES FOLLOWING UP THE RETREATING BOERS AT
PIETER'S HILL.
In their eagerness to get in a final volley the men rushed into the open, disdaining cover.

ed banks, and then smooth, brown slopes, terminating in the three hills which were to be successively assaulted, and which were surmounted by the dark lines of the Boer forts and trenches. It was like a stage scene viewed from the dress circle. Opposite our front a considerable valley, thickly wooded, ran back from the river, and it was our easy and pleasant task to 'fan' this, as an American officer would say, by scattering a ceaseless shower of rifle and machine-gun bullets throughout its length." Covered by the fire of the guns, the infantry filed across the new pontoon bridge and then moved eastwards under cover of the high river banks till they stood in line facing the points of attack.

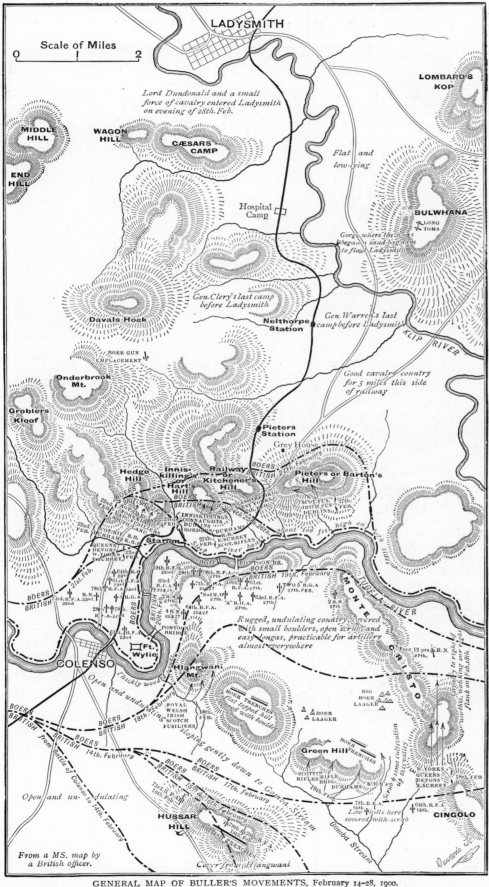

GENERAL MAP OF BULLER'S MOVEMENTS, February 14-28, 1900.
The lines of demarcation between the opposing forces on the various dates are shown by heavy dotted lines. The gradual beating back of the Boers by the successive waves of the British advance is thus graphically illustrated.

Through the army, as it marched out to battle in splendid array—an army of veterans proved upon four battle-fields, and resolved this time to win success—ran an exultant cheer. Great news had come in from the west; the surrender of Cronje with his whole force to Lord Roberts had been put upon the wires the moment it was known with certainty, and it reached Natal in time to breed in the minds of General Buller's men a new confidence and a determination to equal or surpass the glory that had been reaped by the soldiers of the west. To stir their men to the utmost and prepare them for the desperate work which lay before them, the generals who were to lead the attack called upon their men to "Remember Majuba." Never had the Natal army gone out to battle with such a fierce heat of spirit, and the effect was seen when through the smoke and flame the assault began. "I never," says Mr. Atkins, "saw infantry strain at the leash as they strained this day. The renascence of confidence and power and spirit and dash was complete."

The Boers, on their part, as they realised the change in the British plans, must have seen, with their quick insight, that their plight was all but hopeless. In vain they established on the height north of Monte Cristo a false left with a gun which enfiladed the British line of attack.

Their false left failed to deceive, and played no important part in the battle. The storm of shells was now lashing the summit of Pieter's Hill as Barton's men formed up to make their assault; it was terrible to witness. About one o'clock the brigade put itself in motion. The advance was brilliantly, unflinchingly executed by the Scots, Irish, and Welsh Fusiliers, the Scotchmen leading. Two knolls, each crowned with a Boer trench, were carried by two o'clock; the Boer resistance seemed to have been shaken by the bombardment, and the casualties were not heavy. A third knoll remained, but the Fusiliers, with the instinct of men who sought to make their influence felt at the decisive point, paid no attention to it, but swerved to the left, where General Kitchener, with the Lancashire Brigade,

GENERAL LUKAS MEYER.

Lukas Meyer was the first President of the so-called New Republic, which consisted of some 3,000 square miles granted by Dinizulu, son of Cetewayo, to certain Boers who had assisted him against another off-shoot tribe of Zulus. In 1886 Great Britain formally recognized the new Republic; but a couple of years later it was absorbed by the Transvaal. Lukas Meyer was for long a member of the Volksraad, and was among the few "forwards" who were favourable to the Uitlander. He was a bitter opponent of Kruger's retrograde policy, and had many friends among the English. However, he is a true patriot, and took a very prominent part in the war. He it was who commanded the Boer forces when they were defeated at Dundee.

backed by the Yorkshires, was already moving to storm the height which bears his name, and which is

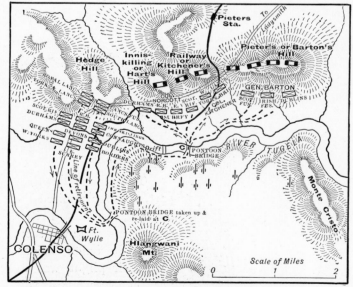

PLAN OF THE FINAL ATTACK ON THE BOER POSITIONS NORTH OF THE TUGELA.

better known as Railway Hill. Kitchener's men passed up the railway, and from the gorge between Kitchener's and Pieter's Hills began to mount, at first slowly, from patch to patch of cover. Over their heads the guns on the slopes of Hlangwane and Monte Cristo had now turned their whole fire from Pieter's Hill to the eminence under attack. At a range of 2,000 yards they made admirable practice, tossing stones and earth high in the air as their projectiles fell. A kopje at the head of the hollow between Railway and Inniskilling Hills was particularly troublesome to the infantry at this juncture, by reason of the deadly fire from the Boers upon it. The gunners saw, and made most determined efforts to overwhelm its garrison. Their fire rose in a terrific crescendo; the hill was now altogether veiled in smoke, and now again dim figures standing against the skyline, in the attitude of men aiming and

COMMANDANT H. P. R. PRETORIUS.
Wounded at Elandslaagte; liberated on parole by
Lord Roberts, but afterwards found in arms.

MAJOR P. E. ERASMUS.
One of the men who opposed Buller at Colenso and
Pieter's Hill.

firing, would show through the lurid clouds. Some Boers were seen to run for their lives, and a tall man twice to go boldly out and bring them back. Then he stood in a pose of dramatic defiance, till an unusually fine shot from one of the naval 4·7's struck right upon him, and he was gone.

Still the bombardment of the height grew—it was afterwards known that it had produced the most demoralising

Storming of Railway Hill.

effect upon the Boer garrison —and then the British infantry in a long graceful line fleeted forward, disdaining cover. The array of Barton's Brigade on the right and Kitchener's Lancashire men in the centre was now prolonged by Norcott's Brigade on the left; with invincible dash and fury from three sides the infantry were pressing forward to storm the two eminences on which the Irish Brigade had made its heroic but ill-fated assault. Ten thousand men were to be put in to make the final attack, while the artillery poured in shell after shell into the Boer entrenchments. The flash of bayonets showed through an indescribable tumult, and suddenly the British artillery fire ceased with a startling suddenness as the line neared the crest of the height. The moment had come when our gunners could no longer co-operate in the assault without endangering the lives of our own men. This was the supreme moment of the war on the Natal side, and all who saw held their breath. Defeat and the fall of Ladysmith, victory great almost beyond imagination and hope, hovered in the scales. If that line halted, if it flinched, all was over. Yet as men watched they saw the scale of victory weigh down the balance; the British infantry with shouts of "Remember Majuba!" swept onward. Towards five o'clock, after three charges with the bayonet, tne Lancashires showed on the summit of Railway Hill; the battle was won, and the Boers on that part of the field took to flight, though they rallied again, reinforced by parties newly come from

Victory at last.

Ladysmith. "Surely nothing so beautiful was ever seen as the advance of Kitchener's Brigade at No. 2 kopje," wrote a witness of this magnificent charge. "The bursting lyddite clothed the summit with a yellow veil; through this flashed the exploding shrapnels, and up and in through the smoke advanced a stately line of infantry, without a pause, until they had command of the kopje, and drove the enemy for ever from the banks of the Tugela. All the money, all the lives, all the misery caused by the war, are well repaid by this glorious battle. In Great Britain the new century has been baptised in the blood of her soldiers, and has opened in the flame of battle, but

CAPTAIN J. J. BOSMAN.

LIEUT.-COLONEL S. P. E. TRICHARDT.

from the holocaust the courage of the British infantry comes pure and unsullied—a sure presage that the safety of the greatest country in the world is secure for ever in the arms of her soldiers." Many prisoners were taken; many burghers were slain at this point. White flags showed from the enemy's trenches; cheer after cheer resounded from the British troops, and men could be seen waving their helmets upon their bayonets in the sudden exhilaration of success. Elsewhere there was a scene of wild rejoicing. Prim and stiff staff-officers threw their helmets in the air as they saw and knew that victory had come at last. Other battalions cheered the stormers, the storming brigades answered back, and a glad tumult swayed the field for some instants. Then men came back to business and remembered Colenso and Spion Kop. With a roar the field guns re-opened, whirling their shrapnel over the hill crest amidst the fugitives. Yet the Boer rearguard was still not to be disregarded. Holding the third kopje on Pieter's Hill, soon after the fall of Railway Hill, it repulsed a determined attack of the Scots Fusiliers and inflicted upon them a loss of about 100 men. This stand prevented a vigorous pursuit, and was all the more creditable to the enemy in that it was made in the face of troops flushed with victory. The cavalry who had been ordered out to press home the defeat were, at this check, stopped at the pontoon bridge and

[Photo by Caney.

LADYSMITH TOWN HALL,
Showing the damage done to the clock tower by a Boer shell, one of three which entered the building whilst it was in use as a hospital and flying the red-cross flag.

directed to suspend their pursuit until next day. Nor did men even now feel altogether certain that in some incomprehensible manner, as before at Spion Kop, the fruits of their sacrifices might not be snatched from them. The Boer guns, as night fell, still flickered with incessant fire

LADYSMITH: THE PRINCIPAL STREET.

on the high land to the left of the Pieters position. As yet there was no tangible sign of a general Boer retreat. Ladysmith had listened all that day in silent agony to the fierce roar of the battle raging barely eight miles away, powerless to give help, had seen Boer waggons moving hurriedly rearward, and had been cheered by the message—" Doing Well "—from General Buller. But the rations had again been cut down, and hope deferred so often had made all sceptical of victory.

The Boer stand on Pieter's Hill was, however, the last flicker of success which came to the enemy. Under cover of night they evacuated their positions, retired their guns and waggons, and fell

Pieter's Hill evacuated by the Boers. back with all possible speed to the north and west. A council of war had been held in the Boer army, and, in spite of the objurgations and entreaties of Botha, Erasmus, and Lukas Meyer, it had been decided to retreat to the Biggarsberg. It was complained by the Boer officers who had conducted the defence of the Pieters position that

s

their appeals for reinforcements, when their commandos, weary with days of fighting, required aid and relief, had been disregarded by Joubert, and it is certain that Mr. Kruger, who visited the burghers just after the retreat had been made, was furiously angry with his Commandant-General. The night was an unquiet one, broken by the noise of heavy rifle-firing in the Boer lines near Ladysmith; the cause was unknown, but was ascribed to panic. All the morning of the 28th the retreat continued; columns of waggons wreathed in dust hurried along every road, while General Buller's army made no effort at pursuit. The continuous fighting and bivouacking of the past fortnight, the desperate exertions of Majuba Day, and uncertainty as to the extent of the victory that had been gained, were the causes of the delay. A further stand on the part of the Boers under the slopes of Bulwana was anticipated. General Buller decided to rest during the 28th and to fight the last battle on March 1. The retreat of the Boers was veiled from his sight. else his action would certainly have been different.

[*After a sketch by Melton Prior.*

THE ADVANCE GUARD OF BULLER'S ARMY ENTERING LADYSMITH.

The final battle and the movements that preceded it are not unfitly described by a correspondent with the army in these words:—" Twenty-five thousand men were moved like clockwork; the loss in the operation was slight. Heavy artillery was taken like a field battery or a mountain battery to the tops of precipitous hills. Finally, the whole position was searched with a deadly fire, and Buller's infantry streamed up after the shells as if it was their first and not their twenty-seventh day's fighting. Courage has always been the glory of the British infantry, and it is hard to add to the laurels of Irish regiments. I think it difficult myself to distinguish any one particular corps, but certainly the Rifles, Devons, Queens, South Lancashires, Dublins, on one side, and the Gordons and Manchesters at Ladysmith, are examples of what results discipline combined with courage will produce."

In the course of the morning of the 28th, Lord Dundonald with the cavalry crossed the pontoon bridge and cautiously pushed northwards, coming into touch with small bodies of the Boers, who, however, after firing a few shots, took to flight. Yet the wiles of the enemy in the past suggested that this might be only a snare for the British horsemen, and justified the utmost care in covering the small space which now parted the outposts of the Army of Relief from the lines of Ladysmith.

A squadron of Imperial Light Horse and another of Natal Carbineers were sent in advance to reconnoitre; they crossed the plain, passed a deserted Boer laager, came in sight of the gorge near which lay the Neutral Camp filled with the fever-stricken from Ladysmith, and of the eminence of Cæsar's Camp. A few shells were fired from the Boer guns in the neighbourhood of Bulwana, but that was the only opposition encountered. Twilight was falling, when Colonel Gough, who commanded the reconnoitrers,and Lord Dundonald, resolved to make a dash for the town. They rode past Intombi camp, and presently out of the growing darkness came

Ladysmith relieved.

Sir G. White. Sir R. Buller.

THE MEETING OF GENERALS BULLER AND WHITE IN LADYSMITH.

This meeting was not prearranged, and took place in the early morning of March 1. General Buller's state entry followed two days later. The photographs on this page are absolutely unique; they were taken by an officer, the only person present who had a camera with him.

a welcome challenge in English—"Who goes there? Halt." At the answer, "The Ladysmith Relief Column," there rose a quavering cheer. A few worn, thin, pale-faced men showed from their shelters, and with indescribable emotion the troopers of the relief force saw that tears were coursing down their cheeks. The end of their trials had come; Ladysmith at last was free.

Heralded by faint cheers, the very weakness of which told eloquently of sufferings endured, the two squadrons rode into Ladysmith in file, two and two abreast, Imperial Light Horsemen and Natal Carbineers, that there might hereafter be no dispute as to which had had the proud honour of entering the town first. The town poured forth to meet them amid tears and cheers. In that hour the limit of human emotion for relievers and relieved was reached. Men's voices broke as they cheered; women and children laughed and cried by turns; a race which ordinarily makes it a boast that it hides and represses its deepest feelings, showed them

MUTUAL CONGRATULATIONS.

The staffs of Generals Buller and White meeting in Ladysmith the morning after the relief of that town.

for once.　General Sir George White and his staff rode forward; about him were Ian Hamilton and Hunter, two of the best and bravest and youngest commanders that the British Army boasts in its ranks, and with the new-comers and the draggled, woe-begone, patient, indomitable soldiers of the garrison, all fell to cheering.　Presently, in a lull of the glad uproar, the General spoke a few measured words of thanks, suited to such an occasion :—

"I thank you, men, one and all," he said, "from the bottom of my heart, for the help and support you have given me, and I shall always acknowledge it to the end of my life.　It grieved me to have to cut down your rations, but I promised you I would not do it again.　I thank God we have kept the flag flying."

The assembly sang "God Save the Queen," that time-honoured anthem of the English peoples, with a strange fervour, and the relief was accomplished.

Deep, indeed, must the gratitude of the nation be to the General and soldiers of the force who had thus opened the way to Ladysmith and saved in the very nick of time a whole British division, one of the finest in the army, from surrender.　Whatever the faults of the past, and there had been none on the part of the soldiers, they were amply retrieved by this immense and glorious success. The Boers up to almost the moment of Lord Dundonald's entry into the besieged town had declared that never, *never* should the British army of relief cut its way through.

F. W. Burton.］　　　　　　　　　　　　　［*After a sketch by F. A. Stewart.*

CAPTURE OF A MAXIM ON PIETER'S HILL.

In the morning after the capture of Pieter's Hill, a colour-sergeant and some men of the West Yorkshires noticed that anyone going near a certain spot on the north slope of the hill was "sniped" at.　They determined to go over and ascertain the reason; and having silenced the snipers, they advanced and found a maxim, partially buried, left behind by the Boers in their hasty flight.

"We didn't believe it possible," said a Boer leader to Mr. W. Churchill.　His tribute to the valour of the British soldiers which had achieved this impossible thing was not ungenerous or ill-deserved. "They do not care for life," he said simply.

The losses of the army in the long series of battles from February 14 to 28 were heavy, yet the price of blood had not been paid to no purpose.　Never again did the Boers make a really

British losses.　determined stand against General Buller's army ; its patience in defeat, its disregard of death, and its obstinate valour in attack, had produced an impression which time could not efface.　Upon their own chosen battleground it had met and conquered the Boers; it had driven them from fortress after fortress, and shown them that no position, however strong, could defy its assault. Two generals, Barton and Wynne, were wounded; seven colonels, Reeves, Harris, Thackeray, Foot, Sitwell, Thorold, and O'Leary, were killed or wounded; in all, the killed numbered 265, the wounded 1649, and the missing 12—a percentage of 10 on the strength of the force engaged. Some regiments suffered terribly. The East Surreys, for instance, lost 140 men on the 22nd–23rd; the Inniskillings, after their attack on Railway Hill, had 414 missing from their roll-call, though afterwards some of the missing rejoined the battalion, and as their strength probably did not exceed 600 men on going into action, their casualties reached a percentage of nearly 60. The Connaughts, in the same fight, had 150 casualties, and the Dublin Fusiliers 100. Of this last regiment, famous for its spirit and heroism, but a shattered remnant now remained. The cavalry, mounted infantry, and artillery suffered in less degree than the infantry, but they, too, had many casualties.

THE ENTRY OF BULLER'S ARMY INTO LADYSMITH.
General Sir G. White and his staff are seen on the extreme right of the picture; the pipers of the Gordon Highlanders can be seen just behind the photographer's cart on the left.

In all, the relief of Ladysmith, from first to last, cost General Buller's army of 30,000 men just 5,000 men, thus distributed, in the battles from Colenso to Pieter's Hill:—

	Killed.		Wounded.		Prisoners and Missing.		Total.
Colenso	135	...	762	...	228	...	1,125
Spion Kop	272	...	1,103	...	358	...	1,733
Vaal Krantz	25	...	344	...	5	...	374
The Relief	265	...	1,649	...	12	...	1,926
	697		3,858		603		5,158

In addition to the losses in men, eleven guns were captured by the enemy at Colenso.

The Boer losses in the long series of combats from February 14th–27th could only be roughly **Boer losses.** estimated, but there is every reason to think that they were heavy. At the storming of Monte Cristo several prisoners were taken, and when the hill was examined after the battle a number of newly-made graves were discovered. On Railway and Pieter's

Hills were many Boer dead and not a few wounded; among the killed were two women, and another was wounded and made prisoner. She asserted that her husband had forced her to fight, as she was a remarkably good shot. One "Pom-Pom" was found buried, and disinterred. In one trench alone lay sixteen of the enemy's dead, yellow with the effect of lyddite; the bushes and dongas through which the Boers had fallen back were littered here and there with corpses. It is probable that their total loss reached at least 500, and it may have been greater. They were under perfect cover, be it remembered, while the British had to advance through the open to attack the trenches, and so were bound to suffer more. Large quantities of stores and ammunition, tents, waggons, equipment, and a searchlight plant, were among the captures made by the Army of Relief.

GENERAL SIR GEORGE STEWART WHITE

Was born July 6, 1835. Son of the late Mr. J. R. White, of Whitehall, co. Antrim; educated at Sandhurst; entered the Army in 1853; served in the Indian Mutiny with the Inniskilling Fusiliers; exchanged into the Gordon Highlanders, 1863; captain, 1863; major, 1873; went through the Afghan War of 1878–80 (in which expedition he won his V.C.): Military Secretary to the Viceroy of India, and Lieut.-Colonel of the Gordon Highlanders, 1881; Colonel, 1885; served in Egypt, 1884–5, and in Burma, 1885–9, was promoted Major-General for his services in the latter campaign; Commander-in-Chief of the Forces in India, 1893–98; Lieut.-General, 1895: Quarter-Master-General to the Forces, 1898–9; appointed to command the troops in Natal, September 1899. On his return after the relief of Ladysmith, he was appointed Governor and Commander-in-Chief of Gibraltar, with rank of General.

[Photo by Langfier.

GENERAL SIR GEORGE STEWART WHITE, G.C.B., G.C.S.I., G.C.I.E., G.C.V.O., V.C.

That exultant Army, its sore trials now past, made its state entry into Ladysmith on March 3. General Buller rode at its head; as the meed of honour, which all men acknowledged fairly won, the **State entry into the town.** Dublin Fusiliers marched behind him in the very van. . Their ranks had been sadly thinned by death and wounds, yet the handful of survivors strode with an elastic swing, buoyantly and splendidly, wearing sprigs of green in their helmets in remembrance of their far-off island. Many broke from the ranks as they passed Sir George White and pressed about him with cheers. After them came in superb array the other brigades; the boots of the men yawned, their clothes were worn with the marches and bivouacs of months, and gaping with the rents torn by the bullets in weeks of battles; beards of many days' growth hid their tanned faces; they might have been an army of tramps but for the trimness of their weapons and the order and confidence and martial vigour of their movements. War had set its seal upon them; they were lions blooded in the terrible business of man-hunting, "with the light of triumph in their eyes and the blood of fighting ancestors in their veins." As they defiled through the streets of the obscure village, now famous for ever to the ends of the earth, cheers greeted each battalion, and were returned by each battalion with interest. Each had had its historic days. This had bravely faced defeat on Spion Kop, that had won its spurs in the advance on Vaal Krantz; this, again, had been pre-eminent in the brilliant and immortal onslaught upon Railway Hill. So the Army of Relief came to Ladysmith and accomplished its Herculean task.

A special Army Order issued by General Buller stated in no exaggerated terms the greatness of the work that had been accomplished and of the difficulties that had been overcome. "The relieving force," it said, "had to make its way through unknown country, across unfordable rivers, and over almost inaccessible heights in the face of a fully-prepared, well-armed, tenacious enemy. By the exhibition of the truest courage, which burns steadily besides flashing brilliantly, it accomplished its object. . . . The general commanding congratulates both forces on their martial qualities, and

[Photo by W. Cohen.

THE GOVERNOR OF NATAL, SIR WALTER HELY HUTCHINSON, ANNOUNCING THE RELIEF OF LADYSMITH AT THE ASSEMBLY HOSPITAL, PIETERMARITZBURG, on March 1, 1900.

thanks them for their determined efforts.   He desires to offer his sincere sympathy to the relatives and friends of the good soldiers and gallant comrades who have fallen in the fight."

To General Buller his victory must have given peculiar satisfaction. By the same heroic persistence in misfortune which marked General Grant, he had reversed the unfavourable verdict passed on his operations at Spion Kop, and justified the belief which his troops, even in the darkest hour, always showed in him. He, too, had profited by his mishaps, and learnt wisdom in the school of misfortune. When, after a long halt, he again took the field, his generalship won the praise of the world, and he closed the war with high distinction. And now

HOW THE RELIEF OF LADYSMITH WAS CELEBRATED AT PIETERMARITZBURG, NATAL.
Kruger as Guy Fawkes. A miniature edition of the great "carnivals" which were organised at home, and, as in England, the street collections were devoted to the funds for the sick and wounded.

there flowed in upon him and his men a great tide of congratulations, all the more eagerly offered because the British people had begun to realise at once the difficulty of the task before him and the all-importance of its achievement. From the Queen came thanks to the general and his troops, **Honours for the Irish.** and especial recognition of the valour of the Irishmen, whose deeds were henceforward to be commemorated by the "wearing of the green" on St. Patrick's Day and by the creation of a regiment of Irish Guards. It was noted that, for probably the first time in history, the green flag made its appearance everywhere in England side by side with the Union Jack.

The enthusiasm in London knew no limits; vast crowds paraded the streets, and the Englishman in his joy seemed to shake off for a few brief hours his traditional reserve. A great weight had been lifted from the shoulders of the nation; the fear had slowly spread that for the first time since Yorktown a large British army might be compelled to surrender to the enemy. For months the Empire had tasted only defeat; and now, when victory came both in the east and west, it came trebly welcome.

HOW THE CAMBRIDGE UNDERGRADUATES CELEBRATED LADYSMITH-DAY.
With the recklessness of youth, they tore down railings, "commandeered" barrows and everything that came to hand to feed the great bonfire in the market place. The fun was costly, perhaps, but at least it was enthusiastic.

F. de Haenen.]

LADYSMITH-DAY IN PALL MALL.

Scenes of the most extraordinary enthusiasm were witnessed in all the principal streets of London. About the Mansion House all vehicular traffic was stopped. Enormous crowds gathered and cheered, and sang, and shouted themselves hoarse. Great numbers of people paraded the streets with flags, and the clubs in Pall Mall lighted their gas torches. Similar rejoicings were reported from all parts of the Empire.

(484)

[Photo by Bassano.

LIEUT.-GENERAL SIR ARCHIBALD HUNTER, K.C.B., D.S.O.,

Was born in 1856 in London ; educated at Glasgow Academy and at Sandhurst ; joined the 4th King's Own Royal Lancashires, 1874 ; Captain, 1882 ; Major, 1885 ; Lieut.-Colonel, 1889 ; Colonel, 1894 ; Major-General, 1896 ; served in the Nile expedition, 1884-5, with the Egyptian Army ; with the Egyptian Frontier Field Force, 1885-6 ; in the operations on the Sudan frontier, 1889, in command of a brigade in the Egyptian Army ; and with the Dongola Expeditionary Force under Sir H. Kitchener in 1896 in command of the Infantry Division ; in 1898 he commanded a division of the Egyptian Army at the battle of the Atbara, and the Infantry Division at the Battle of Khartoum ; Governor of Omdurman, 1899 ; commanded a first-class district in India, 1899 ; joined Sir G. White at Durban to act as his Chief-of-the-Staff until Sir Redvers Buller took command ; promoted to local rank of Lieut.-General and the command of the 10th Division in South Africa, March, 1900. One noteworthy feat since accomplished by General Hunter was the capture of Prinsloo and his 4,000 burghers.

(485)

Lieut.-Colonel Sir H. Rawlinson.
Colonel Frank Rhodes.   Major Bateson.

Sir A. Hunter.   Sir G. White.   Colonel Ward, A.S.C.   Captain Downing, R.A.
          Captain Lyon.   Captain Russell.   Major Ludlow.

SIR GEORGE WHITE AND STAFF, LADYSMITH.

CHAPTER XXI.

THE DEFENCE OF LADYSMITH.

Condition of Ladysmith at the beginning of the siege—Mistakes which might have been fatal—Lines of defence—Positions of enemy's guns—Neutral camp at Intombi—Daily bombardment of the town—War on leisurely lines—Extraordinary escapes—Strange fatalities—Blowing up the enemy's guns at Lombard's Kop—The feat repeated at Surprise Hill—Hopes of relief—"Fools or Heroes?"

HEN, on November 2, 1899, the town of Ladysmith was isolated and surrounded by the Boer forces, the British troops under Sir G. White's orders numbered 572 officers and 12,924 men. In this total there were about 10,000 efficient **Condition of Lady-** combatants of the cavalry, artillery, infantry, irregulars, Natal **smith at the beginning** volunteers, and naval brigade. Over and above the troops were **of the siege.** 2,000 civilians, 750 Cape boys, 2,440 Kaffirs, and 2,470 Indians. The total of mouths to be fed was thus slightly over 21,000, of whom not more than half were fighting men. No immediate help could be anticipated from outside; under the most sanguine assumption the British Army Corps could not take the field in Natal for at least a month, and General White in a message to General Buller had undertaken to hold out for far longer than that period. The first problem was the feeding of the garrison and the inhabitants.

Immense stores, on the outbreak of war, had been accumulated at Ladysmith, and though a large part of these had been sent forward to Dundee and abandoned there—for the use of the Boers—there still remained at the beginning of November in Ladysmith, 979,000 lb. of flour, 173,000 lb. of tinned meat, 142,000 lb. of biscuit, 267,000 lb. of sugar, 23,000 lb. of tea, 9,500 lb. of coffee, 3,965,000 lb. of maize, 1,270,000 lb. of oats, 923,000 lb. of bran, and 1,864,000 lb. of hay, with spirits, wine, and medical comforts. There were in addition 9,800 horses and mules, 2,500 oxen and some hundreds of sheep, all of which could be eaten in the last emergency. But with a foresight which the army in this war too rarely displayed, the senior officers of the Army Service Corps, Colonels Ward and Stoneman, were not contented with this store; at an early date they determined to impound, by process of requisition, paying a fair price, all the supplies and provisions in private hands. In this way they acquired 1,511 cattle, 1,000 sheep, 1,517,000 lb. of maize, about 200,000 lb. of other corn, and considerable quantities of spirits, condensed milk, and tinned provisions. Their timely and judicious action it was that rendered the protracted defence of Ladysmith possible. In some cases the tradesmen were so unpatriotic as to hide their wares, in the hope of retailing them later at an exorbitant profit, but generally such trickery was detected and punished as it deserved.

The troops in Ladysmith might be described as the pick of our foreign-service army, though from the absence of the mature reservists from their ranks they were not of quite such high quality as the troops of the Army Corps. One battalion, the Dublin Fusiliers, which had a reputation

[*Photo by Bradley, Durban.*

GENERAL WHITE'S SCOUTS AND GUIDES.

second to none, had been sent down to Colenso just before the siege began; the losses of Nicholson's Nek had depleted two others. The following were the units present :—

REGULARS.

INFANTRY.		CAVALRY.
1st Devonshire.	1st Leicestershire.	5th Lancers.
1st Gloucestershire (½ battalion).	1st King's Royal Rifles.	19th Hussars.
1st Manchester.	1st Liverpool.	18th Hussars (part only).
2nd Gordons.	2nd King's Royal Rifles.	5th Dragoon Guards.
1st Royal Irish Fusiliers (½ battalion).	2nd Rifle Brigade.	

ARTILLERY.

13th, 21st, 42nd, 53rd, 67th, and 69th Field Batteries (each six 15-pounders).
10th Mountain Battery (two muzzle-loading 7-pounders, two 12-pounder quick-firers).
Also two old 6·3-in. howitzers, firing 80-lb. shell.

IRREGULARS AND NATAL TROOPS.

Imperial Light Horse.   Natal Police.   Durban Naval Volunteers (one Nordenfelt quick-firer).   Border Mounted Rifles
Town Guard.   Natal Artillery (with six 9-pounder muzzle-loaders).   Natal Mounted Rifles.

NAVAL BRIGADE.—Two 4·7-in. guns; four long naval 12-pounders.

At the outset the wisdom of retaining the cavalry inside the town was much questioned; they were all but useless there, whereas they would have been of immense service to General Buller. Sir George White's reason for keeping them was that they were needed as a reserve, in view of the long line of defences which he had to hold with a small force. But to this the answer has been made that, if so, it would have been better to retain the splendid Dublin Fusiliers and send the cavalry down; and that, had full use been made of the Town Guard and had the able-bodied civilians been armed and drilled as at Mafeking and Kimberley, there would have been no want of men. Possibly, in that case, Bulwana might have been occupied, and the garrison enabled to lend a hand to General Buller.

Though works had been prepared upon Bulwana and Lombard's Kop, these heights were not held. The Intelligence Department reported that heavy guns could not possibly be taken to their summits—a lamentable miscalculation—and that light weapons placed upon them would

[Photo by Press Photo Bureau.

MILK FOR INVALIDS.

Mistakes which might have been fatal. not be able to do any damage at so long a range. As traced at the outset, the British line of defence showed a curious ignorance of the power of artillery; it had a perimeter of only eight miles, and did not include Cæsar's Camp, from which the place must have been bombarded at short range with deadly effect. Luckily, the appearance of the Boer heavy artillery on Pepworth Hill revealed in time the risk of allowing the enemy to occupy heights so near the town, and the line was greatly extended by the inclusion of Cæsar's Camp, Helpmakaar Hill, Observation Hill, and other eminences, till it measured about fourteen miles round. Thus much additional space was gained; the assailants were kept at a better distance; and a fairly adequate force still remained to hold the wider perimeter. Though there were less than

WEIGHING AND DISTRIBUTING RATIONS IN LADYSMITH DURING THE SIEGE.

1,000 men to the mile, all the experience of the war showed that a small force of men armed with the magazine rifle behind good entrenchments could defy attack. And here we come to a strange omission: at many of the most important points there were not good entrenchments, but only works of the most indifferent design, giving feeble cover. Cæsar's Camp, for example, and Wagon Hill, the keys to the position, were grievously neglected. The

[*Photo by Bradley, Durban.*

NAVAL 4·7-IN. GUN AT LADYSMITH: WAITING THE WORD TO FIRE.
The photograph shows the carefully constructed shelter behind which the Naval Brigade worked in comparative safety, and the rigid mounting of the gun
as on board ship.

first had no more than weak stone walls, without loopholes, on its summit. The second, in the words of *The Times* correspondent, had "practically no defences of any kind. As to the gentle slope between Wagon Hill and Maiden Castle, a determined enemy, mounted as the Boers are, could gallop up in waves and gain a footing." "This failure carefully to fortify their position cost our troops many a brave life," writes the correspondent of *The Daily Telegraph*. "It was so obvious a duty that its neglect would almost make one think the men careless of their lives, were not the latter supposition controverted by the action of a few of them." Whoever was to blame, whatever was the cause, whether a dangerous over-confidence or mere laziness, it all but brought about the fall of Ladysmith, as will be seen hereafter.

From Cæsar's Camp and Wagon Hill the line of defence followed Maiden Castle, Highlander's Post, Range Hill, Rifleman's Post, King's Post, Cove Redoubt Hill, Observation Hill, Cemetery Hill, and Helpmakaar Hill. The two naval 4·7's, which were **Lines of defence.** the only heavy long-range guns in the town, and which were therefore of the utmost importance to the garrison, were placed one in Cove Redoubt and one on Cemetery Hill, in positions where they could direct their fire upon all the heavy Boer guns on the various heights round the town. They were fixed upon solid platforms and defended by thick

[*Photo by Lieut. J. F. Forbes, Gordons.*

THE SIGNAL TO SEEK SHELTER.
A Hindoo, on a heap of flour bags, announcing with a flag the firing of a shell from "Long Tom." Gordons
getting into shelter.

earthworks. Three long-range naval 12-pounders were upon Junction Hill. Though we have seen that a strange neglect of fortifications was shown at certain points, that neglect was not universal. Several of the hills were crowned with redoubts, which were made as formidable as possible—so strong that no Boer projectile ever penetrated them. The naval guns, in particular, were protected with the greatest care, and on Helpmakaar Hill the Devons—a superb battalion—traced excellent defences. The works were loop-holed, and bomb-proof shelters were dug for the men. To give additional security and prevent the enemy's fire having great effect, the entrenchments, as far as could be, conformed to the undulation of the ground and matched its colour. Dummy parapets were built at points so that the enemy might direct his projectiles where they would do no harm. The mute embrasures of a sham battery south of Helpmakaar Hill were pounded with the most praiseworthy vigour by the Boers, day after day, till at last the enemy's gunners began to suspect that they were being tricked

AMBULANCE WAGGON, LADYSMITH.

The enemy's heavy artillery was thus disposed. On Pepworth Hill was a 6-inch Creusot **Positions of enemy's** fortress gun, firing a 94-lb. **guns.** melinite shell, with a range of seven or eight miles. On Surprise Hill, close at hand, was a 4·7-inch howitzer. On Lombard's Kop was another

AMBULANCE CAMP, LADYSMITH.

howitzer of the same calibre, and a 6-inch Creusot. Upon Bulwana was a third 6-inch Creusot, and on Middle Hill, to the south-west of Cæsar's Camp, a fourth, while just above Intombi Camp a 4·7-in. howitzer made its appearance. All these guns were protected by cleverly designed earthworks of enormous thickness, and as the siege went on one or two more heavy weapons were added to the total. Though a very accurate fire was directed upon them at first, whenever they opened, by the naval guns, they were never silenced for more than a few hours. The Boer heavy guns had the support of a dozen field guns, of a Maxim automatic 1-pounder, of several Maxim rifle-calibre guns and of the British 7-pounders captured at Nicholson's Nek. As for the Boer force in the neighbourhood of Ladysmith, the best sources of information would show it to have been from 20,000 to 25,000 men at the beginning of the siege, when hope ran high and the British armies in other fields were too weak to exert any serious pressure. It never, even in the hour of the Spion Kop and Pieter's Hill battles fell much below 10,000 men, and these were the very pick of the burghers, excelled only, if at all, by Cronje's Potchefstroomers. Its headquarters were at Modder Spruit, only five miles north-east of Ladysmith, where General Joubert and the bulk of his men were usually to be found. Joubert had now grown old and disinclined to a policy of energetic attack; he was uniformly against an assault upon the besieged town, even when President Kruger ordered one, and he, more than any man, must be held responsible for the miserable fiasco which resulted.

BOERS ON THE WATCH AROUND LADYSMITH.

[From a Boer photograph.

He either was, or professed to be, certain of capturing the town by sitting still round it and bombarding it. He forgot, however, that the time which such a feeble plan demanded would allow of the arrival of strong British reinforcements from home, and that such reinforcements would surely be despatched the moment it was realised that Sir George White's division was in danger.

Perhaps the most serious weakness of the garrison was in ammunition. There was not a sufficient supply either for guns or rifles—a fact which almost precluded vigorous action on the part of the troops. Whether the Field Artillery, with its short-range weapons, could have done anything to keep down the fire of the Boer heavy guns is doubtful, but unfortunately the naval guns, which had a great range, were also very ill supplied with ammunition. The full supply required had not arrived when communications were cut, and it was only by strict economy that the heavy projectiles were made to hold out till the end of February. Thus in the latter part of the siege they were unable to reply to the Boer guns and render things uncomfortable for the gunners. The enemy's artillery, therefore, had matters all its own way.

For the sick of the army and for those civilians who did not care to share the misfortunes of the soldiery, by the grudgingly-conceded consent of **Neutral camp at Intombi.** the Boers, a neutral camp was established at Intombi Spruit, four miles to the south-east of Ladysmith and upon the railway to Colenso, as has been described on page 73 of this work, though certain details which

BOER COMMISSARIAT AND POST OFFICE AT MODDER SPRUIT.

Nicholson's Nek.　　　　　　　　　　　　　　　　　　　　　Pepworth Hill.

[*Photo by Nicholls, Johannesburg.*

NICHOLSON'S NEK AND PEPWORTH HILL FROM OBSERVATION HILL.

require attention were not then known, owing to the strictness of the British censorship. The site was an unhealthy one, swampy, and liable to be flooded when the river rose, but it was the best that the enemy would allow. All combatants who entered this camp were put upon their parole to take no further part in the war. The Boers refused to recognise any hospitals within the British lines round Ladysmith; they constantly fired—and fired deliberately—upon buildings over which floated the Red Cross Flag, repeating here their conduct at Kimberley and Mafeking. Infractions of the conventions of war on their part were so numerous that space cannot be spared to chronicle them. Though they were always themselves sending into Intombi Camp for medicines and brandy— which were invariably given them—they attempted to drive Kaffirs and coolies into Ladysmith to eat up the garrison's stock of food; they fired on ambulances, and more than once they strove to detain as prisoners members of the medical staff. Around Intombi Camp they drew a "dead line," and anyone who crossed it—a soldier raving with fever, or hospital attendants in pursuit of him —they mercilessly shot. Though they might well have allowed certain luxuries for the sick and the suffering—who, if they recovered, be it remembered, could take no more part in the war—to pass into Intombi Camp, where men were dying of want by the hundred, they stood and looked on. War must always cause suffering, but unnecessary suffering has never been inflicted by humane commanders in modern times. The British army had to submit and endure in silence; it had no means of retaliation, and was, in these things, utterly at the mercy of a relentless enemy.

The soldiers, with their one blanket apiece, camped out on the hills, and with little or no shelter against the heat of the sun, the torrential rains, or the chilly nights, had nothing to do but endure. "The smudgy khaki uniforms, soaked through and through, stained

LADYSMITH: A TYPICAL SHELTER.

black and green and dingy red with wet and earth and grass," writes Mr. Nevinson; "the draggled greatcoats, heavy with rain and thick with mud; the heavy, sopping boots; the blackened, battered helmets; the blackened, battered faces below them, unwashed and unshaved since the siege began, the eyes heavy and bloodshot, with sun and rain and want of sleep; the peculiar smell—there is not much brass band and glory about us now." Proud indeed may the land be that bore such sons, so patient, so brave, so enduring, so ready to surrender all that man holds dearest.

After the Boer assault delivered on November 9, at the advice of the foreign mercenaries with their forces, and of the younger, more eager burghers in the commandos—an attempt which, by its complete failure, no doubt contributed to the over-security of the British garrison **Daily bombardment of the town.** —the siege languished through November, and the people and troops shut up inside Ladysmith had little more to complain of than the extreme monotony. The one source of interest and excitement was the daily bombardment, which at first was very languidly conducted,

Frank Craig.]　　　　　　　　　　　　　　　　　　　　　　　　　　[*After a sketch on the spot by W. T. Maud.*

GORDONS PLAYING FOOTBALL UNDER FIRE IN LADYSMITH.

The incident here depicted took place on November 18. The Boers dropped a shell into the football ground in the midst of the game, fortunately without injuring anyone; the Gordons filled up the hole and went on with their sports.

so that the casualties were extraordinarily few. It is strange that it was not pushed with greater persistence. Possibly the explanation was that the enemy found it difficult to provide the necessary ammunition. Yet there was every reason to use the most vigorous efforts to compel Sir George White's surrender. If once he could be captured with his 10,000 combatants and his fifty-four guns, not only would a blow be struck against British credit, which would echo throughout South Africa and the world, but also the Boers would be able to detach a large number of men for the invasion of Cape Colony.

Each side at the outset had anticipated that the siege would be a short one. The Boers expected sickness and starvation to make their dreadful presence felt among Sir George White's indomitable soldiers at an early date, and so compel surrender. The British, knowing that a great force was on its way from England, felt certain that they would not be abandoned, and as November drew on looked eagerly for signs of an army of relief on the hills to the south. But day followed day, and the army did not arrive. Instead there came each morning the half dozen of shells from the Boer heavy guns,

LADYSMITH: ENTRANCE TO THE CROWN HOTEL CAVE.
This cave was about 12 ft. deep.

and the pouring rain, converting the low ground round Ladysmith into a miasmatic swamp and the roads into quagmires. Holes and caves were burrowed in the ground, especially in the precipitous banks of the little River Klip, and during bombardment hours many took refuge in them; but the boldest disdained such shelter, and nicknamed the inhabitants of these dens the " Troglodytes."

" It must be said," wrote Mr. Steevens, the correspondent of the *Daily Mail* in the town, " that the Boers made war like gentlemen of leisure; they restricted their hours of work with trade-unionist punctuality. Sunday was always a holiday; so was the day after any particularly busy shooting. They seldom began before breakfast; knocked off regularly for meals—the luncheon interval was 11.30 to 12 for riflemen, and 12 to 12.30 for gunners—hardly ever fired after tea-time, and never when it rained. To do them justice, they did not at first try to do wanton damage in the town. They fired almost exclusively on the batteries, the camps, the balloon, and moving bodies of troops." [This was far from being the case later on, according to other

War on leisurely lines.

correspondents.] " In a day or two the troops were far too snugly protected behind schanzes and reverse slopes, and grown far too cunning to expose themselves to much loss. The inhabitants were mostly underground, so that there was nothing really to suffer except casual passengers, beasts, and empty buildings."

As time went on the misery of living for hours in holes, which in hot weather were stifling and in wet weather miserably uncomfortable,   out-

CAVES OF THE IMPERIAL LIGHT HORSE ON THE KLIP RIVER.
The Imperial Light Horse being mostly from Johannesburg, received many proofs of Boer illwill. Their camp was so persistently snelled that it received the name of " Shell flat."

[*Photo by Caney, Pietermaritzburg.*

BRIGADIER-GENERAL J. G. DARTNELL,
Commanding Natal Volunteers. In the uniform of Chief Commissioner of the Natal Police.

Brigadier-General John George Dartnell has been for 26 years Commandant of the Natal Police. He was born at London, Ontario, in 1838, and received his first commission as Ensign in the 86th Royal County Down Regiment in 1855. He served throughout the Indian Mutiny, and was given special promotion and mentioned in despatches for brave conduct. In the present war he has been of immense service by reason of his knowledge of the country, and he was raised to the rank of Brigadier-General when he took command of the Natal Volunteers at Ladysmith.

weighed the sense of danger, and men preferred to face the peril in the open air, where they could at least see what happened. A flash and a puff of smoke on the surrounding heights was the danger signal. Eight seconds later would come the whistle of the projectile, the crash and violent blast of

BOER AUXILIARIES: CORPS OF FRENCHMEN UNDER THE COMMAND OF LIEUTENANT GALLOPAUD.

its explosion, the sickly smell of melinite, and the rattle of the fragments and of the stones hurled by it upon the roofs of the houses. Now a house would be struck and would dissolve in a crater of fire, as if it had been built of cards; now a shell would explode close at hand to an officers' mess, yet without causing the slightest harm; now, again, with strange perversity, one would spread death and mutilation on every side.

There were many extraordinary escapes. A shell, for instance, burst right upon Mr. Nevinson, the *Daily Chronicle* correspondent, while with a friend he was fording the Klip. "Suddenly," he writes, **Extraordinary escapes.** "there was something more than the usual bang, crash, scream of a big shell; and the water was splashed with lumps and shreds of iron, my hat was knocked off and lay wrecked in the stream, and the horses were dashing this way and that with terror." "Are you killed?" asked his friend. "I don't think so," he replied, and in fact he was not touched. Yet it was one of the narrowest escapes of the siege. The bedroom where Mr. Pearse, the *Daily News* correspondent, did his work was struck and wrecked by another shell; had the projectile come but one minute later it would have found him there and have made an end of his story. This shell blew an officer—who was sitting with his back to a window opposite the room where it burst—ten feet or more, yet did not scathe him. Brigadier-General Dartnell, the

SOME SURVIVORS OF THE NATAL CARBINEERS.

A shell burst in their camp, killing five men and wounding nine. A splinter passed through the box on the left, on which the trooper at the moment was sitting as depicted. Other splinters tore the clothing and blankets as shown.

brilliant Colonial officer to whom—though his name figured in no despatches—the nation owes more than to any other the credit of the retreat from Dundee, happened to have gone outside his tent for a moment, when a shell arrived and destroyed everything inside it. General Ian Hamilton, Colonel Rhodes, and several other well-known officers and civilians chanced to be a little late for breakfast one day; while the breakfast waited for them a shell entered the dining-room and reduced its contents to splinters. Fortunately there was nobody there at the time. Sir George White and his staff were sitting on horseback in a little group, discussing the situation, when a shell came shrieking from the sky and buried itself under the general's horse in earth; it did not explode, but had it done so few could have escaped. The general, it was noticed, did not start; he was speaking as the shell fell, and he continued his sentence without hesitation or alteration of voice.

On the other hand there were some upon whom inevitable doom seemed to have set its seal. Dr. Stark was an instance, a British doctor who believed the war unjust, but had come to Ladysmith to tend the Boer wounded who fell into our hands. He always took shelter in the caves, but the shells

BOER AUXILIARIES: CAPTAIN RICCIARDI AND HIS CORPS OF ITALIAN SCOUTS.

seemed to pursue him, and once a splinter struck and injured one who was in the same burrow with himself; he left the cave and went to another hole, when a fresh shell dropped close to this, knocking

Strange fatalities. a man down by the wind of its flight. The Boers usually ceased firing in the evening, and one night he had come back to the hotel, after what he had supposed the last gun, when several rounds were rapidly fired from the 6-inch Creusot on Lombard's Kop. A shot actually struck him just as he reached the door of the hotel, and inflicted upon him such terrible injuries that he died almost at once. A kitten which he always carried with him to his cave in a basket, that the poor little creature might be safe, was unharmed. His last unselfish words as he lay dying were, "Take care of my cat." A sergeant of the Liverpools who left his shelter out of curiosity just after a shell had burst, was caught by another projectile and torn almost to pieces. As they lifted him back to the shelter he only said, "Wasn't it a pity I went out to see it?" Here, as at Kimberley, it was noted that those civilians who suffered most in life, or limb, or property through the Boer shells were the sympathisers with the Boers. Such is the irony of war.

The soldiers took it all with calm philosophy. At first they felt and showed uneasiness; then they became utterly indifferent—outwardly, at least; and then, again, they were taught not to expose themselves. "If they do start bombarding of us, there ain't only one hymn I'll sing, and that's 'Rock of Ages, cleft for me, Let me hide myself in Thee,'" was a treasured saying of one private of the

Devons.   Mr. Nevinson tells us a tale which illustrates the simple, stolid heroism of the common Englishman.   A private of the Liverpools, who occupied a dangerous and exposed position, kept a diary.   But in it was no word of shells and sniping—no vivid picture of the emotions.   It was a colourless tale of how he rose, went to bed, slept in the rain with one blanket, fought, cut brushwood and made entrenchments, without a single complaint.   Little wonder at the chorus sung by despatches— " The men are splendid."   Nor were the officers less brave or patient.   But their weak point was their want of professional knowledge and of close attention to detail.   " We are only sportsmen," said one of them to Mr. Nevinson, as he crawled, sick with dysentery, to the train for Intombi.   War was their pastime, not the profession and study of their lives.   Yet there were in the town many with whom no man, however captious, could find fault—officers, such as Generals Ian Hamilton and Hunter, destined to win greater renown when endurance was exchanged for action.   Of General Hunter, this

[*Photo by Caney.*
NATAL NAVAL VOLUNTEERS FILLING SANDBAGS AND BUILDING SCHANZES.

incident out of many others is worth chronicling.   The Leicesters and Rifle Brigade were being severely " sniped " by the Boers one afternoon and the men showed signs of uneasiness, when General Hunter arrived.   He stood upright in the sight of hundreds of the enemy, while the bullets hummed round him.   " Let us see whether these Boers can shoot or not," he said ; and after thus exposing himself for a minute or more, decided that they could not.   The effect of his bravery was electrical.

November gave way to December, and now the flashes of search-lights and heliographs to the south told unmistakably of the approach of the relief force.   No one in Ladysmith anticipated that it would have much difficulty in clearing a way through from Colenso.   What, after all, was the fighting power of the Boers?   Even now, perhaps forgetting Nicholson's Nek and Farquhar's Farm, the British could not bring themselves to believe that an army of so little coherence as that of the Boers could long keep in check the trained and disciplined force with which Sir Redvers Buller was moving against it.

In early December Sir Archibald Hunter originated and carried to success a daring enterprise— nothing less than the disablement by a night attack of the heavy Boer weapons on the slopes of

Blowing up the enemy's guns at Lombard's Kop.

Lombard's Kop.   At 10 p.m. on the night of December 7, he marched out with 100 men each of the Imperial Light Horse—" the hard, the valiant, the flower of British South Africa "—and of the Natal Carbineers, who were to do the dangerous work, while 400 more of the Natal volunteers acted as a reserve. With such secrecy had the general acted that even his own staff knew nothing of his intentions until the evening.   The chosen 600 marched cautiously through the brushwood which parted the British outposts from the foot of the hill.   No Boer picket saw them ; no alarm was given ; and in safety the little British column reached the point where the ascent began.

The night was very dark, but the dim outline of the mountain before them could be seen against the sky. The British force now divided. Three hundred men moved off to the right, to guard the gap between Bulwana and Lombard's Kop and prevent the Boers sending up reinforcements from that quarter. One hundred worked round to the left and took post in the bush on that side. Then at last, a little before two, the actual storming party, 200 strong, began its adventurous ascent. The men were extended in single line two or three feet apart. Slowly the steep slope was breasted. It seemed to the forlorn hope marvellous that the rattle of the stones dislodged did not alarm the slumbering enemy or disturb his pickets.

At length, as the top was neared, there came from below a challenge of alarm: "Wie gaat daar? Wie gaat daar?" There was no answer, but a fierce rush for the gun. "Shoot, Martens, shoot! the rooi-neks are upon us!" shouted the picket, and instantly a volley broke from them and from the earthworks at the summit. Major Henderson and half-a-dozen men fell wounded. And now occurred an incident which Mr. Steevens shall tell in his inimitable style :—"A wild fire broke out from above—and from below, as well. Either it was the picket firing or some of the men in rear had lost their heads. The inevitable moment had arrived when success or ruin were balanced on the razor edge. Hunter seized a trumpet, and, for the first time in the British Army's history, a general sounded the 'Cease fire.' It was correct, they say, but quavery. Colonel Edwards, of the Light Horse,

W. *Hatherell R.I.*]　　　　　　　　　　　　　　[*After a sketch by a British officer.*

DESTROYING THE BREECH-SCREW OF THE BOER CREUSOT SIEGE GUN.

tried, and experts think he got more tune out of the instrument. At any rate it was enough, the firing dropped in rear, and in a minute the firing dropped in front too. There were only a couple of dozen Boers or so, and they had been all asleep. The 200 panted on." With a ringing cheer and the shout, "Fix bayonets and give them the cold steel!"—though as a matter of fact there were only four bayonets in the force, and to make the enemy think the steel was really to be used, the men had to clatter the butts of the rifles on the rocks, so as to produce a sound like that of fixing bayonets—the stormers entered the Boer position, General Hunter, Major King, and Major Henderson,

MAXIM GUN CAPTURED FROM THE BOERS, AND SOME OF THE MEN WHO ASSISTED IN THE BLOWING UP OF "LONG TOM" AT LOMBARD'S KOP (OFTEN SPOKEN OF AS GUN HILL).

notwithstanding his wound, at their head; and the enemy fled into the darkness.

It remained to destroy the guns. The heavy weapons were two in number, a long 6-inch Creusot siege weapon and a 4·7-inch howitzer. They were 150 yards apart, each behind a mountain of sandbags, 31 feet thick, proof to the heaviest projectiles, with a Maxim automatic gun between them. The automatic gun and the sights and breech block of the Creusot were carried off as trophies; then twelve artillerymen and four engineers under Captain Fowke and Lieutenant Turner set to work to disable the big weapons. Sledge hammers were used on the breech screws; charges of gun-cotton were inserted in the breeches and muzzles, and the fuses lighted. Captain Fowke waited behind for the explosion while his comrades retired. There were two violent reports, and, examining the guns, he found that two large holes had been blown in the muzzle of the 6-inch weapon, and that its breech was much damaged—probably beyond all possibility of repair. As for the howitzer it was completely ruined.

The forlorn hope retreated, full of exultation, down the steep slope, and without incident or interference from the enemy regained Ladysmith, just as the day was breaking. There at leisure a number of papers and letters, which had been found in the Boer works, were examined. The most interesting was this letter from a young Transvaaler to his sister:—"One month and seven days have passed since we surrounded Ladysmith, and still we do not know what will happen. We see the English walking all over the town every day, though we are bombarding it with our cannon. It would be very dangerous to attack the town, as they have several breastworks outside. They have two of their naval guns close to the town which give us a very warm time—often unbearable on account of their excellence. I think a good deal of blood will have to be shed before the time comes for their surrender, as Mr. Englishman fights hard and well, and our burghers are a bit shaky."

"LONG TOM" IN HOSPITAL: A BOER GUN UNDER REPAIR AT PRETORIA.

A FEATHERED POSTMAN.

This is the pigeon which carried the congratulations of the beleaguered townspeople of Ladysmith to the Prince of Wales on his birthday, November 9. 1899. Shortly before the investment of Ladysmith, Sir George White accepted the use of some carrier pigeons which had been trained by Mr. Hirst, of the Durban and Coast Poultry Club. He volunteered to take charge of some 160 birds in lofts at Ladysmith. It was by means of these birds that news of the condition of affairs in the beleaguered town was conveyed to Durban and thence to Europe.

The British losses in this affair were only one killed and four wounded. The Boers were not slow to express admiration for the courage and conduct of the attacking party. "Every man in it deserves the Victoria Cross," they said to a medical officer, who went out to attend to a mortally wounded trooper, as they ruefully contemplated the havoc wrought by the gun-cotton. They at once removed the 6-inch gun and despatched it to Pretoria, where its battered muzzle was sawn off and its damaged breech reinforced by metal bands. It is then said to have been sent against Kimberley, where its missiles once more caused terror and consternation. The commandant in charge of the gun was sent before a Krijgsraad, convicted of neglect of duty, and disgraced.

To cover the retreat of General Hunter's men, or perhaps, with the idea of attacking Modderspruit camp, the cavalry at dawn of the 8th had made a sortie in the direction of Pepworth Hill. They did not get far. Long before Modderspruit was reached, the hills all about began to crackle with rifle firing, while from Surprise Hill the Boer heavy and light guns opened on the British rear. It was clear that the enemy, far from having weakened their forces in the neighbourhood of Ladysmith, were in great strength. Accordingly, the horsemen were directed to retire, and did so in admirable order, with a loss of two killed and twenty wounded. The 18th Hussars, who were the farthest in advance, suffered most. A fine story, illustrating the pluck of one of their wounded men, is told by the *Daily Telegraph* correspondent. "The horse carrying the spare ammunition for a squadron of the 18th Hussars,"

SIR GEORGE WHITE ADDRESSING THE NATAL VOLUNTEERS AFTER THE BLOWING UP OF THE GUNS ON GUN HILL, LOMBARD'S KOP
"The news of your deed is now ringing through the Empire."

he writes, "had a leg blown off by a splinter, and it became necessary to carry the two boxes of ammunition back to the town, a distance of nearly a mile. Four men performed this service, and when it was finished one of them said to his comrade that some insect must have bitten him during the night, as his shoulder had been smarting for a long time. He took off his shirt, and then it was plain that he had been shot clean through the shoulder, the bullet entering between the shoulder bone and the spine, and passing out in front. For a man wounded in this fashion to help carry a heavy box containing 1,100 rounds of ammunition was an almost unequalled feat of grit and endurance."

Eager to emulate the distinction which the sortie of the 7th had brought the Colonials, the regulars begged Sir G. White to be allowed to repeat the attempt in a new direction. Colonel Metcalfe, of the Rifle Brigade, was the most importunate, and on December 10 he was permitted to deliver a night attack upon the troublesome 4·7 inch howitzer on Surprise Hill. He marched away from camp at 10 p.m. with five companies of the 2nd Rifle Brigade, a few artillerymen of the 69th Field Battery under Major Wing, and a handful of sappers under the gallant Lieutenant Digby-Jones—destined all too soon to pay the inevitable price for his devoted heroism.

The feat repeated at Surprise Hill.

The little column marched to Observation Hill and there halted for ninety minutes till the moon had gone down behind the mountains. Then, without sound or speech, the 469 men rose and marched silently away into the night, crossing the railway which runs from Ladysmith to Harrismith.

SIEGE OF LADYSMITH: BRITISH PRISONERS AT MODDER SPRUIT AND BOER LADY VISITORS TO THE LAAGER.

Beyond the railway stretched the broad, uneven veldt up to the foot of the hill. Just as the storming party reached this point a beam of light struck the sky. It was the Boer search-light on Bulwana. The men threw themselves down and waited for some minutes in momentary expectation that the beam would turn upon them and reveal their movements to a wakeful enemy, rendering them the instant target of every gun and rifle to the north of Ladysmith. But after some instants of errant uncertainty the search-light turned skywards and spent its efforts in meaningless flashes. The British sortie had, after all, not been discovered. The enemy was only busy trying to interrupt the British flash-light signals from the south.

Reassured, the attacking party advanced once more and reached the foot of the hill. Here 250 men were left to secure the retreat; the rest pushed forward rapidly and noiselessly, and gained the summit unchallenged. Then only came a cry, "Wie gaat daar?" and the crepitation of musketry. At once, as if by magic, the whole northern sector of the Boer lines broke into uproar. The crash of field guns and the rapid jarring of the Maxim automatic 1-pounder was heard to left and right, warning the Boer pickets that the "rooineks" were once more upon them. Then this hubbub died away and all interest centred upon the summit of Surprise Hill.

The British advance dashed forward with fixed bayonets and entered the gun emplacement just as half-a-dozen of the enemy took to flight.   The howitzer was found to have been moved some distance to the rear.   Surrounded by the men of the Rifle Brigade with fixed bayonets, Lieutenant Digby-Jones placed the gun-cotton in the muzzle and breech, lighted the fuses, fell back, and waited. Minutes, however, passed, and there was no explosion.   Facing the risk of death or mutilation if the charge went off, Lieutenant Digby-Jones coolly walked back and applied another fuse.   This time there was no failure.   With a roar and blaze of light the charge exploded, and the gun was irreparably damaged.

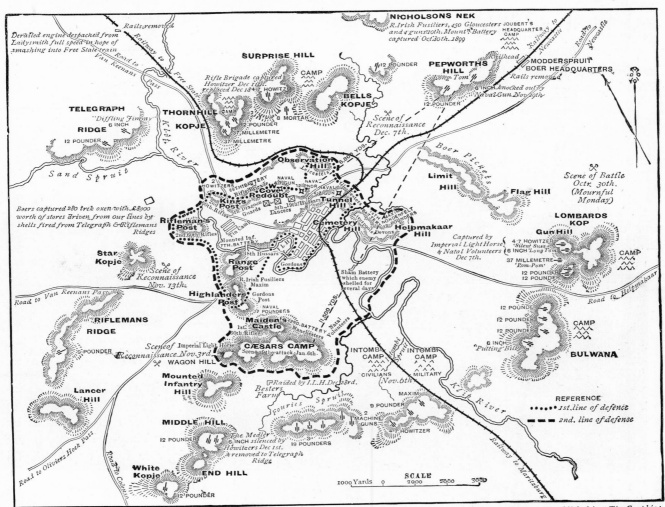

[*Based, by permission, on a sketch-map by Mr. W. T. Maud, published in "The Graphic.'*

MAP OF LADYSMITH.

The delay, however, had given the enemy time to collect men and to concert measures to cut off the British retreat.   As the Rifle Brigade fell back, cheering, the Boers pressed forward on each flank, pouring in magazine fire.   They shouted in English to the British soldiers, endeavouring to decoy them to the rocks on either side, whereupon the soldiers were shot down or made prisoners. In some confusion the foot of the hill was reached; here a fierce tussle took place with a detachment of the Boer Foreign Legion, while the true Boers fired impartially into their auxiliaries and their assailants.   Among the enemies bayonetted at this point were an American, who cried out that he was only a newspaper correspondent—but in whose hands was found a hot rifle—and an Irishman. The struggle was sharp but short; the Boers were driven back, and the British column retreated with all speed to Ladysmith.

This exploit was not performed without considerable loss.   On the British side one man was killed, fourteen mortally and thirty-nine less severely wounded, while eight prisoners were taken by the enemy.   The Boers acknowledged a loss on their part of over a hundred killed and wounded.   It was afterwards known that they had specially detailed 250 men to guard the destroyed howitzer, and had, as they supposed, rendered it secure from attack.

After this they took greater precautions to protect their guns, surrounding them with elaborate wire entanglements, and strengthening the pickets on night duty. Owing to these measures it was impossible for the British garrison to repeat its exploits. Thenceforward till the end of the siege, the Boer works and guns were left unmolested, except by the fire of the howitzers and naval guns.

On December 12 the sound of heavy firing in the Colenso direction filled the garrison with joy. A Flying Column composed of Devonshires, Manchesters, and Gordons, with the main part of the British field artillery, waited all that day for the order to march out and burst in upon the retreating

Hopes of relief. enemy. It waited all the 13th, all the 14th, and all the 15th, while the roar of guns Colenso-wards waxed steadily louder. No message came to Sir G. White from General Buller, and on the 16th there was comparative silence to the south. Only the Boer guns on Bulwana were active. In quick succession they fired twenty-one

SURPRISE HILL, WHERE THE BOER 4·7-IN. HOWITZER WAS DESTROYED, Showing also the Boer trenches at foot of the hill.

rounds to mark that it was Dingaan's Day—the anniversary of the great defeat of the Zulus by the Boers sixty-one years before in this very region. This joyful salute had an ominous sound to the besieged, and next day all was explained in a general order:—

"The General Officer Commanding the Natal Field Force regrets to have to announce that General Sir Redvers Buller failed to make good his first attack on Colenso; reinforcements will not, therefore, arrive here as early as was expected. Sir George White is confident that the defence of Ladysmith will be continued by the garrison in the same spirited manner as it has hitherto been conducted until the General Officer Commanding-in-Chief in South Africa does relieve it."

SHELTER TRENCHES OF THE GORDONS AT LADYSMITH.

In a moment the bright expectations of an early relief faded, and despondency succeeded rejoicing. General Buller had failed; the plight of Ladysmith was grave indeed. From Bulwana the exultant Boers signalled in bitter derision: "Where is your Buller now? He has presented us with ten guns in place of the three you took." "To-day," wrote Mr. Nevinson on the 19th, "there was something like despair throughout the camp."

The Boers mounted fresh guns, and in the weary days of suffering and sorrow that followed their bombardment exacted more victims. One fatal shell pitched among the unlucky Gloucesters,

F. J. Waugh.]

THE RETURN OF THE 2ND BATTALION RIFLE BRIGADE AFTER BLOWING
UP THE BOER GUN ON SURPRISE HILL.

killing six and wounding nine; another fell among the officers
of the 5th Lancers and wounded eight; a third burst among
the Natal Carbineers and accounted for 12 casualties, a fourth
among the Devons laid low 17 men. The garrison began to
feel the pinch of hunger; all luxuries had long since disappeared, and tobacco was unprocurable except for almost its
weight in gold. Eight new potatoes fetched thirty shillings,
a turkey went for £5. Even the water of the river was all
but undrinkable. The Boers systematically poisoned it with
carcases and offal, and it ran a thick stream of tainted mud.

Silent, enduring, cut off from the world, knowing nothing
of what was happening elsewhere or of the great efforts which
were now at last being made at home to turn defeat into
triumph, the garrison spent the last fortnight of December
and the early days of January. It could not be aware that
the eyes of the world were fixed upon it and its fate. "Are
we thought fools or heroes?" signalled

"Fools or Heroes?"
the heliographers one day to General
Buller's men—so near and yet so far off—and the answer
was blurred by the failing of the sun. Christmas under such
conditions was melancholy enough, though the Boers, as a
grim pleasantry, fired shells containing plum-puddings into the

The Ladysmith BOMBSHELL

STEALING A MARCH UPON PIET—
Joubert indignant at the loss of his Guns

[Copyright of Bennett & Davis, Durban.

Endeavours were made by some enterprising journalists
to make up for the lack of news from the outside by inventing
news inside the town. *The Ladysmith Lyre* prided itself
that all its news was thoroughly unreliable; *The Bombshell*,
a weekly manuscript paper, "circulated gratis," was em-
bellished with cartoons illustrating the topics of the hour, of
which one, *apropos* the events related in this chapter, is here
reproduced. The same number puts a pertinent question:
"If the Relief Column takes a day and a half to march a yard
and a half, how much longer will the price of eggs be 10s. 7d.
per dozen?"

[*Photo by S. Cribb.*

ONE OF THE KHAKI-COLOURED NAVAL 12-POUNDERS FROM LADYSMITH, AND ITS CREW.

THE KHAKI UNI-
FORM OF THE
NAVAL BRIGADE.
Portrait of one of the bluejackets
who served in Ladysmith. He wears
on his left arm the good-conduct
badge.

town. For once the men were given a good dinner, and efforts were made by some of the officers to commemorate the season in a suitable manner. All the unbroken toys were bought up, and four great Christmas trees were dressed for the occasion. It is astonishing to read that no fewer than two hundred children attended this festivity. Meanwhile disease was claiming an ever-increasing tale of victims of privation, and the number of sick at Intombi Camp steadily grew. There were over 1,000 towards the end of December. Unfortunately the corruption and mismanagement prevalent at this camp caused the utmost bitterness. Many correspondents allude to the matter, but as the truth of their assertions has been fiercely disputed, Mr. Nevinson, the able and trustworthy correspondent of the *Daily Chronicle*, shall make his own statements. "The 18th Hussar officers," he writes, "at Christmas gave up a lot of little luxuries, such as cakes and things which count high in a siege, and sent them down to their sick at Intombi. Not a crumb of it all did the sick ever receive. Everything disappeared *en route*—stolen by officials or sold to greedy Colonials for whom the sick had fought. It is a small point, but *characteristic of the whole affair.*" And, again, he notes that Colonel Stoneman, upon a visit to the camp, found a "general want of organisation" in the distribution of stores, and was met with objections by the medical authorities, "on the ground of expense," to certain improvements he suggested.

Many of the Boers appear to have been granted leave during the Christmas season, and towards the end of the year they were seen to be trooping back. Forage for the horses in Ladysmith was at this time growing scarce in spite of the fact that 400 men were sent out every day to cut grass upon the hillsides which were least exposed to the enemy's fire.

Thus the year closed, for the besieged, in alternations of hope and misgiving, but with the enemy still at arm's length. The new year, while yet young, was to see the two armies meet in deadly struggle, hand to hand.

SIR GEORGE AND LADY WHITE AND FAMILY AT HOME AT WHITEHALL, CO. ANTRIM.

CHAPTER XXII.

THE DEFENCE OF LADYSMITH—*continued*.

The Boers determine to assault Wagon Hill—The British surprised—The gun-pits taken and retaken repeatedly—Death of
Lord Ava—Homeric fight between Generals—The Boers checked—Attempts to take Cæsar's Camp by stratagem—
Bravery of the Manchesters and of the Field Artillery—The enemy claim to have captured the hill—A critical
situation—Saved by a storm—Devons to the rescue—The Boers fall back—Losses—News of Buller's second repulse—
Privations and Sickness—Supposed attempt to flood the town—Hope revives—The Boers trekking—Relief accom-
plished—Losses—The long agony not in vain.

EARLY in January the Boers, alarmed at the strong reinforcements which had
reached General Buller, and learning from their spies the imminence of another
effort on his part to relieve Ladysmith, determined at last to
The Boers determine assault the place. It is believed that orders to this effect
to assault Wagon Hill. were received from Mr. Kruger, and at a Krijgsraad, held to
consider the question, the advocates for the assault gained the day. The Free
Staters were foremost in requiring either an immediate attack or the abandonment
of the siege, and taunted the Transvaalers with cowardice. Finally, Commandant De Villiers was
instructed to make the attempt on the night of January 5-6. Strong reinforcements were brought up
from all quarters; 7,000 men returned from Colenso; and hope ran high in the laagers that the next
morning would see Majuba triumphantly repeated.

The point selected for the chief attack was the long ridge south of Ladysmith, the western end
of which was called Wagon Hill, and the eastern, Cæsar's Camp. As has already been said, it was
without any fortifications other than a few schanzes, or low stone walls. On Wagon Hill were two

gun pits, prepared for one of the 4·7's and one of the naval 12-pounders, which were in process of being moved to these positions that night; the noise made by the working parties was a factor undoubtedly favourable to the Boers. Wagon Hill was weakly held by the British. About 270 dismounted troopers of the Imperial Light Horse were its garrison, supported by half the 1st King's Royal Rifles, just beyond the nek which parts Wagon Hill from Cæsar's Camp. On Cæsar's Camp were 560 of the 1st Manchesters and the 42nd Field Battery. There were also on Wagon Hill half-a-dozen bluejackets under Gunner Sims, and some thirty engineers under Lieutenant Digby-Jones. Insignificant addition though they made to the total of men on the ridge, they played a great part in the terrible struggle which was now to begin, and both Sims and Jones, by the most heroic and determined valour, won a name for themselves that will never be forgotten. Sims for his splendid conduct was promoted to commissioned rank; Jones met a soldier's death in the battle, and sleeps in the little town which he fought so well to save.

[Photo by Bradley, Durban.

THE MANCHESTERS "SHELL-DODGING" ON CÆSAR'S CAMP.

The night was dark; the lower slopes of the ridge were covered with boulders and brush-wood. Shortly before midnight the noise of a great concourse of men singing hymns in the Boer lines came **The British surprised.** through the blackness to the Light Horse pickets. This should have warned them, but long security had made them careless. The search-light from Bulwana played steadily on the British posts along the ridge, intensifying the darkness and blinding the watchers. No sound of footfalls disturbed the silence; stealthily, with bare feet, the picked Boers made their approach. At last, about 2.30 a.m., a British sentry on the outer slope of Wagon Hill saw a number of dark figures about him. The challenge was given; immediately came the answer: "Friends; don't shoot." Deceived, he held his fire; the Boers closed, poured in a volley, and killed him on the spot, as he stood with rifle raised.

This happened on the south-eastern face of the hill; it gave the alarm at once, but gave it too late. Already another body of Boers had reached the western summit of the ridge, and, as the sound of firing came up from below, dashed forward and carried the gun pits. The surprise was

s

successful and complete. The most vital point of the most vital position of the Ladysmith defences was in the enemy's hands, and, worst of all, one of the 4'7's was in the enemy's midst.

Day dawned and the Boers held fully half the ridge; from the ground gained they were able to direct a deadly enfilading fire upon Cæsar's Camp and upon the handful of British troops on Wagon Hill. Inextricable confusion prevailed; bullets came, or seemed to come, from all quarters, and our men could only fire at the flash of the Boer rifles. It was a struggle in which, on each side, everything depended on the daring and endurance of individuals; but it must be remembered that many of the British were sickly, and all ill-fed, whereas the Boers were in the very pink of physical condition; and, as many of them were Natal rebels, they had a perfect knowledge of the ground.

The Light Horse on Wagon Hill were **The gun-pits taken and re-taken repeatedly.** forced back; the six seamen of the Royal Navy were forced back; the party of Engineers was forced back—but not for far. Again and again this handful of men advanced to capture the gun pits, led by Lieutenant Matthias of the Light Horse, and by Sims and Jones, and again and again was repulsed by an enemy not less brave. At last, however, their courage met its reward. They succeeded in taking the gun-pits and held them for some minutes. But

[*Photo by Johnson & Hoffmann, Calcutta.*

LIEUT.-GENERAL IAN HAMILTON.

Colonel Ian Standish Monteith Hamilton, C.B., D.S.O., commands the Mounted Infantry Division, South Africa Field Force, with rank of Lieut.-General. He was born at Corfu in 1853, is the eldest son of Colonel Christian Monteith Hamilton, and was educated at Cheam and Wellington College. He entered the Army in 1873; served with the 92nd Highlanders in the Afghan War of 1878-80, and was present at the operations around Cabul in December, 1879; Captain, 1882, joining the Staff of Sir Frederick Roberts, then Commander-in-Chief at Madras, as Aide-de-camp; served in the Boer War of 1881; with the Nile Expedition, 1884-5, in the 1st Battalion Gordon Highlanders; Major, 1885; Lieut.-Colonel, 1887; took part in the Burmese Expedition in 1886-7, with Sir Frederick Roberts' staff; Colonel, 1891; Military Secretary to General Sir George White, who had succeeded Lord Roberts in the Indian command, 1893; served with the Chitral Relief Force in 1895; commanded the 3rd Brigade, Tirah Expeditionary Force, 1897-8; Commandant of the School of Musketry, Hythe, in 1898; and held this post till he embarked for South Africa with Sir George White.

the Boers came on in such numbers and with such resolution, that the British were again forced out. The two sides shot desperately at one another across the breast-work of sandbags, where rifles almost touched the target and every bullet dealt a mortal wound. The King's Rifles were brought up

[*Photo by Yuille, Irvine.*
MAJOR MILLER-WALLNUTT, D.S.O.
Killed in the action at Wagon Hill.

[*Photo by Knight.*
MAJOR BOWEN,
King's Royal Rifles.
Killed in the action at Wagon Hill.

LIEUTENANT DIGBY-JONES,
Royal Engineers.
Killed in the action at Wagon Hill.

to support the Light Horse, the rest of whose regiment galloped hard to the scene of fighting; a party of Gordons, too, arrived from Maiden's Castle, and they were thrown into the battle. But they could not turn the scale. Valiantly the Light Horse advanced; they sought to show that the cruel insinuations against their courage, made by some of those Englishmen who delight in disparaging their own country and their own countrymen, were false. Rarely or never have Volunteers fought better, and officer after officer dyed the boulders purple with his blood. But their courage and devotion seemed displayed in vain. The most that they could do was to cling to the northern slope of Wagon Hill and its western extremity, while the Boers could not get beyond the nek and the southern slope. The crest was a no-man's land, the possession of which was disputed by both and made good by neither. To the rear, on Red Hill, two field batteries, unlimbered and loaded, looked on upon the struggle. They could not fire without peril to the British troops fighting on the ridge before them. Another battery shelled with vigour Mounted Infantry Hill, where lay the Boer supports behind excellent cover. Now the fire swelled up furiously, the Boers dashed forward, and to the horror and dismay of spectators in the British line, the King's Royal Rifles were seen to break and retire in great disorder. It was about 6 a.m., and just at this moment the defenders suffered a terrible loss. Lord

Death of Lord Ava. Ava, eldest son of Lord Dufferin, who was serving on General Ian Hamilton's staff, and who had endeared himself to all by his cheerfulness and courage, was shot through the head while looking through his field glasses at the enemy. Hearing that he was shot, Colonel Rhodes and Lieutenant Lannowe went forward to his aid at the risk of their lives, and passing unharmed to and fro through the storm of bullets, carried his unconscious form to safety.

Minutes passed slowly; hours passed like years, and still the struggle raged upon Wagon **Homeric fight between Generals.** Hill. The Boer artillery had opened fire, and its shells and shrapnel perpetually lashed the summit, yet so skilfully did the Boer gunners direct their projectiles, that though the two armies were hereabouts only one hundred yards apart, no stray missile found a target among their own men. Once more the gun pits had been taken by the

[*Photo by the Stereoscopic Co.*
LORD AVA,
Eldest son of the Earl of Dufferin.
Mortally wounded in the action at Wagon Hill.

[*Photo by Amey, Portsmouth.*
GUNNER SIMS,
H.M.S. *Powerful.*
Promoted Lieutenant for bravery at Ladysmith.

British.   Here Major Miller-Wallnutt of the Gordons—a man of great stature and as great courage—was shot dead by Commandant De Villiers; General Ian Hamilton, who was directing the fight, himself shot at De Villiers and missed him, but the Boer general fell to Corporal Albrecht of the Light Horse; Corporal Albrecht fell to a field-cornet; the field cornet to Lieutenant Digby-Jones, who, revolver in hand, fought like a demon.   Once Jones was left alone, and in that time he killed three Boers with three chambers and brained a fourth with the butt.

F.J. Waugh.]

LIEUTENANT DIGBY-JONES'S BRAVERY AT WAGON HILL.

Attempts were made to get the men on the northern slope to charge with the bayonet, but they failed.   The soldiers were shaken by hours of mortal conflict without food, and by the certainty

The Boers checked. of death which faced all who rose from the ground.   Lieutenant Denniss of the Engineers, who had especially distinguished himself, though he was fighting there contrary to orders, Majors Mackworth and Bowen, and two lieutenants of the King's Rifles, were shot down, calling upon the men to follow them.   The fight continued an individual action: man against man and rifle against rifle.   About noon the firing slackened from mere exhaustion, but the

Boers had not loosened their hold. Dismounted men of the 18th Hussars, 5th Dragoon Guards, and 5th Lancers were now pushed up the hill and the enemy were at last brought to a standstill. For the third time the gun pits were carried by the British, and thenceforward remained in our hands. General Ian Hamilton was able to send a message to General White that the hill and the priceless 4·7 upon it were at least safe for a time. But unless the Boers could be cleared off the southern slopes before night, they would inevitably be reinforced in the darkness and must be able to rush the position. Everything, therefore, centred upon the recapture of the southern slopes.

Meantime, to turn to other quarters of the field, an equally fierce fight had raged all day along the ridge of Cæsar's Camp. An outpost of Natal troops on Intombi Spur, the extreme eastern end

Attempts to take Cæsar's Camp by stratagem. of the ridge, suddenly saw a large number of slouch-hatted riflemen creeping up the north-eastern slope, which was thickly covered with bush. They challenged, but the strangers replied in good English: "For God's sake don't fire; we are the Town Guard." The Town Guard were armed civilians of Ladysmith and did not wear uniform,

J. S. *Wells.*]   [*After a sketch by Melton Prior.*

THE MANCHESTERS REPELLING THE BOER ASSAULT.

so that the enemy might easily be mistaken for them; but as they were never employed on the outer line of defences, it seems strange that the Natal men were deceived. By their stratagem the Boers were enabled to approach closely and pour a deadly volley into the colonials. They pushed rapidly up the slope and surprised the pickets of the Manchesters on the summit, taking Lieutenant Hunt-Grubbe of that battalion prisoner, as he was visiting his outposts; he supposed them to be the Border Mounted Rifles, and discovered his mistake too late. One of the pickets was cut off and ordered to surrender, but refusing to do so, was instantly shot down. In this quarter the Boers did not scruple to advance in such a line that no shots could be fired at them without the risk of hitting Intombi Camp, where the British wounded lay: they were within their strict rights, but a more honourable enemy would not have acted thus. In another part a Boer advanced with

R. Caton Woodville.]

THE DEFENCE OF CÆSAR'S CAMP: "FIX BAYONETS!"

the white flag, followed by a hundred companions, slinking through the bush. He shouted as the rifles were turned on him, "Don't fire; I want to surrender," but the trick by this time deceived no one. The British troops emptied their magazines into the treacherous flag-bearer and his comrades, and covered the hill with their corpses.

The bravery of the Manchesters was equal to the strain imposed upon it by the sudden attack of an unknown number of the enemy. Sixteen of the battalion were cut off with the pickets by

Bravery of the Manchesters and of the Field Artillery.

the advance of the Boers, but they held their post all day, and when night fell fourteen lay riddled with bullets, one was desperately wounded, and one man only was untouched. In the whole course of the war there was no finer example of the devotion of the common Englishman, which is faithful unto death. So deadly was the fire of this little party that it played a great part in checking the advance of the

GENERAL JOUBERT AND HIS STAFF AT BREAKFAST AT THE HOOFD LAAGER, MODDER SPRUIT.
On the General's left is his son, and the chaplain sits cross-legged in front of him.

Boers, and thus these men died not in vain. Scott and Pitts were the names of the two survivors —heroes both. The bulk of the Manchesters, like the Light Horse on Wagon Hill, had to give ground, and fell back to the northern edge of the crest, but there they stood fast and no power of the enemy could force them from their position. Now the Boers signalled to the big guns on Bulwana "Maak vecht," and the great Creusot and the three 12-pounders on that height began to rain shells on the Manchesters, enfilading the crest from end to end. From the guns on the heights to the south and south-west of Intombi Camp came a not less heavy fire. The shells pounded the stone walls of the frail schanzes, sending dust and splinters and stones flying, but, miraculous to relate, few men among the British troops were touched. And yet to spectators it seemed that nothing could live upon the hill.

Help was now at hand for the stubborn, hard-pressed Manchesters. Colonel Dick-Cunyngham led out all the Gordon Highlanders, who were not engaged upon Wagon Hill, to clear and hold the north-eastern slope of Cæsar's Camp; Colonel Metcalfe, with half the 2nd Rifle Brigade, hurried up to the ridge and rendered splendid service; Major Addy, with the 53rd Field Battery, which had covered itself with such glory at Farquhar's Farm, pushed boldly out into the open, under the muzzles of all the Boer guns on the south-eastern sector of the line of investment, and exposed to

MEMORIAL CAIRN TO LIEUT.-COLONEL DICK-CUNYNGHAM.
Erected on the spot where he fell, and over which the Gordon Highlanders passed to the assistance of the Manchesters.

the rifles of the enemy. It calmly unlimbered, and began to sweep with its shrapnel the bush on the north-eastern slope, where every thicket hid a Boer. Sometimes, too, it turned its projectiles upon that end of the summit which was held by the enemy. Two Boers were seen through the telescope on Convent Hill, creeping along the ridge—father and son—when a shrapnel caught them both and carried them away in its blast.

The battery was not many seconds in action before the muzzle of the great 6-inch Creusot on Bulwana was slewed round, and began to make the field guns its target. Under its shells the gunners displayed superb coolness. Says Mr. McHugh, correspondent of the *Daily Telegraph* :—" The conduct of the gunners under the fire of this gun—which was throwing shrapnel shell, fortunately with percussion fuse—was simply magnificent. I watched it from the crest of the hill above the battery, and again and again I saw our guns fired right out of the cloud of smoke from the enemy's bursting shell. One gun I noticed in particular. A shell exploded, as I judged, right on the gun, and gunners and all disappeared from view. I gazed, fascinated, through my glasses, expecting to see a dismounted gun and mangled men when the smoke had cleared away. But almost before the first shock of the explosion was over, flash went the crimson lance of flame from the muzzle of the gun I had thought wrecked, and the shrapnel, aimed as true as if at a peace practice, went smash into a group of the enemy, killing or wounding fifteen out of seventeen of them. It was a splendid exhibition of the coolness and nerve of our gunners, and was worth risking something to see. But it was not only one instance; again and again did I notice shells bursting not a dozen yards from the battery, and the men went on with their work without even turning their heads to look at them."

Before the Gordons could reach Cæsar's Camp they lost their gallant

A BURGHER AND HIS SON ON OUTPOST DUTY BEFORE LADYSMITH.

Colonel, Dick-Cunyngham, mortally wounded by a long-range shot; he had only just recovered from his wound received at Elandslaagte, and rejoined his regiment. When they arrived they delivered a brilliant bayonet charge, and recaptured the more advanced schanzes from which the Manchesters had been beaten back. The Boers met the charge with the utmost courage, firing steadily until the Gordons were almost upon them; only then did they break and take to flight. One Boer fell a victim to the bayonet; he and a colour-sergeant each fired simultaneously at and wounded the other, but the Scotchman followed up his shot with the steel. The colour-sergeant, so hot was the fire, was struck in thirteen places; fortunately his wounds were not mortal.

The Rifle Brigade, farther along the ridge, suffered heavily from the field guns, "Pom-Poms," and rifles of the Boers. Though they fought most gallantly they could not gain ground. In the

Gordon Browne, R.I.]   *[After a sketch by H. McCormick.*
THE RIFLE BRIGADE HOLDING THE EASTERN END OF CÆSAR'S HILL.
The sketch was made on the ground occupied by the Border Mounted Rifles.

struggle Lieutenant Hall was severely wounded, and his men compelled to abandon him. He lay in front of their rifles, with another wounded man, under the fire of the two armies. Desperate attempts were made to bring him in, but, as no man could rise without becoming the target for twenty or more Boer marksmen, the attempts were unsuccessful. A gallant colour-sergeant, however, three times crossed the bullet-swept zone with water for the wounded, and crossed it unscathed. Then, as his soldiers watched him in silent agony, Lieutenant Hall was seen to attempt to bandage his arm, which was bleeding badly. In so doing he must have lifted himself and exposed himself to the enemy, for at that instant another bullet struck him and ended his sufferings. And his was only one out of many such cases.

On Cæsar's Camp the fight thus flickered to and fro all the morning and early afternoon, and the Boers could not be driven back, despite their losses, which were, for once, incontestably heavy. They had heliographed in the morning to the head laager: "We have taken Cæsar's Camp," and it almost looked as though their boast was to be made good. The situation was critical in the extreme;

The enemy claim to have captured the hill.

A critical situation.

it was, perhaps, the most critical moment of the whole war, for if Wagon Hill and Cæsar's Camp were lost, Ladysmith must speedily capitulate, when the surrender of a whole British Division, with its more than fifty pieces of artillery, would deal a deadly blow to British prestige in South Africa, and give every encouragement to our enemies in Europe to intervene. More, the fall of the place would have set free at least 10,000, and possibly 15,000, picked Boers for work in other quarters, and this at a time when reinforcements had not arrived from England in large numbers. Many heavy guns would have been available for the bombardment of Kimberley and Mafeking, so that the fate of these two places depended largely upon Ladysmith. Lastly, the surrender of the three besieged towns would have been accepted by the Dutch of Cape Colony as proof that the British cause was hopeless, and the much-dreaded, constantly discussed, and carefully arranged insurrection of the Dutch would have come to pass, increasing ten-fold the danger and difficulty of the war.

But at this supreme moment, when it might almost be said that the fate not merely of Sir George White's 10,000 fighting men, but of the British Empire trembled in the balance, the elements intervened. The battle was still raging, as towards 4 p.m. the sun vanished; the sky grew preternaturally black; and with a fearful crash a thunderstorm, more

Saved by a storm.

BOER GUNNERS: MEN OF THE TRANSVAAL STAATS-ARTILLERIE.

violent than any the army had yet seen, broke over the combatants. The rain descended in such sheets that it was impossible for men 100 yards away to see each other, even when the flashes of forked lightning illuminated with their weird glare the terrible scene. Hailstones, large as eggs, fell at intervals, but they were to the British troops a welcome exchange for the projectiles from the Boer artillery on Bulwana and the neighbouring heights, which was unable to fire in the intense blackness. The rain and hail drove clean in the enemy's faces, utterly disconcerting their marksmen's aim. Now it was that on Cæsar's Camp the gallant Manchesters and Gordons and Rifle Brigade began to force the enemy back. Step by step, yard by yard, they gained ground. One final effort the Boers made in this quarter; one more most desperate onset was delivered with a courage as faultless as that of the men they strove to dislodge, but it was met with the most stubborn determination and repelled. Then through the driving rain dark figures could be seen by the dozen bolting down the hill, under the cover of a tremendous long-range rifle fire. Cæsar's Camp was safe at last.

Upon Wagon Hill scenes even more stirring had been enacted. As the storm broke, the pick and flower of the garrison, Sir George White's mainstay and last hope, three companies of the Devonshires, arrived. If they failed to clear the hill, all indeed was lost. Led by Colonel Park, Captain Lafone, and Lieutenants Field and Masterson, they pushed

Devons to the rescue.

forward with superb coolness, firing as they advanced with such accurate aim, that they unsteadied the shooting of the Boers. About six o'clock they struck the summit of the ridge; officers and sergeants called upon the men to "remember that they were Devons," and the three companies, cheering, with bayonets ready, swept over the level plateau to its southern edge, hurling back the discomfited Boer. The losses of both sides were terrible at this moment, but the Devons were more stubborn than their foes, and they did their work. They reached a low stone wall on the farther edge and there they halted under an appalling fire. Here died Captain Lafone, ending all too early a heroic career, yet pur-chasing with his life-blood the sal-vation of Lady-smith; here also fell, wounded, Lieutenants Field and Masterson, the last a soldier of conspicuous and

[*Photo by Caney.*

LADYSMITH AND CÆSAR'S CAMP.

Cæsar's Camp is the long line of hill in the distance; Wagon Hill is seen to the right of it.

LOMBARD'S KOP, FROM LADYSMITH.

The high distant hill is Lombard's Kop; the outlying spur of that hill to the left at a slightly lower level is Gun Hill, and was the scene of the destruction of the Boer guns by the Imperial Light Horse and Natal Carbineers on December 7. The nearer and less lofty ridge is Helpmakaar Hill.

remarkable valour, who had risen from the ranks. He had been sent back for rein-forcements; on his way three bullets struck him, but none the less he staggered on and gave his message.

The charge, in the opinion of many, was the finest of the war, and it turned the **The Boers fall back.** doubtful fortunes of the day. The Boers fell back, pell-mell, bolting down the hill in utter confusion, while the British troops through the driving rain plied them with magazine fire. Many in their mad flight were caught in the impetuous torrents which now swirled down the dongas and spruits; the deadly fire of shrapnel from the indefatigable 53rd Battery, supported by two guns of the 42nd, drove dozens into Fourier's Spruit, where they were drowned. The sun showed for a few instants through the clouds and gave light for the work of slaughter, disclosing the long disorderly lines of Boers riding rearwards upon their ambling ponies. But there was no attempt at pursuit. The British troops were too exhausted; they had suffered too severely in the protracted and terrible struggle of fifteen hours' duration. As the Boers vanished in the scrub,

THE CHARGE OF THE DEVONS ON WAGON HILL.

our men set about the arduous work of tending the hundreds of wounded who lay out upon the plateau, still exposed to the enemy's long-range fire.

To the north of Ladysmith the Boers had attacked Observation Hill and Helpmakaar Hill. Against Helpmakaar Hill they made little more than a demonstration, but at Observation Hill, held by the Leicesters, Liverpools, and detachments of the Devons and Rifle Brigade, there was sharp fighting. A tremendous shell-fire was directed by the enemy upon the British positions, and about 9 a.m. the Boers endeavoured to charge home. They reached a point only fifteen yards from the outermost British works, but, once there, they could get no farther, and lost at once their leader, Commandant Schutte, and their courage. One by one they took to their heels, and though they kept up a long-range fire upon the hill all day, the situation in this quarter caused no further anxiety.

GENERAL WHITE'S HOUSE, LADYSMITH.
Damaged by shell fire.

Thus everywhere victory was ours, but at what a fearful cost! Fifteen officers and 164 men

Losses. were killed; 33 officers and 287 men were wounded, and two men were missing, a total of exactly 500 casualties. The Imperial Light Horse, the Devons, the Gordons, the Manchesters, and the Rifle Brigade were the heaviest sufferers; the Light Horse in particular had now almost all their officers and four-fifths of their men *hors de combat*—a sad and

[*Photo by the Biograph Co.*

GRAVE OF Mr. G. W. STEEVENS.
Mr. Dickson, the first man to take biograph pictures on the field of battle, is standing by the grave.

splendid testimony to their impugned valour; in one company of the Gordons the commander at the close of the battle was a lance-corporal. On the Boer side the losses are unknown; British estimates varied, at the time, from 1,000 to 2,000, and were based on the fact that 133 Boer dead were collected by the British troops on the top of Cæsar's Camp and Wagon Hill, and then handed to their friends for burial. Many dead were seen in the bush upon which the 53rd Battery had played, but it is none the less probable that the Boer loss did not altogether exceed, if it reached, 1,000. They themselves, with their usual mendacity in such matters, put it at four killed and 15 wounded. Such a statement, if true, would have convicted the assaulting commandos of flagrant and despicable cowardice. This seems to have occurred to their leaders, whereupon they expanded the list—on January 10—to 54 killed and 96 wounded, which was certainly a gross understatement. Their repulse and the slaughter of their best men cowed the commandos round Ladysmith, and thenceforward they made no more attempts to storm the town, but were content with a mere blockade. Even the bombardment was thereafter less severe.

On January 7 a solemn service of thanksgiving was held; eight days later, Mr. G. W. Steevens, the *Daily Mail* correspondent, ended his brief and brilliant career.   He died of enteric, and no braver or more devoted life was sacrificed for the Empire at Ladysmith.   The hand of death was

News of Buller's second repulse.

now indeed heavy upon the garrison: the town and Intombi Camp were crowded with sick and wounded, and as food failed and rations were reduced, privation began to send up the casualties from disease.   For some days men were supported by hope, the great consoler, in their sufferings: they heard and saw the progress of the battle which the Army of Relief was fighting about Spion Kop.   But on January 27 the terrible truth was known: General Buller had been repulsed.   The effect of the mind upon the body was seen in the immediate rise in the number of fever cases.   "Men and horses suffer horribly," writes Mr. Nevinson, " . . . It is believed that not 500 men could be got together, capable of marching five miles under arms, so prevalent are all diseases of the bowels.   As to luxuries, even the cavalry are smoking the used tea-leaves out of the breakfast kettle.   'They give you a kind of hot taste,'

Drakensberg Mountains (30 miles distant).   Spion Kop (14 miles).   Taba Myama.   Boer laager.

W. B. Robinson.]   [*After a sketch by Melton Prior.*

WATCHING FOR BULLER FROM OBSERVATION HILL.

they say."   A message of thanks from Lord Roberts for the "heroic, splendid defence of the garrison" was the only source of satisfaction.   Such is the power of words that the commendation made the hearts of all beat more proudly and led men once more to think with hope of the relief of which they had already begun to despair.

February passed, as January before it, but with ever-growing suffering and fast swelling lists of deaths from disease.   Food was running shorter and shorter; horseflesh and horse-extract or

Privations and sickness.

"chevril" were served out to the garrison; men were wretched and depressed.   "The laughter," said Mr. Nevinson, "has gone out of the siege, or remains only as bitter laughter when the word 'Relief' is spoken."   The troops were not only ill-fed but ragged and miserably clothed.   On January 31 there were no less than 2,145 officers and men in hospital with disease; in the streets of Ladysmith wandered weak-kneed, feeble soldiers begging for a morsel to eat.   The rations were cut down till they barely sufficed to maintain life; at their lowest they were 1 lb. of horseflesh, 4 oz. of biscuit—and such biscuit— 3 oz. of maize meal, an ounce of sugar, a few grains of pepper, salt, and tea, and a spoonful of vinegar. But there is no need to enlarge upon the record of sickness and suffering. Suffice it to say that for the last six weeks of the siege the garrison eked out the most wretched existence, and that when at last relief came, the picked two companies of the picked battalion of the garrison could not march a mile and a half. That is sufficient proof of what these brave men endured.

The scarcity of food and luxuries is shown by the fact that early in February bad tobacco sold for 90s. the pound; fifty bad cigars for 130s.; ten cigarettes for 25s.; and eggs for 4s. each. To the poor privates with their

THE BOER ATTEMPT TO DAM THE KLIP.
The illustrations show the dam in course of construction and after the attempt had been abandoned and the river had broken through. The Boers appear to have undertaken this work as part of a plan for the flooding of Ladysmith with a view to compelling its surrender.

shilling a day such figures were prohibitive, so they suffered and starved, but they did not complain. Life in that terrible monotony and privation passed like some evil nightmare, yet there was never a word of surrender. All were determined to keep the flag flying to the last; the Boers, if they ever entered the town should enter it over their prostrate bodies.

On February 13 came news that Lord Roberts

had entered the Free State and hoped to take the pressure off Ladysmith, and next day heavy firing

Supposed attempt to flood the town. began on the Tugela. It was known that the Army of Relief was once more attacking; the capture of Monte Cristo raised new hopes, rations were increased, and the naval guns shelled more vigorously a mysterious dam which the Boers were building below Intombi Camp, the object of which was, it was supposed, to drown Ladysmith out. On the 21st General Buller signalled " Will be in Ladysmith to-morrow," but he came not. Again rations were put down; again the gloomiest depression set in, and even the Kaffirs began to desert in hundreds. They thought the fall of the town was at hand, in which case they preferred to be found in the Boer lines.

On the 26th General Buller heliographed that he " was going strong, but the country was difficult and progress slow," also that Lord Roberts' army had surrounded Cronje and held him at its mercy. But Ladysmith could scarcely believe good news. All the 27th the fierce and successful fight was seen raging at Pieters, and in the afternoon came definite news of Cronje's surrender. Better still, there were some signs, though not very plain ones, of a Boer retreat. Hope rose, but dropped when in the evening rations were cut down

Hope revives.

Mr. FARQUHAR,
Mayor of Ladysmith during the siege.

for the last time. The staff, it was whispered, believed General Buller's success at Pieters to be after all another Spion Kop affair.

Night passed, and with day the signs of a Boer trek had multiplied. Waggons by the hundred and long lines of horsemen were filing disconsolately off to the north. Over the Bulwana Creusot a tripod was rigged, and the Boers were evidently removing the great gun which had so long showered death upon Ladysmith. At once the naval guns awoke and poured shell upon the enemy. It was the heavy booming of the 4·7's, after days and days of silence due to want of ammunition, that first told the town what was happening. Then about 6 p.m. suddenly great cheering smote the air. Riding up the village street, two and two, were strange horsemen. There they were in real flesh and blood—the vanguard of the Army of Relief. The clouds had broken; the night was damp and miserable, but the elements could not subdue the exultation which filled relievers and relieved. The siege was over; Ladysmith was free. In a moment, hardship, and suffering, and death, were forgotten, and there remained only the memory of a heroic deed, of a famous defence, in which every man of the garrison was proud to have played his great or humble part, and of which he would not have willingly been deprived.

The Boers trekking.

Relief accomplished.

Next day, with splendid energy, the garrison made an effort to interrupt the Boer

[Photo by Russell, Southsea.

CAPTAIN THE HON. HEDWORTH LAMBTON, OF H.M.S. "POWERFUL."
Commanded the Naval Brigade in Ladysmith. He is a brother of the Earl of Durham, and was born in 1856; entered the Navy in 1870; Captain, 1889; served in the Egyptian War of 1882, and was present at the bombardment of Alexandria; Private Secretary to the First Lord of the Admiralty, 1894-7; unsuccessfully contested Newcastle in the General Election of 1900.

retreat; a handful of infantry, two squadrons of cavalry and two batteries of artillery staggered out along the Newcastle road. But the men could scarcely carry their rifles and the horses dropped completely exhausted. The Boers had a strong rearguard, and against their force this debilitated detachment could achieve nothing. That it ever made the endeavour is sufficient credit for officers and men. But why General Buller gave it no assistance was and is still a curious puzzle. Two good brigades of cavalry only waited the word; it was never spoken, and the Boers were allowed to carry off their stores and guns.

The moment the road was open immense quantities of food and clothing were pushed up for the relief of the sufferers, and in a few hours plenty reigned where want had but lately prevailed. Champagne for the sick was given precedence, and no time was lost in emptying the place of all who could be moved. The invalids and wounded were sent down to the sea; the rest of the garrison was distri-

Sir G. White.

SIR GEORGE WHITE RECEIVING THE THANKS OF THE PEOPLE OF LADYSMITH.

After the review of General Buller's troops on March 3, Sir George White was presented by the Mayor with an address from the inhabitants of Ladysmith. In accepting it, he thanked the people for the help they had afforded him, and for their cheerful endurance of the privations of the siege. He specially acknowledged the services of General Hunter, and of Colonel Ward, whom he described as the best supply officer since Moses.

buted among the healthiest camps to be found in Natal, there to recover strength. So saturated was the town with fever germs that immediately after its arrival, an outbreak of enteric occurred in the Army of Relief.

From first to last the siege of Ladysmith cost the garrison 1,640 men :—

	Died or Killed.	Wounded.	Prisoners and Missing.	Total.
Casualties in action	211	609	14	834
Casualties through bombardment	33	232	0	265
Casualties through disease	541	—	—	541
	785	841	14	1,640

while in all no less than 10,688 men were admitted to hospital. The totals in hospital at various dates illustrate the progress of disease; on November 15 there were 374 patients; on December 1, **Losses.** 465; on January 1, 1599; on February 1, 2477, and on March 1, 1996. The strength of the garrison on the last date was nominally 10,164 officers and men, but of these, as has been seen, none were fit for work in the field. So carefully was the ammunition husbanded that most of the guns still had an ample supply left, though the 4·7's had only 42 rounds out of 556; for each available rifle no less than 540 cartridges remained.

In the course of the bombardment the Boers are estimated to have fired 12,500 projectiles, many of heavy calibre, such as 96 and 45-lb., into the town. It will be seen that it took 50 shells to inflict one casualty upon the troops, and 375 or thereabouts to kill one man. A great mistake was made by the enemy in not concentrating their fire upon particular points or employing all their guns simultaneously. Their gunners seemed to fire at their fancy at any target which presented itself, and their guns were so scattered that real combination was impossible.   Had the Boer artillery been in the hands of a French, a German, or a British commander, the consequences to the garrison must have been far more serious.   M. Leon, the French expert, who here, as at Kimberley, selected

[Photo by Russell & Sons, Southsea.

SIR GEORGE WHITE'S ARRIVAL AT SOUTHAMPTON.

On April 14, Sir George White landed at Southampton amid scenes of great rejoicing.   The vessels in the bay cheered lustily as the *Dunvegan Castle* steamed up Southampton Water.   The hero of Ladysmith, bearing traces of the strain of the siege, was greeted on the quay by Lady White and his daughter, and, as he landed, a touching farewell was witnessed between him and the children on board.   Her Majesty telegraphed congratulations, and the town clerk read, on behalf of the Mayor and Aldermen of Southampton assembled on the quay, an address of welcome.   Sir George White, wearing a light-coloured, soft felt hat, is seen on the right of the picture; Colonel Stacpole, in cocked hat, is nearer the centre.   The Mayor, wearing his chain of office, is close behind, followed by Lady and Miss White and the Recorder and other officials.

the positions for the heavy guns, could hardly have been responsible for the tactics pursued. Another disastrous error of the Boers lay in not repeating their assault of January 6 early in February,

They seem to have had good information of the miserable plight of the garrison, and their failure to attack can only be ascribed to the fact that they had been thoroughly awed by the losses incurred on January 6.

Photo by Wallace, Durban.

NAVAL 12-POUNDER AT LADYSMITH,
With its crew and its protecting earthworks.

Before the happy deliverance of Ladysmith there was a **The long agony not in vain.** tendency to regard Sir G. White's action in standing a siege there as a disastrous blunder. But with the wider knowledge which after events have given, it is probable that another view will ultimately prevail and be accepted by posterity; in fact, that his action will be held to have been the best under the circumstances, and to have saved South Africa. Errors in detail he undoubtedly committed; with his rare nobility of spirit he was the first to admit this, and his admission disarms criticism, for there is no soldier in history who has not made such mistakes. But on the larger issues he was not at fault; he judged coolly and decided wisely. His own words, returning thanks at a public dinner at Portsmouth, reveal the strength of mind which carried him through the 119 arduous days of siege.

"I knew," he said, "that even 10,000 gallant men might be reduced to straits which they could not endure, and which a Commander could not call upon them to endure, from famine, and from great depletion of the garrison; but I had seen these troops cross swords with the Boers, and we knew that we could hold out upon the defensive. I could not bring myself to believe that the Ruler of the Universe, who had ordained the centuries to succeed each other, could, after the dawn of the Twentieth Century, hurl the loyal and progressive Colony of Natal back into the Seventeenth Century of darkness and bigotry which is represented by Boer rule. Nor did I believe that I had before me so miserable a fate as to be the principal actor

MARCH OF THE NAVAL BRIGADE THROUGH DURBAN.
The Brigade was met and escorted by their comrades of the *Terrible.*

Frank C aig, R.I.]
BANQUET TO THE NAVAL BRIGADE OF THE "POWERFUL" AT PORTSMOUTH.

More fortunate than their comrades of the Army, the men of the *Powerful* who had fought at Ladysmith, at Enslin, and at Modder River, returned direct to England from the scenes of their heroic labours, and were received both at Portsmouth and in London with overwhelming enthusiasm.

in a tragedy that would have caused such humiliation to my countrymen and to that great Lady whose long and prosperous reign has realised her name of Victory, and who has united the name of England to Empire. In acknowledging this high honour, let me not forget the honoured memory of those who have fallen in its defence—those 600 heroes, many of them known to my friends present, who lie buried in the Oleander Cemetery at Ladysmith, or who, having fallen from fever, lie buried on the banks of the Intombi River; these died as thoroughly in the defence of their country as those who foremost fighting fell."

His courage, his patience, his tenacity, his cheerfulness, and his faith sustained the force he commanded through the most grievous trials which can fall to human lot. He detained the best of the Boer army about his division all through the critical period, when if thrown against the weak British forces in Cape Colony, it might have swept them to the sea. When others despaired he never lost heart, and this though he suffered sorely himself from privation and ill-health. His men believed in him, admired him, and were ready for every sacrifice. And he had the rare good fortune to be served by subordinates such as Generals Hunter, Ian Hamilton, and Dartnell. In British military history the defence of Ladysmith will always remain an honourable page.

[*Photo by S. Cribb.*
NELSON'S "VICTORY" AT PORTSMOUTH SALUTING THE "POWERFUL" ON HER RETURN FROM AFRICA.

REMOVAL OF CAPTIVE BRITISH OFFICERS FROM THE MODEL SCHOOL TO NEW QUARTERS NORTH OF PRETORIA.
This transference was effected about the beginning of 1900, when the number of prisoners was swollen by the officers and men captured in the December battles.

CHAPTER XXIII.

THE MARCH ON BLOEMFONTEIN, AND OPENING OF THE RAILWAY TO THE SOUTH.

Second stage of Lord Roberts' campaign—Proclamation to inhabitants of the Free State—Preparations for the advance—Presumptuous appeal to Lord Salisbury—Boer aspirations crushed—Condition of the Boer army—Positions of opposing forces—Plan of attack—Boers escape from enveloping movement—Isolated engagements—Mr. Kruger in flight—Lord Roberts smiling at failure—Battle trophies—Boers at Abraham's Kraal—Turning movement—Boer tactics effectual—Infantry in difficulties—Splendid artillery fire—Infantry in pursuit—More infractions of the usages of war—Casualties—Advance continued—The Boers helpless—Surrender of Bloemfontein—Hoisting the flag—Halt at Bloemfontein imperative—Conquering heroes—Subjugation of Stormberg district—Repair of the Western railway—Saving Bethulie bridge—Communications restored.

Second stage of Lord Roberts' campaign. WITH the capture of Cronje in the west, and the relief of Ladysmith in the east, the first stage of Lord Roberts' campaign may be said to have ended. The powerful reinforcements sent out from home, and the skilful strategy of the commander-in-chief had turned the scale. The British Army was relieved from its " entanglements " at Ladysmith and Kimberley; Mafeking, it is true, was still besieged, but its garrison, as was known to the British Staff, if not to the nation, could hold out till June. In other ways the situation had changed greatly to our advantage; we were no longer on the defensive in our own territory, but were pursuing a vigorous offensive in the country of the enemy. While of the three main Boer armies one had ceased to exist, more and more British troops were arriving. The Yeomanry, Volunteer Companies, Canadians, Australians, and the Fourth Cavalry Brigade were beginning to land; and at the end of March yet another regular division, the Eighth, under Sir L. Rundle, reached the scene of action. Militia battalions were disembarking weekly. Thus the forces at Lord Roberts' disposal were, notwithstanding the losses of battle, constantly increasing, and at the same time the enemy's capacity for resistance was diminishing. The relief of Ladysmith set free a whole division, the Tenth, which was placed under that brilliant officer, Sir A. Hunter, and transferred by sea to the western field of war. It included Barton's splendid Fusilier Brigade, Hart's famous Irishmen, with the exchange of the 2nd Somersets for the shattered Inniskillings, and three of the Natal Field Batteries—the 63rd, 64th, and 73rd. It was not, however, ready to take part in operations in the Free State before April.

After the capture of Cronje, Lord Roberts gave his troops a well-earned rest, while the transport and supplies for the advance to Bloemfontein were preparing. He had already issued a proclamation

Proclamation to inhabitants of the Free State.

to the people of the Free State, recalling the fact that their own misdeeds had brought about the invasion of their territory, but promising that the persons and property of those who desisted from further hostilities should in no wise suffer. Requisitions were to be complied with, but the full value of everything taken would be paid.

SPORTS IN CELEBRATION OF THE CAPTURE OF CRONJE: STARTING A SACK-RACE.

The interval of inactivity for his army, Lord Roberts filled up by paying, in company with Lord Kitchener, a visit to Kimberley, where he was received with wild enthusiasm. On March 2, after despatching Lord Kitchener to Prieska, in Cape Colony, some miles to the west of the Cape to Kimberley railway, to suppress a troublesome little insurrection which

Preparations for the advance.

had broken out there, and which in some degree menaced the safety of the lines of communication, he returned to Osfontein, a farm a little to the south

of Koodoesrand Drift, where his headquarters had been established since Cronje's surrender. On the Boer side this interval of inaction passed in melancholy reflections and attempts to gain time by peace negotiations. After a conference at Bloemfontein, the Boer Presidents, Steyn and Kruger, on March 5, forwarded a telegraphic appeal to Lord Salisbury. They were, it

Presumptuous appeal to Lord Salisbury.

appeared, deeply impressed by "the blood and tears" of thousands who were suffering through the war; they solemnly declared that they had invaded (and annexed) British territory as a defensive measure, and they required only the "incontestable independence as sovereign international states" of both Republics, and an indemnity for the rebels who had joined them. It is impossible to say whether this preposterous effusion was really meant to secure peace, or only to strengthen the hands of the pro-Boers in England and on the Continent.

VISITORS TO CAMP: DUTCH LOYALISTS BRINGING PRESENTS TO SOLDIERS.

Virtually it requested the British Empire, after two great victories and the successful invasion of Boer territory, to forget the Boer insults of the past six months, and to replace the republics in a stronger position than ever, since the Transvaal had never been "a sovereign international state." Lord

Boer aspirations crushed.

Salisbury's reply was a recital of the Boer acts of wanton aggression, concluding with a flat refusal to recognise the independence of either the Free State or the Transvaal. Thus any hopes the Boers may have entertained of another 1881 settlement were rudely dissipated. Discontent and disorganisation were manifesting themselves in the burgher ranks, and notwithstanding the eager harangues of Mr. Kruger, the farms filled with deserters, who had had quite enough of the war. To meet Lord Roberts, a fresh army had been assembled under General Christian De Wet, on the banks of the Modder. It was nominally seven to ten thousand men strong, made up of commandos from Natal, Colesberg, and the southern frontier, and of the last available burghers called out from the Transvaal and the Free State. To

Condition of the Boer army. join it, journeyed Presidents Kruger and Steyn, but they must have been dismayed by the spirit which they found prevailing among its men. These were demoralised by the news of Paardeberg, and were in no mood for hard fighting. In fact, the last great battle of the war had been fought, and the Boers, though hereafter they

THE PLUCKY POST-MISTRESS OF LADY GREY AND HER FELLOW-LOYALISTS.

| Mr. Sterley, Field Cornet of Lady Grey. | Mr. Vander Byl, (Herschel). | Mr. Court, A.R.M. (Herschel). | Major Hook, resident magistrate of Herschel. | Mrs. Gluck, the brave post-mistress of Lady Grey. | Inspector Ryan, Cape Police. | Sub-Inspector Hutchins, Cape Police. |

Basuto (native) Police.

When the Boers, early in November, 1899, overran the northern part of Cape Colony, on their entry into Lady Grey they endeavoured to take possession of the Post Office, but were met by the postmistress, an Englishwoman, Mrs. Gluck, who declined to turn over to them the office and its contents, and ordered them to leave the premises. The Boers went outside and hoisted the Free State flag, but Mrs. Gluck pulled it down and ran up the Union Jack. They then posted up their proclamation to the Colonists, but this also Mrs. Gluck tore down and substituted the Governor's proclamation against treason. The Boers thereupon gave up the contest and retired. She and other loyalists sent to Herschel to invite Major Hook to come to the relief of the town, but the Boers occupied it and kept possession until about January 6. It is pleasant to learn that Mrs. Gluck was finally reinstated, with an increase of salary, in May, 1900.

showed great aptitude for cutting off and overwhelming small detachments, never again obtained a success against any body of British troops as large as a brigade.

Lord Roberts' army of three infantry divisions (the Sixth, Seventh, and Ninth) and one cavalry division, had been strengthened by the Guards' Brigade from Kimberley and by drafts from the base at

Positions of opposing forces. Capetown. General French with the cavalry was encamped at Bank's Drift, east of Paardeberg, and scoured the country on the British flanks; General Colvile's Ninth Division was in quarters north of the Modder and to the east of the entrenchments once held by Cronje, with General Tucker's Seventh Division encamped opposite it on the south bank, and General Kelly-Kenny's Sixth Division and General Pole-Carew's Guards' Brigade round Osfontein. A screen of mounted infantry held a line of kopjes in advance of the British camps and prevented the enemy from obtaining knowledge of Lord Roberts' movements and dispositions. The Boer headquarters were at Poplar Grove, about fifteen miles from Osfontein. To the north, the right of the enemy's position rested upon a high flat-topped hill, north of the Modder; south of that stream ran a line of kopjes at right angles to the direction of the British advance. These

C. H. Taffs.]

A BOER HORSE-TRAP.
Barbed-wire entanglements under water.

were occupied and formidably entrenched; Krupp field-guns and "Pom-Poms" were placed in strong field-works, and elaborate wire entanglements were constructed by the enemy to hamper the movements of the British cavalry and guns. The total front was about fourteen miles. The weakness of the position was that it was quite open on either flank and could be turned with ease by the British cavalry—a fact which did not escape Lord Roberts when on March 6 he made his dispositions for a battle on the following day. It was anticipated that the most strenuous resistance would be encountered, as those who had examined the Boer position were much impressed by its appearance, while the enemy's force was far stronger than at Paardeberg.

The cavalry, under cover of the night of the 6th, moved round behind **Plan of attack.** the British army from the left to the right, with instructions to make a wide sweep, turning the Boer left, and to come in upon the enemy's rear next day, precluding escape. The Ninth Division was to push forward along the north bank of the Modder; one Brigade of the

Seventh, and the Guards in the centre, were to watch the Boer centre, while to the south the Sixth Division drove in the Boer left. The British front exceeded twenty miles. The plans were admirable, and, if executed to the letter, a second or even more decisive Paardeberg must have been the result. But in war, as in life, practical difficulties and mistakes are the rule rather than the exception, and on this occasion the whole scheme miscarried. Everything depended upon the cavalry, but the cavalry, with horses worn out by half-rations and the hard work of the ride to Kimberley and Paardeberg, and meeting with more opposition than had been anticipated, failed for once to come up to time.

Before daybreak of March 7 the British army was advancing in splendid array. A little south of the Modder the naval 4·7's had moved out, in readiness to shell the Boer centre with their deadly projectiles; from headquarters field telegraphs trailed away to the left and right, maintaining touch between the different divisions on the enormous front, and enabling the Commander-in-Chief to handle his army as though it had been but a brigade. In the bed of the Modder the balloon waited to make its ascent. Just before 6 a.m. the first shot was fired by one of the 4·7's and the action began. But it was already too probable that the enveloping movement which had been intended would fail. General French's Division, instead of being by daylight well round the Boer left flank, was only just approaching it; instead of executing a wide sweep, it had kept much too close to the Sixth Division. The general had with him Major Burnham, the well-known American scout, and, perhaps remembering certain incidents at Colesberg, he had judged it wisest to avoid the risk of stumbling upon the enemy in the dark. That there was sound reason for his action his whole conduct in the war, before and after this affair, would amply prove. He knew the Boers, and was admired and feared by them,

F. de Haenen.]   [After a sketch by F. Baragwanak.

THE CITY IMPERIAL VOLUNTEERS IN A RECONNAISSANCE NEAR BRITSTOWN.

The Dutch element in Cape Colony gave great trouble during the days of Lord Roberts' inaction after Paardeberg. Lord Kitchener was sent to Prieska on March 2 to deal with the rebels in that district. At Britstown a party of Boers raided cattle, and on March 6 the 24th Battery R.F.A. with six guns, a company of the Warwickshire Mounted Infantry, and two companies of the C.I.V. were sent to disperse them, which they did with trifling loss.

because, as they said, "he fights us in our own way." Still, if the enemy would only stand and give battle, time might be gained for the cavalry to complete the envelopment even now.

Boers escape from enveloping movement. But the question whether the enemy would stand was all too soon answered in the negative. The Boers were in no mood to be caught in any of Lord Roberts' traps, with Paardeberg fresh in their minds; they only waited till the last safe moment, and then they "cleared."

So wide was the field that it is hard to describe the action. Like most of the battles of the war, it was a series of detached combats. On the British right General Colvile slowly pushed forward,

Isolated engagements. and worked round the table-topped hill without frontally assailing it. There was a great deal of noise, but very few were hurt on either side. In the centre the Boers made no attempt to deliver a counter-attack, which, in the opinion of good judges, they might have done with success; on the left the Sixth Division tramped, and tramped, and tramped,

s

LIEUT.-GENERAL REGINALD POLE-CAREW, C.B., J.P.,

Was born in Cornwall in 1849 and educated at Eton and Christ Church, Oxford. Entered the Coldstream Guards, 1869; Private Secretary to Sir Hercules Robinson, Governor of New South Wales, 1876-7; A.D.C. to Lord Lytton, Viceroy of India, 1878-9; to Sir Frederick (now Lord) Roberts in the Afghan War, 1879-80, and to H.R.H. the Duke of Connaught in Egypt, 1882; Lieut.-Colonel, 1883; Military Secretary to Sir F. Roberts in India, 1884-90; served in the Burmese Expedition of 1886-7; Colonel, 1888; commanded the 2nd Battalion Coldstream Guards, 1895-9; Brigadier-General in command of a 2nd class District in India, 1899; Major-General, 1899; commands the Eleventh Division in South Africa with local rank of Lieut.-General.

(533)

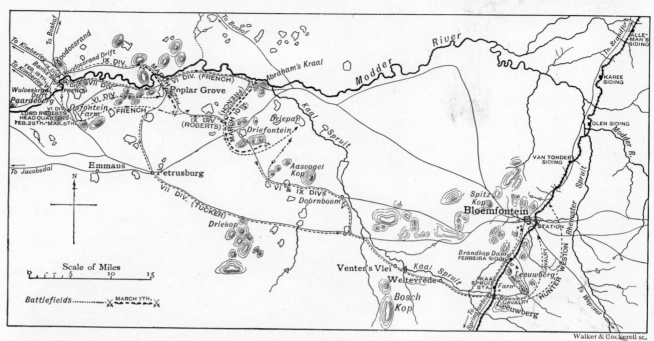

MAP OF THE ADVANCE ON BLOEMFONTEIN.

Walker & Cockerell sc.

changing direction time after time, but burning little powder; while the cavalry on the extreme flank came under a sharp artillery fire and lost a few men, a shell bursting close to General French himself. The moment the cavalry were well round the Boer left, the Boers bolted with the utmost precipitation, notwithstanding the tearful entreaties of President Kruger and the sjambok of President Steyn. It was just as well for the burghers that they refused to listen to the appeals of their

Mr. Kruger in flight. Presidents; had they waited, the only possible result would have been complete disaster. At last a shrapnel from the British artillery cut short Mr. Kruger's harangues and objurgations. He scuttled into his carriage, and drove hastily off to Bloemfontein, leaving his followers to themselves. The guns and most of the baggage were got away under cover of a brave and skilful stand by a small rearguard of Johannesburg police. About 10 a.m. the Boers were everywhere in flight, and the botched battle was over. Lord Roberts received the failure of his plans with the serene coolness of a general who knows what war is. "Those all too ready with censure," wrote Mr. Battersby, a correspondent with his army, "should have been here to witness how the great little man who leads us took the upset of his conception, and the

Lord Roberts smiling at failure. vanishing of a battle which might have left the Free State at his feet. He stood there with the quiet smile on his face, when many another man would have been mad with anger, knowing well where the blame

GENERAL HECTOR MACDONALD AT POPLAR GROVE.
General Macdonald, who was suffering from a wound in the foot (page 411), watched from a high kopje the advance of the Highland Brigade, under Colonel Hughes Hallett.

should be laid, but speaking not a word of it as he twisted his moustache. 'In war you can't expect everything to come out right,' was all he had to say about the blunder, and in the strength of that smiling silence lies the greatness which we revere."

Among the trophies were a Krupp field-gun, abandoned by the enemy, a small camp, probably that of the Boer rearguard, in which food was found ready prepared, and, it was claimed by the **Battle trophies.** cavalry, Mr. Kruger's silk hat. Not only these, but two of the foreign attachés with the Boers fell into British hands. They were Colonel Gourkho, the Russian attaché, and Lieutenant Thomson, representing Holland. Their waggon came under a heavy shell fire from both armies; the horses took fright, and a wheel was lost. Naturally the Boers would not stop to help these foreigners. The two attachés demanded, as of right, to be at once sent back through the lines to the Boer army, a request which was unreasonable, and with which Lord Roberts was unable to comply. He sent them down to Capetown, whence they made their way back by Delagoa Bay. The British casualties were four killed, forty-nine wounded, and one missing; the Boer losses were probably slightly larger.

[*Photographed in Pretoria.*]

MR. KRUGER'S STATE CARRIAGE AND POLICE ESCORT.

The enemy were finally rallied, though not without difficulty, at Abraham's Kraal, fifteen miles farther to the east. Here was the strongest position on the road to Bloemfontein, and here rough **Boers at Abraham's Kraal.** works had already been prepared. The key to it was a cluster of kopjes seven miles to the south, round the farm of Driefontein. These kopjes were in shape like a **W**, but they had the usual defect of positions in the Free State—from the Boer point of view—that they lay in the plain, and could be turned by cavalry on the south. To the north some small and awkward kopjes linked them with Abraham's Kraal.

Lord Roberts' dispositions, as usual, were daring and skilful, but as at Poplar Grove, and for much the same reason, they failed to secure a complete success. The cavalry were divided up **Turning movement.** between the three infantry divisions, a brigade to each. The advance was to be made in three columns; on the left, following the course of the Modder, General French was to march, slightly ahead of the other columns, past Abraham's Kraal, with the Sixth Division, the First Cavalry Brigade, and a regiment of mounted infantry. In the centre, passing round the south of Driefontein, Lord Roberts, with the Ninth Division, the Guards, two regiments of mounted infantry, the Second Cavalry Brigade, and the heavy artillery, was to advance. The track to be followed by his men was one which the Boers had never expected to see used by a British army;

from lack of water it could only be traversed in rainy weather, and was shown in few of the maps; it had the great advantage of turning the Boer position. In case, however, the enemy prolonged their line to the south, General Tucker, with the Seventh Division, the Third Cavalry Brigade, and one regiment of mounted infantry, was to march due south to the village of Petrusberg, and then to press along the main Bloemfontein road to Driekop, which would bring him well to the rear of the Boers. He encountered no serious opposition, and played no part—except an indirect one—in the action which followed.

Late on March 9 the three columns were put in motion, and on the 10th the advance continued. But almost at once the left column under General French found that the awkward-looking kopjes, of **Boer tactics effectual.** which mention has already been made, near Abraham's Kraal, barred its way, and that these were held by the enemy in some force. The total strength of the Boers in this battle, it should be said, was placed by British authorities at 16,000, though the Boers themselves estimated it at no more than 8,000. Probably the truth lies between the two figures.

J. *Finnemore, R.I., R.B.A.*]   [*After a sketch by W. B. Wollen, R.I.*

ROBERTS' HORSE TURN THE TABLES ON THE BOERS.

"Roberts' Horse" surprised a party of Boers retreating from Kitchener's Kop, near Poplar Grove, on March 9, and killed or wounded thirty-five of them.

As his orders were not to make any frontal attacks, to avoid serious detention by the enemy, and to keep touch with Lord Roberts, General French, instead of fighting his way through—a course which would have placed him on the enemy's line of retreat, and which in all probability would not have cost more in blood than the attack upon Driefontein to which he was ultimately forced—turned southwards, passing along the base of the Boer kopjes. He left the 2nd Dragoons with the mounted infantry to keep the Boers busy at Abraham's Kraal—a work which they skilfully performed. His deflection from the more direct road complicated matters, as it brought his division directly in the line of Lord Roberts' column, which in turn had to edge southwards.

As General French was advancing southwards near Driefontein the Boers opened upon his flank a sharp artillery fire from the uppermost angle of their **W**-shaped series of kopjes. They seemed to have at least four Krupps and a "Pom-Pom" in action, and the men of the Staats Artillery, in khaki uniforms, could at times be made out working one of the weapons. Five British batteries replied and shelled the kopjes and the Boer guns; but though our weapons were six to one they could not silence the Boer fire. The 1st Cavalry Brigade, weak though it was in numbers, and growing daily and hourly weaker from its losses in horses, after considerable delay to permit of the approach of the infantry, who were some hours behind, endeavoured to work round to the Boer left flank. As it pushed along the front of the enemy's position it received some very unpleasant attentions from one of the Krupps and from a "Pom-Pom." The shells burst all among the horsemen, and yet, strange to say, only one man was hit. The farther the cavalry advanced, the farther the Boer lines extended. They appeared quite interminable, and it was scarcely surprising that the risk of stringing out six or seven hundred cavalrymen along such a protracted front, with no effective support at hand, at last compelled General French to suspend his turning movement long before the right arm of the **W** had been rounded. He determined to occupy the enemy's attention by skirmishing until the infantry of the Sixth Division should arrive, and until the Ninth Division came into line upon his right. After three hours of desultory firing and slow advance, however, the 2nd Cavalry Brigade, attached to Lord Roberts' column, came up, and the two brigades of cavalry were at last able to reach a low kopje on the Boer left. Endeavouring to push home the small success, and to get in upon the Boer rear, General French was checked by a Krupp which opened a sharp fire, using smoke-producing powder and bursting its shrapnel just over the heads of the men. Efforts were made to

[*Photo by Raju Deen Daya.*

LIEUT.-GENERAL CHARLES TUCKER, C.B.

He was born in 1838, in Devon, and in 1855 joined the old 80th Foot (now 2nd Battalion South Staffordshire Regiment); Captain, 1860; Major, 1872; Lieut.-Colonel, 1879; Colonel, 1883; Major-General, 1893. Served in the Bhootan Expedition of 1865; in the Perak operations of 1876; and commanded the left attack in the operations against Sekukuni in 1878, the 80th Regiment in the column on the Swazi border in the Zulu War of 1879, and the troops at Luneberg. Later on he led his regiment, attached to Sir Evelyn Wood's column, on its march through Zululand, and in the action at Ulundi. From 1895 he was in command of the Secunderabad District in Madras Presidency, until he left for South Africa to command the Seventh Division of the South Africa Field Force, with local rank of Lieut.-General, in December, 1899.

silence this piece, but with no great result. First, P Horse Artillery Battery engaged it, then a second British Battery began to fire upon it; yet it continued defiantly to reply. "There was," says Mr. Bennet Burleigh, "a distinct feeling at the divisional headquarters that our guns fired indifferently, and were so slow in changing direction and getting ranges that hundreds of Boers and waggons escaped that should have been smartly 'slated.'" Gradually Kitchener's Horse worked round the Krupp to its rear, threatening its retreat. The Boers were seen to be busy about it, limbering up and preparing to retire, and when this was noted the 10th Hussars and the 12th Lancers were sent to cut it off as the mounted infantry rushed the hill. But the mounted infantry arrived just four minutes too late; the horses of the cavalry were weary and in bad condition, and though the Hussars got near the gun their beasts were in no condition to charge the small escort of Boers. The enemy's men dismounted, and opened so sharp a magazine fire that the pursuit was checked. The Boer tactics were admirable, and nothing could exceed the coolness and determination of the little force that thus held at bay a British regiment. The Hussars had drawn ahead of the Lancers, so that on

RUSSIAN AMBULANCE BATTLE-CART WITH THE BOERS.

their part they had no support at hand. They dismounted and exchanged fire with the enemy, but they could not capture the gun, and as darkness was now coming on had to retire with a loss of six men.

Meantime, farther to the British left a fierce and unexpected infantry fight was raging. The Boers on the inner angle of the **W** gave no sign of life, and it was generally thought that they had retreated.

Infantry in difficulties. About 1.30 p.m. the Sixth Division appeared upon the field and was ordered to occupy what, it was supposed, was the abandoned line of kopjes. General Kelly-Kenny with his staff rode forward to reconnoitre, when there came a rude surprise. A terrific fire was on a sudden directed upon the little group of officers and upon the two brigades of infantry advancing in close order behind them. Bullets came from front and flanks, and so hot was the fire that it seemed amazing anyone should be left alive. The position was awkward, if not dangerous. Here, exactly as at Paardeberg, the division found itself in battle before proper deployment could take place, and was compelled to advance and deliver a frontal attack, notwithstanding Lord Roberts' express orders to the contrary. Retreat would have been even more dangerous than a continuance of the advance. At the head of the two British brigades were the East Kents and the 1st Welsh, who both suffered severe loss before they could open out and begin the attack. The situation was complicated by the fact that the men were marching light with only fifty rounds of ammunition apiece. There was no time to fill the pouches from the waggons; the division had to fight as it stood. Opposed to the British infantry was the very pick of

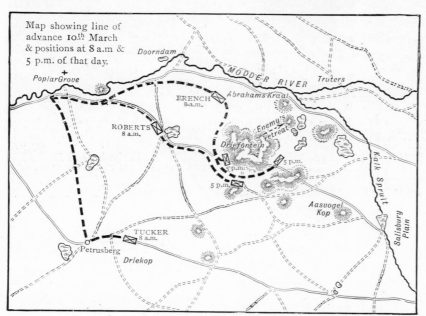

[*From the sketch-map supplied by Mr. Battersby to the "Morning Post."*

PLAN OF THE BATTLE OF DRIEFONTEIN.

the Boer army—indeed, the only disciplined body of men which it contained—in the Johannesburg Police and the Pretoria commando, who wore uniforms and always distinguished themselves by their courage. The Boers, too, had good cover in the shape of schanzes and in the usual, inevitable boulders.

The artillery of the division at once opened a heavy—and as it proved afterwards, an effective—fire upon the Boer position, while the Welsh Regiment opened out upon the left and the East Kents upon the right. Gradually the Yorkshires prolonged the right of the line, and the Essex and Gloucester

Splendid artillery fire. Regiments gave further support. "In the long semi-circular skirmishing line," says Mr. Filson Young, a correspondent with the army, "strung like a girdle round the hillside, a man suddenly turned and ran backwards for half-a-dozen paces, and then tumbled, rolling over and over like a shot rabbit. . . The ground was becoming dotted with writhing and motionless forms; it was a horrible sight." The conduct of all was magnificent; U and T Batteries of Horse Artillery and the 76th Field Battery especially distinguished themselves, their gunners working the guns most steadily under a terrible rifle and "Pom-Pom" fire. The Boer "Pom-Pom," indeed, struck two men of the T Battery just as it was coming into action, while there were several of the narrowest escapes, yet the very gun at which the men were killed was firing inside two minutes from the moment of unlimbering, and the gunners carried the ammunition past the bodies of their dead comrades as coolly as if nothing had happened. Of the infantry, the East Kents suffered most at this juncture, as the ground which they had to cover was bare and devoid of shelter. "It was a beast of a time," said one man;

[Wal. Paget.]   *[After a sketch by W. B. Wollen, R.I.*

THE ESSEX MEN CLEARING A KOPJE AT DRIEFONTEIN.

"we crawled half the way with only that long grass in front of us, thick with streaks of lead. . . We hadn't seen a man nor the flash of a rifle."

The East Kent, Welsh, Essex, and Yorkshire regiments, though pelted by explosive and other **Infantry in pursuit.** bullets, gained the crest of the Boer line of kopjes by a series of daring rushes— the last cheering and with bayonets fixed. Evening was falling, and from the rear Lord Roberts witnessed their splendid and spirited advance. Many of the officers were down;

the Welsh and East Kents being the hardest hit in this direction, but the colour-sergeants carried the men forward. The Boers did not wait. They fell precipitately back, their retreat covered by a rear-guard, which at short range, poured in a storm of bullets upon the pursuing infantry. The old disgraceful white-flag trick was re-enacted under Lord Roberts' own observation **More infractions of the usages of war.** when the Welsh were charging. A party of Boers dropped their rifles and held up white flags, whereupon several officers and privates advanced to accept their surrender. Without more ado, they, or men close at hand, fired a volley, bringing all the British who had thus exposed themselves to the ground. Such indignation did this incident cause that after the battle Lord Roberts telegraphed, remonstrating in the strongest terms with the Boer Presidents and warning them that, if such an infraction of the customs of war occurred again, he would be compelled to order his troops to disregard altogether the white flag. He complained, too, and with good reason, of the murderous explosive bullets employed by the Boers.

As darkness came down, the serried mass of infantry of the **Casualties.** Ninth Division arrived, and the enemy took to flight, retiring in a north-easterly direction. The battle was over. Once more the Sixth Division had distinguished itself by its marching and fighting, for the action followed directly upon a hard march of six hours under the burning sun. The heaviest loss was suffered by the Welsh regiment, which had 130 officers and men killed or wounded, and this out of a total strength not exceeding 800. Lieut.-Colonel Giffard, who had replaced Colonel Banfield, wounded at Paardeberg, was wounded ; Captain Lomax was killed, and five lieutenants wounded. The battalion had now

Allan Stewart.]　　　　　　　　*[After a sketch by Fred Villiers.*
AID AT LAST.
A surgeon at work in the field after a battle.

lost all its field officers, the adjutant, and eight lieutenants ; only twice in its history had it been harder hit. Next in order of losses came the East Kent, Essex, and Gloucester battalions. The total number of British casualties was 426—killed 24, wounded 400, and missing 2.

When the Boer position was examined next day, 102—some say 127—of the enemy's dead were discovered, besides a large number of dead horses. The Boer losses must therefore have been heavy, though, as most of the bodies found had been struck by shrapnel, it is probable that the proportion of killed was unusually high. A number of Boer wounded were found in the field and carefully tended by the British ambulances, but the great majority of the injured, as was the Boer custom, had been removed before the retreat.   About 20 prisoners were captured, most of them by the Welshmen.   They stated that the Boer force was composed of men withdrawn from before Ladysmith and from Colesberg. With their usual effrontery the Boer newspapers pretended that their losses were only 7 killed and 18 wounded, and represented the battle as a brilliant success for the Federal arms.   By this time, however, most men in the Republics must have begun to guess the truth.

The night of the battle was spent by the Sixth and Ninth Divisions at Driefontein, while the cavalry bivouacked at Driepan.   Next day the advance was resumed.   The two divisions did not again part **Advance continued.** company, but, cutting absolutely loose from all their communications, and taking with them in the waggon train only the barest necessaries, marched along the central of the three Bloemfontein roads, leaving the left-hand road, along the course of the Modder, unwatched—except by Boers.   The enemy's force gave no more trouble ; it had evidently had enough of

THE AMBULANCE TRAIN FROM THE FRONT PASSING THROUGH THE KAROO.

Much kindness was shown by the ladies to the wounded at the different stations.   Touws River Station is about 60 miles N.E. of Capetown.

fighting for the time, and was now retiring hastily in the direction of Brandfort, having been deflected from Bloemfontein.   " What can we poor Boers do ? " said President Kruger, about this date, to Captain Allum, the Norwegian attaché.   " The English have 100,000 soldiers at one place, 40,000 at another, and 30,000 at a third."   Though he exaggerated our strength, the fact remained that the Boer plight was desperate, and no attempt was made on their part to defend the strong position which existed at Aasvogel Kop.   There was some insignificant skirmishing between the scouts and flanking detachments on either side, and from time to time small bodies of Boers were seen.   East of Aasvogel Kop, the army bivouacked at Doornboom, face to face with a line of kopjes commanding the direct Bloemfontein road, which were reported to have been entrenched and manned with burghers brought down by rail from the north.

On March 12, when the army once more put itself in motion, the Boers were seen in considerable strength.   An attempt to force a passage must necessarily have cost the army dear.   But Lord

The Boers helpless.   Roberts was equal to the occasion.   Swinging off his forces to the right, he marched them southwards along the front of the Boer position, but well out of range, to Venter's Vlei, where, next morning, he effected his junction with the vanguard of General Tucker's column.   The Boers were able to do nothing, and they must have raged as the 20-mile line of waggons and transport passed under their noses.   Meantime, the cavalry division had been reassembled under General French with orders for one brigade to halt during the night at Weltevrede,

keeping touch on the one hand with the infantry divisions at Venter's Vlei, and on the other with the two remaining cavalry brigades, which were to reach Leeuwberg, a height immediately to the south of Bloemfontein, by the evening of the 12th, and to break the railway south of Bloemfontein.   This order was skilfully exe-

[Photo by J. F. J. Archibald.

GENERAL FRENCH AND STAFF.

The famous cavalry General sits in front of the group. Standing behind him, wearing a peaked cap, is Sir John Milbanke, Bart., V.C., and next him, also in a peaked cap, is Colonel Haig, General French's Chief of Staff. At the extreme right of the picture stands Major Foster, and on the extreme left, Captain Jos. Laycock, of the Imperial Yeomanry.

cuted; Leeuwberg was seized, a force of 200 Boers flying like frightened rabbits before the British cavalry and abandoning their camp; President Steyn's brother was made a prisoner on his farm, the railway was cut, and the Horse Batteries were placed in position to shell Bloemfontein.   During the night a most daring exploit was successfully performed by Major Hunter-Weston, of the Engineers, with a small party of picked men.   He rode round the Boer lines to the

PRESIDENT STEYN'S BROTHER.

The photograph represents Mr. Steyn with his little daughter by the "stoep" of his house. It was here that General French stayed on March 12, and here also that Lord Roberts breakfasted on the following morning.

north of Bloemfontein, and blew up a culvert on the railway at dawn of the 13th, completely isolating the Free State capital.   General Joubert, with a force of Transvaalers, was thus prevented from arriving in time to help the Free Staters.

Meantime, utter panic and confusion prevailed in Bloemfontein.   General French had already sent in to demand its surrender under threat of bombardment.   Mr. Steyn pleaded eagerly with the citizens for a desperate resistance, and promised assistance from the Transvaal, but his entreaties fell upon deaf ears.   Bloemfontein was an open town with no means of resisting or replying to the fire of the 120 guns which Lord Roberts could speedily bring to bear upon it.   This was pointed out, and finally the defeated President, about 6.30 p.m., fled hurriedly northwards, announcing that henceforward Kroonstad must be considered the capital of the Free State.

With daybreak of the 13th, while the 1st Cavalry Brigade held the ground to the south of the town, the 2nd pushed eastwards with instructions to stop any trains attempting to leave, as it was not yet known that the line to the north was cut. The batteries of the 1st Brigade were already in action, but it was not many minutes before messengers arrived from the town with the news that all resistance had ceased, and that the place surrendered.

Surrender of Bloemfontein.

Meantime, from Venter's Vlei the Sixth and Seventh Divisions, followed later by the Ninth, set out in majestic progress to complete the last stage of their eventful march. The men were worn with hard work and short rations, yet as they realised that the goal was already in sight, new vigour marked their movements. The unending column, veiled in dense clouds of dust, headed south, and at Brand Dam found the cavalry in possession of that point. Resistance had been anticipated here, as there was a fair position for the Boers, but now it was clear that no further fighting was to be expected before Bloemfontein. As Lord Roberts' staff breasted a steep rise from which the first view of Bloemfontein is obtained by those approaching from the south, a deputation from the municipal authorities came out to make the formal surrender. Then Lord Roberts, at the head of his army, rode forward. Behind him came his secretary, his aides-de-camp, his

J. Finnemore, R.I., R.B.A.]

THE SKIRL OF THE PIPES.

The weary marching of the Highland Brigade on March 12 was enlivened by the pipes of the Black Watch

GENERAL VIEW OF BLOEMFONTEIN.
The large building on the right is the Raadzaal, or Parliament House.

Bloemfontein lies in a plain with low hills surrounding it. It is 4,518 feet above the sea, 450 miles from Port Elizabeth, and 750 miles from Capetown. Its normal population is about 10,000, of which some 7,000 are whites. The town is laid out rectangularly, and there are some fine buildings, many of which are of stone quarried in the neighbourhood. Electric light and water supply are both good. The climate is exceptionally salubrious under normal conditions.

subordinate generals, and the foreign attachés ; and after them again cavalry and guns, and more cavalry and guns.   The squadrons and batteries were in their fighting dress ; colour was wanting to relieve the dingy hue of the stained and torn khaki, yet all who looked upon the men were moved by their magnificent appearance.   Browned and tanned by the sun, they were in the very pink of physical condition —lean and lithe and hardy, worthy representatives of the nation whose honour they had so well sustained. On his entry into the capital the British Commander-in-Chief was received with cheers, and it was noted with some surprise that the population of the town seemed English by race and English in sympathy. As he passed the Artillery Barracks, Lord Roberts' quick eye noticed a band of Kaffirs looting the place ; at once he signed to his aides-de-camp, and the dukes and lords who formed his retinue fell to arresting the culprits.   Then the silken flag which Lady Roberts had prepared was hoisted

Hoisting the flag.　upon the staff in front of the President's official residence, while the troops and people sang " God Save the Queen."   Simultaneously Union Jacks had appeared as if by magic in all quarters.   A police to protect the inhabitants was organised without a moment's delay, and there was not a single breach of public order, though 30,000 fighting men were in or around the town.   Thus quietly, without incident or excitement, Bloemfontein fell, and the Free State paid its first instalment of the penalty for interfering in a war with which it had no concern.   So easily was success obtained that we are prone to forget the skilful strategy by which a strong Boer force was dislodged from position after position with the loss of less than 500 men, and was compelled to an ignominious retreat northward ; we are apt to overlook the supreme daring which cut loose from base and line of communications and left the Boers, if they would, to gather in the army's rear. The operations, indeed, illustrated the helpless position of an inferior force when attacked by a general of commanding ability.   If the Boers stood, they were certain to be enveloped and captured *en masse :* if they ran they gave up their country to the enemy.   Among the spoils captured were large quantities of ammunition and dynamite, 25 locomotives, certain parts of which, though abstracted and buried, were speedily disentombed and replaced, 124 trucks and about 20 carriages.   This rolling stock was of immense service to the army, and it was entirely due to Major Hunter-Weston's daring that it was secured.

There was a tendency both in the army and at home to think that with the fall of its capital the resistance of the Free State had collapsed—a tendency which found encouragement in the easy successes of the next few days. Perhaps, if the army had been in a condition immediately to follow up the Boers the war might have speedily ended, but in fact, it was not in such condition. From the 7th to the 13th most of the infantry battalions had covered over seventy-seven miles, and this, be it remembered, not along good or even passable roads, but upon sandy tracks of indescribable badness. They had had to endure short rations and bivouacs in pouring rain upon the open veldt. The strength of the brigades and divisions had been reduced by casualties and sickness till divisions had shrunk almost to brigades. The Sixth Division, for example, instead of 10,000 men could muster only 5,300, though it is

Halt at Bloemfontein imperative.

THE HOISTING OF THE BRITISH FLAG AT BLOEMFONTEIN.

The honour of hoisting the flag—a small silken one, made by Lady Roberts' own hand, and bearing a shamrock in one corner—fell to Lord Herbert Scott, A.D.C. to Lord Roberts. After the ceremony had been performed, the small flag was run down, and a full-sized Union Jack substituted.

true that its losses had been exceptionally heavy; the cavalry brigades, from the enormous expenditure of horseflesh which had characterised the march, were in yet worse case; and many of their regiments had shed two-thirds of their strength on the road. Thus, the arm upon which most depended—by which all Lord Roberts' turning moves had been effected, and which had been the cause of the envelopment and capture of Cronje—had been weakened till it was rendered useless, or all but useless. The artillery, horse and field, was in as bad case. Its losses in horses had been prodigious, and the beasts that remained alive could scarcely drag the guns at a walking pace. It was a matter of paramount necessity to remount the cavalry and re-horse the artillery before the advance was resumed upon a great scale. The infantry, too, needed boots and warm clothing for the winter, now fast approaching; above all, it needed rest. Not less urgent was the accumulation of reserves of ammunition, food, and clothing at Bloemfontein. But, to effect this, the railway to the south had first to be cleared, and then, day by day, a surplus, over and above the current needs of the army, forwarded along a single narrow-gauge, ill-laid, poorly-equipped line, 350 miles long. The roads to

A FIELD HOSPITAL FOR SICK HORSES.
This picture represents the veterinary surgeon at work amongst the sick horses in the Worcester Imperial Yeomanry Camp, near Belmont.

Kimberley across the veldt by which the army had been kept supplied during its great march were so bad, so devoid of water, that it was practically impossible to meet requirements by waggon transport. It had been expected that efforts would be made to lay a field railway from Kimberley to Bloemfontein, which would have relieved the congestion; there was an ample supply of Kaffir labour available, yet nothing was done to build such a line. Probably the reason was that the whole energy of the Kimberley-Capetown railway had to be concentrated upon the supply of Lord Roberts' army until the end of March, and that trucks could not be spared for the despatch of rails and sleepers or of subsistence for the men who would have been required to construct the strategic line.

All these considerations compelled a suspension of the forward movement, and for the next six weeks Lord Roberts was busy securing his hold over the south of the Free State. The halt, necessary though it was, gave the enemy time to reorganise their forces and to recover from the extreme dejection which the capture of Cronje's army, the relief of Ladysmith, and the march of Lord Roberts' army to Bloemfontein had caused. Had an ample supply of remounts and strong reinforcements been available upon the spot, it is just possible that the Field Marshal might have seen his way to continue the vigorous offensive, though even then, in the light of after events, it is doubtful if this would have

[*Photo by Alfred Ellis.*

MAJOR HUNTER-WESTON,

Entered the Royal Engineers in 1884, and served with the Bengal Sappers and Miners in the Miranzai Expedition in 1891, and with the Waziristan Delimitation Escort in 1894. He received his brevet of major for services with the Waziristan Field Force under Sir W. Lockhart in 1894–5, and he has since served under Sir H. Kitchener in the Dongola Expeditionary Force in 1896. He has frequently rendered great services to the Army under Lord Roberts by cutting the railways on the Boer lines of communication.

brought the submission of the Boers. Like the low organism, which is susceptible of infinite injury without complete loss of vitality, the enemy displayed a surprising endurance. And yet, perhaps, to speak thus is to be guilty of a certain injustice to the Boers. They were passionately attached to their independence, and, like the Confederates in the American Civil War, would never renounce their hopes and aspirations till their armies were completely crushed and their territory in the enemy's hands. We may respect and honour them for their self-sacrificing devotion, inconvenient though it was to ourselves.

On March 14 the infantry of the British army entered Bloemfontein and marched past Lord Roberts. They made a

Conquering heroes.

superb show, notwithstanding their dirty khaki uniforms, creased and sodden with the torrential rain of the night before. They wore the look of conquerors, not of sufferers, and seemed to ask for envy, not sympathy. "They were," says Mr. Ralph, "no longer hungry; the stains and wrinkles on their clothing were well earned and proudly borne. I turned aside and whispered under my breath, 'God bless Tommy Atkins. He has done his duty and is satisfied with the reward of merely marching through the capital of the rich new territory he has given to his Queen and nation.'

The Oxfords swept by thinned in ranks; the Welshmen, fresh from the lurid jaws of Hades-like Paardeberg, strode lightly past; the brave men of Essex, covered with new glory, marched proudly along; the splendid Yorks, whose ranks had just been tattered by battle strokes, trooped jauntily by. Looking on at them all were thousands who never had heard of the feats these men were fresh from, or the dangers they had braved. But what did the soldiers care?"

To the Guards who defiled before him, fresh and jubilant, notwithstanding their amazing forced march of thirty-eight miles in the last twenty-eight hours, Lord Roberts addressed especial congratulations upon their splendid appearance and not less splendid spirit. And, tactful as always, mindful of their primacy in the Army, he told them that only accident had prevented his marching at their head into Bloemfontein. He promised, however—and he kept his word—in recompense for this to lead them into Pretoria. It was such acts as these that made him the idol of his men. "Every **march**, every movement, and every victory," wrote the *Times* correspondent, "increases his popularity and strengthens the Army's confidence in him.'

[*Photo by Duffus Bros.*

MR. T. R. PRICE,

General Manager of the Cape Government Railways, has been a railway man all his life, and under his able supervision the system attained a high degree of efficiency, considering the enormous disadvantages, natural and economic, which had to be overcome. Mr. Price was heavily handicapped at the beginning of the Boer War by lack of support on the part of the Cape Ministry, of which Mr. Sauer, his official chief, was a member.

He now turned to opening up communications with General Clements, whom we last left at Arundel, and with General Gatacre, whom we left at Bushman's Hoek. General Gatacre, after his reverse at Stormberg, had been steadily reinforced by excellent Colonial troops,

Subjugation of Stormberg District.

and eventually by General Brabant's division of Cape Colony Mounted Volunteers. On December 25 he was able to occupy Dordrecht with a force of Cape Mounted Rifles and Police under Colonel Dalgety. The Boers were seven miles north of this place, at Labuschagne's Nek, where a sharp skirmish was fought on the 30th and 31st, between De Montmorency's scouts and the enemy, in which the latter had much the worst of matters. On January 3, the Boers, with ardour undiminished by their reverse, made a surprise attack upon a small detachment near Molteno, but reinforcements arrived in time from the camp at Bushman's Hoek, and they were beaten off. Yet their appearance in this place compelled General Gatacre to withdraw from Dordrecht, which thus once more fell into the enemy's hands. On January 27 General Brabant arrived, to take command of the Colonial Division, with secret instructions to advance on General Gatacre's right, through Dordrecht and Jamestown to Aliwal North, as soon as Lord Roberts was ready to open the new campaign in the west. He paraded his men on the eve of the advance, and promised them that the greatest glutton for fighting should have his fill of it. On February 15 he pushed forward from his camp at Penhoek, south of Dordrecht, to Dordrecht and delivered a night assault upon the Boer entrenchments defending the place; the enemy were in weak force, and fled precipitately. A day later Dordrecht was taken by the British

THE COLDSTREAMS TAKING POSSESSION OF THE OLD FORT AT BLOEMFONTEIN, March 13, 1900.

for the last time. Continuing his advance, on March 4 he seized a height which dominated the Boer position at Labuschagne's Nek, when the enemy hurriedly retired. They were promptly followed up; Jamestown was occupied on March 9; on the 11th General Brabant entered Aliwal North and crossed the Orange River, thus winning with his gallant Colonials the proud honour of being the first British force to invade the enemy's territory from the south. So rapid and skilful were his movements that the extreme north-eastern corner of Cape Colony was virtually cleared of the enemy without serious loss. The rebels in panic began to surrender, protesting that they had only taken up arms against the British under constraint. For the most part they were sent to their farms to await punishment.

General Gatacre did not move till the effect of General Brabant's advance began to be felt. On February 24 he was so unfortunate as to lose Lieutenant de Montmorency, who had organised the corps of scouts that bore his name, and who was famous as one of the bravest officers in the British

R. Caton Woodville.]

IN THE COLESBERG DISTRICT: A RECONNAISSANCE UNDER DIFFICULTIES.

(549)

F. Dadd, R.I.]   [After a sketch by an officer.

FIRST OVER THE FRONTIER.

Montmorency's Scouts led General Brabant's forces across the bridge at Aliwal North, and were thus the first regiment to invade Boer territory from the south. As they passed over the bridge each man cheered. We gave on p. 49 a photograph of a Boer force crossing the same bridge to invade Cape Colony.

Army. De Montmorency fell by the wayside in a skirmish.   The enemy's force at Stormberg was greatly weakened by desertion and the despatch of detachments to other parts of the field of war at

Repair of the Western Railway. the end of February ; finally, on March 4, the Boers abandoned the position which had been the scene of General Gatacre's defeat, and on the following day he occupied it without incident. He at once began the repair of the railway to the west, so as to open up through communication by land with Colesberg, Capetown, and the west ; at the same time he continued his advance northwards, and on March 7 occupied that great Mecca of the rebels and the Afrikander Bond—Burghersdorp.   Four days later his outposts were a mile south of the Orange River and of the two important bridges, road and railway, which cross near Bethulie ; on the 13th, the main British force neared the bridges, and skirmishing began.   The Boers had taken

A NASTY FALL:
Trying men for the Mounted Infantry at Bushman's Hoek, January 1900.

the precaution of demolishing the railway bridge by blowing up with dynamite five of its spans ; the piers, however, were left standing, and for their own purposes the enemy refrained from destroying the road bridge. They mined it in readiness, placing charges of dynamite and detonators at several points in holes cut in the stonework of the bridge ; they also laid an electric cable from the bridge to their trenches on the Free State soil, but did not connect it with the charges.   Finally, they placed several boxes of dynamite on the farther bank, under the last span of the bridge, in case of any failure in their other arrangements.

To save the bridge was a matter of extreme moment to the British. Late in the afternoon of the 13th a party of the 1st Sherwood Foresters crossed the bridge, and, unobserved, while the Boers, after their usual habit, were at tea, removed the cable and detonators.   Then, under cover of night, Lieutenant Popham, with a little

Saving Bethulie Bridge.

handful of men of the same battalion, stole across, got down under the bridge, and, finding no trace of a Boer sentry except a bandolier, removed the boxes of dynamite one by one to the roadway.   The lieutenant, thinking that perhaps the enemy had retired, crept towards their trenches, when he trod by ill-luck upon a dog, and a hail of bullets speedily showed him that the Boers were there.   Returning, he and his men boldly carried the boxes of explosives over the bridge to the British camp under a heavy fire.   Fortune favoured them and no one was hit.   There still remained a possibility that the enemy might succeed in exploding the charges next day by means of shell fire.   To remove this source of peril Captain Grant of the Engineers crept over the bridge, and withdrawing the charges in succession from the holes in which they had been placed, flung them one after the other into the river.   By this series of acts of superb gallantry the bridge was saved.

On March 14 the dust raised by the retreat of the Boer

Communications restored.

waggon train could plainly be seen, moving towards Smithfield, but the British force did nothing.   Only on the 15th did General Gatacre cross the river and enter Bethulie.   On the 16th touch was established with Lord Roberts at Springfontein Junction, where General Gatacre captured two en-

Stanley Berkeley.]

A VICTORIA CROSS INCIDENT.

During a reconnaissance near Colesberg on Jan. 5, 1900, Lieut. Sir John P. Milbanke, Bart., while retiring under a heavy fire with a small patrol of the 10th Hussars, and notwithstanding the fact that he had himself just been wounded in the thigh, rode back to the assistance of one of his men, whose horse had become exhausted.   He took him up on his own horse, and got him safely back to camp.   For this act Sir John Milbanke was awarded the Victoria Cross, and he was shortly afterwards promoted from Lieutenant to Captain.

gines, forty trucks, a number of prisoners, and 500 or 600 rifles, and whither General Pole-Carew, with the 1st Scots Guards, 3rd Grenadiers, four guns, and a section of mounted infantry, had been despatched by Lord Roberts from Bloemfontein on the 15th.   General Pole-Carew then turned southwards towards Norvals Pont and established communication with General Clements on the 17th.

General Clements, when the Boer force in his front felt the effect of Lord Roberts' operations in the Free State and had to think of its communications, was able in his turn to advance.   But

THE RAILWAY BRIDGE AT NORVALS PONT.

before this he had on February 20 to repulse a last determined attempt on the part of the enemy to work round his flank to the south, threatening the De Aar and Naauwpoort Railway. On the 23rd the Boers fell back to the positions near Rensburg, from which, weeks before, General French had dislodged them. Here they were attacked by General Clements next day, but without result. In view of his growing strength and of their increasing weakness, they retired farther before him, and on the 27th Rensburg was occupied by the British; on the 28th, Colesberg. The Boers in this quarter had apparently retired across the Orange River, for on March 2 the mounted infantry reconnoitred up to the road bridge without seeing the enemy, but the bridge was not immediately seized. At Norvals Pont it was ascertained by reconnaissance that the enemy was still in some strength. On March 6 they blew up the railway bridge there, as also the Colesberg road-bridge farther to the west; on the 8th General Clements reached Norvals Pont and made arrangements for bridging the river. The ferry was seized through the daring of a few Colonials, who crossed by a ford and threw up trenches. On the 15th a pontoon bridge was ready, and General Clements' column began its passage a few miles below Norvals Pont. There was no opposition, and he was able to push his outposts forward as far as Donkerspoort, where a day or two later General Pole-Carew met them. The repair of Norvals Pont Bridge was at once undertaken, but could not be completed for some weeks. Meantime, railway traffic between Cape Colony and Bloemfontein was carried on by means of a light line carried across Bethulie road-bridge. In this way the main army was kept supplied, though only with extreme difficulty.

ERECTING THE TEMPORARY RAILWAY BRIDGE AT BETHULIE.

The Boers having destroyed the fine iron girder bridge, part of which is seen to the right of the picture, the Royal Engineers, as soon as the Boers had been driven away, set about the construction of a deviation railway and a trestle-bridge. In the meantime a light line was laid across the road bridge; but as this structure could not carry the weight of an engine, the trains were cautiously backed on to it and picked up on the other side.

S. Paget.]

HOW FOUR VICTORIA CROSSES WERE WON.

[after a sketch by W. B. Wollen, R.I.

The story of the disaster at Koorn Spruit, relieved as it was by the superb gallantry of the Royal Horse Artillery, is told in this chapter. The illustration above represents Q Battery wheeling into action.

CHAPTER XXIV.

THE HALT AT BLOEMFONTEIN.

Excessive clemency—Expedition to Thaba N'chu—Skirmishing north of the capital—The Karee kopjes captured—Broadwood's retreat from Thaba N'chu intercepted—The ambuscade at Koorn Spruit—The alarm given—Magnificent conduct of the Royal Horse Artillery—No help from Bloemfontein—Retreat and losses—The water-supply cut off—The Boers threaten Dewetsdorp—Surrender of Captain McWhinnie's force—Gatacre's relief force barred—Rundle and Kitchener guard the railway—British occupy Wepener—The town besieged—Assault repulsed—Closer investment—Sufferings of the garrison—Final attack repelled—Arrival of relief columns—Plans for capturing the Boer force—Fruitless pursuit—Recovery of Bloemfontein Waterworks—Entry into Thaba N'chu—Operations against surrounding heights—Disappearance of the Gordons—Infantry surprised—Skilful withdrawal—Attempt to capture Boshof—Disturbance in north-west of Cape Colony—Death of Joubert.

FOR the first week after the arrival of Lord Roberts' army at Bloemfontein all went well, and the general disposition to suppose that resistance in the Free State had collapsed received new support from the number of burghers who made their submission, and from the stories which they told of profound disagreement between the Free Staters and Transvaalers. Touch had been

Excessive clemency.

established with the British armies advancing from the south; the country traversed by our soldiers was outwardly friendly; Lord Roberts' proclamation to the effect that burghers who surrendered their arms, took an oath of neutrality, and remained upon their farms, would not be molested, was, it seemed, well received, though it was noted that the worthy Free Staters handed in, not Mausers or good modern rifles, but Martinis, Enfields, and even ancient flint-locks, and that these were accepted

THE GOAT WHICH ACCOMPANIED THE WELSH FUSILIERS THROUGHOUT THE CAMPAIGN.

The Royal Welsh Fusiliers have the privilege of passing in review preceded by a goat with gilded horns and adorned with flowers. The custom is an ancient one whose origin is lost in obscurity.

by British officers, with amazing simplicity, as evidence of disarmament. But, fixed in the belief that the Boers were "sick of the war," the military authorities appear to have supposed that they had only to post up the proclamation to effect an immediate pacification. There was a natural—perhaps a statesmanlike—desire not to press the enemy too severely. And though after events proved that in pursuing this course a great error was committed and that the character of the resistance to be expected was dangerously underrated, it is impossible to blame a man of such wisdom and experience as Lord Roberts. He wished to conciliate the conquered and to try clemency before recourse was had to sternness.

After the fall of Bloemfontein it had

THE SIEGE TRAIN ON ITS WAY TO BLOEMFONTEIN.

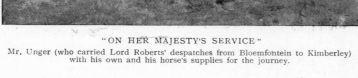

"ON HER MAJESTY'S SERVICE"

Mr. Unger (who carried Lord Roberts' despatches from Bloemfontein to Kimberley) with his own and his horse's supplies for the journey.

been hoped that the Boer forces from Colesberg and Stormberg, at least 5,000 men, and possibly 10,000 men strong, would be cut off and captured. The only safe line of retreat for them lay along the roads which run north-eastwards through Thaba N'chu and Ladybrand. But either their mobility and determination were underrated, or the "wreck of an army"—as it was not unjustly called—at Bloemfontein was unequal as yet to a new and severe campaign in the mountainous region of the eastern Free State. In any case Olivier and Grobler were able to march northwards, well ahead of the columns of Generals Brabant, Gatacre, and Clements, until they could come into touch with De Wet and the burghers who had fought at Poplar Grove and Driefontein. No vigorous attempt was made to intercept their retreat; instead, resort was had to half-measures with mortifying consequences.

On March 18 a composite force of mounted men comprising the Household Cavalry, the 10th Hussars, a hundred or so of Rimington's Guides, Roberts' Horse, the Queensland and Burma Mounted Infantry,

Expedition to Thaba N'chu. and Q and U Batteries of Horse Artillery, the whole under Generals French and Broadwood, left Bloemfontein for Thaba N'chu, to receive the submission of the farmers in that district, distribute proclamations and show the British uniform. Thaba N'chu was reached without incident on the 19th; on the 20th Colonel Pilcher with about 250 men pushed on yet further towards Ladybrand. Natives reported that a Boer commando, 4,000 strong, was in the neighbourhood, and the flashing of a heliograph was seen away to the east, but the small British detachment was not as yet attacked. It occupied the important flour mills on the Leeuw River, a little to the west of Ladybrand, remained there some days unmolested, and actually pushed on into Ladybrand itself on the 26th. Colonel Pilcher seized a few prominent Boers, administered the oath to others, and was calmly searching the place for a sum of Boer gold, when the enemy appeared all round the village. An immediate retreat was the only possible course. The detachment fell back covered by the fire of its Maxims to Leeuw River, losing a few prisoners; and thence continued its retirement under cover of night to Thaba N'chu, joining, east of that place, a small force which had been sent out to its

GOVERNMENT BUILDINGS, BLOEMFONTEIN.
During the stay of Presidents Kruger and Steyn.

support. The enemy were now showing in strength along a curving line from Karee Siding, north of Bloemfontein, through Thaba N'chu to Dewetsdorp, and their attitude was becoming hourly more threatening. General French was recalled to Bloemfontein to operate against the right of this line, and General Broadwood's

INTERIOR OF THE RAADZAAL, BLOEMFONTEIN.

The first illustration on this page is a view of the old Raadzaal, which was afterwards used as the Law Courts. In front of the building is a statue of President Brand, who was in office from 1864 to 1888. A good Town Hall adjoins the municipal offices, which are simple and unpretentious. The other illustrations give the interior and the exterior of the new Raadzaal, a rather imposing building of freestone, with Doric columns and a domed tower over 90 feet high. It cost nearly £60,000, and has been used as a hospital during the war. The late Government of the Orange Free State was constituted in 1854, and consisted of a States President at the head of the Executive Government, elected every five years and possessing a casting vote, assisted by an Executive Council (consisting of the Landdrost or magistrate of Bloemfontein, the Government Secretary, and two unofficial members), and, lastly, the Volksraad of fifty-eight members, representing the district towns and wards, whose membership lasted four years, and half of whom retired every two years. There have been six Presidents, named respectively Hoffman, Boshoff, Pretorius, Brand, Reitz (since State Secretary of the Transvaal), and Steyn.

EXTERIOR OF THE RAADZAAL, OR PARLIAMENT HOUSE, BLOEMFONTEIN.

2,000 men were left at Thaba N'chu, in a very dangerous position, to watch the Boer centre and left.

Meantime, the British outposts to the north of Bloemfontein had been pushed out as far as Glen, where the railway bridge over the Modder, destroyed by the Boers on their northward retreat,

Skirmishing north of the capital. was under repair. On March 23 a party of four British officers rode boldly from Glen to Karee, where they sighted a picket of Boers and gave chase.

The chase was most unfortunate, as the enemy took shelter in a kopje and shot down all their opponents, killing Lieutenant Lygon, and wounding the other three. Reconnaissances located the Boers in some force at Karee, and on March 27 General Tucker with the Seventh

W. Small.]   *[After a sketch by G. D. Giles.*

CARRYING OFF THE LANDDROST OF LADYBRAND.

On March 26, after driving in the Boer outposts, Colonel Pilcher entered Ladybrand and seized several officials, including the Landdrost. As the enemy shortly afterwards appeared in force, Colonel Pilcher decided to retire, but he carried off the Landdrost and Field Cornet with him, the 10th Hussars compelling the native driver to keep up with them by holding a pistol to his head.

Division was despatched to Glen. There, next day, he was joined by General French with the 2nd and 3rd Cavalry Brigades, and by Colonel Le Gallais with a brigade of mounted infantry. The programme was for General French to turn the Boer position from the west while Le Gallais worked round it from the east, and the infantry attacked from the south. In garrison at Glen, and available to support the Seventh Division, were two battalions of Guards. All the troops engaged were much below the nominal strength, from the losses in men and horses on the march to Bloemfontein, which had not yet been made good. The odds were by no means heavily in their favour.

Early on March 29 the two turning columns of mounted men moved off. The Boer position consisted of three parallel lines of kopjes, running at right angles to the railway, with considerable stretches of level ground between the lines. The northernmost of these three lines lay 1,000 yards to the north of Karee Siding. About 10 a.m. signals announced the fact that General French's men

H. W. Koekkoek.]

CAVALRY SEARCHING A DONGA.

(557)

were on the enemy's right rear, and at once the infantry advance began. The Boer force was under Commandant Grobler; it numbered about 5,000 men, and included the famous "Zarps," or Johannesburg Police—the best fighters in the Boer army. The turning movements forced the **The Karee kopjes captured.** Boers to abandon the first two series of kopjes; only at the third, near Karee, did they make a stand. Hereabouts, on his eastward advance to get in upon their line of retreat, General French found himself entangled in an intricate maze of woods and dongas, admirably adapted to give the Boers shelter. These had to be carefully shelled, examined and turned in succession, which rendered his progress slow; finally, after persistent skirmishing, he found himself, with horses and men worn out by his wide turning movement, face to face with a long

donga, which made a natural trench, running north and south. The donga was filled with Boers; unless it was captured it quite precluded the continuance of the turning movement. Remembering, it may be, the manœuvre which had opened the road to Kimberley, General French prepared to charge, when the roar of firing from the south told that at last General Tucker's infantry attack had begun, and led the Boers gradually to fall back. On the British right Colonel Le Gallais' mounted men had been held in check in much the same manner, and were prevented from cutting off the Boer retreat.

General Tucker's two brigades—the 14th on

BRIGADIER-GENERAL WAVELL AND CAPTAIN DAVIDSON, A.D.C., AT KAREE.

the right and 15th on the left— advanced in open order towards the kopjes north of Karee Siding, seeing nothing of the enemy. It was the old Boer trick, yet it deceived, and the opinion began to gain strength that the enemy had retired. The mounted infantry

MAKING UP THE MAILS OF THE 15TH BRIGADE AT KAREE.

scouted as far as the base of the kopjes, and reported no Boers and drew no fire; then the infantry, in a long waving line, advanced. Two companies of the King's Own Scottish Borderers went forward, and were only a few hundred yards from the summits of the two kopjes between which passes the railway, when suddenly the bushes and boulders before them broke into flame, and a sheet of lead decimated their ranks. The enemy were absolutely invisible; it was impossible to say whether there were a hundred or a thousand Boers on the slope; but the fire was so terrific that it forced the British troops to recoil to a donga under the kopjes, where, fortunately for them, good shelter could be found. The Boer artillery opened with effect, bursting shrapnel accurately among the battalions of the 14th Brigade. To reply to it, one of the 7th Division's batteries attempted to push to the top of a steep hill facing the extreme left of the Boer position, but the horses, worn out and exhausted, were unequal to the work, and could not make the ascent. Practically, the battery was out of action for the rest of the day.   The other two batteries nearer the British centre opened fire upon the kopjes commanding the railway; but whether the cordite ammunition—as some said—was defective, or the gunnery was bad, the shots seemed to go wide of the mark.   The enemy's rifle fire could not be got under; it continued to be so heavy that no

advance was practicable. The whole division remained extended flat on the ground, engaged in an interminable, resultless, long-range rifle fight. At last the East Lancashires, about 4 p.m., made an effort to storm the kopje on which the Boer right rested, but they received a hail of bullets which quickly brought them to a standstill. Not till some minutes later did General French's manœuvres in the enemy's rear make themselves felt. His shells were seen bursting well behind the Boers, and simultaneously there were signs of a Boer retreat. Horsemen were observed hurrying rearwards; guns limbered up and bowled off over the plain to Brandfort. Now was the time for a stern and vigorous pursuit, but unfortunately the cavalry horses, after the exhausting work of turning the Boer position, were in no condition to complete the rout of the enemy; moreover, the plain across which the Boers retreated, for all its level and open appearance, was full of hidden dongas, and was no place for British cavalry with night coming down. The British infantry pushed forward and fired a few volleys, but probably did not inflict any very heavy loss. However, the chief object of the

BRIGADIER-GENERAL BROADWOOD.

[*Photo by T. Fall.*

Brigadier-General Robert George Broadwood was born in 1862, and joined the 12th Lancers in 1881; Captain, 1888; Major, 1897; Brevet-Lieut.-Colonel. 1897, and Brevet-Colonel, 1898; served with the Dongola Expeditionary Force under Sir Herbert Kitchener in 1896, and the Sudan Campaign of 1897-8, and took part in the battles of the Atbara and Khartoum; for the latter he received the brevet of Colonel. Throughout the Nile campaign he proved himself an able cavalry officer, and was particularly successful in reconnaissance. Though a Major in his own regiment, the 12th Lancers, he has commanded the 2nd Cavalry Brigade, South African Field Force, since February 1900, with the rank of Brigadier-General whilst on the staff.

battle was attained, as the immensely strong positions round Karee fell into our hands, and in our hands they afterwards remained.

    The fight was, in its details, of much the same type as Poplar Grove and Driefontein.   The artillery was insufficient in strength to beat down the Boer sharpshooters' fire, the infantry were all but powerless, and the cavalry had to cover so much ground that they were unable to strike at the close of the day.   It was an action won by manœuvring, not by hard fighting, and as such struck no severe blow at the enemy's morale. To edge an enemy out of a position by dodging round his flanks has not the stunning effect of going at him and gripping him by the throat—the course which

we had pursued in the earlier battles of the war—but then it is far less bloody work. Still, the British losses were somewhat heavy for the result obtained— 21 men were killed and 161 wounded. The Boers reported their own casualties as small; probably they were much the same in number as those among our troops.

The Boer right had thus been pushed back, but their centre **Broadwood's retreat from Thaba N'chu intercepted.** still threatened Thaba N'chu, where General Broadwood's position was growing daily more critical. Such was the importance of Thaba

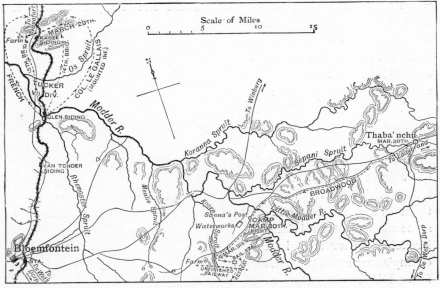

MAP OF THE OPERATIONS AROUND KAREE, THABA N'CHU, AND KOORN SPRUIT.

N'chu to the British Army that at least a brigade of infantry might have been expected to be sent out to his help, but either the situation was misjudged, or the difficulty of keeping a force of 5,000 or 6,000 men supplied at such a distance forbade the move. Finally, on March 30, General Broadwood came to the conclusion that further delay would mean destruction, and having reported his position and asked for reinforcements he began to retreat on Bloemfontein. The enemy were in touch with him all day, but by the night of the 30th he had crossed the Modder River and encamped near the Bloemfontein Waterworks, only 22 miles away from Bloemfontein, at a point known as Sanna's Post. To support him, Colonel Martyr, with some companies of mounted infantry, was sent out from Bloemfontein that same night, with orders to reach and hold the waterworks. General Colvile and the Ninth Division were to follow at daylight of the 31st.

But before these troops could arrive upon the scene the Boers were able to plan and execute a terrible surprise for General Broadwood. Under General De Wet a thousand or more burghers with four guns rode rapidly south, under cover of night, to Sanna's Post, where the bulk of the commando placed themselves between the British column and Bloemfontein. The road from the waterworks to Bloemfontein, along which the British were expected to retreat, crosses, some five miles from the waterworks, the rivulet Koorn Spruit. Like all South African rivers, this stream flows in a wide

"AWKWARD—FOR THE COO."

The photograph represents a scene not infrequent in South Africa—a cow "bogged" whilst in the act of drinking. The incident here depicted took place at Abraham's Kraal.

bed with high banks; on each side a track has been cut down through the banks to the level of the water, so as to enable vehicles to cross.   The track drops steeply on the one side and rises steeply on the other.   In the bed of the river the Boers ensconced themselves and lined its banks, which were covered with brushwood.   A little to the south of the drift was the low embankment of an unfinished railway, running at right angles to the spruit; behind this other parties hid themselves.   The place might have been made for an ambush; it was capable of concealing hundreds of men and horses.   Meantime other commandos of Boers pushed westwards from Thaba N'chu, and in the night placed artillery in position upon heights overlooking the British camp.   Thus General Broadwood, though he did not know it, had

The ambuscade at Koorn Spruit.

WINNING A VICTORIA CROSS AT BLOEMFONTEIN.

On March 13, 1900, the men who had destroyed the railway north of Bloemfontein (p. 542) had to get through several spruits under fire.   Sapper Webb's horse failed to get up the bank of one spruit, whereupon Sergeant Engelheart returned to Sapper Webb's help, and was at last successful in rescuing both man and horse in the face of the enemy.   For this gallant action he has received the V.C.

enemies in front and behind.   In the direction of Bloemfontein—as the road was traversed daily by troops and convoys—he would naturally expect security, the more so as he knew that the Ninth Division had been ordered to his aid.

If the Boers can be believed, the British column had neglected every precaution essential in war, in an enemy's country, with strong hostile forces in close proximity.   "There were no pickets, no outposts, and none of the usual safeguards of an army," says an American correspondent with the Boers.   Yet it is not certain that, even had outposts been properly placed, what followed could have been averted.   The drift lay too far from the camp to be held with safety by a small detachment.   It was natural, too, for officers who had seen how the Boers ran whenever their retreat was threatened, to jump to the conclusion that never would they venture to place themselves between the troops on their way from Bloemfontein and General Broadwood's retreating column.

Day broke, and over the dreary veldt the tall chimney of the water-works showed through the grey light to the eager watchers in the spruit; then fires appeared here and there in the British camp as the cooks prepared breakfast; last of all tents could be discerned and all the bustle of an army making ready to march. Mules and oxen were being inspanned; officers and men were eating their rough fare in complete unconsciousness that two or three thousand enemies watched them from within easy artillery range; when suddenly there came a heavy boom—a flash and whistle in the air—and from the hills on the east dropped a heavy shell right in the midst of the camp. Another and another followed, and rifle-firing broke out. The camp was thrown into the completest confusion by these untoward happenings, and it would seem that the faculty of judging coolly and calmly was paralysed by the surprise. No one realised that the attack from the east was merely designed to do the work of beaters in a great battue, and to put up the birds to be shot down by the party in the spruit to the west.

There was as yet no sign of the enemy to the west, and the waggons and guns were ordered to retire by the drift. Once across the stream the guns were

[Photo by J. Bowers.

INGENIOUS COOKING DEVICES.

The upper illustration represents a Boer State-artilleryman boiling his pot in an ant-hill, from which he has extemporised a fire-place. The lower shows a not less ingenious oven contrived with the aid of an old biscuit box by one of the cooks of the Lancashire Fusiliers.

to take post on the farther bank and cover the retirement of the main force. The movement of the transport was accelerated by the Boer shells, which were now falling very freely. The waggons, three abreast, galloped eagerly down the wide mouth of the funnel-shaped descent which led down to the Koorn Spruit. The Horse Artillery batteries, anxious as quickly as possible to get into action, thundered along among them. Had the gunners looked they might have descried a man with gestures of agonised apprehension, waving, as sign of danger, a red handkerchief. It was Burnham, the famous scout, but no one saw him, and presently he was marked by the Boers and seized and moved to where he could not signal. There was a fearful babel of cracking whips and shouts to the oxen and mules, while from behind the advancing torrent came ever the boom of artillery and the crackle of multitudinous rifles. As the foremost waggons tore down through clouds of dust to the level of the river bed, half-a-dozen Boers in slouch hats were seen to be quietly standing in the spruit. They gave no sign of hostility—this was one of the many cases where a uniform worn by the enemy might have saved British troops from disaster—and they were regarded as friends rather than foes. The convoy did not arrest its movement for them. The first waggons descended

THE DISASTER AT KOORN SPRUIT: THE ROYAL HORSE ARTILLERY WORKING THEIR GUNS.

into the river bed. which hereabouts widens so as to give a great sheltered area, and then, to their

stupefaction, drivers and team-sters found that these same benevolent-looking Boers were the enemy in very truth. As each waggon entered the trap the drivers saw rifles aimed at their heads and heard the cool and collected order, "Drive to the right," or "Drive to the left." Resistance was out of the question; the waggons were without escort—what the escort was doing still remains a puzzle; they were shepherded, parted, and sent this way or that, like a flock of sheep by a few silent, snapping dogs. Men were too benumbed with astonishment to lift a hand or disobey. It was all, says a correspondent, as orderly and methodical as the

A TRIFLING HURT.
Australian scouts and medical officer.

handing-in of luggage at a cloak-room window. And the mischief was that the surprise seemed capable of indefinite extension; the teamsters and gunners descending towards the ambush could see nothing of what was happening, as the road made a slight bend at the foot of the steep-cut descent. "The operation of substituting drivers," says a correspondent with the Boers, "was done so quickly and quietly that none of those approaching the drift from the other side noticed anything extraordinary." And so the convoy poured steadily on, and the hidden Boers reaped their harvest of plunder as they lay by the hundred with their rifles aimed at the hapless *rooibatjes* and with their fingers on the triggers, waiting only the moment of alarm to pump death from their magazines upon the tumult of horses and men.

Exactly how the alarm was given is a matter of dispute. The Boer story, which has a good deal of evidence in its favour, is that an officer came riding along, and before he could resist was "held up"; that De Wet saw him, told **The alarm given.** him the British column was surrounded by an overwhelming force, and called upon him to bid his men surrender "in order to save lives"; that the officer gave his word of honour he would do this, and was told by De Wet that if the promise was not kept his life should be the forfeit. Then, runs the story, he galloped back, was seen to parley with his men, who instantly wheeled and fled, and in the same moment De Wet's rifle cracked and he was dead. The British story

INDIAN AMBULANCE WAGGON WITH LORD ROBERTS' ARMY.

is that Sergeant Green, of the Army Service Corps, was the first man to fire a shot. Covered by a dozen rifles he **shot** a Boer dead, and himself paid with his life the price of so great courage and devotion. Whichever story is true, and no one seems to have heard the shots fired by or at Green, U Battery dashed rattling and clanking into the spruit, and five guns were surrounded and captured in a moment; Q Battery, which was behind with Roberts' Horse, was also riding down to its destruction, when Major Taylor and a Sergeant-Major of U Battery, who had slipped away from the confusion in the donga, appeared and shouted " Files about." At once from all sides broke out a fearful fire : the bushes seemed to glow with death as the Mausers got to work; the concourse of guns and waggons and men, jammed in the narrow descent, fell into the wildest disorder; horses and mules stampeded or dropped dead; oxen refused to stir; and in and out among the waggons and guns Briton and Boer fought furiously hand to hand. Boer cannon began to fire into the convoy and their shells tore the beasts limb from limb and set the waggons on fire. " Shoot, burghers, shoot ! " the Boer leaders could be heard shouting, and the wonder was that anything passed unscathed from out the hail of lead.

ONE OF THE GUNS CAPTURED AT KOORN SPRUIT,
With the Boer commando under Field Cornet De Fosse. Photographed at Winburg, May 22, 1900. The British gun is the nearer one.

One gun of U Battery wheeled and escaped; the six guns of Q Battery went bowling backwards when the horses could be got round. Friend and foe alike marvelled at the superb gallantry and coolness of the gunners and drivers under such a fire. Only heroic valour had extricated even seven guns of the twelve—a sorry remnant. From both flanks, from front and rear, came shells and bullets; yet the seven guns, with Roberts' Horse, thundered back to some corrugated iron sheds, which marked the future Koorn Spruit Station, and there their flight was checked. The guns turned into the firing position— one weapon upset as it wheeled, and its horses fought in wild panic with the traces and strove to free themselves from their trammels—and at a range of less than a thousand yards, exposed to rifles handled by skilled and composed marksmen behind perfect cover, came into action. The fire of the guns was fast but ineffective, because the enemy were simply invisible; yet it was noted by the prisoners who watched the manœuvres of the gunners that they shot as steadily as on parade. The influence of their example was incalculable. Men suddenly bowed and fell as they stood erect handling the guns; their bodies were instantly cast aside, and their comrades took up the

Magnificent conduct of the Royal Horse Artillery.

24*

devoted service. Now an artilleryman would drop as he carried ammunition, now again an officer as he directed the fire. The gun-crews shrank steadily, but the fire did not abate. Once more the British artillery redeemed by its heroism defeat complete and dishonourable; once more it inspired by its action confidence in wavering and shaken men.

Nor, if the fire failed to kill and wound the enemy, was this sacrifice of noble lives in vain. "Had it not been for those terrible guns," says Burnham, "the Boers told me they would have charged, closing in on all sides upon General Broadwood's men . . . The Boers were astonished at the courage and endurance of the artillerymen." Meantime Roberts' Horse had rallied and deployed in a long line of skirmishers. The terror and anguish of the scene were increased by the fact that

J. Charlton.]

A RUNAWAY GUN-TEAM.
One team of the R.H.A., having lost all its drivers, broke away in fright and careered madly about the field.

a number of women and children of British nationality and sympathy, from Thaba N'chu and the neighbourhood, were with the British force. Some of these poor souls fell victims to the Boer fire. The crackling roar of rifles came from every side, except the ground immediately to the south of General Broadwood's camp. That way lay the only possible means of escape.

And where were the British troops from Bloemfontein that should have been at hand to support the hard-pressed column and cover its escape? No sign of their approach could be discovered. The

No help from Bloemfontein.

roar of battle, one would have thought, must have reached Colonel Martyr's mounted infantry and the head of General Colvile's Division, but though troops under such conditions, with the note of the cannon ringing in their ears and the hope of succouring comrades in their hearts, are capable of almost any exertion, it does not seem that desperate exertions were made. The artillery officers with General Colvile did, in fact, hear the ominously rapid fire of the guns, and guessed what it meant, but they could not accelerate the movements of the division. There was a want of energy and combination. It may be that the mounted infantry were too weak to help, or that the Ninth Division had been ordered to put itself in motion too late; but the fact remains that, almost in sight of 30,000 British soldiers, three or four thousand Boers were permitted to work their will upon the 2,000 horsemen and gunners of General Broadwood. It was a fact so extraordinary as to provoke the biting comment of the world.

Retreat and losses. While the gunners were falling one by one, and the mounted infantry holding off the Boers with the utmost difficulty, Captain Chester-Masters was sent by General Broadwood to the south with a small party of men to examine the river, and discover, if possible, another crossing. He found a practicable point two miles to the south, placed men to hold it, and returned. And now the attempt was made to withdraw the remnant of the column by this passage. First, the seven guns had to be retired, and this, under the ceaseless hail of lead, was as desperate and dangerous work as can be imagined. The

[*Photo by Charleton.*

SERGEANT PARKER, V.C.
Selected by the non-commissioned officers.

[*Photo by Charleton.*

GUNNER ISAAC LODGE, V.C.
Selected by the gunners and drivers.

THE V.C.'S OF SANNA'S POST.

[*Photo by Jacolette.*

MAJOR PHIPPS-HORNBY, V.C.

FOUR V.C.'S.

Lord Roberts considered that all ranks of Q Battery were equally brave and deserving of the V.C.; he therefore determined to follow a course probably unprecedented, though authorised by the Victoria Cross Warrant, viz., to direct that one officer, one non-commissioned officer, and two gunners or drivers should be nominated for the honour by their equals in rank. Major Phipps-Hornby and Captain Humphreys being the only two unwounded officers left to save the guns, each nominated the other for the V.C., which eventually fell to the Major by right of seniority.

gunners and many of the teams had been shot down, but, as at Colenso, volunteers were ready to plunge into the vortex of death. Major Phipps-Hornby, Gunner Gudgeon, and Driver Glasock were foremost at this moment. Glasock had six horses shot under him, and was wounded himself. Five of the seven guns were at last got away—the fifth run back by hand, as every horse had been shot down—and the other two were abandoned to the enemy. "As the mutilated remnant of two batteries of Horse Artillery tottered through the line of prone mounted infantry covering its withdrawal," wrote *The Times* correspondent, "the men could not restrain their admiration. Though it was to court death to show a hand, men leapt to their feet and cheered the gunners as they passed." It was a memorable picture, and it remained burnt into the minds of all who gazed upon that terrible scene—the men who had defied death acclaimed by the men who were defying death, in a spirit of exultation that knew no fear.

DRIVER HORACE H. GLASOCK, V.C.
Selected by the gunners and drivers.

The retreat of the guns was covered by the troopers of Roberts' Horse, Rimington's Scouts, the New Zealand Mounted Infantry, and the 3rd Regular Mounted Infantry. They met with singular steadiness and courage the repeated onsets of the Boers, who were constantly growing in numbers and daring, and who at times advanced within 300 yards of their opponents. Here died Major Booth, of the Northumberland Fusiliers, with four men, all of the Regular Mounted Infantry, who would neither retire nor surrender. An attempt was made to take the pressure off the retreat by the 10th Hussars and the Household Cavalry, who were directed to cross the river by the newly-found drift; the movement, however, was carried out but slowly, and was met with a terrific fire through which the cavalry could not charge home. "Horses and riders fell," says a correspondent with the Boers, "officers leaped to the

SOME OF THE MEN WHO WERE FIGHTING LORD ROBERTS.
The man sitting in the foreground wearing a white shirt front and a watch chain is Chief Commandant Wessels; next him on his left is Chief Commandant Delarey. The other members of the group are officers who fought under these men at Kimberley and Bloemfontein.

ground and shouted encouragement to their soldiers, men sprang behind rocks and discharged their carbines. Minutes of agony passed. . . Burghers crept around . . . and emptied their rifles into the backs of the cavalrymen, cannon poured shell upon them from three different directions, and these men on the open plain could not see even a trace of Boers to fire at." The cavalry were compelled to suspend their attack and fall back. The last hope of recovering the lost guns and waggons vanished; but at least the retreat of the remnant of the column had been assured, and under a heavy fire General Broadwood succeeded in reaching Boesman's Kop, where the mounted infantry from Bloemfontein were in position to cover his further movements.

The losses of the column were heavy, for though the killed numbered only 19, no less than 134 men were wounded and 425 taken prisoners. Moreover, 90 waggons and seven of the Horse Artillery 12-pounders were captured by the enemy. U Battery had 122 men missing; Q Battery 33 killed or wounded and 7 missing; while Roberts' Horse lost 22 killed or wounded and 54 missing. The wounded were treated with great kindness and consideration by the Boers, though there are stories that the enemy shot down certain of the Kaffir waggon drivers and some Free State farmers captured with the baggage. It is certain that in the heat of the fight they fired into the midst of the mass of waggons and prisoners, thereby killing or wounding some of their own men. This may be the foundation for these reports. The manner in which the enemy got the prisoners and the great bulk of the captured waggons away, in the presence of a superior British force—for in the afternoon General Colvile's Division arrived, followed by General French with a strong body of cavalry—was worthy of admiration. The captives were sent north to Winburg and thence by train forwarded to Pretoria.

Not less serious than the loss of so many men and guns and so much transport was the capture of the Bloemfontein Waterworks by the Boers. They at once, of course, cut off the supply of water from the Free State capital, and the British army in the vicinity was compelled

F. J. Waugh.]

"THOUGH IT WAS TO COURT DEATH TO SHOW A HAND, MEN LEAPT TO THEIR FEET AND CHEERED THE GUNNERS AS THEY PASSED."

to fall back upon wells which were neither numerous nor free from pollution. One of the immediate consequences was a terrible increase in the epidemic of enteric fever among the conquerors. The seeds of the malady had been brought from Paardeberg, and before the month of April had ended, 2,000 British soldiers were carried off by disease. It is difficult to explain why so important a point as the Waterworks was not strongly guarded, or why, having been lost, it was not at once recovered. Its recapture could scarcely have cost the army as dearly as did the disease engendered through its loss.

The water-supply cut off.

General Colvile with his men reached the neighbourhood of the disaster about 3 p.m., some hours after Broadwood had retired. He had marched twenty-five miles on bad tracks, but had he attacked with vigour there was at least a bare possibility of retaking some of the prisoners and guns.

RIMINGTON'S "TIGERS," WHO HELPED TO COVER THE RETREAT OF THE ROYAL HORSE ARTILLERY AT KOORN SPRUIT.

General French with his cavalry manœuvred to the south, as if to turn the Boer position on the Koorn Spruit. But the enemy seemed to be in great force; they were now estimated by the British generals at 10,000 men—which seems a great exaggeration—and nothing was done that day. Only, three of the Field Batteries opened a long-range fire on the Boer position. Next day the infantry pushed up the west bank of the Koorn Spruit, and at once the Boers were seen in strength near the Waterworks. No further action was attempted. The cavalry were recalled, and General Colvile with his division marched rapidly back to Bloemfontein, leaving behind him the scene of death and disaster in the ill-fated drift of the Koorn. Among the wounded who were removed by his division was a Dutch military attaché, Lieutenant Nix, mortally injured in the fight. He died in British hands. Even as the Ninth Division retired, far away on the hills towards Dewetsdorp could be seen a large Boer commando travelling south, which indicated that the enemy were now suspending their retreat and assuming the offensive. What this movement meant was soon made painfully manifest.

OFFICERS AND ORDERLIES OF THE NEW ZEALAND MOUNTED RIFLES.

Of the prisoners taken at Koorn Spruit, Burnham, the American scout, alone managed to escape. Feigning to be wounded in the leg—so as to lead his captors to suppose that there was little risk of his attempting to get away —he obtained a seat in the rear waggon of the convoy as it proceeded north under escort, and though he was specially watched by a bushman, he dropped off the waggon while his custodian was busy with the harness of the team of oxen, ran to a kopje near at hand and hid in a drain, where he remained motionless for hours, with Boers constantly passing near him. At nightfall he started, steering by means of the stars, and forty-eight hours later, having eaten nothing more than a biscuit on the way, reached General Broadwood's camp.

The Boer commando seen towards Dewetsdorp, moving south, was 1,400 strong, and intended, in co-operation with another commando, 800 strong with six guns, to attack a small British force which had been receiving surrenders in the Dewetsdorp district. The British detachment consisted of three companies of the Royal Irish Rifles, which had left Smithfield on March 29, and two companies of mounted infantry. The latter joined the Irish Rifles unexpectedly on the evening of April 1, and were at first taken for Boers, and all but fired upon by the infantry. The detachment belonged to General Gatacre's Division; it had with it no guns; was outside the reach of prompt support; and is said to have received no orders as to what it was to do. In command was Captain McWhinnie. On April 1 the British had entered Dewetsdorp and received from the Landdrost the keys of the public buildings, though the public records and the arms and ammunition in the place had been hidden, and so were not captured. Several of the inhabitants took the oath of neutrality,

The Boers threaten Dewetsdorp.

MAJOR BURNHAM, THE SCOUT.
See the biographical note on page 418.

and these, like their brethren in misfortune at Thaba N'chu and Ladybrand, had afterwards to pay dearly for their belief in the protecting power of the great British army. It was, however, supposed by them that the Boers had finally retired from the south-eastern corner of the Free State, and no danger of vengeance seems to have been anticipated. News of the affair at Koorn Spruit had not yet reached the British commander or the Free Staters. The same day Captain McWhinnie telegraphed to General Gatacre that the Boers had been reported in some force in the neighbourhood, and about the same time, it would appear, the general learnt that there had been a British disaster near Bloemfontein, and that the troops east of the Free State capital had fallen back, uncovering the roads to the south. Accordingly, he sent orders to his small detachment to retreat. He did not, however, take steps to support it, though it was obvious that it might be attacked at any moment.

ON THE WAY TO DEATH.
The centre figure in this group, in uniform, is Lieut. Nix, the Dutch Attaché, who was mortally wounded at Koorn Spruit. On the extreme right of the picture is Lieut. Raoul Duval, the French Attaché.

Captain McWhinnie received the order to retreat at 3.30 a.m. of April 2, and without any delay began to move towards Reddersburg and Bethanie. The weather was most unfavourable; rain fell in sheets; and on the muddy roads the teams and horses at once began to show signs of exhaustion. Slow progress was made, and the force was compelled to encamp east of Reddersburg, at Kelly's farm, that night. It was followed by De Wet and the Boers, who kept touch with it, though themselves out of sight. On the morning of the 3rd the retreat was resumed, when, while passing to the south of a long line of kopjes at Mozar's Hoek, an ominous cloud of dust was seen to the north-east. Fire, too, was suddenly opened from the south upon the mounted infantry. On this Captain McWhinnie ordered his men to seize the long line of kopjes, at either end of which was a spur. The western spur was occupied by the mounted infantry, the eastern spur and the ridge connecting the two by the Royal Irish Rifles. Under the eastern spur were parked the six ox-waggons, the water-cart, the two ammunition carts, and the three ambulances which formed the baggage of the little column. Almost as soon as this had been done the Boer attack began. A rifle-fire was opened by the enemy upon the eastern and western spurs, and about noon a cannon arrived and began to bombard the kopjes. It was clear from the first that the position was

BOERS OF THE LADYBRAND COMMANDO.
It will be noticed that several of these men carry umbrellas as well as rifles.

hopeless unless reinforcements should arrive. There was no water, except that in the carts and in the men's water-bottles, the enemy were on all sides in superior force, and they had artillery. De Wet sent in a letter by a flag of truce, stating that he had 2,200 men and six guns—which seems to have been the truth—and urging surrender to avoid bloodshed. Captain McWhinnie very properly tore the missive to fragments and answered with indignant refusal.

On this a second gun began to shell the kopjes. All the afternoon fighting continued. There was good cover, and the men at the officers' orders made the best use of it, so that they exposed themselves but little to the enemy's projectiles. Neither side, in fact, could see the other. The British fire was cool, slow, and accurate, under very trying conditions. Towards evening the Boer shells began to fall among the British transport and inflicted some loss. A third piece of artillery opened and the shrapnel threw up the stones and dust along the ridge, while the enemy crept closer and closer. Captain Casson and Lieutenant Barclay had already been killed; Captains Dimsdale and Kelly were severely wounded, but the losses otherwise were not serious. Night fell, but no fire could be lighted, as the enemy shot freely whenever an Englishman showed himself, and the utmost vigilance was required to prevent the small force from being rushed. The men were greatly in want of food and water but, worn out with the strain of a long day's fighting, they fell asleep where they lay. In the darkness the officers held a consultation. A proposal to cut their way out was considered and dismissed as impracticable—which it probably was—and it was decided to hold on another morning. A brave scout was sent through the enemy's lines to ask for the prompt dispatch of reinforcements.

At 6 a.m. of April 4, after a bitterly cold and miserable night, the Boer fire re-

Surrender of Captain McWhinnie's force.

commenced. First the rifles opened and then came the shrapnel. Once in the early morning the little column fancied that it heard the sound of volley-firing far away, which could only proceed from a British force. But, as it listened, the noise died

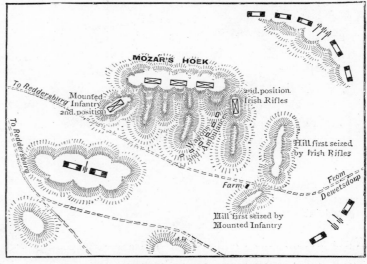

PLAN OF THE ACTION AT MOZAR'S HOEK.
⬟ British. ▬ Boers.

away and seemed to have no other origin than the eager fancy of anxious men. A fourth Boer gun had now opened fire, and from all sides bullets and shells rained on the crest and spurs held by the British. Yet so good was the cover that the losses still continued small. The eminence held by the mounted infantry was especially singled out for concentrated fire, and at last the men on it were forced back. The Boers seized the summit, and from it could enfilade the long ridge held by the Irish Rifles. This marked the end. First one and then another white flag showed; the fire instantly ceased on both sides, and 405 unwounded British officers and men laid down their arms. Their losses were only 12 killed and 35 wounded, or about 10 per cent. of the original strength. It was the first time in the war that a British force had surrendered with such light casualties. There is reason to think that if only the resistance could have been protracted by a couple of hours, relief might have arrived. But in justice to the men their physical exhaustion and want of food and water should be borne in mind. The reports that the British ammunition had been exhausted do not seem to have been true.

Meantime, where were the supports? On the afternoon of April 3 Lord Roberts heard that the detachment had been attacked, and at once tele-

Gatacre's relief force barred.

graphed to General Gatacre's headquarters at Springfontein, directing him to go to Captain McWhinnie's aid. At the same time the Cameron Highlanders were sent south from Bloemfontein to Bethanie to co-operate. From Springfontein to Bethanie, the nearest station to Mozar's Hoek, was, however, 55 miles along the railway, and from Bethanie to the Hoek 15 miles over bad roads. It was not therefore very probable that he would arrive in time, even if he had trains and rolling stock ready. Yet, if he had made a mistake in not previously supporting the detachment, he must now have acted with vigour, since early on the morning of the 4th his advance guard under Colonel Sitwell reached Bethanie, and, hearing heavy firing to the east, turned in that direction. Colonel Sitwell, on nearing Reddersburg, found his further advance barred by a Boer force on a line of kopjes. With this force he exchanged fire—probably the volleys

A HALT AT SPRINGFONTEIN STATION.
The chaplain is handing round tea; the men are holding out their pannikins with the air of happy school-boys.

heard by the detachment at Mozar's Hoek—but as he thought himself too weak for a frontal attack on the Boer position, attempted to turn the enemy's northern flank, and was so hotly received that he had to retire and wait for the main British force. This came up some hours later, but by this time the action at Mozar's Hoek was over, and the noise of battle had ceased. General Gatacre therefore did not go farther than Reddersburg, which he entered, and shortly afterwards evacuated, as the enemy were showing in strength to the north of the town. He retired to Bethanie and there remained, protecting the railway line to Bloemfontein, till some days later he was removed from command. It has, however, been since denied that he was responsible for the despatch of the detachment to Dewetsdorp, and the matter remains one of the innumerable mysteries of the war.

[*Photo by S. E. Hill.*

THE VOLKS' HOSPITAL, BLOEMFONTEIN.

With two remarkable successes to their credit, the Boers were now expected to attack the railway line **Rundle and Kitchener guard the railway.** south of Bloemfontein in earnest, and great efforts were made to guard against such a contingency. General Rundle, with the Eighth Division, was hurried from Kimberley to the south of the Free State, and Lord Kitchener, who had returned victorious from Prieska, moved every man who could be spared to this quarter, to protect the all-important line of communication upon which the very existence of the army at Bloemfontein depended. But as a matter of fact the Boers showed a great want of strategic insight at this critical juncture.

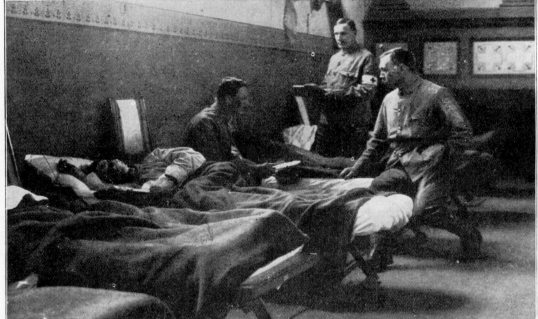

DR. CONAN DOYLE, THE CREATOR OF "SHERLOCK HOLMES," ATTENDING SICK CANADIANS IN THE CLUB-HOUSE AT BLOEMFONTEIN.

Instead of making a determined effort against the railway, they turned aside to attack a small force of Colonial troops from General Brabant's Division which had occupied Wepener. This town lies 80 miles by road from Aliwal North, on the eastern confine of the Free State, and close to Jammersberg Drift, where is an important bridge over the Caledon River.

The British force at Wepener was 1,600 strong, under Colonel Dalgety. It consisted of detachments of the 1st and 2nd Brabant's Horse, Cape Mounted Rifles, Kaffrarian Rifles, Driscoll's Scouts, Royal **British occupy Wepener.** Scots Mounted Infantry, and Royal Engineers, and had with it seven guns, two of which were 7-pounder muzzle loaders, two naval 12-pounders, two field artillery 15-pounders, and one Hotchkiss 12½-pounder quick-firer. The first British detachments entered Wepener on March 29, and subsequently the rest of the force followed in its tread. The inhabitants gave the newcomers a hostile and sullen reception. On April 1 the enemy were reported by scouts in some strength to the north ; on the morning of the 4th two German officers rode up to the British outposts with a flag of truce and asked to see the officer commanding, who at that time was Major Maxwell, Colonel Dalgety not yet having arrived. The messengers were blindfolded and taken into the village, when a letter was produced couched in the following terms : " I am here with a few thousand burghers, and in the cause of humanity, to prevent such terrible slaughter as occurred in our last battle at Thaba N'chu, I ask your immediate surrender.—Banks, General." Major Maxwell refused to return any reply to this effusion, and, by way of bantering the German emissary, asked whether it was not really General Banks who wished to surrender to the British.

On April 5 Driscoll's Scouts came into contact with the main body of the enemy 15 miles north of Wepener, and carried off eight Boer prisoners. Next day Captain Driscoll was attacked when out

CAMP OF THE OXFORDSHIRE YEOMANRY WITH THE PRIESKA COLUMN.

reconnoitring, but by fine management got his men away in the face of a vastly superior force. All preparations for a stubborn defence were made. The camp was moved three miles to the north of Wepener, where it rested on the south upon the Caledon, on the east upon a series of kopjes facing Jammersberg Mountain, and on the north upon another series of kopjes. Only on the west was it open to easy attack. Schanzes of boulders were constructed, the area enclosed being about three miles by one mile ; trenches were also dug where they would prove most serviceable, and where the ground permitted digging. On the western front the pick of the force—the Cape Mounted Rifles and Driscoll's Scouts—were stationed to meet the expected onset.

Not until April 9 did the Boers begin the siege, though on the 8th rockets were seen to the north and the Boer patrols closed in upon the camp. At 4 a.m. on the 9th the whole force was called to arms ; little more than an hour later a shell fell in the lines. A small party of men at Wepener had to ride for their lives and were all but cut off from the camp as the Boers approached. The enemy lost no time in developing the attack. Gun after gun opened fire till there were five pieces of artillery and a " Pom-Pom " in action against the western front. Their riflemen, too, poured in a hail of bullets at long range, and the Cape Mounted Rifles, who bore the brunt of the onset, were hard put to it to hold

The camp besieged.

J. H. Thornely.]   A RIDE FOR LIFE AT WEPENER.

their own. Driscoll's Scouts, who had hitherto been acting as a reserve, were sent in to their relief. They lost heavily. So terrible was the fire of the Boer artillery, and so well directed, that in the earlier hours of the day it seemed as if the defence could not be made good. The great ironstone boulders of which the schanzes were built were hurled and splintered in all directions, and under the rain of bullets the damage done could not be repaired. Fortunately for the British garrison, the enemy could not see or ascertain the effects of their fire, and, after their invariable fashion, relaxed its vehemence at the most critical moment. Fortunately, too, the British guns were able to put in some good work and presently disabled a Boer weapon. Two attempts were made by the enemy to move three guns to a position which would have enfiladed from the south the western line of defences, but the accurate fire of the British guns and rifles on each occasion drove them back. At dusk, after a terrible day, the fight ended. The casualties were heavy —11 killed and 41 wounded. As the men were eating their suppers in the darkness, and as the ambulances were recovering the wounded, two more shells were fired by the Boers into the camp, one of which killed a man.

[Press Photo Bureau.
AN ARMOURER AT WORK REPAIRING A RIFLE.

Unceasing efforts were made that night by the weary men to improve the defences. More boulders were rolled up and placed in the schanzes, and the trenches were deepened. The enemy on their part were not inactive. The guns to the south were protected by a strong breastwork, and at dawn of April 10 opened an enfilading fire on the western front. To build traverses—and build them quickly—was all important for the besieged. Accordingly, blankets and greatcoats were filled with earth, and, thus converted into sandbags, were placed every thirty feet to catch and stop the raking fire of shrapnel. At the same time the 7-pounders and naval 12-pounders got to work to "knock out" the Boer guns, and did succeed in keeping their fire down. In the course of the afternoon the ammunition of the men lining the western defences was exhausted, and in efforts to bring up a fresh supply from a store eighty yards to the rear, six out of eight men were shot down, including the gallant Major Sprenger, who persisted in standing erect in the open, superintending the work.

Night fell—a night brightened only by the fitful beams of the new moon—when the firing of shots in the Boer lines suggested that an attack was impending. Ammunition was issued in ample quantities to the men guarding the western front, and parties of the Cape

Assault repulsed.

Mounted Rifles and Driscoll's Scouts crawled out on either flank of that front, so as to be in position to enfilade any assaulting force. Then suddenly from the front came the heavy roar of a rapid fusillade, and a large force of Boers showed against the sky line not 300 yards away. They were 300 strong, and had sworn to fight their way into Wepener or die. They advanced by quick rushes, in alternate sections, the advancing sections covered by the rapid fire of the others. But the men they were fighting were cooler and more determined than themselves. The Cape Rifles and Driscoll's Scouts, fine shots to a man, fired with terrible effect "into the brown" of the

A FRENCH AMBULANCE CART.
Inscribed: "Homage to the Boer people." This cart strayed into Dewetsdorp whilst that town was in the hands of the British.

advancing body. Now the enemy were so close that words of command and oaths in English and Dutch could be heard; now the British rifles grew hot with the rapidity of the magazine fire, and men listened in the din for the order to use the cold steel. But once more the superiority of a defensive fight was to be demonstrated; thirty yards from the schanzes the crowd of assailants melted, halted, fell prone; and then one by one the Boers fled for their lives, covered by the fire of their marksmen. The British, from their weakness in numbers, dared not venture forth and charge. But the assault had been completely, ruinously repulsed.

The Boer losses in this desperate affair are not known. Probably they were between 100 and 200; by the British they were placed at 800; but this is certainly an exaggeration. Still, at such close quarters was the fight, and so exposed were the enemy in their advance to storm the works, that they must have suffered terribly. The British lost only 8 killed and 30 wounded, having the immense advantage of good cover.

During the next few days the Boers began the systematic construction of trenches and

Closer investment.

parallels, under shelter of night, working slowly towards the British lines. Nothing could be done to prevent this slow approach, but a steady fire was maintained upon the Boer sap, and it is probable that the enemy lost considerably in their work. The British troops, obeying strict orders, never exposed themselves, and suffered but little. Unhappily, the enemy's unaimed fire played on the building used as the hospital, and killed three men in or near it, wounding six others. On April 12 one of the British 15-pounders placed several shells in a farm to the north of the lines, where a large party of Boers had been seen, and caused the enemy so much annoyance that they attemped to capture the gun on the night of the 12–13th. A general advance began under cover of darkness, but, probably cowed by their losses on the night of the great attack, the Boers did not push home the assault. The main body never got within 750 yards, and the affair resulted in nothing more than a heavy exchange of fire on either side.

As the Boer parallels drew nearer, the garrison was eager to sally out and use the

Sufferings of the garrison.

bayonet. But Colonel Dalgety, who combined in an eminent degree caution and bravery, would not allow this; the besieged force was too small to run any serious risks.

[Photo by Healey, Queenstown.

COLONEL DALGETY.

Colonel E. H. Dalgety is the second son of the late Colonel Dalgety, R.A. He was educated at Wellington College, and from there entered the 21st Foot and served for some years in India. He left the Army in 1876, went to the Cape, and joined the Cape Mounted Rifles. He took part in the Basuto War and the Bechuanaland Expedition of 1897. In the past four years he has commanded the Cape Mounted Rifles. He is a first-rate scout and rider, and distinguished himself by his manœuvring in the district of Stormberg and in the occupation of Dordrecht, and later on by his gallant defence of Wepener.

He was in communication with Lord Roberts by way of Mafeteng in Basutoland, with which place he constantly exchanged signals, and had good reason to think that relief would arrive before the sap could approach too closely for safety. The enemy, though maintaining an intermittent bombardment, no longer attacked with the old vigour. The sufferings of the garrison, however, in this period were severe. As in Cronje's laager at Paardeberg, there had been a large number of horses and oxen with the column, and these were killed by the Boer long-range fire, when their carcasses, in so small and confined an area, polluted the air. Only fourteen oxen were left in the camp, and but 15 per cent. of the horses; the others had either been killed, and now lay putrefying in the sun, or had strayed into the Boer lines. Moreover, food was short. Dalgety's devoted Colonials had started the siege with only four days' rations, and had been compelled, when these were exhausted, to feed upon trek-ox or horse. Under the circumstances their endurance was remarkable; not many days had passed, before, from the bad sanitary conditions prevailing and the extreme monotony of the diet, almost every member of the garrison was visited by a more or less mild form of dysentery. Yet, so splendid was the spirit of the men, so resolute their determination not to give in to their maladies, that not one soldier went into hospital, invalided by sickness. There was no malingering; not even Cronje's stubborn burghers surpassed in resolution these officers and privates of English and Colonial birth and training. And if the British had not to face the terrible fire of the 5- and 6-inch howitzers and 4·7-inch guns, they had to endure steady bombardment by nine field-pieces and two "Pom-Poms," without any such shelter as the bed of the Modder afforded at Paardeberg.

But now to the south and north-west heliographs began to twinkle, and the garrison at last obtained palpable evidence of approaching relief. British columns appeared to be converging from all sides, and

Final attack repelled.

hope ran high that the Boers might find that they had exchanged the rôle of would-be captors for prisoners. As yet, however, they gave no sign of alarm. Their sap continued to approach, till on April 20 it was within 160 yards of the western defences. With determination on their part, an assault should now have proved successful. The sound of guns on all sides and the advance of the British relief columns precipitated their attack. The Boer force round the camp now mustered about 7,000 men. On the morning of April 21 a heavy fusillade was opened from ten of the Boer guns and "Pom-Poms" upon the weak western front of the camp. For three-quarters of an hour the artillery preparation continued, but then, instead of the whole Boer strength advancing to the assault, only a couple of hundred men left the nearest parallel. Such an attack inspired no terror in Colonel Dalgety or his battle-tried Colonials. They poured a terrific fire upon the storming party, and in less than a minute drove it back to the earth from which it had sprung. Never was there a more complete and miserable

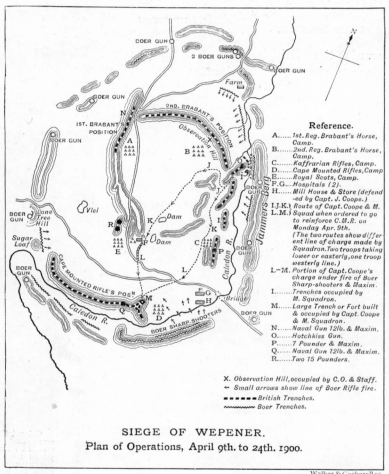

Reference.

A......1st. Reg. Brabant's Horse, Camp.
B......2nd. Reg. Brabant's Horse, Camp.
C......Kaffrarian Rifles, Camp.
D......Cape Mounted Rifles, Camp.
E......Royal Scots, Camp.
F.G....Hospitals (2).
H......Mill House & Store (defended by Capt. J. Coope.)
I.J.K.) Route of Capt. Coope & M.
L.M.) Squad when ordered to go to reinforce C.M.R. on Monday Apr. 9th. (The two routes show different line of charge made by Squadron. Two troops taking lower or easterly, one troop westerly line.)
L–M. Portion of Capt. Coope's charge under fire of Boer Sharp-shooters & Maxim.
I......Trenches occupied by M. Squadron.
M......Large Trench or Fort built & occupied by Capt. Coope & M. Squadron.
N......Naval Gun 12lb. & Maxim.
O......Hotchkiss Gun.
P......7 Pounder & Maxim.
Q......Naval Gun 12lb. & Maxim.
R......Two 15 Pounders.

X. Observation Hill, occupied by C.O. & Staff.
← Small arrows show line of Boer Rifle fire.
▪▪▪▪ British Trenches.
⌇⌇⌇ Boer Trenches.

SIEGE OF WEPENER.
Plan of Operations, April 9th. to 24th. 1900.

Walker & Cockerell sc.

fiasco. The rest of the day passed in the usual exchange of long-range fire, but the Boers had made their last effort and failed. None the less, the close proximity of the enemy in a superiority of at least six to one caused some unrest in the garrison, and the question of falling back some hundreds of yards was debated. But before a decision had been reached, on the night of the 24th, the patrols to the north-east of the camp heard the sound of waggons and large bodies of men moving along the road which skirts the Basuto frontier. With dawn it was seen that the enemy were undoubtedly in retreat. In the British camp only two rounds of artillery ammunition remained, and though these two shots were at once fired, the guns could not effectually harass the retreat. Eighteen of Driscoll's Scouts, however, were allowed to sally forth on the last serviceable horses, and these captured two prisoners and two waggon-loads of ammunition. Thus ended a memorable defence, most honourable to Colonel Dalgety and his Colonials. The total British casualties numbered 33 killed and 132 wounded, but this figure did not include the slightly wounded, of whom there were at least another 50. In recognition of the gallant and skilful conduct of all concerned, Lord Roberts addressed special thanks and congratulations to the garrison, and promised its members a special medal.

VISITORS IN CAMP AT BETHULIE.

On April 25 a British column **Arrival of** came in **relief** sight to **columns.** the south of the town, and a few hours later another to the south-west. But it is now time to turn to the measures taken by Lord Roberts for the relief of the place, and to explain how and whence

these columns came. As soon as the Commander-in-Chief learnt the plight of Wepener, he ordered the new Eighth Division, under General Rundle, to concentrate at Springfontein, while fifty miles to the north the Third Division, under General Chermside, who had replaced General Gatacre, assembled at Bethanie. Upon Bethulie General Hart with the Irish Brigade from Natal was directed, and General Brabant with all those of his Colonial Division who were not besieged in Wepener, assembled at Rouxville. Hither General Hart marched to join him. The first moves directed by Lord Roberts had in view merely the relief of Wepener, and not the capture of the Boer force besieging it. Accordingly, General Rundle was ordered to proceed north to Edenburg and then to strike eastwards to Wepener, through Reddersburg and Dewetsdorp, while Generals Hart and Brabant advanced north from Rouxville. General Rundle was reinforced —as his division was not yet complete—by troops from General Chermside's command, and by 1,400 Yeomanry and mounted infantry under General Brabazon. Without encountering any serious opposition Rundle pushed through Reddersburg, and on April 19 was at Oorlogs Poort, seventeen miles from Dewetsdorp. Next day he came into contact with the enemy. The Yeomanry advanced, found the Boer position covering Dewetsdorp, and seized and held a commanding kopje under a heavy " Pom-Pom " fire. In front of this position the column waited all the 21st, to concentrate and permit the 16th Brigade, which had had to cover more

[*Photo by Knight.*

LIEUT.-GENERAL CHERMSIDE.

Sir Herbert Charles Chermside, G.C.M.G., C.B., R.E., was born near Wilton, Wilts, in 1850, the second son of the Rev. Seymour Chermside. Educated at Eton, he entered the Army in 1868 ; Captain, 1882 ; Brevet-Major, 1882 ; Brevet-Lieut.-Colonel, 1885 ; Brevet-Colonel, 1887 ; Major-General, 1898. He accompanied the Turkish troops as Military Attaché in the Russo-Turkish War of 1876-8 ; served in the Egyptian War of 1882, in the expedition to the Sudan in 1884 with the Intelligence Department, in the Sudan Campaign of 1885 in the Egyptian Army, and as Governor-General of the Red Sea Littoral and Egyptian Military Commissioner, and in the operations in the Sudan in 1887. Between 1889 and 1897 he was Military Attaché at Constantinople ; from that time till 1899 British Military Commissioner and commanding H.M. troops in Crete ; in 1899 he commanded the Curragh District till he took command of the 14th Brigade, 7th Division, in South Africa. In April 1900 he was appointed to the 3rd Division South Africa Field Force, with rank of Lieut.-General.

ground, to reach the scene of action. The mounted men in the interval worked round the southern flank of the Boer line, but when the enemy saw that the British infantry were not following and supporting, they at once delivered a counter-attack and pressed the horsemen hard, inflicting some loss on them. On this occasion, for the second time, Mr. Winston Churchill, then acting as correspondent with the column, had a marvellous escape. Half-a-dozen Boers opened fire upon him not 120 yards away; his horse took fright and galloped off; and had not a devoted scout stopped and given him a stirrup, he must have been captured or shot down.

The enemy's position had now been fully located, and it was determined to attack it next day. But in the night arrived orders from Lord Roberts not to press the Boers as yet, since new movements

Plans for capturing the Boer force. were in progress, designed to cut off and capture the enemy's force at Wepener. In the course of this night an unfortunate incident happened, as thirty-five men of the Worcestershire Regiment in the darkness blundered into the enemy's lines and were captured. The fresh columns put in motion from Bloemfontein were as follows:—General

C. H. Taffs.]   [*After a photograph.*

CONSTRUCTING THE DEVIATION RAILWAY NORTH OF BETHULIE BRIDGE.
Magnificent work has been done by the Royal Engineers and the Railway Pioneer Regiment—the latter a body of expert engineers, mainly from Johannesburg—in relaying, under all sorts of adverse conditions, the broken-up railway lines and bridging the rivers.

Ian Hamilton, who after the relief of Ladysmith had been summoned by Lord Roberts to take a command in the west, with 2,000 mounted infantry, was to strike eastwards and threaten at once the Waterworks and the Boer retreat; General French, with his two brigades of cavalry and several batteries of Horse Artillery, was to march past Leeuw Kop, and, then, striking due east, to place himself on the Boer line of retreat; finally, General Pole-Carew, with the newly-formed Eleventh Division, consisting of the Guards' Brigade and the 18th Brigade, reinforced by the 4th Mounted Infantry Corps and the 4th Cavalry Brigade, was to advance down the road from Bloemfontein to Dewetsdorp, maintaining touch with General Rundle on his right and General French on his left. The mounted infantry of his force on April 22 attempted to turn a formidable Boer position at Leeuw Kop, but here, as in the case of the Yeomanry at Dewetsdorp, were compelled by the stout resistance of the

[*Photo by Lambert Weston.*

LIEUT.-GENERAL SIR HENRY MACLEOD LESLIE RUNDLE, K.C.B., C.M.G., D.S.O., R.A.,

Commands the Eighth Division, South Africa Field Force. He was born at Newton Abbot, Devon, in 1856, is the second son of the late J. S. Rundle, Captain, R.N., and was educated at the Royal Military Academy, Woolwich; entered the Royal Artillery in 1876; Captain, 1885; Major, 1885; Lieut.-Colonel, 1889; Colonel, 1894; Major-General, 1896; He served in the Zulu War of 1879 with Wood's Flying Column; with the Field Artillery in the Boer War of 1881 (taking part in the defence of Potchefstroom); in the Egyptian War of 1882; in the Nile Expedition of 1884-5 (receiving the Brevet of Major). He was with the Sudan Frontier Field Force as Assistant-Adjutant-General, and for his services received the D.S.O.; joined in the operations on the Sudan Frontier in 1889; served with the Dongola Expeditionary Force under Sir H. Kitchener in 1896 as Chief of the Staff; promoted Major-General for distinguished services in the field. He was General of Communications during the operations on the Atbara in 1898, and afterwards Chief of the Staff. Commanded S.E. District, 1898-9.

Boers to await the arrival of the infantry. During the night of the 22nd, however, the enemy withdrew most of their force, and next day General Pole-Carew's men carried the position magnificently, with the trifling loss of two killed, twenty wounded, and two missing, and this in spite of an unlucky misunderstanding which deprived the force of the best part of its artillery. The manner in which the infantry when attacking the height availed themselves of cover, was particularly noticeable, and, no doubt, accounted for the smallness of the casualty list. Meantime, General French swept round Leeuw Kop to the south. On the 24th the advance continued, the chief feature being constant skirmishing with small parties of Boers who hung on the flanks of the British and caused some trouble. They repeatedly fired upon the scouts and reconnoitring parties from farms flying the white flag, and at last, provoked by these outrages, General Pole-Carew gave orders that a farm belonging to a Boer named Richter should be burnt. Unfortunately, it would seem, in some other cases the occupants were innocent; they had made their submission, and to punish them, their own countrymen wantonly fired from their windows, anticipating the result, and then made good their escape. Such incidents will always occur in a war of this kind; they are, probably, unavoidable, but that does not render them the less melancholy. On this particular occasion no doubts could arise, and Richter and his brother were arrested for their treacherous action.

R. *Caton Woodville.*]   [*After a sketch by Melton Prior.*

A PAINFUL DUTY.

In the earlier part of the campaign in the Orange Free State great leniency was shown to the Boers, even when they treacherously fired from houses flying the white flag. This dishonourable practice, however, became so prevalent that sterner measures were forced upon the British generals, and the order was given that houses used for such dastardly purposes should be burnt and their contents confiscated. It is of this fact, and of the resulting hardships which it necessarily entailed upon the families of the Boers, that ex-President Kruger repeatedly endeavoured to make capital in his speeches at Marseilles, Paris, and elsewhere, ignoring the villainy which made such drastic measures necessary.

On the 24th General French, who had turned off too much to the right, found himself at Dewetsdorp, where he was speedily joined by General Rundle, from whose front all opposition had

Fruitless pursuit. melted. Unfortunately they made no "bag" of Boers, and the whole series of operations miscarried, if its purpose was to capture the enemy. On April 23 Commandant-General Louis Botha had reached Dewetsdorp and, realising the extreme danger of the situation, had ordered a general Boer retreat. It was only just in time. By the skin of their teeth the Boers from Wepener and Dewetsdorp succeeded in getting away to Thaba N'chu and Ladybrand with all their guns, stores, and waggons. As soon as Lord Roberts heard of their retreat, he directed

General French to give chase, with all possible speed. Early on April 25, accordingly, General French started for Thaba N'chu. But his horsemen were heavily laden and did not know the country well:

the Boers rode light and knew every foot of the ground. The pursuit had, therefore, no result. Forthwith General Pole-Carew was recalled to Bloemfontein to take part in the advance on Kroonstad, and General Rundle was charged with the task of protecting the extreme British right by operating in the direction of Thaba N'chu and Ladybrand. His mounted men under General Brabazon were sent to Wepener to bring away the garrison —as soon as Dalgety's men could be remounted, which was

COMMANDANT-GENERAL LOUIS BOTHA AND MRS. BOTHA.
See the biographical note on page 565.

speedily accomplished by the purchase of ponies and horses in Basutoland—and to open communications with General Brabant. When Brabazon had done his work he returned by way of Dewetsdorp to Thaba N'chu, on his way rescuing a convoy from attack by the enemy.

General Ian Hamilton, whose operations have not yet been detailed, left Bloemfontein on April 22 with 2,000 mounted infantry and a battery of Horse Artillery. On the 23rd he reached the all-important Waterworks, examined

Recovery of Bloemfontein Waterworks. them, found them weakly held, and made himself master of them with little difficulty, at the same time seizing Strachan's Drift over the Modder. This done he asked for reinforcements, as the enemy appeared to be in force on the hills to the east, and both brigades of the Ninth Division were sent to his assistance. Counting little done while aught remained to do, he now asked permission to push eastwards to Thaba N'chu. Leave

THE BUSINESS SIDE OF WAR.
Telegraph office of Lord Roberts' headquarters at Bloemfontein

to act thus was granted, and he was given General Ridley's Brigade of Mounted Infantry, General Smith-Dorrien's Brigade of Infantry (the 19th), and two Field Batteries, as well as a Horse Battery, for the work. On April 25 he began to march eastwards along a road bordered on either side, north and south, by high ridges. Six miles west of Thaba N'chu the road was barred at Israel's Poort by a series of rocky kopjes at right angles to and connecting the parallel ridges north and south. On these kopjes and on the northern ridge the enemy were presently located in considerable strength.

To capture the position by a frontal assault was not to be thought of, after the Field Marshal's general order forbidding such exhibitions of energy. The Canadians were, therefore, deployed in front of the row of kopjes with Marshall's Horse on their flank. They worked forward to a distance of 800 yards from the Boer position. Then General Smith-Dorrien, with the Cornwalls, Shropshires, and Gordons advanced along the northern ridge, supported by the fire of the two batteries. Finally, the mounted infantry made a wide sweep backwards, crossed the ridge, at a point where it was not held, by a nek, and struck at the enemy's line of retreat. The result of this admirably executed turning movement was seen at once. As soon as the mounted infantry had made good progress the Boers bolted, and the kopjes were occupied by the Canadians and Marshall's Horse, with the trifling loss of twenty killed and wounded.

[Copyright of the "Review of Reviews."

President Kruger.   Doctor Heymans.   Commissioner Bredell.

ON THE STOEP OF THE PRESIDENT'S HOUSE AT PRETORIA.
Photographed April 24, 1900.

Doctor Heymans is a Dutch physician of some repute in the Netherlands. He has taken no part in politics, but Mr. Kruger chose him a few years ago to act as his body physician and oculist. Commissioner Bredell was formerly in the Transvaal Police Service, and had influence in government circles. A man of some education, with plausible, agreeable manners, and a moderate in politics, he may have exercised some restraining influence over Mr. Kruger.

Entry into Thaba N'chu.

Thaba N'chu was entered the same night without further resistance, and there on the next day General French arrived. The enemy still held the heights of Thaba N'chu mountain, a lofty and broken ridge which rises north of the town and runs generally east and west. To dislodge them was necessary, as a further advance was impracticable till they had been forced to retreat.

Operations against surrounding heights.

Disappearance of the Gordons.

On April 26 the mounted infantry seized a point near the western end of the ridge known as Kitchener's-Horse Hill, from the regiment selected to occupy it; but at nightfall, being much "sniped," they abandoned it, and, retiring, were hotly attacked by the Boers. They beat off the attack with the loss of a dozen men and reached safety. The firing, however, and vague reports that they were cut off led General French to despatch the Gordons to their help, and this battalion had a disagreeable—if not a dangerous—experience. It lost itself in the darkness, wandered off, and was lost by the army, so that nothing more was heard of it till late next day, and some fear was felt that it had been captured. On the 27th operations against Thaba N'chu Mountain were resumed.

General Smith-Dorrien seized Kitchener's-Horse Hill, supported by a turning movement against the Boer right, which was executed by the mounted infantry of General Ridley's Brigade. Then General

THE FINISH OF A FORCED MARCH.

The Highlanders here represented formed part of the reinforcements sent to General Ian Hamilton after his recapture of the Bloemfontein Waterworks, and the photograph was taken as they joined his command.

Dickson, with the Fourth Cavalry Brigade, made his way across the ridge, to the east of Kitchener's-Horse Hill, and descended to the other side. At the outset General Gordon, with the Third Cavalry Brigade, had been despatched to turn the Boer left, and to cross the ridge by a defile some miles to the east. It was hoped that the action of the cavalry would bring them in upon

the enemy's rear, on open ground, where they would be able to charge and cut up the retreating Boers. General Rundle's troops, tired with hard marching, were set the task of linking these wide movements and demonstrating against the Boer front.

On the British left everything went like clockwork. Ridley's Mounted Infantry and Dickson's Cavalry descended into the plain to the north of the ridge, and began to work along eastwards to a corrie in the northern side of the mountains, where the Boer laagers were

Infantry surprised.

supposed to lie. As they did so, a few Boers galloped north-westwards, seized an isolated kopje on the flank of the British advance, and opened fire. There was as yet no sign of General Gordon, but hopes of enveloping a large part of the enemy's force ran high. General Ian Hamilton pushed his tired infantry eastwards along the ridge, when suddenly came a sad surprise. Gordon's cavalry should have swept round the Boer left, and when from that quarter of the field a mass of 4,000 horsemen

"COMMANDEERING."

A photograph showing how the Boers obtained supplies for the war. The payment for such supplies usually took the form of quite valueless paper acknowledgments.

advanced with order and precision, it was, with good reason, at first taken for the expected body of British troops. But it proved, instead, to be a mass of Boers, who speedily proceeded to attack Dickson and Ridley, and threatened to cut them off in their turn. As a matter of fact, Gordon had found the enemy too strong, and had not been able to force the required passage. The British plan had therefore failed; it now remained to extricate the forces engaged. This was accomplished by the skill and coolness of the officers and men, but several carts belonging to the Fourth Cavalry Brigade were taken by the enemy. The casualties were absurdly small; only about a dozen men were placed *hors de combat* on the British side. In view of the fact that all the dispositions made assumed the Boer strength to be but 2,000, and that it proved

Skilful withdrawal.

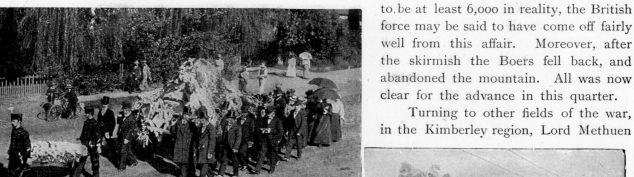

to be at least 6,000 in reality, the British force may be said to have come off fairly well from this affair. Moreover, after the skirmish the Boers fell back, and abandoned the mountain. All was now clear for the advance in this quarter.

Turning to other fields of the war, in the Kimberley region, Lord Methuen

FUNERAL OF GENERAL JOUBERT AT PRETORIA, March 29, 1900 (p. 588).

early in March occupied Boshof, a small place to the north-east of Kimberley. There he placed a detachment of the 2nd Yorkshire Light Infantry, who were later relieved by half the 3rd South Wales Borderers—a militia battalion. It seems to have occurred to the Boers, after the convoy affair, that this detachment offered a favourable opportunity for another surprise. Accordingly, Colonel de Villebois-Mareuil, with the "European Legion" and a commando of Boers, moved towards Boshof, and drew up elaborate plans for the capture of the village and its garrison. "Whatever happens," ran the instructions issued by the French filibuster, "the assailants should remember that their morale is crushing, and that, even in the case of retreat

Attempt to capture Boshof.

being necessary, they have every facility in the darkness for gaining their horses and departing." Unhappily for the success of this expedition, native scouts observed it in camp at the farm of Twee-fontein, eight miles south-east of Boshof, and informed Lord Methuen of its presence on April 5. Seemingly without the knowledge of the Boers, he had just arrived at Boshof with about 2,000 of the Yeomanry, Kimberley Mounted Corps, and Royal Artillery. He at once moved out to Tweefontein, and presently located the enemy on a kopje some miles off. The Boer commando had discreetly retired, but at least the "Foreign Legion" remained, though it was only sixty-eight men strong. The British force opened out, pushed forward its flanks, and surrounded the kopje. Then the Yeomanry dismounted and began to advance under a smart fire. For two hours skirmishing continued, terminated only by the boom of the British field guns, which opened fire as soon as their front was clear. Three shrapnel were discharged with perfect accuracy, and on this the white flag appeared on the kopje. The Yeomanry stood up and rushed in to take the prisoners, when a rifle cracked on the kopje and the gallant Captain Cecil Boyle fell dead. The man who had killed him was instantly shot and the survivors were captured. The unwounded

[*Photo by Hill & Saunders.*
CAPTAIN CECIL BOYLE,
Killed at Tweefontein.

numbered fifty-four; eight had been killed, and six wounded. The British loss was in all four killed and seven wounded. Villebois-Mareuil's body was among the dead; some say that he had fired the treacherous shot in ignorance that the white flag was flying. He was buried that night, and over his grave Lord Methuen erected a monument. With the "Foreign Legion" was captured a cart containing dynamite and engineers' tools, whence it was supposed that Villebois-Mareuil intended, after the capture of Boshof, to push south and cut the Kimberley railway. Unhappily for him and his comrades, he found himself the trapped instead of the trapper.

From Boshof Lord Methuen pushed out north-eastwards to Zwartkopjesfontein, but only to be ordered back some days later. On his way back he had a sharp brush with the Boers, who attacked his column while on the march, on April 20, but were repulsed with some difficulty. The British loss was twenty men, of whom, however, only two were killed. The Boers were some hundreds strong, with four guns, under the younger Cronje, son of the Paardeberg soldier.

AN IMPERIAL YEOMANRY ROUGHRIDER.

The burlesque rebellion among the poor farmers and the mean whites of North-Western Cape Colony, which broke out in the Prieska and Carnarvon districts, was rapidly and effectually suppressed by Lord Kitchener in March, with a force largely consisting of Colonials and City Imperial Volunteers. The Boer invaders had given out the false report that Lord Roberts had been surrounded and his army destroyed

Disturbance in the North-West of Cape Colony.

at Jacobsdal, and so ignorant were the Dutch of these districts that the fable was believed. The British troops, however, speedily overran the country, occupying Kenhardt, Prieska, and Van Wyk's Vley, but the greater part of the Boers and many of the rebels succeeded in making good their escape.

Among the blows which the Boers sustained in March was the death of General

A GROUP OF C.I.V.'s: INNS OF COURT CYCLISTS.

CYCLISTS IN CAMP: REPAIRING THEIR MACHINES.

The cycle and the road-locomotive have both been largely used in this war, for the first time, and both have fully justified their inclusion in the Army's equipment. In a land where the mortality among horses has been so great, the ever-ready cycle has been of great value.

Joubert. The Commandant-General had been ailing in health for months, and it is possible that the mental chagrin caused by the complete failure of his operations in Natal aggravated his malady. He died on March 27, regretted, perhaps, most of all by the British, against whom he had fought, but who could respect his

Death of Joubert.

many noble qualities. He had been against the war from the first, considering the British demands reasonable. He was succeeded by Louis Botha, as the Boer Commander-in-Chief. One other internal Boer event in this period demands notice: this was the explosion at the ammunition factory which had been improvised in Begbie's Works at Johannesburg, on April 24. It was at first ascribed to British treachery, but was really due to accident and gross carelessness.

BEGBIE'S FOUNDRY AND ENGINEERING WORKS, JOHANNESBURG, AFTER THE EXPLOSION.

OFFICERS OF THE MAFEKING RELIEF COLUMN.

[*Photo by Taylor, Mafeking.*]

Top row (left to right): Major Karri Davis (Imperial Light Horse), Major Baden-Powell (Intelligence Department), Captain Robinson, R.A., Major Weil (Transport), Captain Peakman (Kimberley Corps), Prince Alexander of Teck, A.D.C., Captain Cobb, A.S.C.
Second row: Captain Donaldson (Imperial Light Horse), Captain Maxwell (Kimberley Corps), Colonel King (commanding Kimberley Corps), Colonel Mahon, Colonel Edwards (Imperial Light Horse), Captain Bell-Smyth (Brigade-Major), Captain Barnes (Adjutant, Imperial Light Horse).
Bottom row: Captain Ker (commanding Infantry detachment), Sir John Willoughby (D.A.A.G.B.), Colonel F. Rhodes, D.S.O. (Chief of Intelligence Department), Captain Smyth (Galloper), Captain Du Plat Taylor (R.H.A.).

CHAPTER XXV.

THE RELIEF OF MAFEKING.

The Relief Force and its commander—Rapid advance of the Column—Halt at Vryburg—The younger Cronje across the line of advance—Colonel Rhodes' ingenious message—Skirmish with the enemy—Junction with Colonel Plumer's force—Artillery fight – Cronje outwitted—The relief effected.

The Relief Force and its commander.

AS Lord Roberts' army moved out of Bloemfontein on that great march to Pretoria, which it will be our business to record in a succeeding chapter, a small column in the western field of war struck north from Kimberley upon an even more arduous and incalculably more dangerous enterprise— the relief of Mafeking. Colonel Mahon, an officer of Egyptian renown, was in command, and with him rode a force of picked men. There were 900 selected troopers of the Imperial Light Horse—the salt and flower of South Africa—and of the Kimberley Mounted Force; 100 infantry from the Scotch, Welsh, Irish, and Royal (English) Fusiliers of Barton's brigade; four guns of M Battery of Horse Artillery; two "Pom-poms"; three Maxims; and last, but not least, 55 waggons laden with forage and supplies for the long journey of 230 miles over the arid veldt. Though attempts had been made to maintain complete secrecy as to the composition and movements of the column, the Boers were, as usual, perfectly informed on every vital point, and the younger Cronje, with a force 1,500 strong, was directed to arrest its march. Since Colonel Mahon could not dispose of more than 1,200 men, the odds were distinctly against him, and it was only by his rapidity of progress and his dexterous tactics that he succeeded in his perilous mission. To support him, General Hunter with the Tenth Division attacked the enemy on the Vaal, near Windsorton, as the march began.

On May 4 the column crossed the Vaal and left Barkly West, marching through difficult country, bush-covered and abounding in kopjes, towards the far-off village in the north. Great caution was observed, for though the district had already been swept by a mounted column co-operating with General Hunter's division on the Vaal, the Boers might well have returned. The first march was

Rapid advance of the column.

only nine miles long, but on the 5th the column advanced with great speed, covering no less than thirty-one miles. All day the boom of Hunter's guns could be heard; his shells in that clear air could be seen bursting on the kopjes to the right, and his balloon was marked hovering at great height over the battle. But the Boers put in no appearance, though the scouts reported that they were present in force at some distance. Presumably, Hunter's attack was for the time occupying all their attention. At nightfall, the most stringent precautions were enforced; no lights or fires were allowed after 8 p.m., and even pipes and

cigarettes were not to be lighted in the dark. For all the men knew the Boers might be all round the column, sheltered by the bush and rocks, and any hour might see the beginning of a fierce attack. At 2 a.m. of the 6th the force silently up-saddled and moved on through pitchy darkness, the men benumbed by the icy cold of the night air. Even as the march began a shot rang out, and for an instant it was taken for the signal of the enemy's presence; fortunately, however, it was

THE VAAL RIVER AT
BARKLY
(near where Mahon's column
crossed).

found to have been fired by some careless soldier while charging his magazine.

On the 6th again the march was unmolested and uneventful, save for the capture of several Boer waggons on their way westward from Fourteen Streams. They

"FOURTEEN STREAMS."
The railway bridge can be seen to the left of the central clump of trees.

were moving peacefully and happily through country which the burghers had occupied now for seven months without their occupation being disputed by any British force, and their owners had seemingly not been informed of the advance of Colonel Mahon; so they fell an easy prey. The noise of Hunter's guns in action now grew fainter in the right rear, and on the 7th the column was close to Taungs. All the morning its attention was centred upon a dense line of dust, which could be made out moving north-westward; this was the pillar of cloud denoting Cronje's rapid advance to cut off the column from Mafeking. Boers, too, were reported to the south and east; the column was in the midst of the enemy. But here no precautions were neglected. Colonel Mahon was a man who took no unnecessary risks, and exacted the utmost activity from his patrols. "Any little neglect in the matter of patrolling and choosing bivouac positions," writes Mr. Filson Young, a correspondent with the column, "might mean complete disaster to the column, and the frustration of its end. These little things have often been neglected in this campaign; and whenever there has been a convoy captured, it has been because someone has taken for granted that someone else was holding a drift or pass. So we move warily through a placid country that may become at any moment full of menace; travelling may at any moment be exchanged for fighting, and the roadway for the battlefield; even the green slopes that front us may hide the greatest danger, and the river bed, with its grasses and lapping waters, become a pit of death."

On this day a patrol entered Taungs, cut the telegraph wire, destroyed the instruments, and examined the messages; among these an order from Mr. Kruger was found directing a general retreat to Christiana. On the 8th the column hurried through Pudimoe, where several rebel farms were looted and burned, to Brussels Station, only fifteen miles from Vryburg. At Pudimoe the Boers had intended to take up a position astride of Colonel Mahon's route, but the celerity of the British movements prevented the accomplishment of this purpose. Next day the

Halt at Vryburg.

British rode into Vryburg, and found that a Boer outpost there had taken to flight. The few English in the town hurried out to greet the newcomers, who seemed to them to have started suddenly from the earth; the long nightmare of Boer invasion had ended at last. But Colonel Mahon could make no protracted stay; as night of the 10th fell, the troopers with buoyant hearts and the waggons were again faring forward, after the unusual experience of a twenty-four hours' halt. Already the

[Photo by Elliott & Fry.

BRIGADIER-GENERAL BRYAN THOMAS MAHON, D.S.O.,

Belongs to a County Galway family. He joined the 21st Hussars in 1883, and later on the 8th Hussars; Captain, 1888; in 1896 he was transferred to the Egyptian Army; Major, 1897; Brevet Lieut.-Colonel, 1898; Brevet Colonel, 1900; Lieut.-Colonel (12th Lancers), 1900; served with the Dongola Expeditionary Force under Sir H. Kitchener in 1896 as Staff Officer, and received the D.S.O.; distinguished himself in the Atbara and Omdurman battles, and especially in the final destruction of the Khalifa. When war broke out he was on the borders of Abyssinia, but on receiving a telegram from Lord Kitchener, at once hastened south. He has been appointed to the local rank of Brigadier-General on the Staff, South Africa, his promotion dating from May 4, 1900.

losses in horses and mules had been serious, owing to the forced marching and the exiguity of the supply of forage; nearly 100 had been left behind on the way. The night's journey was a weary one, as the guides mistook the whereabouts of water, and it was not till 2 a.m. that the force bivouacked, waterless and disconsolate. Even then only three hours' rest was conceded; but in the morning the anxiously-looked-for water was reached, and a long halt was called. Again, on the night of the 11th, a long march was accomplished, and on May 12 the column stood a little to the west of Kraaipan, where, in the affair of the armoured train, the first blood had been shed in the war. Since then what sufferings and what sacrifices for two peoples!

Photo by Underwood.

A BOER LASSIE.

The younger Cronje across the line of advance. That day the scouts reported Boers in considerable force to the east, and during the night the enemy pushed forward to a hill on the Metsima Spruit, which bore the familiar name of Koodoesrand, hoping thus to bar the way. But Mahon was by no means eager for a fight. He heard that the enemy were throwing up entrenchments with their usual lightning speed, and decided that it would be best to leave them alone. Accordingly, he turned westward, and marched in that direction nine miles before resuming his northward course. Manœuvre was met by counter-manœuvre. The Boer scouts stealthily watched him, crawling through the thick bush in which a stranger without his bearings is as helpless as a ship without compass on the trackless ocean, and, on the information which they gave, Cronje marched swiftly north, and a second time placed himself on the British line of advance. Already runners had come in to the British camp from the north. One, from the brave and steadfast Colonel Plumer, announced that that officer would effect his junction with Mahon north-west of Mafeking; the other, from Colonel Baden-Powell, asked for information as to the numbers, guns, and supplies of the column. Such information was not lightly to be entrusted to any messenger; there was no cipher of which Baden-Powell had the key; but in these straits, Colonel Rhodes, the intelligence officer with the column, succeeded in inventing a most ingenious reply, unintelligible to the Boers, but clear as daylight to the British. It is thus given by Mr. Filson Young: "Our numbers are the Naval and Military multiplied by ten; our guns, the number of sons in the Ward family; our supplies, the officer commanding the 9th Lancers." The key to the message was that there were 940 men, 94, Piccadilly being the number of the Naval and Military Club; that the guns were six, that being the number of sons in the house of Dudley; and that the supplies were Little.

Colonel Rhodes' ingenious message.

Skirmish with the enemy. All the morning of the 13th the advance continued through the bush veldt, "which consists," says Mr. Young, "of long, rank grass, with thorn bushes at small intervals, and hardwood trees at greater distances —the whole something like an English paddock or park of young

MAP OF THE ROUTE OF THE FLYING COLUMN WHICH RELIEVED MAFEKING.

F. Dadd, R.I.

[After a sketch by F. J. Mackenzie.

COLONEL PLUMER'S ATTEMPT TO RELIEVE MAFEKING.

On March 31, Colonel Plumer was within six miles of Mafeking, and a portion of his force, consisting of about 200 mounted men, came into collision with the Boers who were investing the town. The engagement lasted from 3 till 6 o'clock in the afternoon, and Colonel Plumer, who was himself slightly wounded, and who lost 10 killed, including 3 officers, about 25 wounded, and 7 missing, was compelled to retire to Ramathlabama.

SOME OF THE MEN WHO WERE BESIEGING MAFEKING.

The photograph, taken in the early days of the siege, shows General Cronje (afterwards captured at Paardeberg), whip in hand, standing by the breech of the 94-pounder "Long Tom," nicknamed "Creechy" (abbreviation of Marguerite), or "Creaky," which had frequent duels with the little Nordenfeldt. On his right, pipe in mouth, is Commandant Snyman—the man who deliberately fired on the women and the sick—and on his left is Captain Van der Merwe. In the foreground are some of the shells, the fragments of which, when fired into Mafeking, were eagerly sought as mementos of the siege.

LIEUT. SMITHEMAN,
Of the Rhodesian Regiment, who got through the Boer lines into Mafeking, and returned with reports to Colonel Plumer.

trees." The going was so heavy that the waggons straggled, and this in spite of the fact that Boers were from time to time seen on the right flank, and in spite of heavy clouds of dust which were made out, slowly converging on the British route. About 3.30 p.m. the "pip-pop" of the Mauser was heard to the south-east, while the column was in the bush; the convoy was at once ordered to close in, and M Battery was called upon to open fire on the nearest dust cloud. The range, however, was too great, and the guns had to wait. Then from the south-east the roar of a heavy rifle fusillade ran with the swiftness of a forest fire along the front. Bullets came in showers; Mr. Hands, the cheerful and capable correspondent of the *Daily Mail*, was severely wounded, and in a few minutes a dozen men were prostrate. Yet there was nothing whatever to be seen. Of the Boers' presence there was no sign or token except the whistling bullets and the crackling musketry.

The convoy closed up with the troopers around it. There were some narrow escapes, and many casualties. Major Baden-Powell, brother of the famous Colonel, had his watch smashed to pieces, but himself escaped without a scratch. Mahon showed imperturbable coolness with the bullets flicking up the dust at his feet; at an order from him the four horse guns and the two "Pom-Poms" changed position and opened in the direction from which seemed to come the fiercest fire. As if by magic the situation changed. A few fierce blows from the "Pom-Poms," a dozen rounds from the guns, and the Boer fire ceased as suddenly as it had begun. The enemy had had enough, and the fight was over. Yet the casualties in that half hour's skirmish were serious. Six men lay dead, twenty-four were wounded, and one was missing. The force bivouacked where it had fought, though Cronje had the effrontery to pretend that it had only escaped because it took to precipitate flight. He marched north once more, drawing in reinforcements from Snyman's commandos in front of Mafeking, and yet again took post athwart its line of advance.

On his part, Mahon rode swiftly north-westward all the 14th and early 15th, and as day of the 15th broke, struck **Junction with Colonel Plumer's force.** the first outposts of Colonel Plumer's force at the Kaffir kraal known as Jan Masibi's. As the column from the south appeared on one side, that from the north marched in amid clouds of dust from the other. There were the 350 stalwart soldiers of the Rhodesian Regiment, who for seven weary months had been incessantly skirmishing with the Boers, and attempting to relieve Mafeking; there were 200 Queenslanders of enormous stature; there were six quick-firing guns of the C Canadian Battery, manned by the hardy militiamen of the far West, fresh from a journey which is without parallel in the annals of war. In the short space of a month they had travelled by sea from Capetown to Beira, by rail from Beira to Marandellas, by road from Marandellas to Buluwayo, and by rail again from Buluwayo to Ootsi, whence they had marched, covering 70 miles or more in two days, to Jan Masibi's, completing 3,100 miles of journeying by steamer, rail, and road, from Capetown. Their guns were an invaluable reinforcement to Mahon, who could now dispose of 1,500 men and 15 pieces of artillery, two of which, however, were muzzle-loading 7-pounders of little value. No shadow of gloom marred the meeting. Though both forces were eating their last rations, and retreat was out of the question, the men were absolutely determined to force their way into Mafeking or perish. It was neck or nothing.

On the 16th the combined force struck south-westward down the Molopo, on the last stage of its great march. And now the far-away village, with whose story the whole world was ringing, came into sight. Over the veldt could be seen the sheen of tin roofs and some white specks of houses. At mid-day a halt was called, seven miles from the beleaguered town, on the northern bank of the Molopo, while the mules were watered. The position occupied by the British was not favourable; all around the ground rose considerably, and here, as elsewhere, it was covered with bushes. The artillery took post on a gently swelling eminence to the north; the convoy halted in a saucer-like depression; the Imperial Light Horse watched the left flank, and Colonel Plumer the right; the Kimberley Mounted Corps guarded the rear. Soon after 1.30 several shots put the

ONE OF THE BOER FORTS OUTSIDE MAFEKING.

British on the alert. As yet nothing could be seen of the enemy, and it was not certain where they were. Gradually their fire swelled and developed on the right front, and the British artillery took position

Artillery fight.

ARTILLERY IN MAFEKING WAITING TO CO-OPERATE WITH THE RELIEF COLUMN.

—horse guns on the left, Canadian guns and "Pom-Poms" on the right, ready to open. As they waited, the Boers got to work with three 15-pounders, a 7-pounder, and a "Pom-Pom." Their shells dropped everywhere, but did infinitesimal damage. With a prodigious banging the British pieces replied, and a hot artillery duel, the roar of which dominated the incessant crackle of the rifle fusillade, was immediately in progress. The enemy were now showing in considerable strength in front and on both flanks.

The British artillery preponderance, however, was overpowering. M Battery speedily cleared its front and forced back the Boers; the Canadian quick-firers rained shells upon a donga in which the enemy were seen to be hiding, and with some trouble induced them to depart. The last stand was made by them at Israel's Farm, upon the British right front; here they checked Colonel Plumer, but when the guns of M Battery and of the Canadian Battery, as well as the "Pom-Poms," concentrated upon the farm, the fight came abruptly to an end. It had lasted five long hours with little incident; it was an incessant "sniping" upon a prodigious scale, in which the casualties were by no means heavy. In all, sixty men on the British side were killed or wounded; the Boers suffered far more severely, as was only to be

H. C. Seppings Wright.]　　　　　　[After a sketch made by an officer who was present.

THE MEETING OF BADEN-POWELL AND MAHON.

S

THE RELIEF OF MAFEKING: THE PROCESSION THROUGH THE MARKET SQUARE.
Colonel Baden-Powell and his Staff were on horseback between Dixon's Hotel and the adjoining house, which was the Colonel's headquarters.

expected in view of the strength of the British artillery. Among the trophies of the victory was a waggon with 2,000 shells for the Boer "Pom-Pom."

The rapidity and energy of the British attack stood Mahon in good stead. Spades and picks were found in numbers just to the rear of the line which the Boers had held, whence it was plain that they had intended to entrench themselves. Behind earthworks, such as they were capable of constructing, with the advantage of superior numbers, their defeat would have been no easy task, especially when it is remembered that the British had not sufficient supplies or provisions to permit of any elaborate manœuvring. Even now the tenacious Cronje did not feel thoroughly beaten.

Cronje outwitted. There is good evidence to show that he intended calling up more men from Snyman's commandos before Mafeking, and offering further resistance before Mahon reached the besieged town. But he was outwitted by a stratagem of the British leader.

Mahon had already exchanged heliograph signals with Baden-Powell. He had announced that his force would halt where it had fought, and would march into Mafeking at 4.30 a.m. of the 17th.

The relief effected. Meantime he sent Major Karri Davis with eight of the Light Horse to reconnoitre the road. They sped straight into the besieged town without let or hindrance, and sent him back word to the effect that the way was open. The defenders of Mafeking had watched with sickening anxiety the clouds of dust and flashes of guns on the horizon, all the afternoon and evening of the 16th, and as this handful of men rode into the town they had the first clear evidence of a British victory. A crowd swiftly gathered; there was tumult and cheering and singing of "God Save the Queen," and after that again three cheers for Baden-Powell, the steadfast, the wily, the invincible.

Nor was the rest of the column long in following in their footsteps. At 11 p.m. Colonel Mahon

THE FIRST TRAIN INTO MAFEKING.
This is the train of supplies which Colonel Plumer had kept in readiness. As can be seen in the photograph, its passage through the veldt had been as far as possible disguised with foliage, so that when at rest it could scarcely be distinguished.

happened to wake—men thought there was design in this seeming accident—and gave orders for the waggons to inspan. The night was bright with a full moon, and the last stage of the march was accomplished without incident. In absolute silence the train of men and waggons passed through the Boer patrols, who were so careless and unobservant that next day they could not believe that Mahon had stolen through their lines and entered the town till they had ocular demonstration of the fact. At 4 a.m. of the 17th the first of the Mafeking outposts was encountered by the relief force, and amidst general exultation pipes were lighted and conversation opened in tones louder than a whisper. A few minutes later Colonel Baden-Powell rode up. There were no dramatic acts or words. Mahon said, simply : " Glad to meet you. How are you ? " And Baden-Powell replied : " Good. How are you ? It's a long time since we met." Thus in true Anglo-Saxon fashion two of the heroes of the war exchanged greeting. As day broke the relief force halted and breakfasted in Mafeking.

For the splendid success of this enterprise Colonel Mahon deserves the highest credit. His leadership was perfect throughout. In ten days of actual marching he covered 223 miles of arid country, though perpetually threatened by a superior enemy. He met that enemy twice in action, and on each occasion discomfited them. So certain were the Boers that he must fail in reaching Mafeking that some of their number who were prisoners in the town told Baden-Powell that he had not a chance of success. They counted upon capturing him and his whole force. The intense anxiety which Lord Roberts and General Hunter, both admirable judges, are known to have felt for him is, perhaps, the best measure of the difficulty of his task. There was no more brilliant feat of arms in the whole campaign than this meteoric rush through the desert. But while giving all due credit to Mahon for his achievements, Colonel Plumer's energy and decision in moving so swiftly to reinforce the southern

[*Photo by Lafayette*

COLONEL (NOW MAJOR-GENERAL) BADEN-POWELL IN HIS HUSSAR UNIFORM.
This portrait is one of the few in which the popular officer appears uncovered.

column should not be overlooked, nor the patience and caution which he displayed in the weary months when his tiny force was the only bulwark between the Boers and helpless Rhodesia, the only hope in the eyes of beleaguered Mafeking. Moltke has said that it is the highest achievement of the General's art to unite two forces in the face of the enemy. And before Mafeking this was accomplished with faultless precision under Lord Roberts' guiding hand by his two gallant subordinates, Mahon and Plumer.

The result of the expedition was awaited with breathless interest all over the civilized world ; its success was a disappointment to those of our enemies who were already clamouring for intervention.

COLONEL BADEN-POWELL AND HIS MILITARY AND CIVIL STAFFS.

[Photo by E. J. Ross.

Top row (reading from left to right): Major Panzera (commanding the Artillery), Captain Ryan (Commissariat Officer), Captain Greener, Lord Edward Cecil (Chief Staff Officer), Captain Wilson, A.D.C., Lieut. the Hon. A. Hanbury-Tracy (Press Censor, Military Intelligence Officer), Captain Cowan (Bechuanaland Rifles).
Second row: Major Godley (commanding Western Outposts), Colonel Vyvyan, Mr. C. Bell (Civil Commissioner), Colonel Baden-Powell, Mr. Whiteley (Mayor), Colonel Hore (in command of the Western Fort), Dr. Hayes (Principal Medical Officer).
In front: Lieut. Moncrieff.

CHAPTER XXVI.

THE SIEGE OF MAFEKING.

Mafeking's defences and defenders—Leisurely bombardment—The trenches flooded by a storm—Disquieting rumours—Attack on Game Tree Fort—The assault fails—Improvised artillery—Plumer at Gaberones—Relief delayed—Food supply—British lines pushed out—Sniping—Cattle raiding—Capture of the Brickfields—Dearth of food—Escape of Kaffirs—Plumer's repulse—Casualties—Messages to and from Lord Roberts—Attack on the Kaffir stad—Colonel Hore surrenders—The Boer advance checked—Eloff trapped—Surrenders to Colonel Hore—Snyman's inaction—Relief at hand—The Boers driven away—Review of the troops—Losses during the siege—Baden-Powell's work and its reward.

WHEN we left Mafeking, in Chapter III., that beleaguered town had defied the Boers for a month. Information, which has become available since the siege ended, and which was not likely to be allowed to pass through the British lines while the Boers were still surrounding the town, has enhanced the brilliance of the early days of this defence. It is now known that at any time in these first weeks the place might have been rushed by 2,000 determined men. The terrible mines which Baden-Powell professed to have planted all round the town were in real truth "scarcely capable of damaging a cow," as one of the garrison writes. The artillery at the disposal of the defence was miserable, both in quantity and quality—a good sample of the carelessness and want of foresight of the British authorities. There were four muzzle-loading 7-pounders with worn rifling, dilapidated carriages, and rusty elevating gear; a Nordenfeldt machine gun, and a Hotchkiss gun.

Mafeking's defences and defenders.

"LORD NELSON." Dated 1770.

This was an old gun presented to Montsioa, father of Wessels, the Kaffir chief. It had lain buried for twenty years, but at the commencement of the siege was unearthed and handed over to the military by Wessels, and by them used throughout their later operations. It was a smooth-bore muzzle-loader, over a century old, firing round balls, and, curiously enough, the initials of the founders stamped upon it were "B. P. & Co." The Boers did not relish its missiles, which from every point of view were "uncanny."

(599)

Presently to these was added a venerable specimen of smooth-bore cannon, dating back to last century, and firing round cannon balls. Such was the equipment with which the progressive British nation supplied Colonel Baden-Powell for the encounter with the high velocity breech-loaders of the retrograde and stupid Boer. Yet the more inadequate the means, the greater the glory of the defence. On the other side were the very best and most modern guns, and here, as at Ladysmith and Kimberley, had these guns been intelligently used, and their fire concentrated upon one point to prepare the way for an assault, the town must have fallen.

MAFEKING'S ARTILLERY.
On the extreme right is "Lord Nelson," and next is "The Wolf," the little howitzer made in the town.

The garrison of Mafeking was composed of the most heterogeneous elements, agreeing only in this respect—in the possession of fine physique and of the high courage which is the inheritance of the British race. It included the mounted men of the Protectorate Regiment, sturdy, intelligent volunteers; two detachments of Cape Police; a detachment of British South African Police; the Bechuanaland Rifles; the Railway Employés, who were enrolled and armed; and the other whites in the town, who formed the Town Guard. The total strength at the outset did not exceed 1,200 men, and was rapidly reduced by casualties. Surprising to many of the British officers was the high efficiency of this curious medley of odds and ends. Even the Town Guard, without discipline and training, shaped admirably, enduring terrible hardships in the trenches—scorched by the sun in the day, shivering in the cold of the frosty nights, and in rain storms, which were frequent, holding the lines in a foot or more of slimy mud. For water, the town

THE PROTECTORATE REGIMENT ARRIVING FROM RAMATHLABAMA BEFORE THE SIEGE.

depended upon wells near the Molopo River, which ran through the lines; the river itself was undrinkable, but it served for washing. The total civilian population in Mafeking included 700 English and Dutch women and children, who were placed in the women's laager, under protection of the Red Cross flag, and no less than 7,000 Kaffirs of the Baralong tribe and refugees from the Rand, who were allowed to take no part in the fighting. These Kaffirs were a most serious encumbrance and source of danger. Though they loved the Boers less than the English, it was always possible that they might turn against the latter, if they saw any prospect of an ultimate Boer victory. The enemy steadily shelled the Kaffir "stad" with the express object of irritating the Baralongs against the British, who would naturally come to be considered as the ultimate cause of all the suffering.

The Boer tactics were to bombard the town with long-range guns, while slowly pushing trenches forward towards the British positions. As the sap drew nearer and nearer the garrison hourly dreaded an assault. It has been reported that the Cronjes were eager to deliver an attack, and that they telegraphed to Mr. Kruger that they could easily carry the place by hand-to-hand fighting. But Mr. Kruger, with a strange want of prescience and an utter ignorance of the immense importance of time, replied that an assault was not worth the lives of fifty burghers, and that Mafeking was certain to succumb to the mere process of blockade. Never was a more disastrous mistake made. The garrison under Baden-Powell displayed a capacity of

THE CHIEFS OF THE BARALONGS.

In the centre sits Wessels, with Melema on his right and Lekoko on his left. The "headmen" of the tribe stand behind. The separate portrait is that of Matsatse, the "Queen-Mother."

A KAFFIR WEDDING PARTY.
The Christianized Kaffirs delight to mimic European ways, often with results calculated to raise a smile.

THE WOMEN'S LAAGER, MAFEKING.
A trench was dug round the laager, but because of persistent Boer firing, this was afterwards covered over and used as a shelter.

endurance which must have been as astonishing to the Boers as it was to the anxious spectators in England; and the enemy, who had at the outset of the war boasted that in two days they would breakfast in Mafeking, saw ten weeks pass without the place being appreciably nearer its fall.

The bombardment was at first conducted with the same curious regularity as at Ladysmith. "At dawn we had half a dozen shells," says Mr. Neilly, a correspondent imprisoned in the town;

Leisurely bombardment.

at luncheon time three, at 4.30 another half dozen, and at 7.45 one for 'good night.' The people became so used to the times at which the gun was fired that I heard of some who timed their watches by the fire, and occasionally, when somebody heard the gun, he would say: 'There's the afternoon gun. My! I must hurry up. I'm ten minutes late already for an appointment I had.'" After a time, however, the enemy saw the mistake of their shelling at fixed hours, and fired more irregularly. Generally speaking, the bombardment was most ineffective. Mafeking was built of soft, sun-dried bricks, through which shells would pass without bursting. The roofs were of corrugated iron, and the houses much scattered. Bombproofs had been prepared, and in these the people took refuge when the Boer shells were falling; yet complete safety was not to be had, though the number of casualties among the whites was not large until men grew careless. Here, as in the other sieges, it was noted as curious that the Dutch and their sympathisers suffered most.

The heavy 6-inch gun, with its 94-lb. shell, at Mafeking, as at Kimberley, was most feared, but whereas Kimberley had to endure only a few days' shelling with its ponderous projectiles, Mafeking was deluged with them for months. Efforts were made to annoy the Boer gunners by "sniping," with considerable success. At times the enemy fired incendiary shells, but these caused no serious damage. Signals were arranged by which the inhabitants were informed, not only when the big gun had been fired, but also the direction in which its ugly muzzle pointed. Here, as at Kimberley and Ladysmith, the enemy from time to time shelled the hospital, the convent, in which the brave Irish sisters of mercy held their ground undismayed, and the women's laager, notwithstanding the Red Cross flags which flew above and in spite of Colonel Baden-Powell's frequent remonstrances. General Snyman in this matter sinned more than Cronje, and the feeling in Mafeking against the Boers grew exceedingly bitter in consequence.

CAPTAIN MARSH,
Commanding Cape Mounted Police at Mafeking.

On November 30, there was hot rifle firing on either side, but the only result was a prodigious waste of ammunition, by which one or two Boers were wounded. The British trenches were being steadily pushed out to meet the enemy's approach, for Baden-Powell, with rare judgment, saw that the best way to cow the Boers

The trenches flooded by a storm.

was to show them that the garrison was ready to take the offensive and would not sit still to be attacked. On December 5 one of the most tremendous storms experienced in South Africa passed over the town. It opened with a terrific display of thunder and lightning, after which the rain descended in a veritable Niagara, flooding the trenches and bombproofs in a few minutes and driving all into the open. Had the Boers seized the opportunity and attacked, the drowned-out garrison could have offered little resistance; as it was, the trenches had to be pumped out by the town fire-engine or baled with buckets. But the chance, like so many others, was allowed by the enemy to slip past unimproved. The soaked garrison stood to arms all the night in the awful slime of the trenches, and the Boers contented themselves with firing purposeless and useless volleys; yet the dawn of day brought indescribable relief to all who knew the danger.

[Photo by Barnett.

COLONEL BADEN-POWELL IN HIS SOUTH AFRICAN OUTFIT.

In these days, rumours of British defeats began to reach and depress the garrison. It was known, more or less certainly, that in

Disquieting rumours.

Natal affairs had gone badly, but General Snyman professed in his harangues to the Boers that the British now held only two points in South Africa, Capetown and Mafeking; and though, of course, these absurd fables were not credited, it was thought that they had some foundation in fact. To diminish the elation of the burghers Baden-Powell prepared a proclamation to the Boers, and with amusing audacity sent copies of it to the various Boer positions. It warned the enemy that there was no chance of foreign intervention, and asked them humorously whether it was worth their while to attempt to take a town which, if taken, would be of no use to them; adding that Mafeking could never be captured by "sitting still and looking at

SOUNDING THE ALARM.

The mounted orderly, stationed in front of Dixon's Hotel in the market place, is sounding the bugle-call which required every man to go to his allotted post. A cyclist orderly beside him awaits orders. On the roof of the adjoining house (which was the Colonel's headquarters) is the original look-out, with an officer on the watch. Large bells were used for the purpose of warning the townspeople when the Boer artillery began to fire.

it," as the garrison had ample supplies. However, if they would go home to their farms by the 14th, their misdeeds should be forgiven. This piece of banter was not altogether appreciated by the Boers, though many of them confessed to the British flags of truce that they were thoroughly sick of the siege.

The weeks of December passed with no more striking incident than a hot exchange of fire between the two opponents on Dingaan's Day, December 16, when the Boer gunners were con-
Attack on Game Tree Fort. siderably incommoded by the projectiles of the British 7-pounders and Nordenfeldt. Christmas went by peacefully; the garrison feasted; but for many on that day it was a case of "Let us eat and drink, for to-morrow we die," since Colonel Baden-Powell had determined to make a desperate attack on the 26th upon the Dutch position known as Game Tree Fort. This work lay to the north of Mafeking, distant from the town about two miles. Its capture was desirable for two reasons—to open up communication with the north and to extend the area of pasturage for the large number of cattle in the town. Indeed, the live stock could not be kept in condition on the limited grazing ground, which was all that was available,

THE BOERS MANNING THEIR TRENCHES OUTSIDE MAFEKING.
The men could be clearly distinguished from Mafeking by the aid of glasses. The intervening scrub is like worn-out cocoanut matting, in which a Boer could creep up to the village unseen.

so long as the fort was in the hands of the Boers. On Christmas Day the work was carefully reconnoitred and examined. It was seen to be a low sandbag breastwork with one tier of loopholes, perfectly easy to storm. But, though the utmost secrecy was maintained by Colonel Baden-Powell and his staff, the Boers must have been informed by spies of the British plans, since after the reconnaissance they raised the height of the sand-bag rampart from three to twelve feet, provided three tiers of loopholes, trebled the garrison, placed two commandos near at hand as a reserve to give support or deliver a counter-attack, and tore up the railway track near the fort, to preclude any movement by the armoured train in Mafeking. Thus, all unconsciously, the British were preparing to march into a skilfully laid trap. It was afterwards remarked that the Dutch women in the women's laager had behaved in an unusual manner, singing Psalms with unprecedented vigour, and it was conjectured that this was a pre-arranged method of giving the enemy a hint of what was intended.

Long before dawn the troops were in position. Two squadrons of the Protectorate Regiment were to attack from the east, under the command of Captains Vernon and Fitzclarence, supported by 300 men of the garrison with all the available artillery and the armoured train. As the first

s

MAJOR-GENERAL ROBERT STEPHENSON SMYTH BADEN-POWELL

Was born in 1857, son of the late Rev. Professor Baden-Powell, of Oxford, and educated at Charterhouse; joined 13th Hussars, 1876; Captain, 1883; Major, 1892; Lieut.-Colonel, 1896; Brevet-Colonel, 1897; Major-General on Staff, 1900; served as Assistant Military Secretary and Intelligence Officer to the General Officer commanding the operations in Zululand, 1888; Assistant Military Secretary at Malta, 1890-3; on special service in Ashanti, under Sir Francis Scott, in command of native levies, and as war correspondent to *The Daily Chronicle*, 1895; Chief Staff Officer in the Matabeleland Campaign, 1896; promoted from the 13th Hussars to command the 5th Dragoon Guards, 1897; sent to Rhodesia to organise a local levy early in the summer of 1899; promoted from Colonel to Major-General, 1900, in recognition of his gallant defence of Mafeking. He is extraordinarily versatile, being noted as soldier, scout, author, artist, musician, actor, athlete, and sportsman. His peculiar personality equally impresses whites and natives.

(605)

26

faint glimpse of breaking day showed over the veldt, at 4.15 a.m., the guns opened their fastest fire. The Boers immediately replied; a volley from the direction of the fort showed that they were upon the alert, and with a heavy boom the great 6-in. Creusot joined in the battle. In the dim, grey light the flashes of cannon and rifles flickered along the horizon like summer lightning. From Cannon Kopje, an outwork in the Mafeking defences, a 7-pounder did its feeble best to keep down the fire of the big gun.

Major Panzera, who was in charge of the British artillery, was anxious to breach the walls of the fort, so as to render an assault easy. He fired steadily at the work, but from the manner in which it had been strengthened by the Boers, and from the inferior quality of his guns, could make little or no impression. A few shrapnel were burst just over the fort, and may have caused the enemy some loss; most of the projectiles, however, exploded against the sandbag face without result, without even battering down the rampart. Then about 5 a.m. the signal was given to the artillery to cease fire; the armoured train blew a deep blast on her whistle; the rifle fusillade of the two opponents blazed up furiously, and through a sheet of bullets the Protectorate Regiment advanced to the assault. The men dashed forward in swift rushes, keeping admirable order, their officers well in front, with such spirit and gallantry that all who saw were filled with admiration. A few fell, but the losses were not heavy at this stage, despite the bullets which seemed to come at once from every quarter. Half the distance had been covered, when the men, by order, lay down to

H. C. Seppings Wright.]

THE ATTACK ON GAME TREE FORT.

recover breath, and, as they lay, opened fire with their rifles. Then the order "Fix bayonets" was given; the steel glinted in the rays of the early sun, and the sixty prone figures rose as if by clockwork from the ground and swept with a cheer towards the fort, now only 300 yards away. Captain Sandford was one of the first to fall in this rush; in an instant he was hit twice; one wound through the spine was mortal; but he died calling upon his men to go forward, with his face to the foe.

And now the Boer fire blazed up with a fury and intensity that appalled the onlookers. The fort vomited bullets in sheets from every loop-hole. Yet the Protectorates did not halt or check for a

INTERIOR OF GAME TREE FORT.
From a photograph taken immediately after the town was relieved.

moment. Captain Fitzclarence was down with a bullet through his thigh; Captain Vernon was wounded also, but he was still in front, refusing to go to the rear. The men were worthy of these officers. As they closed in on the fort they sent up cheer after cheer, and the spectators, from the note of triumph which rang in their shouts, were certain that victory was as good as won. But the cry of triumph was, after all, only that of men who stand in the presence of death with the consciousness that they have done supremely well. For the last 25 yards of the rush, every man in that little band of heroes had seen that success was not to be dreamt of, and that only one thing remained —to die with honour. From a deep ditch there rose before them a perpendicular rampart, with row upon row of loop-holes; and even if the rampart were climbed the work was roofed in with iron, so that access would still be difficult. Yet the wounded Captain Vernon, Lieutenant Paton, Corporal Cooke, Corporal Pickard, and Sergeant Ross, broke desperately forward, crossed the ditch, and strove to reach the loop-holes, into which the officers emptied their revolvers. At the sight of these figures scrambling up the face of the fort, all in the rear felt certain that the work had been carried. Cooke was now on the iron roof with the bullets swishing round him at the shortest point-blank range, yet, strange to say, though his tunic was riddled, he himself came off without a scratch. Paton was shot dead with Sergeant-Major Paget, both fighting to the last; Vernon, an officer of faultless bravery, fell dead with his third glorious wound; there was no one left to lead and none to follow.

The attack had failed. Yet the handful of survivors did not **The assault fails.** break or run. They sauntered backwards, many of them still facing the Boer fire, with such incredible calmness, that the spectators could not divine what had happened. "Swift in the advance, slow in the retreat," is indeed a British axiom; but this leisurely, reluctant withdrawal under a hell of fire was something that evinced dæmonic courage and covered the day's disaster with immortal honour. The nine who returned were all that was left of the 63 men who

[*Photo by Taylor, Mafeking.*

CAPTAIN SANDFORD AND HIS GUN.
From a photograph taken on Christmas Day—the day before the assault on Game Tree Fort, in which Captain Sandford was killed.

had gone in to the attack. The others were not in the fort, but dead, dying or wounded, upon its outer slope. Yet the fierceness of the assault, the determination with which it had been pressed home, and the spirit shown by the survivors in the retreat, had made so deep an impression upon the Boers, that they did not attempt to follow up their success. As the British troops retired on Mafeking, the Red Cross flag was shown by Baden-Powell's orders, and the Boers at once responded, hoisting it over the fort. Stretcher-parties went forward into the terrible arena of death. There they found twenty-one of the best and bravest dead. Many of them had five or six wounds, with such fury and resolution had they fought; few had less than two; all the bodies had been looted. The wounded numbered thirty, and there were three prisoners in the enemy's hands. The Boers poured out of the fort and talked with the stretcher-parties. They were depressed, rather than exultant, at their success. The valour of the English had made upon them the profoundest of impressions, and they expressed sorrow that so many brave men had fallen, saying that they could not have believed that men could fight so well. It was gathered from their talk that they had been upon the very verge of surrender; indeed, it was afterwards learnt that the garrison had only been held fast by the resolution of one man, who swore he would blow out the brains of the first burgher to hoist the white flag.

[*Photo by Bassano.*]

CAPTAIN CHARLES FITZCLARENCE, V.C.,

Of the Royal Fusiliers, showed conspicuous bravery in commanding the Protectorate Regiment during the attack on the armoured train at Mafeking, October 14, in leading his troops into the enemy's trenches at night about a fortnight later, and particularly in the attack on Game Tree Fort, December 26, when he was severely wounded.

[*Photo by Bassano.*]

CAPTAIN VERNON.
Repeatedly wounded and at length killed in the attack on Game Tree Fort.

Though the affair ended so unfortunately, it was not without effect upon the Boers. They showed less stomach than ever for an assault upon Mafeking, and were themselves so alarmed for the security of their own positions that they did not dare to detach more men to the south. They set to work in all directions to strengthen their defences. Moreover, night after night they seemed to be seized with panic, so that suddenly their whole line of trenches would open fire, without cause or reason.

BOMBARDING MAFEKING: STATE-ARTILLERYMEN LAYING THE BIG CREUSOT GUN, "CREECHY."

F. Dadd, R.I.]

A GLEAM OF SUNSHINE BETWEEN THE STORMS.

A scene on the battlefield of Game Tree Hill during the truce, December 26, 1899.   The Boers on this occasion crowded round the British wounded with sympathetic interest.

[*After a sketch by a British officer.*

(609)

The dead were buried that night in the little cemetery of Mafeking, while the thunder rolled and the lightning played over the veldt. We may echo, as their epitaph, the famous words—"In such a death there is no sting, in such a grave there is everlasting victory." They had fallen, bequeathing to the nation for which they had died, a new and glorious example, worthy to rank with the heroism of Grenville, of the *Revenge*, at Flores, of the Light Division at Albuera, and of the Light Brigade in the death-ride of Balaclava. In Pericles' great words, spoken over those who had fallen in the same way, "They lost their lives, but they won ageless renown. No tomb is so splendid as theirs; they are not buried, but embalmed in undying glory."

After the fight at Game Tree Fort some weeks passed without further incident than the usual daily dose of shells. The Protectorate Regiment, which had lost so heavily in the fighting, having

Improvised artillery. 110 men down out of 400, was reorganised in three, instead of four, squadrons.

As ammunition for the old 7-pounder was running low, the energy of the town was concentrated upon casting shells, which were ultimately turned out by an engineer named Conelly, with an ingeniously improvised blast furnace. Round shot were also made for the old smooth-bore, but the triumph of Mafeking was the manufacture of a 4½-in. howitzer, by shrinking rings of iron upon an old iron drain pipe. The smooth-bore was found most serviceable. At the risk of his life Major Panzera loaded it with heavy charges, and sent the ridiculous cannon balls of another age skipping over the veldt towards the Boers, who did not at all appreciate the attention. When the garrison had a particularly successful day, the Boers retaliated by shelling the women's laager or the hospital. A young child was killed by this treacherous fire.

CASTING SHELLS FOR "LORD NELSON."
The old naval gun illustrated on page 599 was sometimes known as "Lord Nelson," sometimes as "B P.," from the founders' initials.

Meantime, as the months drew on, Mafeking grew more and more anxious for relief. But of this there was no sign as yet, either from the north or from the south. On the north, Colonel

Plumer at Gaberones. Plumer with a little force of six or seven hundred men was working slowly south, but the protection of his line of communications, running for 250 miles close to the Boer frontier, and open to interruption by any body of raiders, absorbed a great part of his strength and left him too weak to make his way to Mafeking. Nor would it be enough for him to enter the place; he must be able to throw into it stores and provisions if his arrival was to be more than an embarrassment to Baden-Powell. His headquarters at this date were at Gaberones, a station on the railway ninety-two miles north of Mafeking. It was through him that Mafeking maintained touch with the outward world; to his camp came the runners who forced their way through the Boer lines, as southward to Kimberley the stretch of country to be covered was too great.

It was to the south that the garrison looked for real assistance. That way would come the British army when the tide of fortune set in favour of the Union Jack. Not a day passed without the soldiers and townspeople gazing eagerly forth in that quarter; vague rumours persistently ran round the place like wildfire. Now it was a Kaffir woman who had seen near Maritsani a bag in the sky, and in the bag two men who looked through sticks; now it was some imaginative person who spied, night after night, strange coloured lights on the horizon. But as story after story was disproved, and week after week passed without the advent of any force, men grew too sick and disgusted to talk of relief. What news filtered through was bad news. Colenso, Magersfontein, Stormberg, seen through Boer glasses by Boer reporters, were not encouraging incidents. All had made up their minds from the first that there was to be no surrender, but at the outset it had not seemed that any great feat of endurance would be demanded of the garrison and townspeople. One or two months' siege was the most anticipated. But now—though the moment Lord Roberts had landed in South Africa he had sent through a runner with a promise of certain relief, and with warm thanks and congratulations which made the ears of every man of the garrison tingle with joy—it was understood that the month of May must arrive before anything could be done. So weeks or months of ennui had still to be faced resignedly. As yet, so excel-

Relief delayed.

MR. B. WEIL, THE MAN WHO FED MAFEKING.

lent had been the care and economy of supplies, the whites were not hard-pressed for food—though of course it goes without saying that they did not live in plenty. The natives, however, were beginning to suffer, and to suffer severely. The greatest difficulty which confronted the Commissariat officer, Captain Ryan, was the maintenance of the bread ration, as there was a scarcity of corn and flour. At first a pound and then a quarter of a pound of biscuit was allowed the garrison, and this biscuit, largely made of oats crushed with the husks, was so indigestible that it caused epidemics of dysentery. In addition to biscuit, there was a ration of from a pound to three-quarters of a pound of "scraggy" meat. All luxuries here, as at Ladysmith, rose rapidly in value, and by the end of January whisky was 18s. a bottle, and the coarse Cape brandy, usually obtainable at 1s. 4d. a bottle, fetched from 12s. to 16s. Supplementing the Government stores, which were by no means large, were enormous quantities of food in the warehouses of the well-known South African firm of contractors, Julius Weil & Co. It was thanks to the Weils that the town was able to hold out as it did till the middle of May.

Food supply.

In early February the British lines were pushed out to the south-east so far that it was possible to get a firm hold of the Brickfields, whence, earlier in the siege, the Boer "snipers" had caused much trouble. The British outposts were now only 110 yards away from the nearest Boer works; so close indeed were the two enemies that the men lining the trenches on each side were able to exchange derisive remarks. The work in these advanced positions was extremely hazardous. The Boers had

British lines pushed out.

[*Photo by John E. Shaw, Huddersfield.*

MR. FRANK WHITELEY,
Mayor of Mafeking during the siege.

many excellent marksmen always ready to fire, who could be trusted to put their shots into the British loop-holes. "If so much as a finger be shown above the top of the sandbags," says Mr. Angus

Hamilton, *The Times* correspondent, "there is every likelihood of its being perforated by a Mauser bullet. . . . There is one man who seems to put the bullets precisely where he wishes, since at least once during the day he will test the accuracy of his aim by emptying his entire chamber through the port-holes." But if the Boers had good marksmen, the British also had good shots, and the enemy got back as much as they gave. In this warfare Corporal Currie particularly distinguished himself, repeatedly bringing down the enemy's sharp-shooters.

The design for this note was made by Colonel Baden-Powell. "The Wolf" (or, more accurately, "The wolf that never sleeps") was the native name for the Colonel, and was applied by the white men to the little 4½-inch howitzer made by Major Panzera from a drain-pipe, and firing round cannon-balls, which appears in the centre of the design. The notes were reproduced photographically by the ferro-prussiate process.

Through February the siege went wearily on, without any exciting incident, though the casualties from the bombardment mounted steadily, and on the 10th, Mr. Dall, a town councillor,

Sniping. while serving with the town guard, was struck by a projectile and blown to pieces. The sadness of this loss was increased by the fact that his wife was in the women's laager, distracted with grief and anxiety. On the last day of the month, the *Daily Mail*

The figures, supposed to represent a Boer and a Briton, are rough reproductions of drawings by Colonel Baden-Powell.

correspondent, Mr. Whales, had an extraordinary escape. He was talking to two men in his office when a 94-lb. shell fell in it, exploded, and wrecked the place, but without doing more injury to the human beings within than the infliction of a few slight scratches. On this day at last there came good news from the south—that Kimberley had been relieved and Cronje surrounded. Meantime, in the Brickfields, the war of "sniping," of sap and counter-sap, steadily proceeded. At the end of the month the enemy were within 80 yards of the foremost trench and were still drawing in. The British outposts at this point had to be strengthened. Then they, too, trenched forward, holding the vigorous aggressive the wisest policy. On March 2 the two foes were only 30 yards apart, and it seemed to the garrison that an assault could not be longer delayed. That night the enemy attempted to dislodge the garrison by flinging dynamite bombs into the British trench, but the bombs were a sad failure. The British, too, had bombs ready, but the range was too great for these simple projectiles, and they were not used. At dawn of the 3rd the big Creusot was turned on the British works, killing several Cape Boys and mortally wounding Serjeant-Major Taylor. The position rapidly became untenable, and, profiting by a lull in the bombardment, when the Boers at the most critical moment went to breakfast, as was their custom, the most advanced trench was abandoned. The mouth of the sap had to be banked up, as the enemy were now firing down it; and on the night of the 3rd the Boers seized the whole sap. They did not, however, keep it for long. On the 5th a party of Cape Boys, supported by Captain Fitzclarence and the Protectorate Regiment, plied them with dynamite bombs, when the Protectorates rushed the trench without loss or misadventure. The enemy fled precipitately, having

F. de Haenen.]   SERIO-COMIC WARFARE.   [*After a sketch by Major-General Baden-Powell.*

General Baden-Powell writes: "The advanced trench in the 'Brickfield' was garrisoned by the Colonial contingent. It was pushed out to within sixty yards of the Boer trench. Our men plied the enemy with grenades and bombs, which Sergeant Page threw with a fishing rod. The rifle shooting was so accurate at this close range that the ordinary sand-bag loopholes were no protection, and we used steel loopholes. The garrison also used a very well-made mechanical dummy to draw the enemy's fire." The "grenades and bombs" were made from fruit-tins.

apparently had quite as much as they wanted of meddling with the British works. Thenceforward the two sides watched each other and "sniped" each other. So deadly was the Boer fire that it was still most dangerous to show the head above the sandbags. Some amusing incidents took place in this quarter. On St. Patrick's Day a concertina was played in one of the British trenches, and the men behind the shelter of the earthwork sang and danced. The Boers became so curious to know the explanation of the noise, that at least a dozen of them put their heads over their works. The British sharpshooters were waiting, and at once fired, hitting two Boers. Then the enemy in their turn would shout: "Say, Englishmen, put up your heads and talk. Don't be afraid. We won't shoot you." But woe betide the man who listened to this assurance. If he showed himself he was as good as dead. The Cape Boys would put up bottles on the top of the works for the Boers to shoot at, and would jeer when the enemy shot wide or high. Sometimes the two sides took to

26*

exchanging a high-angle fire of stones and rocks. But, despite such diversions, the service was most dangerous. At such close quarters bullets would sometimes come clean through the sandbags and earth, while the Boer gunners constantly dropped shell and shrapnel among the trenches. It was the bravest men who fell here as elsewhere, because they would not take full advantage of shelter.

The pressure of the British forces in other fields of the war began to make itself felt in March at Mafeking, and the Boer commandos round the town were seen to be diminished in strength. But they were still stronger than the garrison, and they had the enormous advantage on their side of a powerful artillery, so that Colonel Baden-Powell could not hope to force them back. News, too, came through of the relief of Ladysmith and capture of Cronje, causing general exultation and producing an important moral effect upon the Baralongs, who were showing some restiveness. As the Boers

Cattle Raiding. had carried off the Baralong cattle and shot Baralong women, this tribe retaliated with effect, stealing out of the town, attacking the Boer outposts, and raiding the Boer cattle. The animals they carried off were driven back into Mafeking, and, when they were not consumed by the Kaffirs themselves, were sold at a high price to the British authorities, so that the business

THE MAFEKING MINT.
Mr. Ross manufacturing £1 notes.

was profitable to the natives and satisfactory to the garrison, whose supplies were thus augmented.

On March 24 the Boers, weakened by the withdrawal of detachments

Capture of the Brickfields. to other fields of the war, abandoned the Brickfields. They were, however, good enough to leave behind them a great quantity of dynamite, which they had carefully connected by wire with their lines, intending, when the British

WHERE MAFEKING DID ITS BANKING BUSINESS.
The photograph shows also some of the effects of shell-fire on the buildings in the town.

occupied their evacuated works, to send the "rooineks" sky high. But their elaborate preparations were foiled by Major Panzera, who quietly cut the wires. The final capture of the Brickfields was a source of great relief to all in Mafeking. The outposts in that quarter had gone for weeks in hourly fear of attacks, and the "sniping" fire from the Boer trenches had rendered it unsafe to walk the streets of the town by day. About the same date the bombardment was visibly relaxed after a heavy shelling from dawn to dusk, in the course of which no less than 79 big Creusot shells and at least 200 smaller projectiles were fired into the centre of the town. The big gun now remained silent, except when it was deliberately provoked by the projectiles of the British artillery. The members of the garrison could ride or walk on the veldt near Mafeking, unmolested by shell or bullet. In short, the enemy were losing heart and energy, though they still held stubbornly to their investment. But for the scarcity of food, and the utter dearth of news, life would have been by no means intolerable. The supplies, however, were beginning to run low, and the Kaffir refugees,

KAFFIRS SHOOTING DOGS FOR FOOD.

Dearth of food. who had not, like the Baralongs, cattle and farms of their own near or in Mafeking, suffered cruelly. "Hundreds," says Mr. Neilly, " died of starvation . . . many were found dead. When the Colonel got to know of the state of affairs he instituted soup kitchens, where horses were boiled in huge cauldrons, and the savoury mess doled out in pints and quarts to all comers." These wretched people, in their desperate hunger, stole any food upon which they could lay their hands, though the penalty of this was death, and it was a penalty that for military reasons had to be sternly visited upon offenders. When ownerless dogs were killed, the Kaffirs would go to the veldt, where the bodies were buried, and dig them up. There was no remedy for their misery. Even for the fighting men the rations now barely sufficed to maintain life. " We got," says Mr. Neilly, " four ounces of the most abominable kind of chupatty, plentifully mixed with chaff, a little horse, mule, or donkey meat, and black coffee without sugar."

Attempts were made to induce the natives to creep through the enemy's lines, but without much success, though, with a little courage and energy on their part, the Kaffirs should have had no **Escape of Kaffirs.** difficulty in eluding the Boers. Many native women did, however, get away. On April 15 a party of thirteen tried to run the blockade. The night was a bright one; they were seen by the Boers, and were at once fired upon, when seven were killed and others wounded. Several more native women on another occasion were seized by the enemy, sjamboked

NATIVES WAITING FOR THEIR RATIONS OF HORSE-MEAT SOUP.

The announcement of the relief of Mafeking was made somewhat unconventionally by an excited footman at the Mansion House at 9.35 p.m. of May 18th. In an instant the news for Baden-Powell, Roberts, and all the generals they could think of. The scenes in the West End were

PICCADILLY CIRCUS.

as all over the crowded space in front of the building, and as if by magic scores of Union-Jacks made their appearance, whilst the crowd sang "God Save the Queen" and cheered
qually exciting; not even on Ladysmith day had the sombre metropolis witnessed such rejoicings.

THE MUSTERING OF PLUMER'S VOLUNTEERS AT BULUWAYO.
Colonel Nicholson reading instructions to the men. The mounted troopers in front
belong to the British South Africa Company's force.

within an inch of their lives, and driven back into the town. These cruel measures did not prevent further attempts at escape, and between April 10 and 26 803 Kaffirs passed through the Boer lines.

Meantime, Colonel Plumer was not inactive to the north. Leaving Gaberones, he had pushed south to Lobatsi in March, but, finding his force much too weak to attack the Boers with success, was compelled to fall back. At the end of the month he once more advanced, and on March 31 runners entered Mafeking with the important news that he was outside the town, and would attempt to fight his way through. All was excitement within and without. Within, the garrison stood to arms, and attacked the Boers in the direction of Game Tree Fort. Without, large bodies of the enemy with guns could be seen moving northwards. As men watched anxiously from Mafeking, they saw through their glasses figures on the hill crests, ten miles away to the north, and were aware that for the first time since the siege began a British force was watching the town. Then the roll of firing swelled up in that quarter, and the battle began. The afternoon ended, and men felt certain that Plumer had won, and would march in under cover of darkness. But the night passed, and with day came a sad awakening. A flag of truce from General Snyman entered the lines with a message that Plumer had been thoroughly beaten, and that the British dead strewed the field. The Boer general gave the garrison permission to recover and bury these dead.

Plumer's repulse.

Ambulance waggons went out on this melancholy errand, and returned. But the disaster was not so black as the Boers had painted it. Only three bodies were found on the scene of action, though the enemy had buried a few others. The three dead were

Casualties.

THE LOCUST

which Europeans were compelled by hunger to eat during the siege of Mafeking. The locusts arrive in vast clouds, darkening the sky, and quickly eat up anything green which lies in their path. The natives esteem them a delicacy and eat them raw, merely removing the wings. The eggs are made into soup.

tenderly borne into the town which they had come so far to save. They had been stripped of their belongings; there was no means of identification; and though all who had travelled and fought in Rhodesia were called in to name them, none knew them. Unknown, they were laid to rest by unknown friends. Two days later a despatch from Colonel Plumer, with a true account of the engagement, entered the town. It placed his loss at—Captain Crewe, mortally wounded; Lieutenant Milligan, the famous Yorkshire cricketer, and ten men killed; 29 officers and men, among them Plumer himself, wounded, and eight missing, among whom was Captain McLaren, severely wounded, a prisoner with the Boers. On April 4, Lieutenant Smitheman, Plumer's intelligence officer, succeeded in getting into the town, and, after some days' stay, returned, having, it is to be presumed, concerted measures with Baden-Powell and informed him fully of the British plans.

Daily now the outlook became blacker. Men who knew the Boers and the difficulty of the country to the south questioned the possibility of relief. The food ration was steadily reduced. Horseflesh and black bread, of the consistency of papier maché, were the miserable diet of all, and the whites, in the pangs of hunger, took to eating locusts, food from which in

[Photo by Bassano.

BRIGADIER-GENERAL HERBERT C. O. PLUMER

Was born at Torquay in 1857, educated at Eton, and joined the 65th Foot (now the 1st Battalion York and Lancaster Regiment) in 1876; Captain, 1882; Major, 1893; Brevet Lieut.-Colonel, 1897; Local Brigadier-General on the Staff, July, 1900; served in the Sudan Expedition of 1884, under Sir Gerald Graham, as Adjutant of his Regiment; served in the operations in South Africa under Sir F. Carrington in 1896, when he organised, raised, and commanded a Corps of Mounted Rifles (Brevet of Lieut.-Colonel). He embodied his experiences in this campaign in "With an Irregular Corps in Matabeleland." D.A.A.G. at Jersey, 1890–3; D.A.A.G. at Aldershot, 1897–9. When the present war broke out he was put in command of the Rhodesian Irregular Forces to protect the border to the north of the Transvaal, fixing his camp first at Tuli, then at Gaberones.

[Photo by E. J. Ross.

LADY SARAH WILSON AND HER "DUG-OUT."

This adventurous lady, who represented the *Daily Mail* in the beleaguered town, is the wife of Captain Gordon C. Wilson, and daughter of the seventh Duke of Marlborough. At the beginning of the siege she left Mafeking and rode to Setlagoli, and afterwards went to Mosuti and Vryburg, arranging for the running of despatches to and from Mafeking. She endeavoured to get back into the town, but the Boers refused to give her up except in exchange for Viljoen, a notorious horse-thief. It was one of her silk dresses, "commandeered" by General Cronje, which graced the arm of Mrs. Cronje as she stepped into the train for Capetown on the way to St. Helena.

ordinary times they would recoil with disgust. Milk was scarce, and the women and children suffered sorely for want of it, while in the hospital drugs and medical stores were running low. Yet still the spirit of all was splendid. "They shall take a cemetery and not a town," was a typical message. Mafeking would uphold the honour of the Empire to the last, and, if it fell, abandoned and unrelieved, would at least fall with glory. On the 200th day of the siege, Colonel Baden-Powell sent out the following telegram to Lord Roberts:

Messages to and from Lord Roberts.

"After 200 days' siege I desire to bring to your Lordship's notice the exceptionally good spirit of loyalty that pervades all classes of the garrison. The patience of everybody in Mafeking in making the best of things under the long strain of anxiety, hardships, and privation, is beyond all praise, and is a revelation to me. The men, half of whom are unaccustomed to the use of arms, have adapted themselves to their duties with the greatest zeal, readiness, and pluck, and the devotion of the women is remarkable. With such a spirit our organisation runs like clockwork, and I have every hope that it will pull us successfully through."

MAJOR GODLEY'S LOOK-OUT AT THE WESTERN OUTPOST.
Major God'ey sits at the corner of the platform and is using an opera-glass.

On April 18 Lord Roberts had sent a despatch promising relief by May 18. The next few weeks passed monotonously. Early in May, Lady Sarah Wilson telegraphed: "Breakfast consists of horse sausages; lunch, minced mule and curried locusts." Another inhabitant of the town sent out the message: "All well; hungry." From the Boer lines, Eloff, Mr. Kruger's grandson, and one of the best and most daring Boer officers, forwarded taunts, to which Colonel Baden-Powell, who was much more than his match in humour, replied with derisive irony. Rumours were current that the Boers, hearing of the advance of a relief force, would assault the town, and after events proved that such was indeed their intention. Eloff had been sent from Pretoria with express orders to achieve this object, for in the tottering state of the Boer fortunes it was felt by the Transvaal Government that a success must be won to infuse fresh spirit into the burghers. Mafeking appeared to offer an easy opportunity of achieving such a success.

The night of May 11–12 was selected by Eloff for his enterprise. The earlier hours of the night were lighted by a brilliant moon, and everything was still as death, both in Mafeking and the Boer lines. Suddenly, without any preliminary notice, at 3.50 a.m., a terrific fire broke over the town from the Boer lines to the east. The alarm bell beat its heavy note; the bugles sounded to fall in; and from all quarters there was a scurry of hastily aroused bandoliered men to their posts. As yet the true direction of the attack could not be determined. The edge of the moon was sinking below the horizon, and darkness, intense and profound, wrapped the interval between the British and Boer lines. Yet the quick foresight of Baden-Powell had already divined the enemy's intentions. The attack, he

COLONEL HORE'S FORT, CAPTURED BY ELOFF.
The British South Africa Police Fort, held and then surrendered by Colonel Hore, and re-surrendered to him by Eloff. is the low building on the left.

said, would be delivered against the Kaffir stad on the west of the town, and he made his preparations accordingly.

More than an hour passed. The first rays of the sun showed to the east, when to the west tongues of flame leaped to the sky, and in a moment it was seen that the Kaffir stad was ablaze.

Immense volumes of smoke rolled towards the defenders, who were now hurrying to this quarter, and in a few minutes the stad was one roaring

Attack on the Kaffir stad.

sheet of flame. Heavy firing broke out; there was a babel of cries and shouts; and in the glare and smoke figures could be seen moving to and fro. Here was the real attack; the firing to the east was only a feint to draw off the attention of the British garrison. The Boers, with seven hundred men, had stolen up the bed of the Molopo. The Baralongs, who were entrusted with the defence of their own town, had seen and allowed about three hundred men to pass. But then they had opened a terrific fire and driven back the other four hundred. The situation was at this moment that there were 300 Boers under Eloff within the Mafeking defences.

A little to the rear of the native town stood the British South Africa Police Fort, a low, one-storied stone building, held by Colonel Hore and 22 men. Round it were several outbuildings which gave shelter

COLONEL HORE AND HIS ADJUTANT, CAPTAIN MUNDELL, B.S.A.P.

PAPER CURRENCY PRINTED AND USED IN MAFEKING.

to an assailant and interfered with the fire of the defence, so that the position was not a strong one. Towards it Eloff now rushed at the head of his men. In the obscurity his burghers were taken for the British outposts in retreat, and the troopers in the fort were ordered to hold their fire. Not till the enemy were only sixty yards away and in possession of the outbuildings in front and flank was the mistake discovered. Then it was too late. Guided by a treacherous deserter from the Protectorate Regiment, Trooper Hays, the Boers closed in upon the work, and Eloff demanded its immediate and unconditional surrender, threatening that if this were refused, every man in it should be put to death. The triumphant cheering of the enemy could be heard on every side; Colonel Hore was cut off from all hope of support; withdrawal was impossible; to hold the fort was equally impossible under the fire which could be poured into it from such close quarters. Assuredly there was no want of courage on the part of Hore and his men of the Protectorate Regiment; they had proved that in the magnificent

Colonel Hore surrenders.

attack upon Game Tree Fort. At 5.25 he surrendered. But of his men there was one who would on no terms accept life from the Boers. Trooper Maltuschek, when the enemy called upon him to throw down his rifle, replied: "I'll see you damned first," and in an instant fell with five shots through him—a victim to that defiant spirit of valour which disdains death.

The Boers now manned the fort and shouted exultantly through the telephone to headquarters:

MAFEKING SIEGE STAMP.
Made in the town.

"We are Boers. We have taken Mafeking." "Have you, indeed?" was the answer of the orderly, with the aside, "Please disconnect the wire." But Mafeking had not yet fallen—had not nearly fallen. Three hundred yards to the rear of the fort was a corrugated iron fence, enclosing the railway yard and the gaol. The

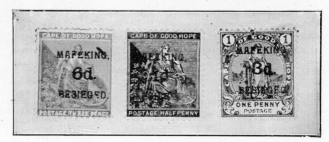

CAPE OF GOOD HOPE POSTAGE STAMPS.
Surcharged "Mafeking Besieged."

prisoners in the gaol had already been set free and armed by the jailor, Heald, who, a minute or two later, was blown to pieces by a shell; they played an honourable part at this critical moment, fighting the enemy as zealously as any of the garrison. Behind the corrugated fence, and on either flank of the British South Africa Police Fort, the garrison was forming up. The Town Guard, Railway Division, and the Bechuanaland Rifles,

A STREET TRAVERSE IN MAFEKING,
Showing a corrugated iron barricade similar to that which held Eloff in check.

took post at the fence; the Cape Police came in hot haste from the Brickfields; the British South Africa Police hurried up from Cannon Kopje; and when the confusion had abated, and what had happened had been clearly ascertained, opened a heavy fire on the fort. The Boers found that further advance was quite out of the question. They had already split up into two parties, the one in the fort and the other in the Kaffir

The Boer advance checked.

stad. Communication between the two was difficult, as a stream of bullets swept the intervening space; retreat was yet more difficult, as the Baralongs had closed up in the rear. Snyman, who should have put in every available man to a general assault, hated Eloff, while the burghers had no appetite for a desperate advance in daylight against enemies of the calibre encountered at Game Tree Fort.

MAKING GUNPOWDER IN MAFEKING.
The garrison and townspeople of Mafeking exhibited ingenuity and versatility scarcely inferior to that of Colonel Baden-Powell himself. They made their own powder, their own shells, even in one case their own cannon; they established a mint with currency of its own, printed their own postage stamps, and ran their own theatre, with the Colonel himself as a leading "star."

"THE WOLF"; THE LITTLE HOWITZER MADE IN MAFEKING.
(See note to illustration on p. 612.)

Thus Eloff was actually in a trap. The fire directed upon the fort prevented the Boers from showing themselves, and caused them considerable loss. Nor was the position of the British prisoners an enviable one. The deserter Hays stole Colonel Hore's watch,

Eloff trapped.

and wished to place the captives on the roof, or to make them stand in the verandah by way of checking the British fire. Finally, at Eloff's order, they were confined in an evil-smelling storehouse, where, in spite of the heavy patter of the bullets, they were tolerably safe. But they suffered much from want of water, as the tanks, early in the day, were perforated by the British bullets, and they were in constant fear of shells from the British guns. Eloff chatted with them from time to time, in the lulls of the fighting, expressing bitter anger against the cowards who had failed to support him. He could not have held out many minutes had it not been known to Colonel Baden-Powell that he had prisoners with him, which led the British artillery to refrain from firing. Had it been otherwise, the 7-pounders and Hotchkiss would speedily have knocked the fort to bits.

As the morning went on, the Cape Police and Protectorate Regiment forced the Boers in the stad back from point to point, and at last drove them into a cattle enclosure, where they were

[*Photo by E. J. Ross.*

ON TRIAL FOR HIS LIFE.

The photograph represents the Court of Summary Jurisdiction in Mafeking at which a native was tried before Lord Edward Cecil (with black band on arm, and whose face is a study of utter absorption in the question of the moment) and Mr G. H. Bell (resident magistrate) for stealing a goat. The reason why extreme measures had to be taken in such cases has already been mentioned (p. 615). In this case the thief was sentenced to death, and the warrant for his execution, duly certified as carried out, appears on the next page. The man standing on the right of the photograph is Heald, the jailor, who was killed in the fight with Eloff. On the left, in front of the bare-headed prisoner, stands the attorney. J. W. de Kock; and Melemo, the Baralong Chief, in the centre of the picture, is watching the case with anxious interest.

shelled by one of the 7-pounders. A bayonet charge was made, and 25 prisoners were taken. The remnant of the Boers in this quarter was closely hemmed in, but they fought on till dusk, and the British were too weak from want of food—most of the men had had nothing all day—and too weary with fighting to effect their capture. They were allowed to run the gauntlet of the British fire, which they did, escaping one by one. Several were killed or wounded; others were dealt with by the Baralongs; those who finally got away were in no temper for further assaults.

It still remained to deal with Eloff and his party. A Frenchman with the Boers got on the roof of the fort with a bottle of Burgundy and proceeded to drink to the toast, "Fashoda is avenged." The vengeance was not very satisfactory or long-lived, since he was speedily tumbled down by one of the British marksmen. As the fire grew hotter and hotter, bullets began to come through the walls, to perforate the windows, and to splinter the door. On all sides the party was hemmed in by a ring of fire. Night was falling and the only light was the flash of the rifles. The Boers were losing heart, and it was all that Eloff could do to persuade them to protract their resistance. They saw themselves abandoned by their friends and surrounded by their foes, without water, and with every prospect of ammunition speedily failing. A hundred or more attempted to bolt, and probably Hays, the deserter, was among these, since he knew that there was a price of £50 upon his head. But when Eloff detected them slinking away he ordered his men to shoot them down. Bullets came at them from before and behind, and it is not likely that many of them escaped. Whether or no Hays was slain in this wholly appropriate manner, history does not relate. The Baralongs are thought to have accounted for a number, whose bodies were never found, and of whose fate the natives said nothing, wishing to keep the white men's rifles as their spoil.

At about 8 p.m. Eloff saw that his plight was hopeless. He gave orders to

Surrenders to Colonel Hore.

cease firing, and then, calling upon Colonel Hore, promised to surrender if the Colonel would induce the

DEATH WARRANT AND CERTIFICATE OF EXECUTION.

rest of the British garrison to stop their persistent fusillade. For a moment the prisoners feared treachery, and, seeing their anxiety and hesitation, Eloff offered himself as a hostage. On this, Colonel Hore and his twenty-two comrades shouted to the British troops to cease fire, disarmed their late captors, and mounted guard upon them. As soon as the result was known, there came a burst of triumphant cheering, and, to relieve their long pent-up feelings, men, women, and children shouted " God Save the Queen." Mafeking had delivered itself from the enemy's hands, and had crowned its seven months' defence by inflicting a terrible blow upon the Boers.

EXAMINING HORSE-MEAT INTENDED FOR RATIONS.

With Eloff 67 men surrendered, making the tale of prisoners captured in that long day's fight 110. Of these 19 were wounded, and, in addition, ten dead Boers were found. The British casualties were only four killed and seven wounded. When the prisoners were marched through the town, they were treated with all the respect that brave men deserve. The natives, indeed, jeered at them, but the British preserved an honourable silence and saluted them as they passed. All night, "Rule Britannia," and "God Save the Queen," echoed round the lines, and men in their joy shook each other by the hand with the words "This is a great day for England."

The attack was well and bravely made; splendidly repulsed. Had Eloff been properly supported, it is at least probable that he would have taken the town, though only at the cost of terrible sacrifice of life. The garrison, under such a leader as Baden-Powell, would have **Snyman's inaction.** fought to the last; though the outer line of defence had been penetrated, the inner line yet remained, and could have been held by determined men. But General Snyman behaved badly, even treacherously, to his subordinate. He watched Eloff fighting for life without lending a helping hand, and by this extraordinary inaction at once ruined the Boer chances and covered himself with discredit. The best men with Eloff were not Boers, but French and German mercenaries, who expressed the utmost contempt for those whose cause they had espoused.

The day after the assault the approach of the relief force from the south was known to all, and no one could do anything but speculate when the column would arrive. Great activity was observed in the Boer laagers, and commandos were seen moving to the west. On the **Relief at hand.** 15th news came in that Plumer and Mahon had formed their junction, but that the Boers were prepared to offer determined opposition to their entry into the town. On the 16th,

H. M. Paget.]   [*From materials supplied by Major Baillie, correspondent of the "Morning Post."*

ELOFF'S ATTACK ON MAFEKING: B.S.A. POLICE ESCORTING BOER PRISONERS TO THE LOCK-UP.

Some of Lord Edward Cecil's Cadet Corps boy orderlies, who played a prominent part in the siege, are seen on the right of the picture. They ranged from nine years old to fifteen or sixteen, used donkeys and bicycles, and became quite expert in dodging shells.

the flash of the guns and the roar of firing showed that they were hotly engaged. A sally to the west was made by the Protectorate Regiment and Bechuanaland Rifles, but evening came on before they could get into touch with the relief force, and they were ordered to retire. At 7 p.m. Major Karri Davis, with seven of the Light Horse, suddenly entered the Market Place. What followed has already been told. The town went wild with joy. But the exultation was even greater next day when the garrison and relief force paraded together, before their start out to harry General Snyman. "I did not think it was possible for human joy to reach such a white-hot pitch," says Mr. Neilly, an eye-witness.

Major B. F. S. Baden-Powell,
1st Batt., Scots Guards.
Miss D. S. Baden-Powell,
the only sister.
Mr. Frank Baden-Powell,
Painter and Sculptor.
Colonel R. S. S. Baden-Powell,
the hero of Mafeking.

The late Sir George Baden-Powell, M.P.
Mrs. Baden-Powell
and one of her grand-children.
Mr. Warrington Baden-Powell,
Q.C., Admiralty Court.

THE BADEN-POWELL FAMILY

About 9 a.m. of the 17th the force moved out towards the chief Boer laager. The artillery, no longer the miserable short-range 7-pounders, but the Horse Artillery 12-pounders, Canadian quick-firers, and "Pom-Poms," got to work to shell the hostile camp, with results that were astonishing. The Boers swarmed out like ants, and hurriedly retired. There was a wild stampede of horses and waggons over the veldt. A 5-pounder gun remained to cover the retreat, but its gunners waited too long, were charged by the British, and had to abandon their weapon. From the laager the relief force made the circuit of the enemy's lines and looted the abandoned camps, in which pots and kettles with soup still boiling served at once as seasonable refreshment to the British troops and as full evidence of the hurried nature of the Boer retreat. At midday the force returned to Mafeking, and passed in review before Colonel

The Boers driven away.

Baden-Powell. First marched the clinking and rattling Horse Artillery; then the various mounted bodies; then again the men of Barton's Brigade, who had, three months before, known such another day, when they cleared the way into Ladysmith; here,

Review of the troops. too, they were received with the wildest enthusiasm; last came Plumer's valiant Rhodesians. "It was," says Mr. Neilly, "a sight that will ever be remembered by those who saw it—this going past—the wild joy on the hunger-stricken faces of the recently beleaguered ones, the tears that flowed unbidden from the eyes of dozens of those who spent the time in alternately cheering and choking down sobs. More than one woman—and man too— turned away from the crowd for a moment or two to wipe their

MISS CRAUFURD.   MRS. BUCHAN.

These two ladies, under Boer escort, carried food and medical supplies to the captive officers in Colonel Hore's fort, under heavy fire from both friends and foes.

eyes, or to go where nobody was to gather up composure. It was evident enough that the gallant 'B.-P.' himself was not unmoved. There were visible signs of the emotion that was within him as he sat on his horse and witnessed the wild outbursts of the people he had worked so well to protect. His eyes, too, were within an ace of overflowing."

Of the garrison, 273 were killed, wounded, or captured, in the siege—the killed numbering 69. The

Losses during the siege. losses from disease were also considerable. In the hour of victory a solemn memorial service was held over the dead who had so valiantly given their lives; with bared heads the lines of soldiery stood around the graves of the heroes of Game Tree Fort, of Cannon Kopje, and countless other fights, and paid them

A PAGE FROM BADEN-POWELL'S SKETCH-BOOK.

the last honours. One by one the glorious roll of names was passed in review; three volleys were fired, and the "last post" sounded. Hearts were full, and the ceremony was not unduly protracted. But the cemetery of Mafeking, where sleep these dead, will, in years to come, be a place of pilgrimage for men of British blood.

Thus ended the siege—the most memorable and heroic episode in the chequered

THE CONVENT, MAFEKING,

Showing the damage wrought by Boer shells on a building known by them to be in use as a hospital. Two of the sisters who acted as nurses were received and complimented by the Queen at Windsor, in December, 1900.

story of the South African War. Assailed at first by 8,000 Boers, and then by 3,000 to 4,000, pounded by 1,498 94-pounder shells and 21,000 projectiles of smaller calibre, for seven months cut off from the world, Mafeking had held its own and kept the flag flying, with a force which at the relief did not muster a thousand rifles. For this, infinite credit is due to the soldiers who fought so finely under Colonel Baden-Powell, and to Baden-Powell himself. The insight of the British race has already recognised the greatness of his work, and it is needless to expatiate upon his achievements. He

F. J. Waugh.|

"WHAT'S NEAREST THE EYE IS HARDEST TO SEE."
Native woman escaping through the Boer lines.

Baden-Powell's work and its reward. combined, with the most resolute courage and determination, a reticence, a sagacity, an alertness, an insight into the enemy's plans, which are the marks of the great general. His tact and cheerfulness were not less conspicuous than his untiring energy. He had no troubles or disputes with the civil population, or with the mettlesome volunteers and irregulars whom he commanded. He was the very man for the work to be done, and without him it is doubtful if the work could or would have been done. Deservedly, he was promoted Major-General the moment news of the relief reached England.

The British nation had watched the later stages of the defence of Mafeking with singular emotion. This spectacle of a handful of men, hundreds of miles away from the outposts of our army, on the confines of the enemy's territory, holding its ground undismayed through good and evil report, confronting starvation, and beating off

the assaults of the foe, had touched all hearts. And so it was natural that when the good news of the relief came in, the Empire should explode with joy. The occasion was no ordinary one, and the very unanimity and fervour of the exultation were evidence to Britain's enemies that the heart of our race was in the war.

THE NORDENFELDT IN THE EXTREME OUTPOST TRENCH.

J. Finnemore, R.I., R.B.A.]

BULLER AWARDING V.C.'s.

At Ladysmith, on March 18, at a special parade held for the purpose, General Buller presented Victoria Crosses to Captain Reed and Corporal Nurse, who attempted to save the guns at Colenso on December 15, 1899. See the account of their action on page 99.

(629)

27

FAMILY OF LOYAL BOERS SEEKING PROTECTION WITHIN THE BRITISH LINES.

The photograph depicts some of the domestic miseries which war brings in its train. These loyal people have been driven from their home by fear of vengeance. They are conducting their morning toilet in the open; the woman on the left is inspecting the result in a small hand-mirror. In the centre, by the sewing-machine, a mother is dressing a baby who lies sprawling on the ground, whilst another little one sits by and plays with the household goods. Pots, pans, beds, and clothing lie in confusion around.

CHAPTER XXVII.

BLOEMFONTEIN TO PRETORIA.

Reorganisation of the Army—Disposition of component forces—Progress of the wings north and east—Main Army reaches Zand River—Kroonstad occupied—A halt necessary—Safeguarding the line of communication—Buller's progress through Natal—Expediency of rapid advance on Johannesburg—Hamilton reaches Heilbron—Roberts crosses Rhenoster and Vaal Rivers—Attack on Klipriversberg—Seizure of Elandsfontein Junction—Surrender of Johannesburg—Pretoria in terror—Rapid advance—Louis Botha counsels resistance—Capture of Pretoria forts—Fall of the town—French's movements to the west and north—Entry into Pretoria—Treatment of British prisoners—Condition of the Field Hospitals—Lord Roberts' great march.

BEFORE the advance upon Pretoria was resumed, Lord Roberts completed the necessary work of reorganising his army. The troops pouring into South Africa had to be formed into new divisions and brigades, and redistributed for the advance. General Hart's Brigade, when Wepener was relieved, was directed upon Kimberley, where it met Barton's Brigade, and composed with it the new Tenth Division under General Hunter. This division, with the Imperial Light Horse, had been moved round by sea from Natal. In the Kimberley district there was also at this time Lord Methuen's First Division, made up of the 9th (Douglas's) Brigade, which had fought so well at Enslin and Modder River, and the new 20th (Paget's) Brigade, with four batteries and four battalions of Imperial Yeomanry.

Reorganisation of the Army.

Garrisoning Bloemfontein and the places near was Kelly-Kenny's Sixth Division, which had suffered so severely in the fighting of February and March. South of Bloemfontein was disposed Chermside's Third Division, consisting of the 22nd (Allen's) Brigade—the battalions of which were the 2nd Royal Irish Rifles, 2nd Berkshires, 2nd Northumberland

Disposition of component forces.

BREAKFAST ON THE VELDT.

Fusiliers, and 1st Royal Scots—and of the 23rd (Knox's) Brigade of Militia. Available for offensive operations Lord Roberts had the following troops, all of which were actively engaged in the fighting of May and June :—

ARMY OF THE CENTRE.

SEVENTH DIVISION.
LIEUT.-GENERAL TUCKER.

14TH (MAXWELL'S) BRIGADE.
15TH (WAVELL'S) BRIGADE.
18th, 62nd, and 75th Field Batteries.

NINTH DIVISION.
LIEUT.-GENERAL COLVILE.

3RD (MACDONALD'S) BRIGADE.
5th Field Battery.

ELEVENTH DIVISION.
LIEUT.-GENERAL POLE-CAREW.

GUARDS (INIGO JONES') BRIGADE.
18TH (STEPHENSON'S) BRIGADE.
2nd Royal Warwick.   1st Yorkshire.
1st Essex.   1st Welsh.
And three Field Batteries.

CAVALRY DIVISION.
LIEUT.-GENERAL FRENCH.

1ST AND 3RD BRIGADES.
4TH BRIGADE.
7th Dragoon Guards.
8th Hussars.   17th Lancers.
And six Horse Batteries.

1ST MOUNTED INFANTRY (HUTTON'S) BRIGADE.
Four Howitzer Batteries.
Several Field Batteries.   Siege Guns.
5-in. Guns.   Naval Brigade.

ARMY OF THE RIGHT.
LIEUT.-GENERAL IAN HAMILTON.

19TH (SMITH-DORRIEN'S) BRIGADE.
21ST (BRUCE-HAMILTON'S) BRIGADE.
1st Derbyshires.   1st Cameron Highlanders.
1st Royal Sussex.   City Imperial Volunteers.
2ND (RIDLEY'S) MOUNTED INFANTRY BRIGADE.
2ND (BROADWOOD'S) CAVALRY BRIGADE.
And four Field and two Horse Batteries (74th, 76th, 81st, 82nd, P, Q),
two 5-in. guns, two "Pom-Poms."

[*Photo by Elliott & Fry.*

MAJOR-GENERAL ARTHUR FITZROY HART, C.B.,

Commanding the 5th Brigade, Tenth Division, South Africa Field Force, was born at Portsmouth in 1844, educated at Cheltenham and Sandhurst, and at twenty entered the Army as Ensign in the old 31st Foot (now the 1st East Surrey). In 1873 he accompanied Sir G. Wolseley to the Gold Coast on special service; trained and commanded the Sierra Leone Company of Russell's Regiment throughout the Ashantee War of 1873-4, including the capture of Coomassie; surveyed the Cape Coast, and the road from the Prah to Coomassie; Captain, 1874. In 1878 he was again on special service in South Africa, and served throughout the Zulu War, first as Staff Officer of the 2nd Regiment of the Natal Native Contingent, then as Staff Officer in the Ekowe Relief Column, then as Brigade-Major of the 2nd Brigade, First Division, and lastly as Principal Staff Officer of Clarke's Column. In the Boer War of 1881 he served under Sir Evelyn Wood as D.A.A. and Q.M.G.; next year he was on special service throughout the Egyptian War as D.A.A. and Q.M.G. in the Intelligence Department, taking part in the reconnaissance from Alexandria, the engagements of Kassassin and Tel-el-Kebir, receiving the Brevet of Lieut.-Colonel for his services; Colonel, 1886; made C.B. for military services in 1889. In 1891 he took command of a Battalion of the East Surrey Regiment and in 1897 became Commander-in-Chief of the 1st Infantry Brigade at Aldershot; Major-General, 1898. He served under General Buller at Colenso and Spion Kop, in the relief of Ladysmith, and afterwards in the operations under Lord Roberts. He edits "Hart's Army List."

ARMY OF THE SOUTH-WEST.

EIGHTH DIVISION.
LIEUT-GENERAL SIR L. RUNDLE.

16TH (CAMPBELL'S) BRIGADE.
2nd Grenadier Guards.
2nd Scots Guards.
2nd East Yorkshire.
1st Leinsters.

17TH (BOYES') BRIGADE.
1st Worcesters.
1st Royal West Kents.
1st South Staffords.
2nd Manchesters.
Three Field Batteries (2nd, 77th, and 79th).
A Brigade of Yeomanry.

COLONIAL DIVISION.
LIEUT.-GENERAL BRABANT.

1st Brabant's Horse.   2nd Brabant's Horse.
Cape Mounted Rifles.   Cape Police.
Kaffrarian Mounted Rifles.   Border Horse.
Frontier Mounted Rifles.   Driscoll's Scouts.
Queenstown Volunteers.

The effective total of these three armies which we have named, of the centre, right, and south-west, at this date probably did not exceed 45,000 combatants, with somewhere about 180 guns, howitzers, and weapons of position. Against these the Boers had not far short of 20,000 men—10,000 near Brandfort, and another 10,000 to the north of Thaba N'chu and on the Free State slope of the Natal passes. On each side the men were seasoned by war, hard and fit, for the most part veterans of many battles. Lord Methuen and General Hunter, who formed the army of the left, may have had 15,000 men, with not more than 3,000 Boers against them. In Natal General Buller disposed of three Divisions—the Second, under General Clery; the Fourth, under General Lyttelton, made up of the battalions which had garrisoned Ladysmith; and the Fifth, under General Hildyard, who had replaced Sir Charles Warren. There was also a cavalry division of three brigades, so that the effective total of men in Natal was about 25,000. Pitted against them were

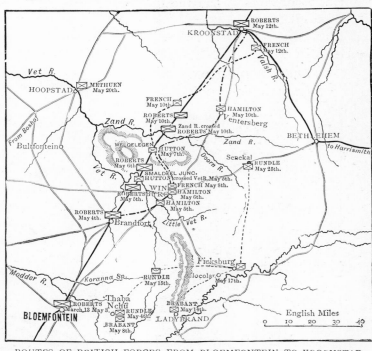

ROUTES OF BRITISH FORCES FROM BLOEMFONTEIN TO KROONSTAD.

5,000 Boers in the Biggarsberg. Preparing to act upon the northern frontier of the Transvaal was General Carrington, with a force of about 6,000 Canadians, Australians, and Yeomanry, who, under our treaty rights with the Portuguese Government, were disembarking at Beira and moving thence by rail to Marandellas, from which point they were to march southward and reinforce Colonel Plumer's 750 men to the north of Mafeking.

The capture of Thaba N'chu had to some extent cleared the right flank of the army. On May 1 the troops began to get into their positions for an advance. General Pole-Carew, with the

Progress of the wings north and east. Eleventh Division, fresh from the campaign in the south-east, marched out from Bloemfontein to the north along roads which the continual rains and the resultant mud had rendered nothing less than infernal. At Karee he took post on the left of General Tucker's Seventh Division, which had on the previous day pushed out some seven miles and reconnoitred the Boer lines south of Brandfort. The 21st (Bruce Hamilton's) Brigade, hitherto on Tucker's left, made a long march behind the army now in course of deployment, with the object of joining General Ian Hamilton on the right. General Colvile's weak division maintained touch between Tucker's left at Schanskraal and the army of the right. From east to west the British front covered a space of fifty miles, reaching from Karee to Thaba N'chu. The right, however, was still thrown considerably back, and it was not thought well to

GENERAL CARRINGTON AND STAFF AT MARANDELLAS.

strike at Brandfort till General Ian Hamilton had worked his way some distance to the north. General French was at Thaba N'chu with two brigades of cavalry; his orders, however, were to move to Bloemfontein, rest his horses, and then take post on the left of the main army.

On April 30 Ian Hamilton led his troops out from Thaba N'chu to Houtnek, and in spite of the enemy's long-range fire succeeded in seizing Thoba Mountain, a commanding height on the Boer left, from which his men delivered a flank attack on the hostile position. Here occurred one of the most dramatic fights of the campaign, Captain Towse, with 22 men of Kitchener's Horse and the Gordons, charging 150 of the Boer mercenaries and driving them back in utter confusion. Captain Towse unhappily lost the sight of both eyes, but his gallantry was so magnificent, so fruitful in tactical result, that for his conduct he was awarded the coveted Victoria Cross. All day the fight swayed to and fro. The British held Thoba fast, but though their losses were insignificant they could not advance; indeed, the enemy were probably much superior in force to General Ian Hamilton. Night fell upon an indecisive field; at dawn on May 1 the battle recommenced, and strong reinforcements began to reach the British commander.

[Photo by Winter, Derby.

CAPTAIN TOWSE, V.C.
1st Battalion Gordon Highlanders.

This officer has twice performed signal acts of gallantry. At Magersfontein, on December 11, 1899, he tried to rescue on his back the late Colonel Downman, who was mortally wounded, and, finding it impossible to carry him, remained with him in the firing line until assistance arrived. Captain Towse's second deed of valour, described in the text, resulted in his being invalided home, and in the bestowal on him of the V.C. by Her Majesty, who, it is said, shed tears when pinning on the decoration. Probably at her instance, the War Office has awarded a special wounds pension of £300 a year to Captain Towse. He had previously distinguished himself with the Chitral Relief Force in 1895, and in the campaign on the North-West Frontier of India in 1898. He has now been appointed Sergeant-at-Arms in Ordinary to Her Majesty.

The 21st Brigade was coming in upon the left, General French had detached cavalry from Thaba N'chu, and the ever-dashing, irresistible Canadians, supported by the Gordons and Shropshires, had pushed eastward from Thoba; while the cavalry turned the Boer right and threatened the enemy's rear. An assault was delivered in the most gallant style; the Boers bolted precipitately, and

FRIENDS FAITHFUL UNTO DEATH.

The incident here depicted took place at Karee Kloof, near Spytfontein, on April 30, and is one of many such acts of devotion recorded in connection with this war. Four friends, indigo planters of Behar, Crane (an officer), Firth (corporal), Daubeny, and Case, all of Lumsden's Horse, were holding a kopje in an exposed position, when the order to retreat reached them. Crane was shot in the head, and, when he recovered consciousness, saw that his three friends had remained behind with him. They tried to carry him back, but Daubeny was wounded, and they had to lay down their burden. Nevertheless they would not desert Crane, but in face of a terrific enfilading fire made a stubborn defence until Firth and Case were killed. Daubeny, though wounded, still continued to fire till he was too weak to do so any longer. He and Crane were picked up by the Boer ambulance.

at the cost of 100 British casualties the pass of Houtnek was won; the Boers certainly lost more heavily. After a day's halt, on May 3, Ian Hamilton encamped at Isabellafontein, only one long march from Winburg. On May 4 he pushed forward, skirmishing continually, and General Broadwood, with the cavalry, succeeded in preventing a junction between the Boer eastern force and a second force retreating from Brandfort. On the 5th Winburg surrendered to the column, in spite of the passionate remonstrances of Philip Botha, brother of the Boer commandant-general, who happened to be in the town when the British officers sent to demand its submission arrived. For a moment it appeared that the officers would be shot down, in spite of the flag of truce, but happily counsels of prudence prevailed; Botha fled, and Winburg hoisted the Union Jack.

DESTRUCTION OF THE VET RIVER BRIDGE BY THE BOERS.

Meantime, Lord Roberts had not been idle. On May 3 the Army of the Centre pushed rapidly forward, and without encountering any serious opposition occupied Brandfort. Next day the infantry rested, but the mounted men rode on to Eensgevonden, the next station on the line, and reconnoitred. On the 5th the whole army marched to the Vet River, where was a strong position which the Boers were expected to hold. In face of a desultory fire the mounted infantry seized a drift close to the railway, and another drift further to the left. The Boers, it proved, were only fighting a rearguard action, and on the 6th, without anything like a battle, Smaldeel was entered by our troops. Here two days' halt was made to allow of the repair of the railway, the bridges on which had been destroyed by the Boers, and to give time for General French to come up with his cavalry and take post on the extreme left. The mounted infantry on the 7th, however, rode out as far as the Zand River, and had a fierce little skirmish with the Boers, in which the West Australians distinguished themselves.

At the Zand River was another strong series of positions, which it was understood the Boers would defend to the last. The dispositions for the attack were these: French on the left, advancing ten miles west of the railway, was to attempt to work round the enemy's right; Ian Hamilton, on the British right was similarly to turn the Boer left, marching from Winburg to Ventersburg; while in the centre the Seventh and Eleventh Divisions, considerably behind the two wings, maintained contact between them. Thus the advancing army might be likened to a crescent, the horns of which were turned towards the Boers with the object of enveloping them.

LORD ROBERTS AND HIS DAUGHTERS WATCHING THE DEPARTURE OF TROOPS FROM BLOEMFONTEIN, May 3, 1900.

On May 9 the British Army of the Centre moved rapidly forward, and by night was close to the Zand. On the left General French succeeded in seizing and crossing Diamond Drift; on the right Ian Hamilton, after a day's skirmishing, was on the river to the south of **Main army reaches Zand River.** Ventersburg, but with the Boers in some force threatening his flank and rear. He, too, seized a drift on his front, and General Tucker did the same; thus at three points a crossing was secured. The enemy in front numbered about 10,000, with 25 guns, but when next day the British attacked all along the line, small resistance was offered. The Boers were once more fighting a rearguard action; their line was of such length and such tenuity that at no point could it withstand the rude assault of the British divisions. On the left General French, making a wide detour, endeavoured to strike and cut the railway to the rear of the Boer main force, but the country was so difficult, and the foe so expert in delaying tactics, that he failed. The 6th Dragoons were badly mauled by a body of Boers, who, from their khaki uniforms and the regularity

W. B. Wollen, R.I.] [*After a sketch by T. Baragwanath.*

CHARGE OF THE SUSSEX REGIMENT AND THE C.I.V.'s AT THE ZAND RIVER.
Advancing across the plain, under support of the 57th and 81st Batteries, at 500 yards they fixed bayonets, cheered, and charged the kopje.

of their movements, were taken for our own mounted infantry; a little later the 8th Hussars and 7th Dragoons charged a party of Boers with some success. In the centre, after a long preliminary bombardment to give time for the British wings to work round the enemy, the Eleventh and Seventh Divisions advanced, and found the Boers gone. On the right, Ian Hamilton had a harder task. Bruce-Hamilton, with the 21st Brigade, crossed the Zand about 6 a.m.; the Sussex Regiment and City Imperial Volunteers assaulted an eminence beyond and carried it with admirable dash; Broadwood, with the cavalry, hurried forward, to ride might and main for the railway, and cut it, when a mistaken order brought him back to the south-east, where Ian Hamilton's baggage was being threatened by the enemy in his rear. The danger passed, and before night Ventersburg had been occupied by the cavalry; but the delay prevented any serious interference with the Boer retreat. The road to Kroonstad—the second capital of the Free State—was opened at a cost of 250 casualties to the British. The Boers probably lost 400 men.

Pole-Carew, Tucker, and Ian Hamilton were to march direct upon Kroonstad, French to make a detour and come down upon it from the north-west. As the army marched north on the 11th great clouds of dust revealed its majestic progress. Geneva Siding was reached in the evening; here prisoners related that Mr. Steyn had been present at the Zand River skirmish, and had implored his men to fight, all to no purpose. Reconnaissances ascertained that a small Boer force was to the south of Kroonstad, but it was found to be so weak that it was clear no desperate resistance was contemplated by the enemy. That night French reached Valsch River Drift, eighteen miles north-west of Kroonstad, and discovered that the enemy were there. A small party, which included Burnham the scout and Major Hunter Weston, was sent through the Boer lines to break the railway north of Kroonstad, and with almost incredible coolness and daring effected its mission, but too late to cut off any rolling

Kroonstad occupied.

BOERS SURRENDER-
ING ARMS AT
VENTERSBURG.
Those behind the wall on
the right are prisoners.

stock. The party rejoined the British cavalry next day. At dawn of the 12th it was found that the Boers had retired, and at midday Lord Roberts entered Kroonstad at the head of the Guards, with Lord Kitchener at his side. There he passed in review the Eleventh Division, to the cheerful music of the Scots Guards' drums and fifes.

CAVALRY AT VENTER'S SPRUIT AWAITING, UNDER COVER, THE ORDER TO ADVANCE.

Thus Kroonstad had been reached in nine days from the beginning of the general advance. A halt was now necessary to repair the railway, allow of the concentration of stores and supplies, and to place the troops in position for the next move. The enemy had already split up into two distinct and separate bodies, as the British army by its rapid movements

A halt necessary.

Lord Roberts.   Lord Kitchener.

LORDS ROBERTS AND KITCHENER ENTERING KROONSTAD.

thrust itself between the Boer force retiring from Thaba N'chu and the commandos under Louis Botha which had fought on the Zand River. The former had gone east, the latter north. The force on the east threatened the British right flank and line of communications if the advance was continued northward in pursuit of Botha. How serious this threat was, we, in the wisdom which comes from after-knowledge, can see; indeed, the greatest mistake which Lord Roberts ever made was probably that of under-estimating the strength and capacity of this force to inflict damage. It was led by the two De Wets—Christian and Piet—of whom Piet offered to surrender with his commando if he were not sent to St. Helena, an offer which Lord Roberts judiciously refused to entertain—by Nel, Olivier, and Prinsloo. They knew the country perfectly, and were admirably supplied with information by burghers who had made their submission, but had not surrendered their hatred for the English. Though for the moment inactive, they only waited an opportunity to strike.

THE CIVIC AUTHORITIES OF KROONSTAD RETURNING UNDER AN ESCORT OF THE BRITISH AFTER DELIVERING UP THE KEYS TO LORD ROBERTS.

27*

PRESIDENT STEYN ORDERING HIS FLEEING BURGHERS TO RETURN TO THE FRONT.
This photograph shows Steyn in the act of stopping the retreat of some of his frightened burghers after the skirmish at Zand River. He threatened them with his sjambok (whip) and is even said to have used it with effect.

Meantime, behind the main British army, Generals Rundle, Brabant, and Colvile, had been advancing. General Colvile followed in Ian Hamilton's steps, a march behind; on May 10 Rundle moved out of Thaba N'chu with the "Brabanditti," as Brabant's men were nicknamed,

Safeguarding the line of communication. from their reported love for loot, to close the gap between Thaba N'chu and Basutoland. On the 13th he was at Brand's Drift; on the 18th he reached Trommel, an important road-junction between Winburg and Ficksburg, sweeping the country clear. Difficulties of transport—for his division was wretchedly equipped —delayed his march, inflicted terrible sufferings on his troops, and compelled him to live on the land. Here he formed the extreme right of the main army. The extreme left was formed by Lord Methuen's division at Boshof; this, on May 14, some 6,000 strong, began to move north-eastwards on Hoopstad, so as to close upon the main army. From Hoopstad it followed the Vaal River to Bothaville, whence it turned south-eastwards to Kroonstad, where it arrived on May 28. Its task was to safeguard the line of communication and deal with the Boer forces in the north-east of the Free State. General Hunter, with the Tenth Division, had earlier crossed the Vaal at Windsorton, defeated the Boers at Rooidam, and advanced to the small village of Christiana in the south-west Transvaal. Thus this gallant and capable officer was the first British general to enter Mr. Kruger's country from

COMMANDANT KOLBE AND COLONEL MAXIMOFF,
Who fought against us at Zand River.

G. D. Giles.]

WITH THE AUSTRALIAN TROOPS IN SOUTH AFRICA: RIDING FOR A FALL.

During the advance on Pretoria "a body of mounted Australians found their progress checked by a wire fence, which they were unable to get through, having no wire-cutters with them. One of their number, a steeplechase jockey, gallantly rode at the fence at the risk of his life, and burst through it, thus enabling his comrades to get through. Luckily, neither man nor horse was badly hurt."

[Photo by W. H. Gill, Viljoen's Drift.

THE TRANSVAAL BOERS RETREATING BEFORE ROBERTS ACROSS THE VAAL RIVER AT VILJOEN'S DRIFT.

It is said that very few Free Staters entered the Transvaal, preferring to remain and fight in their own land, especially as there was some friction between the burghers of the two States, the Transvaalers complaining that their brothers-in-arms had given up too quickly, while the Free Staters considered with justice that they had borne the brunt of the fighting. The Boers shown here were actually the last of the enemy to leave the Free State in any numbers.

the south. Co-ordinated with the general advance in the centre and west was a forward movement in Natal on General Buller's part. While the Fifth Division demonstrated in front of the Boer

Buller's progress through Natal.

lines on the Biggarsberg, and the Fourth garrisoned Ladysmith and watched the passes to the Free State, the Second Division, by a great detour to the east, turned the enemy's flank, and compelled the Boers to fall back. The strategy was brilliant, and resulted in the all but bloodless re-conquest of Northern Natal up to Laing's Nek. On May 15 Dundee was re-occupied; on the 18th Newcastle was gained; on the 19th the army of Natal halted before Majuba, in sight of the sad battlefields of nineteen years ago. One mishap, however, occurred during this advance. Bethune's Mounted Infantry, who were covering the extreme right of General Buller's advance, were on the march from Nqutu in Zululand to Vryheid on May 20, when E Squadron, pushing on too hastily, fell into the midst of a Boer ambush at Scheeper's Nek. Before they could dismount a withering fire was poured in upon them, which laid low half the squadron. The survivors fought with the most desperate gallantry; C and D Squadrons strove to cover the retreat; but the killed numbered twenty-seven, the wounded twenty-five, and the prisoners eleven, and two Maxims were captured by the Boers. No doubt there was rashness on the part of the officer in command of the squadron, who paid the penalty with his life. He was admired for his pluck, and followed by his men with the utmost devotion, yet this was one of the many occasions in the war when "slimness" would have been better than impetuous daring. It has, however, been asserted that there was treachery on the part of one of his own troopers.

WITH RUNDLE'S DIVISION: THE TRENCHES AT FICKSBURG, SHOWING HOW THEY WERE CONSTRUCTED.

In the Free State, preparations were now almost completed for the final advance on Pretoria. The British army was still short of supplies, and none too well equipped with winter clothing; thousands

[*Photo by W. H. Gill, Viljoen's Drift.*

LORD ROBERTS AND STAFF ON THE TRANSVAAL BORDER.

Lord Roberts and Staff entered the Transvaal at Viljoen's Drift on May 27 (Sunday). The photo shows Roberts and Kitchener at the moment of pausing to arrange about the railway staff at Viljoen's Drift Station, where the line crosses from the "Orange River Colony" to the Transvaal.

of thick great coats had not as yet reached the front, but Lord Roberts, believing that vigorous action would bring about the collapse of the war, and remembering the manner in which the enemy had rallied as the result of the long halt at Bloemfontein, wished to press forward at all costs. The risks he took were tremendous. In spite of the approach of Lord Methuen's army from the west, he could not dispose of a sufficient force to guard his ever-lengthening line of communications, and at the same time to crush all resistance on the part of Botha and the Transvaalers in his front. The north-east of the Free State had not been thoroughly cleared of the enemy; indeed, there were many signs that the Boers in this broken and mountainous country were regaining spirit and confidence; they had been troublesome enough in the course of Ian Hamilton's and Colvile's northward march, and had been taught no severe lesson. Were the line of communication left open and ill-guarded, it was practically certain that they would attack it. In that case the plight of the army, moving on and across the Vaal would be more than dangerous. For its supply of food and ammunition that army depended on a single line of railway, running from Kroonstad to Viljoen's Drift, through eighty miles of territory abounding in kopjes, and inhabited by a bitterly hostile population—a country lending itself to a guerilla warfare of ambuscades and surprises. Lord Roberts' force, like all invading armies, grew daily weaker from the need of detaching bodies of men to hold the various important points which it left

Expediency of rapid advance on Johannesburg.

behind it, and from the wastage produced by the loss of horses and men in its rapid marching. Yet the risk was taken, probably because it was held imperative to deprive the Boers of the vast resources which the gold fields and engineering works of Johannesburg afforded, and because it was thought that the movement to Pretoria would end the war.

VILJOEN'S DRIFT PONT, ON THE VAAL RIVER.

On May 15 Ian Hamilton, with his army, left Kroonstad, under orders to march due east to the village of Lindley. He was then to turn north and head for Heilbron, where Mr. Steyn had established for the nonce his peripatetic capital. The roads were abominable—mere tracks over the veldt; the question

Hamilton reaches Heilbron.

of supplies was a serious one, as little or no wood could be obtained to cook the men's rations; the enemy were omnipresent, though unable to prevent the advance of a column of 8,000 men and forty guns. On the 17th, Lindley was reached and seized. The convoy of baggage and

THE VALSCH RIVER AT KROONSTAD.
This is one of the very few South African rivers which run perennially.

supplies, however, owing to the badness of the roads, dropped behind, and there was some sharp skirmishing with the Boers before it got through and rejoined the column north of Lindley. This village was evacuated on the 20th, to the great disgust of the few British sympathisers, who were thus handed over to the vengeance of a by no means scrupulous enemy. A rearguard action began, and continued the greater part of the 20th with a loss to the column of sixty men. A company of mounted infantry had a narrow escape; its horses were stampeded; the Boers closed in, and only the appearance of the rest of the rearguard, who turned and rode back on hearing the crackling of rifles, extricated it from its dangerous plight. On May 22 the column reached Heilbron, and surprised and gave chase to a Boer convoy of sixty waggons in charge of Piet De Wet and about a thousand burghers.

BOER AUXILIARIES: MEN OF HOLLANDER CORPS AT ZANDSPRUIT.

The cavalry and horse artillery under Broadwood succeeded in making a bag of fifteen waggons and a few prisoners, but by clever handling of his rearguard De Wet got most of his charge away. At Heilbron Hamilton was across the Rhenoster, and in a position to drive in the enemy's left in case the Boers attempted to oppose Lord Roberts' main advance along the railway from Kroonstad to Vereeniging.

On May 22 Lord Roberts led out his main force from Kroonstad. It consisted of the Seventh Division, advancing on the west side of the railway, and the Eleventh Division on the east side, with two corps of mounted infantry and a battalion of yeomanry. On the far left, General French, with his cavalry, was well in advance, having quitted Kroonstad with orders to make a wide sweep round the enemy's right. On the Rhenoster, 40 miles north-east of Kroonstad, was a strong position which the Boers had sworn—as usual—to defend to the last. Entrenchments had been dug, gun-pits blasted, and about 12,000 men concentrated to meet the British onset. But in face of the turning movements on either flank, Louis Botha saw that it would be dangerous to make a stand. If he waited and fought, he must inevitably be enveloped and destroyed. On the night of the 22nd, then, when

Roberts crosses Rhenoster and Vaal Rivers.

G. Soper.]   [*After a photograph by a British officer.*

HOW THE ARTILLERY OF THE SEVENTH DIVISION CROSSED THE RHENOSTER RIVER.

the British infantry were seen at Honing Spruit, he fell back. On the 23rd, Lord Roberts reached the Rhenoster to find that the enemy had vanished, after destroying the road and railway bridges. The tireless, indomitable French, with his cavalry, was still well in advance; on the 24th, practically without opposition, he forded the Vaal at Parys, and led the main invasion of the Transvaal.

To reinforce him was necessary, as his cavalry brigades were steadily shrinking, and besides them he had only General Hutton's mounted infantry. Accordingly, Ian Hamilton's whole column was brought in from the British right, and on May 25 was moved across the front of Lord Roberts' army to the left, and directed upon Lindeque's Drift. This manœuvre completely nonplussed the Boers, who had mistaken Ian Hamilton's column for the main army, and, making sure that it would march due north from Heilbron to the Vaal, had concentrated all their means of resistance at Engelbrecht's Drift, twenty miles east of Vereeniging, whereas now Hamilton was hurrying to a point twelve miles west of Vereeniging. On the night of the 25th, Hamilton's cavalry seized Lindeque's Drift, and next day the column crossed, pushing forward eighteen miles on the 27th and coming into touch on the left with French's horsemen, and on the right with Lord Roberts' main army at Vereeniging. Supplies were running low, and but for a lucky find of forage it must have gone hard with the horses. The mounted infantry with Lord Roberts' column were on the Vaal on the morning of May 26, at Viljoen's Drift, in a country of collieries and pit heaps, among surroundings strangely familiar to many of the men. As they entered the river, one span of the railway bridge was blown up; a few shots were exchanged; a battery of horse artillery came into action; and the drift was won. On the 27th the Seventh and Eleventh Divisions crossed the river. Only one day's supplies now remained in the army waggons. To reach Johannesburg with the least possible delay was a matter of life or death to Lord Roberts. On the Klipriversberg,

R. B. M. Paxton.]   [*After a sketch by W. B. Wollen, R.I.*

THE INVASION OF THE TRANSVAAL: LORD ROBERTS AND HIS STAFF CROSSING THE VAAL.

a little to the south of the Golden City, the last stand of the Boers was expected to be made. To Klip River the main army marched on the 28th.

On the left General French was to make his usual wide sweep round Johannesburg, and, if he could, was to seize Driefontein, a station on the Pretoria-Germiston railway; Ian Hamilton was to move on Florida, west of Johannesburg; Lord Roberts was to seize Germiston. But on the 21st French was unable to force his way through, as he encountered the enemy in considerable strength, and came under a heavy fire from the Boer long-range cannon and "Pom-Poms." He was, indeed, compelled to fall back across the Klip River, which he had crossed earlier in the day. On the 29th, with about 3,000 men and twenty-two guns, he moved off once more to the west, endeavouring to

Attack on Klipriversberg. turn the enemy's position, and leaving a weak screen of mounted infantry to hold the ground he had won. The ground was difficult, and he made little progress, while the mounted infantry on his right were steadily forced back by the Boers. At this juncture Ian Hamilton's column opportunely appeared upon the scene, and, detaching all its cavalry and mounted infantry to French's support, advanced to assault the Klipriversberg. The troops were eating their last biscuit; no manœuvres or leisurely turning movements could be attempted; a successful frontal assault was the only means of staving off starvation. Bruce Hamilton was to be put in on the left, the Nineteenth Brigade on the right. The hour was late before the attack could open; there was no time for artillery preparation, though to good judges the strength of the Boer position appeared terrible.

In open order the men advanced, covered by a heavy artillery fire. The City Imperial Volunteers were in the foremost line on the left, and, supported by the Derbyshires and Camerons, went forward

with splendid dash. Already General French's guns could be heard booming on the enemy's right rear. The battlefield in this quarter was upon the very ridges which four years before had witnessed Jameson's disastrous defeat at Doornkop. On the right the Gordons delivered the main attack, and "in perfect discipline and with disdainful silence," as Mr. Winston Churchill, an eye-witness, writes, closed with the enemy and stormed the ridge, aided by the fire of the 82nd Field Battery, which was pushed forward into the very firing line. The Boers fell back in disorder and confusion upon the ridge of the Witwatersrand and Johannesburg, and

AN ENGLISH HOWITZER
OF 1879,

Found in the fort at Johannesburg, and since used for firing the one o'clock gun.

as night fell the battle was won. The British losses were slight; only 150 men had fallen; of these a great proportion were Gordons. That famous regiment left upon the field nine officers and 88 men, out of a strength which probably did not exceed 500.

[*Photo by Nicholls, Johannesburg.*

FORT AT JOHANNESBURG, ERECTED SINCE THE "JAMESON RAID."

With dawn of the 30th, the Boers under De la Rey, Viljoen, and Botha, were found to have retreated to the north, and General French was able, without serious resistance, to push round Johannesburg to Driefontein, capturing on the way a gun and some prisoners. Ian Hamilton's column entered Florida and found the food which it required. Meantime, events of great importance had been transpiring in Lord Roberts' front. Early on May 29, Colonel Henry, with the Australian Mounted Infantry, rode out from Klip River and headed for Germiston and Elandsfontein Junction, where the branch railway from Springs unites with the lines to Pretoria, Johannesburg, Bloemfontein, and Natal. The seizure of Elandsfontein would secure all the rolling stock west of that point, and, in the plight of the army, rolling stock was as necessary as the supplies, which, without it, could not be brought up from the rear. Already the indefatigable Burnham had, single-handed, left his mark upon the railway to Pretoria, but the damage he had caused was not sufficient to delay the Boer

**Seizure of Elandsfon-
tein Junction.**
trains for long. Henry worked his way round the Boer left, eastwards from Natal Spruit station, where skirmishing began, and presently came in sight of the junction, which lay in a valley "bristling with chimneys and head shafts, coloured by heaps of tailings and with a great town filling its western end." Here was the first trace of that almost fabulous wealth upon which Mr. Kruger's power had been built, and with which the great conspiracy against British rule in South Africa had been fostered and fed. In the station, trains were peacefully shunting. The British skirmishers pushed forward, and a sharp fire rattled over the open ground to the south of Germiston; a rain of bullets came from the blue heaps of tailings by the famous Simmer and Jack mine. But the British troops were not to be denied. By the afternoon the Boers had had enough fighting and fell back, when the junction was at once seized. The casualties were by no means heavy; only a dozen of the Mounted Infantry were killed and wounded; and the results

LORD ROBERTS REVIEWING THE TROOPS ON THEIR TRIUMPHAL ENTRY INTO JOHANNESBURG.
Of the passing troops only the shadows are seen in this photograph. Lord Roberts sits on horseback just in front of the flagstaff, with Lord Kitchener, on a white horse, next on his right. Against the flagstaff itself may be seen one of the Indian orderlies who accompanied him throughout the war.

purchased by their daring were of incalculable importance. Within Johannesburg reigned complete chaos. The Boer main force was in confused retreat; the British army had closed in, victorious and

**Surrender of
Johannesburg.**
terrible; under the circumstances further resistance was out of the question. On the 30th the town was summoned to surrender; Dr. Krause, the Boer Commandant, complied with the summons, only asking 24 hours' delay to permit of the withdrawal of the armed burghers in the place and to prevent the horrors of a hand-to-hand fight in the streets of the town. This respite was granted. On the 31st the British flag was hoisted, and the 11th and 7th Divisions defiled before the Commander-in-chief in imposing array. Only three Boer guns, all of old pattern, were captured in the town, but a considerable number of burghers either were taken prisoners or came forward and made their submission, to be released on parole.

Thus, not only had the gold mines and the commercial capital of the Transvaal been secured, with insignificant bloodshed, but large stores of supplies, sufficient to maintain the army for weeks, had passed into our hands. Ammunition would now be Lord Roberts' chief source of anxiety, though the news from the south was bad in the extreme—worse even than the pessimists could have anticipated.

Only for two days did the army halt; this short respite was imperative to allow the men and horses to recover after the hard marching and continual skirmishing of the past week. On June 2, General French, with the cavalry, began to move toward the final goal—Pretoria—where all reports indicated a frightful condition of panic and con-

Pretoria in terror.

fusion. Dismayed by the rapid advance of the conquering army from the south, President Kruger fled from the capital on May 29 with two millions sterling of gold stolen from the mines, to Watervalboven, a station far away upon the Delagoa Bay line. He had previously paid the employés of the Transvaal Government with worthless cheques, which were at once dishonoured because the Government had left no balance with its bankers. A committee of surrender was formed, and, in alarm lest the 4,000 or more British prisoners at Waterval, north of Pretoria, should break out and loot the town, the British officers in prison at Pretoria were approached, and requested to send 24 of their number to maintain order. This they agreed to do on the express stipulation that none of the prisoners should be

F. J. Waugh.]

LORD ROBERTS AND THE INN-KEEPER'S CHILD.

The day of the entry of the troops into Johannesburg, May 31st, closed with a little incident characteristic of Lord Roberts. He took up his headquarters in an inn bearing the sign "Orange Grove." Early in the evening an officer of his staff, wishing to consult him on an important matter, found him with one of the inn-keeper's children on his knee, trying to teach the mite to trace the letters of the alphabet. On the entry of the officer, Lord Roberts looked up with a smile, saying, "Don't come now; can't you see I'm busy?"

removed—a stipulation which was shamelessly violated by the Boers a few days later. The enemy's terror was increased by the movements of a small cavalry force, escorting Major Burnham, the scout, who was attempting to reach and cut the Delagoa Bay Railway. Though the attempt was dashingly made, the Boers were too strong and active to allow their line of defence to be penetrated and their communications to be interrupted. Burnham and the cavalry were compelled to retire.

On June 3 the rest of the army began to advance. French, with the **Rapid advance.** cavalry, formed the left of the army; he was to strike north-westwards, cross the Magaliesberg, 25 miles west of Pretoria, and then to ride north-east and place

KRUGER'S FAMOUS STOEP.

The President is here seen sitting in his accustomed seat on his stoep or verandah at Pretoria, smoking his habitual pipe. Two State-artillerymen are on guard. On either side of the door is a marble lion, presented to Mr. Kruger by Mr. Barney Barnato.

himself astride of the Pietersburg railway. Ian Hamilton was to form the centre and support French; Lord Roberts moved with the Army of the Right, composed of three Brigades of the Seventh and Eleventh Divisions—the fourth (Wavell's) had been detailed to defend Johannesburg—Gordon's Cavalry Brigade, the Mounted Infantry, and the Corps Troops. He followed the course of the railway. On the night of the 3rd, without opposition, he reached Kaalfontein station; next morning he pushed swiftly forward to Six Mile Spruit—also called Nyl or Hennop's Spruit on many of the English maps—and there found the Boers present in some force, holding both banks of the stream. A change of opinion had occurred at Pretoria. **Louis Botha counsels resistance.** General Louis Botha had entered the town with a large force of burghers, deposed the committee of surrender, and substituted more determined men; he hoped now to delay or repulse the British advance. But he reckoned without his Boer troopers, who were in no mood for a strenuous and desperate encounter, in which they ran the risk of being surrounded, penned-up in Pretoria, and compelled to surrender.

KRUGER AS A YOUNG MAN.

This portrait is from a daguerreotype, and is consequently reversed. The hand which has lost the thumb is really the left hand. Mr. Kruger had the member shattered by a gun-accident, and amputated it himself with a knife.

To force the Boers back, Ian Hamilton was ordered to turn eastwards and march to Elandsfontein, a town ten miles west of Pretoria, while Gordon on the right was directed to strain every nerve to place his horsemen upon the Delagoa Bay Railway, and thus cut off the Boers' last avenue of escape.

Capture of Pretoria forts.

Meantime Lord Roberts pressed his attack in the neighbourhood of Irene. The Mounted Infantry pushed forward and drove the Boers back from the southern bank of Six Mile Spruit; Stephenson's Brigade of Infantry supported the movement; the heavy guns, 4·7 and 5-in., with the field batteries of the Seventh Division, opened fire on the Boer artillery, which, after

CRUSHING BATTERY AT A JOHANNESBURG MINE.
The output for the year ending October 1899 of the gold mines of the "Witwatersrand," the district identified with Johannesburg, was about £12,000,000.

their usual fashion, the enemy had cunningly concealed on a ridge of kopjes running westward from the eminence crowned by Fort Schanzkop—a great earthwork constructed years before by the Boers for the defence of Pretoria. This work was empty; its guns had been removed; its formidable breastworks were held by no Boers. But on the left of Stephenson's men the enemy began to make unpleasant demonstrations, and there was some fear for the British flank, as no sign of Ian Hamilton's approach could as yet be discerned. Henry's Mounted Infantry, holding the left of a long ridge facing Schanzkop, had about as much as they could do to maintain their position under a heavy Mauser and cannon fire. J Horse Battery, however, was pushed up to their assistance, and, when its six guns began to thunder, all risk of Henry's being forced back was removed. Seven field and horse batteries and six or eight heavy guns were now in action against the Boer front; overhead the balloon hovered menacingly; and behind the guns the infantry deployed for the assault. The naval 4·7's, as they came into action, were suddenly attacked by a "Pom-Pom," which emptied a belt of snapping shells among their gunners,

[*Photo by Freeman & Co., Sydney.*

MAJOR-GENERAL E. T. H. HUTTON, C.B., A.D.C. to the Queen,

Was born at Torquay in 1848. and educated at Eton. Joined the King's Royal Rifles in 1867; served in Zululand in 1879; in the Boer War of 1881 (with the Mounted Infantry); Egyptian War, 1882. and Nile Expedition, 1884–5; as D.A.A.G. raised and commanded the Mounted Infantry at Aldershot, 1888–92; Lieut.-Colonel, 1889; A.D.C. to the Queen, 1892. In 1893 he went to New South Wales to organise the military forces there, with temporary rank of Major-General, and in 1898 he was appointed General Officer Commanding the Canadian Dominion Militia, having in the meantime (1896-8) held the appointment of Assistant-Adjutant-General for Ireland. In March, 1900, he left Ottawa to take command of the 1st Brigade of Mounted Infantry in South Africa.

wounding Commander de Horsey severely in the foot, but presently the hostile weapon was located and silenced by one of the Yeomanry Colt guns. The British fire was directed upon the ridge in front, upon the Pretoria forts, and upon the railway station and magazines.

About 3 p.m. Pole-Carew's Division began to advance on the right. At the same hour, on the left, Ian Hamilton came into action, and Smith-Dorrien's and Bruce Hamilton's brigades, pushing forward, speedily took the pressure off the Mounted Infantry, who were now withdrawn and sent round the Boer right. This flank movement alarmed the enemy, and they at once began to fall back. By nightfall the whole line of defence was in the possession of the British troops, with the trivial loss of 70 killed and wounded. The Australians, under Colonel de Lisle, dashed forward so impetuously, as day was falling, that they succeeded in reaching a point within easy rifle-shot of the town, capturing on the way a Boer Maxim. Thence De Lisle despatched a flag of truce to demand the immediate surrender

HOISTING THE BRITISH FLAG ON THE RAADZAAL, PRETORIA.
See the note to illustration on opposite page.

of the capital. Late in the night the Burgomaster came out to Lord Roberts' lines with the reply. Botha had recognised the inevitability of submission, but had given instructions that terms similar to those granted Johannesburg were, if possible, to be obtained. Lord Roberts, however, refused to consider any such proposal, and required, under pain of bombardment, unconditional and immediate

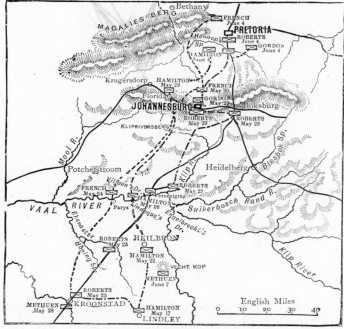

MAP SHOWING ROUTES OF THE BRITISH FORCES FROM KROONSTAD TO PRETORIA.

Fall of the town. surrender of the town and all within it. The Boers had no choice but to agree, and before midnight of June 4-5, Pretoria fell.

The fortunes of the cavalry on the right and left of the army have still to be followed.

French's movements to the west and north. Gordon, with his cavalry brigade, in the attempt to strike the Delagoa Bay line, was foiled by the superior strength and advantageous positions of the Boers, and was unable to achieve his object. On the extreme left French had entered the sombre mountain region of the Witwatersberg, which runs due west from Pretoria, late on the afternoon of June 3, and was proceeding through a narrow mountain pass, in country most unsuited to the action of cavalry, when suddenly the enemy showed in some force ahead and opened with rifles and cannon upon the column. Nothing could be done except to reply with artillery; two British

Horse Artillery guns and a "Pom-Pom" were brought into action, and, as darkness came down, shelled the Boer position with deadly effect, killing, it was afterwards discovered, no less than 33 Boers, while the British loss was only 2 killed and 7 wounded. But the enemy's intention was to cause delay rather than to offer desperate resistance. Under cover of darkness the Boers retired, while French bivouacked in the pass. At daylight of June 4 he continued his advance, and as he reached the highest point of the pass, his troopers looked down upon a land flowing with milk and honey, odorous with multitudinous orange groves, the garden of the Transvaal, a land shut in on the south by the frowning heights of the Witwatersberg, and on the north by the bold, fantastic range of the Magaliesberg. Far away the roar of Lord Roberts' guns could be heard. Striking off to the right, to open communications with the British centre and right, Hutton's Mounted Infantry seized Daspoort Fort without encountering difficulty or resistance. The main body of French's force pushed northwards, and, crossing the Magaliesberg by Mosilikatse's Nek, rode eastwards on the 5th to seize the Pietersburg railway. On their way parties of disarmed Boers were met who announced that the British army had already entered Pretoria, and that the war was over. Thus ended the cavalry's great march of 280 miles from Kroonstad, a distance covered in a fortnight by horses overladen and in bad condition, with a uniform success and rapidity that cowed the Boers, and reflected the utmost credit upon the active and daring General French.

THE FLAG AT PRETORIA: THE SCENE IN THE SQUARE ON JUNE 5, AT THE MOMENT THE FLAG WAS RUN UP ON THE RAADZAAI.

The flag used here was again the silken Union Jack made by Lady Roberts, shown in the illustration on p. 544. It was about 3 ft. by 2 ft., and can be seen fluttering up past the triangular pediment near the roof of the building on the extreme right of the picture. It was almost immediately replaced by the full-sized flag shown on opposite page.

Early on the 5th the first British troops entered Pretoria, but not before, in defiance of their promises, the Boer authorities had hurried off some train-loads of British prisoners from Waterval.

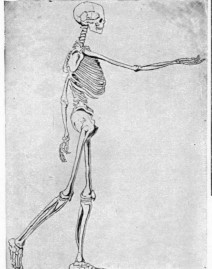

DRAWINGS ON THE WALLS OF THE MODEL SCHOOLS, PRETORIA.

These drawings were made by the British officers in captivity. The map represented the movements of Buller's army in northern Natal, and was added to from time to time as new prisoners arrived.

Entry into Pretoria. Three other empty trains, which were just about to depart, were compelled to wait by the Guards, who fired a few shots near the engine-drivers. The offices of the Netherlands Railway Company, the Residency, and the State Buildings, were occupied at once. At 2 p.m. Lord Roberts made his State entry. In the chief square of Pretoria the Union Jack was hoisted with every accompaniment of pomp and splendour; the National Anthem was sung; and then the troops defiled past their great leader. First came the Guards with the easy swing of veterans; then Stephenson's Brigade and the Artillery; then again the Mounted Infantry, among whom rode the lithe Canadians, the towering Australians, the magnificent troopers who had responded to the call from within the boundaries of Cape Colony, and the middle-sized but wiry English regulars. After them, again, Ian Hamilton's men marched past the Field-Marshal, the two brigades of Smith-Dorrien and Bruce Hamilton making a splendid show. Thus, after nineteen years' absence, the British flag came back to Pretoria, thence never to depart.

While the troops were entering Pretoria, the Duke of Marlborough and Mr. Winston Churchill rode post-haste to the place where the captive British officers were confined, and had the satisfaction of setting free 129 officers and 36 soldiers. A force of cavalry was at once detached to Waterval to liberate the others, and, notwithstand-

Treatment of British prisoners. ing the fire of several Boer guns, early on June 6 it was able to set free 3,187 privates and non-commissioned officers and to capture the Boer guard. As there had been reports that the prisoners had been badly treated by the enemy, Lord Roberts appointed a Court of Inquiry to investigate the matter. It was shown that the

COMMANDANT HERMAN AND THE MEN IN CHARGE OF THE WATERVAL MILITARY PRISON.

captured officers of the regular Army had not been badly used. They were not given much space, indeed, nor were the rations issued to them by the Boer Government of high quality, but they were at least permitted to supplement the food provided, by purchase from their own pockets. At first they were confined in the Pretoria Model School, from which Mr. Churchill had made his escape and from which, in March, Captain Haldane, Lieutenant Le Mesurier, and Sergeant Brockie succeeded in getting away. The three hid in an excavation under the floor of one of the rooms, and there remained from February 27 to March 16, when the prisoners were removed to a building on the hill north of Pretoria. Haldane and his comrades were missed on February 27, but, as a hole had been cut in the roof of one of the buildings, the Boers concluded that they must have got out of the prison, and so never thought of examining the floor, under which they were quietly lying. On March 16 they stole out of the now empty and unguarded building, and started on their way to the coast. Brockie was an Uitlander, and knew the country. Though Le Mesurier sprained his ankle at the very outset, all three in the end reached Delagoa Bay. Brockie parted from the other two, and for some days acted as a bar attendant at Kaapmuiden, without being identified. The others were fortunate enough to enlist the sympathy and assistance of some Britishers employed at the

MAJOR-GENERAL BRUCE MEADE HAMILTON.

In command of the 21st Brigade, South Africa Field Force, with rank of Major-General. Was born in 1857, son of the late General H. Meade Hamilton, C.B. He joined the 15th Foot (afterwards the East Yorkshire Regiment) in 1877; Captain, 1886; Major, 1895; Brevet Lieut.-Colonel, 1896; Brevet Colonel, 1897. He served with the 15th Regiment in the Afghan War in 1880; in the Boer War of 1881 as A.D.C. to his brother-in-law, Sir George Colley, being present in the engagement at the Ingogo River, and afterwards as A.D.C. to Sir Evelyn Wood; joined the Burmese Expedition in 1885, and the Ashanti Expedition under Sir Francis Scott in 1895 (Brevet of Lieut.-Colonel); he was with the Benin Expedition in 1897 in command of the Niger Coast Protectorate Force (Brevet of Colonel). He went out in the present war as Chief of the Staff to General Clery, and distinguished himself under General Smith-Dorrien in the fighting before Johannesburg.

Douglas coal mine, near Balmoral, on the Delagoa Bay Railway, who had previously helped Mr. Churchill, and who now concealed the fugitives in a truck-load of bales of wool. Though the truck was searched in a perfunctory manner at Komati Poort, the escaped prisoners were not detected.

The new prison in which the officers were confined is described as a "long, white shanty, with a fairly large compound, enclosed by formidable barbed-wire entanglements. . . . There are electric lights all round the enclosure, making escape a matter of difficulty. Inside, the place looks more like a cattle shed than anything else. A long galvanised iron building, divided into sleeping rooms, and four small bath rooms, a servants' compartment and kitchen, and eating rooms. . . . There is no flooring. The drains consist of open ditches, while the sanitary arrangements are enough to disgust any civilised being."

Here the prisoners were much more carefully guarded, and further escapes were rendered practically impossible.

But the plight of the captured Colonial and Uitlander officers was far worse. They were treated as common felons and thrown into gaol. Colonel Hunt, in a letter to Lord Roberts, has pointed out that many of them died because the Boer medical officer would not, or dared not, do his duty and order their removal to hospital when sick. "This morning," says Lieutenant Frankland, a prisoner, in his diary, "an officer of the South African Light Horse was buried. To all intents and purposes he was murdered by the Transvaal Government. Although he had typhoid fever, he was thrown into prison, and not until the authorities were pretty certain he would die was he sent to hospital." Vigorous protests against such treatment were made by Lord Roberts and the British Regular officers who were prisoners, but in vain. The Boers persisted in regarding the captured Colonials as criminals. The civilians whom they seized in Griqualand West and the east of Cape Colony were, if anything, worse used. "They were enclosed," says a witness, "in a sort of cattle kraal . . . They were mostly storekeepers and farmers, and had not taken up arms at all. The men had to sleep on the bare ground with nothing but an overhead shelter, and were poorly fed and clothed."

HOW THE BRITISH PRISONERS WERE GUARDED AT WATERVAL.
Notice the elaborate barbed-wire fences within which the prisoners were confined.

As for the non-commissioned officers and men, Lord Roberts' conclusion is that their "food is shown to have been quite inadequate in quantity and inferior in quality. There was no excuse for this, as supplies of excellent meat, bread, and vegetables are easily procurable in the Transvaal at a moderate price." The sanitary arrangements were disgracefully bad and, in the opinion of a trustworthy witness, "the state of affairs was absolutely deplorable . . . The men complained greatly of being in a constant state of hunger." The scale of

INSIDE THE WATERVAL PRISON.
News has arrived of the approach of the British troops, and Tommy's spirits have risen in consequence.

diet, says the report of the Court of Inquiry, was not adhered to, and this though it was in the matter of meat "a starvation ration." Even more heartless and disgraceful was the treatment of the sick. When typhoid broke out, as the result of the filthy conditions under which these British soldiers were compelled to live, the patients were neglected. "I found men with typhoid fever in its worst stages," says a witness, "quite inadequately supplied with proper nourishment. . . The orderlies told me the sick were almost starving, but they had no milk nor any proper nourishment to give them. . . The sick would have been well-nigh starved but for the efforts of private individuals in Pretoria." Other witnesses speak of "the terrible state of affairs existing at Waterval," and tell us that "the prisoners became very weak and liable to disease," so that many had to be admitted to hospital with constitutions wrecked by the deliberate neglect and cruelty of Mr. Kruger and his satellites. It was Andersonville, with all its nameless horrors, over again, and without the faintest shadow of excuse. Meanwhile, the Boer prisoners in the hands of the British were living in plenty and comfort at St. Helena.

For this inhuman treatment of the sick Lord Roberts expressly blames a man of English descent, Dr. H. P. Veale, M.B., of Cambridge, "whose heartlessness in ignoring the disgraceful treatment of the sick prisoners, and the remonstrances addressed to him by the medical officers in immediate charge of them, calls for the severest reprobation." This stern judgment certainly demands action on the part of Dr. Veale's university. As for religious ministration, that, too, was often withheld from the sick and dying. "Ministers

[*Photo by J. F. Archibald.*

THE CONSUL FOR THE BRITISH PRISONERS AT PRETORIA.

Hon. Adalbert S. Hay, American Consul-General at Pretoria, who attended to the wants of the British prisoners and acted for British subjects during the war. He stands by the railway carriage. Behind him is Mr. John G. Coolidge, Vice-Consul; they are bidding good-bye to attachés leaving Pretoria, and Mr. Hay is talking to Captain Slocum, United States Army, American attaché. Other travellers seen in the picture are the Japanese and Russian attachés.

of religion," says a prisoner, "were only allowed to visit us for the purpose of holding services once a month. . . . When a man was dying and wished to see his minister, the Boer authorities did not notify the ministers concerned, and the burial of the dead had to be conducted by a soldier comrade, no clergyman being notified or summoned." This denial of the last and greatest of consolations was a piece of refined cruelty for which there was no excuse. But what is to be said of the Reverend J. Godfrey, priest of the Church of England at Pretoria, who, after the escape of Mr. Churchill,

WATERVAL AFTER THE LIBERATION OF THE PRISONERS.
Boers discussing the situation with the rescuers.

discontinued his religious ministrations, because, to quote his own words, "I desire to maintain the honour due to my position"? "I was sick and in prison, and ye visited Me," were the Master's words; quite otherwise the action of that Master's servant.

Yet where many failed to show the most elementary sense of patriotism and duty, some were true to their trust. Doctors Haylett and Van Gernet, the latter a Boer, did their best, like Christians, for the sick, and the English residents in Pretoria, notably Mr. Wood, of the Natal Bank, raised funds to diminish their sufferings. Such absolute necessaries as scrubbing-brushes, soap, and beds were supplied from these private funds. Mr. Hay, the American Consul, also acted in the most exemplary manner. But for the Boer Executive no words of condemnation can be too strong.

While these things happened to the British prisoners and sick at Pretoria, a great storm of indignation was raised at home by the indictment levelled by Mr. Burdett-Coutts, *The Times* Commissioner,

Condition of the field hospitals. against the treatment of the sick in the British hospitals at Bloemfontein. His charges were based upon observations taken during April and May. "Hundreds of men," he wrote, "were lying in the worst stages of typhoid with only a blanket and a thin water-proof sheet

AN ATTEMPT TO ESCAPE FROM WATERVAL.

The three men shown in the lower photograph succeeded in tunnelling beneath the fence with the aid of the tools which are also shown in that picture. They were detected; but relief came the day before their intended escape. The upper illustration shows where the tunnel was to have opened, outside the fence.

(not even the latter for many of them) between their aching bodies and the hard ground, with no milk and hardly any medicines, without beds, stretchers, or mattresses, without pillows, without linen of any kind, without a single nurse amongst them . . . and with only three doctors to attend to 350 patients. . . . About the same time a convoy of wounded men were being subjected to nameless torture for want of any ambulance transport or the simplest comforts, huddled together in rough, springless ox-waggons, jolting over spruit and drift for 40 miles." Field hospitals, designed to accommodate 100 men, were divided, and one half the hospital packed with patients—sometimes as many as 496, or nearly ten times as many as the section could accommodate, being forced upon it. Terrible suffering to the inmates resulted. Much criticism, too, was aimed at the state of the hospitals at Kroonstad. It was alleged that the hospital requirements of the Army had been altogether under-estimated, that the number of medical officers was utterly inadequate, and that the doctors were overwhelmed with unnecessary paper work in the shape of returns to the War Office, on which every pennyweight of drugs and every yard of bandages expended had to be entered, till they could scarcely find time to attend to the sick. Many independent witnesses confirmed these charges in certain details; other witnesses testified to an unsatisfactory state of things at the base hospitals.

The answer of Lord Roberts to Mr. Coutts' charges was in the main this—that war is always war, and involves infinite suffering, especially where the lines of communication are insecure.   In this

LOOTING THE GOVERNMENT   STORES AT PRETORIA.

When it became evident that Pretoria could not be defended by the Boers, word was passed that the Government stores were at the disposal of any who chose to help themselves, as the British would respect goods in private possession, but would appropriate all public property to their own uses.   Then ensued a scramble for everything portable, and carts, barrows, cabs, and trolleys were requisitioned for the purpose of carrying away the spoil.

case the sick were stinted, but, it was said, of necessity.   "The very existence of my force," telegraphed Lord Roberts from Pretoria on June 16, "depended upon the supplies coming up by train along a line of railway nearly 900 miles long, every bridge of which for the last 128 miles had been destroyed by the enemy. . . . It is obvious that a certain amount of suffering is inseparable from the rapid advance of a large army in the enemy's country, when railway communication has been destroyed. . . .

[*Photo by Russell & Sons.*]

THE EARL OF ROSSLYN.

The nation owed its first news of the position of affairs in Pretoria to Lord Rosslyn.   He went to Africa as correspondent of *The Daily Mail* and *The Sphere*, served with Thorneycroft's Horse at the relief of Ladysmith, and was following the movements about Thaba N'chu when he was captured at Dewetsdorp on April 2.   He escaped, and was recaptured at Mozar's Hoek on April 4, and carried with other prisoners to Pretoria.   Released on parole with 20 British officers who were sent to Waterval to keep order amongst the prisoners there, he succeeded in getting a telegram through to the *Mail*, days ahead of official news, announcing the release of the prisoners and conveying the welcome information that Pretoria would offer no resistance to Lord Roberts.

I can quite understand that people who have no practical experience in such matters are much concerned to hear the hardships which sick and wounded soldiers have to undergo in time of war."

This is a strong defence, but it does not meet the charges which have been brought against the base hospitals, where the "Absent-Minded Beggar" Fund had to supply many obvious necessities and even clothing to the invalid soldiers returning home. Moreover, Doctors René Konig and Jacques de Montmolin, of the Swiss Red Cross Society, who were perfectly independent and unbiassed witnesses, stated, to an interviewer, that the British medical service was "shamefully undermanned" and full of "inexperienced youngsters." At Johannesburg, where mattresses and shelter could easily have been obtained, they declared that British typhoid cases were left for four days lying in the open, and they strongly censured the authorities for not "commandeering" milk and eggs for the sick. That the hospital organisation was not all that it should have been may be taken for certain; an army which was notoriously unprepared for a great war is not likely to have been found perfect in its arrangements for the care of the sick and wounded. But for this the system, not the generals, must be blamed. A Commission to investigate and report upon the question was appointed by the British Government as the result of Mr. Coutts' letters.

The distance from Bloemfontein to Pretoria is 300 miles, which had been accomplished in two days over a month. It has been said with truth by a brilliant writer, Colonel Henderson, that " A march of eighty or one hundred miles into an enemy's country sounds a simple feat, but, unless every detail has been carefully thought out, it will not improbably be more disastrous than a lost battle." And as the country traversed was for the most part unproductive and scantily peopled, and the roads of execrable nature, the greatness of the feat in this instance is immensely enhanced. A force of 30,000 men

Lord Roberts' great march. operating on a front of 30 to 40 miles was handled with clockwork precision. Confident of himself and of his men, the Field-Marshal did not hesitate to make demands upon them, to which only the finest spirit enabled them to respond. He ran the terrible risk of the severance of his communications behind him, because he believed in the expediency of pressing an apparently

[Photo by Cane].

THE RAADZAAL, PRETORIA.

About twelve years ago the Landesvaders or patres conscripti met for their very informal conclaves in a tiny one-storied thatch-roofed building on the Church Square, which was as undignified as it was uncomfortable. After a time they migrated to a long, low, barn-like structure, also on the Church Square. Soon, however, the need of a real Parliament House, or Raadzaal, became apparent, and a lordly and magnificent pile was erected facing the Church, of imposing solidity and effect. It cost rather more than a quarter of a million pounds sterling, without furnishing. It is of the neo-Palladian order, and is surmounted by a gigantic statue of Liberty. Inside, the rooms are spacious and exceedingly well-planned; there are two magnificent council chambers and innumerable offices. Paul Kruger's private room was the most plainly furnished apartment in the building.

THE GOVERNMENT OF THE TRANSVAAL.

The Government of the Transvaal, by the "Grondwet" (fundamental law) of 1856, was Republican. The President, elected by the votes of the burghers, was the highest official in the state, receiving a salary of £8,000 a year, and a "coffee" or entertaining allowance of £300. He possessed the executive power, proposed laws, was responsible to the Volksraad, and had once a year to visit all the towns of the Republic. He was debarred from engaging in trade, or leaving the country without consent of the Volksraad. He was aided by an Executive Council, which included the Commandant-General (elected by the people for ten years), two non-official members (elected by the Volksraad for two years), the State Secretary (elected by the Volksraad for four years); others might be included, on certain conditions, by invitation of the President. The Volksraad, the highest legislative authority, formed one chamber until 1890, when, owing to agitation for representation of the new mining population, a second Raad or chamber was formed. The First Volksraad consisted of twenty-four members, men born in the country, who had been duly enfranchised burghers for fifteen years, were of Protestant religion, thirty years of age, owners of landed property, and possessing the right of burghership before 1890, or after then by birth. The same qualification as to burghership had to be possessed by burghers who elected the members of both Volksraads. The Second Volksraad consisted of twenty-four members, men of Protestant religion, resident in the Republic, possessed of landed property, and duly enfranchised burghers for two past years. They were vested with a partial and strictly limited power to regulate mining affairs, make roads, posts and telegraphs, protect patents and copyrights, control insolvency, civil, and criminal proceedings, and other matters, subject to the approval of the President and of the First Volksraad. Members of both Chambers had allowances of £3 per day while on duty; the chairmen, £3 10s. per day. All debates were in Dutch. A foreigner might become naturalised after two years' residence and on payment of £5, but had to renounce all political rights; he might then vote for or sit in the Second Volksraad, but only after fourteen years' residence could he vote for or sit in the First Volksraad, and then only provided two-thirds of the burghers voted for him. These qualifying clauses in practice excluded persons of foreign origin (even if British, although Great Britain was the suzerain power, and had expressly retained "equal rights" for her subjects) from all control of taxation, whilst as a matter of fact such persons contributed five-sixths of the revenue.

INTERIOR OF THE RAADZAAL, PRETORIA.

disorganised enemy to the utmost, and because, with all the imposing total of British troops in South Africa, he could not muster sufficient men to hold the line behind him securely. There were moments when he was near disaster. Had the Boers made a determined stand at Johannesburg or at Pretoria, his plight would have been grave indeed. But that they did not do so is justification of his strategy.

[Photo by W. H. Gill, Viljoen's Drift.

THE MAIN AVENUE OF SUPPLIES FOR JOHANNESBURG AND PRETORIA.

This photograph shows the deviation-railway over the Vaal River at Vereeniging (Transvaal), made necessary by the blowing up of the great bridge at this point. It is a fine piece of work, of which our Royal Engineers may well be proud.

CHAPTER XXVIII.

OPERATIONS IN THE OUTLYING DISTRICTS.

Boers encouraged to resist—Battle of Diamond Hill—Casualties—Annexation of the Orange Free State—The Yeomanry in difficulties—Fruitless appeals for help—Surrender at Lindley—De Wet captures a convoy—Disaster on the Rhenoster— De Wet wreaks destruction on the railway—Operations of Rundle and Brabant—Battle of Biddulphberg—Warren subjugates Griqualand West.

Boers encouraged to resist.

WITH the occupation of Pretoria it was hoped at first that the end of the war had come, and that the Boers would submit. Negotiations were opened with General Botha, and that distinguished leader seemed not disinclined to make his surrender. But, unhappily, at this juncture, news reached him that De Wet, operating in the Orange River Colony against the British communications, had won a remarkable series of successes; while, at the same time, spies informed him that Lord Roberts' army was far weaker than he had supposed. Smith-Dorrien's brigade had been despatched south to hold the line from Kroonstad to the Vaal; the Seventh Division had been absorbed by the necessity of garrisoning Pretoria and Johannesburg; only the Eleventh and part of Ian Hamilton's Divisions remained available, while French's cavalry had shrunk, till its two brigades, nominally 3,000 strong, mustered scarcely 700 troopers. The Mounted Infantry had diminished in much the same way: Hutton's brigade, for example, instead of 3,000 men, now counted only 600. "Invading armies," it has been said, "melt like the snow," and Lord Roberts' force was no exception to the universal rule. At the outside the British field army mustered 16,000 men, but it had with it 80 guns, since artillery does not vanish as do the other arms. The Boer force, under Botha and De la Rey, was about 10,000 strong, with numerous guns, and held a strong position on a ridge which rises steeply from the plain, and which cuts across the Delagoa Bay Railway, fifteen miles east of Pretoria, near Eerste Fabriken. The general configuration of the ridge is crescent-shaped, the horns pointing to Pretoria. Here the Boers had every chance in their favour, and had the spirit of the burghers been that of good soldiers, they ought to have inflicted a severe repulse on Lord Roberts.

June 8 was a day of armistice to allow of negotiations; on the 9th, Lord Roberts was to have personally conferred with Botha, but early in the morning the Boer general declined to entertain any further proposals. Lord Roberts there- fore determined to attack him on the 11th. French, with the 1st and 4th Cavalry Brigades and Hutton's Mounted Infantry, was to turn the Boer right, Broadwood, with the 2nd and 3rd Cavalry Brigades and Ridley's Mounted Infantry, the Boer left; while Pole-Carew and Ian Hamilton with their divisions were to threaten a

THE BRITISH RESIDENCY, PRETORIA: LORD ROBERTS' HEADQUARTERS.

frontal attack upon the enemy's centre. Botha, on his part, had de- termined to hold the British in the centre, while his flanks were to sweep round and sever their army from Pretoria. Thus the strategy on each side was identical. General French speedily came into collision with De la Rey, who was facing him, and the two forces, each of which was to have turned the

[*Photo by the British Biograph Company.*

LORD ROBERTS RECEIVING DESPATCHES ON THE LAWN OF THE BRITISH RESIDENCY, PRETORIA.

This picture is enlarged from a Biograph film. The operator happened to have his camera in position at the very moment when a cyclist despatch-rider rode up with papers requiring immediate attention, and Lord Roberts was photo- graphed in the act of opening them.

other, merely checkmated each other. The weak British cavalry could not press back the Boers, and were hard put to it to hold their own. A body of Boers even attempted to charge the 1st Cavalry Brigade, and were only repelled by the fire of the three horse batteries and "Pom-Poms" with the column. On the British right Broadwood found that the Boer line stretched in a semi-circle right

Battle of Diamond Hill. round his flank; the most important point in it was the ridge known as Diamond Hill, which extended four or five miles south-east from the railway. Yet, not- withstanding a galling fire, he pushed steadily forward, aiming at a gap, or " poort," immediately to the south of Diamond Hill, and guarding his right flank with Gordon's Cavalry, his left with Ridley's Mounted Infantry. To clear the ridges before him, two guns of Q Battery of Horse Artillery were brought up and ordered to shell the Boer position. At this instant the enemy did a thing which they had never done before. Two hundred men mounted and rode forward towards the guns as if intending a charge. They came on with spirit, though the guns, handled with absolute steadiness by the superb soldiers of the Horse Artillery who had so nobly sacrificed themselves at Sanna's Post, were pouring case shot into their ranks as fast as the weapons could be loaded and discharged. The situation looked critical in the extreme when Broadwood gave the order to Lord Airlie to charge with the 12th Lancers. The Lancers wheeled, opened into line, and dashed forward at the best pace at which their exhausted horses could carry them; their mere appearance was enough, and though they were only 150 strong, the enemy fled precipitately, but not without losing a dozen men impaled upon the much-dreaded lances. In the excitement of the charge and pursuit, however, the Lancers had drawn too close to Diamond Hill, with the result that they came under a terrible fire. At this moment Lieutenant Wright

F. Dadd, R.I.]   [*From a sketch by Lionel James.*

AN AWKWARD MOMENT: THE ENEMY CHARGING THE Q BATTERY OF ROYAL HORSE ARTILLERY.

was shot by a Boer who rode off. Wright's troop-sergeant dashed furiously at him, on which the man threw up his hands and called for mercy. "I'll give you the mercy, you ——, you gave the captain," shouted the sergeant. Lord Airlie, whose piety was exemplary, called to him in the heat of battle, "Sergeant! sergeant! moderate your language." An instant later Lord Airlie met his death. He was a splendid officer, devoted to his profession and beloved by his men, so that his loss was no ordinary one. Captain Fortescue, too, was killed at this juncture, and there was some confusion, but the regiment effected its retreat with a total loss of only 19. Its retirement encouraged the Boers, who came on with greater determination on Broadwood's right, and that general ordered the Household Cavalry to charge. The Guards rode at their enemy waving their huge swords, whereupon that enemy once more precipitately fled. There was no further trouble on the British right, but, in face of opposition so strong and active, the cavalry could not gain more ground.

To relieve the pressure upon the cavalry, Ian Hamilton had, notwithstanding contrary orders from Lord Roberts, pressed home his frontal attack upon Diamond Hill. His artillery and position guns

were already bombarding it; now Bruce Hamilton's Brigade deployed and advanced up the rocky,
bush-covered slopes, the City Imperial Volunteers
on the right, and the Sussex Regiment and
Derbyshires on the left. Just beneath the summit the troops halted, while the great 5-in.
"cow-guns" and the Field Artillery searched the
top of Diamond Hill. About 3.30 the Sussexes
began to push back the Boers. The British
troops had so far suffered little loss. They had
profited by the teaching of war, and their line
of skirmishers, says Mr. Winston Churchill, went
forward, making use of every scrap of cover and
presenting no target to the Boers. As the enemy
gave ground, the City Imperial Volunteers advanced, but only to find that before them, beyond
a slight hollow, rose another and a steeper ridge,
where the Boers could be made out in force.
From this ridge came a sharp fire which speedily
dropped seven of the Volunteers. The day was
declining and further advance was out of the
question. The line captured was strongly
picketed, and the troops withdrew to a hollow

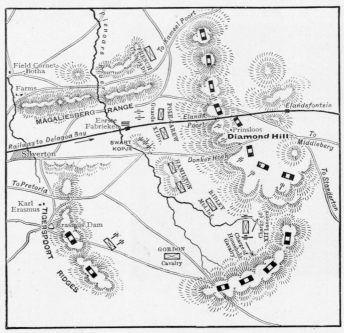

PLAN OF THE BATTLE OF DIAMOND HILL.

under the height which they had just won, and there bivouacked. At dawn of the 12th, after a
bitterly cold night, the action was resumed.

Noting the strength of the Boer position fronting Ian Hamilton, Lord Roberts had given orders
that the Guards Brigade from Pole-Carew's division should reinforce the attack upon Diamond Hill.
The morning passed in shelling the enemy's line and in waiting for the Guards. The Boers replied
at intervals with one long-range gun, and a shrapnel bullet from one of its missiles struck Ian Hamilton
on the shoulder, bruising him severely, but fortunately without disabling him. Meantime the Sussex
Regiment on the left, the City Imperial Volunteers in the centre, and the Derbyshires on the right,

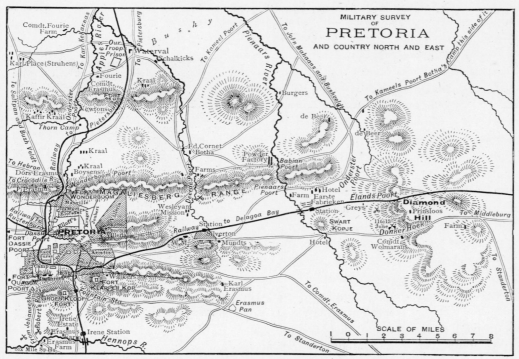

MAP OF THE COUNTRY FROM PRETORIA TO DIAMOND HILL.

advanced to the ridge
which they had won
on the previous even-
ing, and lay there,
waiting the order to
charge. The cover
was good, and though
the Boers maintained
a sharp rifle-fire, be-
stowing most of their
attention on the
Derbyshires, the losses
were small. About
1 p.m. the Guards
came into sight, march-
ing steadily towards
the hill, but still some
three or four miles
away. They were,
however, near enough
to give moral support,
and the 21st Brigade

was at once put in motion against the crescent-shaped ridge held by the enemy, which ran generally parallel to that now occupied by the British troops. So excellent had been the artillery preparation that the line of men was able to gain the foot of the ridge almost without loss. Then followed a short halt while the troops took some food and while the 5-in. guns continued the bombardment of the ridge, hurling their whistling lyddite shells at the enemy. "It was a comforting sound to us," writes Corporal Barclay Lloyd, of the City Imperial Volunteers, "fraught with something restful and confidence-inspiring, as though some unseen power was at our backs, cheering us on with the assurance of strong and watchful help."

LORD AIRLIE.

David, eighth Earl of Airlie, served with the 10th Hussars in the Afghan War, and, later, in the Sudan and Nile Expeditions. He was transferred to the 12th Lancers, and went to South Africa with his regiment in 1899. Lieut.-Colonel, 1897.

[Photo by Bassano.

The artillery's ammunition, however, was running low, and with De Wet victorious behind the army and breaking the lines of communication, it could not easily be replenished. It was for the British a case of "conquer or die." The advance was resumed, the City Imperial Volunteers forcing their way up a rounded hollow, which promised easy access to the summit of the precipitous ridge. On this hollow, however, the Boer guns played incessantly, while from either flank a vigorous rifle-fire was directed on the advance. Yet ever upwards pressed "the regular lines of widely scattered men, who advanced, lay down, rose up and advanced, with splendid precision, quite heedless of the singing in the air above and the spurting of the dust beneath. . . . Away upon our right came that ominous, deadly knocking, now but too familiar, of the ever-present Vickers-Maxim; and hurtling between the open lines of our brother battalion burst the series of one-pound shells." Notwithstanding the fire, the second ridge was gained. To the disappointment of all it was seen that beyond it, and looking down upon it, there was yet a third ridge, held by the enemy.

The position of the British troops was thoroughly unfavourable. They found themselves on the edge of a wide plateau, dominated both in front and flank by eminences still in the hands of the Boers. The situation, indeed, was much the same as that of the stormers on Spion Kop, in the battle of January 24. On this occasion, however, the mistakes which had been made in Natal were not repeated, nor did the enemy attack with the same determination. The firing became very heavy, and the advance in the centre could not be pressed, in view of the fact that each step forward brought the City Imperial Volunteers more and more into the midst of the crescent, from all points in which the enemy's marksmen were pouring bullets. The cover was good, however; there were many large stones on the plateau, and behind these the infantry found excellent shelter, while shell and shrapnel hummed through the air overhead, or at times scattered their splinters of steel and heavy bullets right and left among the prone soldiers. Behind them, the men could now see the Guards coming into action, and the sight gave new confidence. But yet more cheering was the appearance of the 82nd Field Battery on the summit. With characteristic boldness Ian Hamilton had ordered it into the very firing line. Only by the most desperate exertions was it dragged up the steep slope. Arriving, it came under a terrific fire. As the six guns spun round and unlimbered, ten horses fell and several of the gunners were placed *hors de combat.* But here, as throughout the war, the artillery did not flinch. "The men served their weapons," says Mr. Churchill, "with machine-like precision, and displayed a composure and devotion which won them the unstinted admiration of all who saw the action." Their self-sacrificing coolness decided the

[Photo by Maull & Fox.

COLONEL W. W. MACKINNON.

In command of the City Imperial Volunteers, and present at the action of Diamond Hill, June 11–12, 1900.

day. "As if by magic," says an eye-witness, "the situation changed." The Boer rifle-fire suddenly sank, as the riflemen found the steady hail of shrapnel bullets by no means to their liking, and the British fire swelled up. On the left the Guards and Derbyshires gained ground fast and rolled up the Boer line. They had the aid of the 83rd Battery, which emulated the prowess of the 82nd. In this last battery no less than one quarter of the gunners were now out of action. Night fell with the roar of firing still swelling over the plateau and with the Boer position still untaken. The battle ceased and the troops remained fronting the enemy. Pole-Carew and Ian Hamilton conferred, and decided to bring up the 18th Brigade and with its help renew the attack next day.

In other parts of the wide field the battle had gone with varying fortune. On the British right De Lisle's Mounted Infantry had won a lodgment on the crest, some distance from the infantry. On the extreme left French had great difficulty in keeping the enemy in check. His cavalry had to be strung out on the summit of the hills which he held, repelling by carbine fire the incessant attacks of De la Rey. Here O Horse Artillery Battery greatly distinguished itself, remaining in action all day under a heavy rifle-fire. The British were kept well extended, and in consequence the losses of

R. Caton Woodville.]

THE C.I.V. BATTERY ENGAGED OUTSIDE PRETORIA, June 11, 1900.

The Battery furnished by the Honourable Artillery Company to the City Imperial Volunteers was in action with Paget's force outside Pretoria, whilst the infantry division of the same corps was carrying on its gallant fight with the Boers at Diamond Hill.

the cavalry only totalled twenty-one, but the horses were utterly worn out by the hard work demanded of them. In spite of General French's energetic employment of his weak force, the Boers in small numbers did succeed in working round his flank, and the escort of an officer, sent back on the night of the 12th to report to Lord Roberts, was captured. But by the early morning of the 13th the Boers had fallen back. French was able to push on to Tweefontein; his horses were in such a wretched condition that anything like a vigorous pursuit was out of the question. He had already telegraphed that he required 5,000 remounts—an indication of the state to which his cavalry had been reduced. On June 14 he rode into Eland's River, but found De Lisle was there before him.

The enemy had in similar fashion evacuated the positions facing Pole-Carew, Ian Hamilton, and De Lisle, marching east in good order. Hamilton and De Lisle promptly followed them up, but they had got too good a start to be overtaken, and were able to carry off all their guns and almost all their waggons. De Lisle only caught the last of their convoys, pouring into it a heavy fire and inflicting upon it serious loss. The Boers on their part had had enough of fighting for the time, and retreated towards Middelburg and the north, where they ceased to give further trouble during June.

[*Photo by the Biograph Co.*

PROCLAIMING THE ANNEXATION OF THE ORANGE FREE STATE AT BLOEMFONTEIN, May 28, 1900.

The proclamation was read by General Pretyman, Military Governor of Bloemfontein. From this date the State became the "Orange River Colony." The spectators are here photographed in the act of saluting the flag, which had been hoisted by Lord Acheson. The Sixth Division under General Kelly-Kenny formed the guard in the Market Square.

The British losses in this action were 14 killed, 144 wounded, and 4 missing. The Boer losses were certainly in excess of the British, and may be placed at 300 to 400. But the enemy succeeded

Casualties.

in making good their escape and, though forced back, sustained no shattering defeat. It was the old story on our part of a cavalry with worn-out horses and attenuated numbers, unable to get in upon the enemy's flanks, or to pursue the Boers when they had taken to flight.

During the course of the battle Lord Roberts had been compelled by the bad news from the Orange River Colony—for the Free State had been annexed to the British Empire

Annexation of the Orange Free State.

under that title by Lord Roberts in a proclamation issued on May 28—to hurry back to Pretoria, so as to be able to deal with the situation in the south. On Ian Hamilton's march northward from Heilbron in May, General Colvile, with Macdonald's Brigade, had been ordered to follow from Ventersburg by way of Lindley and occupy Heilbron. The 13th Yeomanry Battalion, under Colonel Spragge, reached Kroonstad on May 25, and was at once directed to march to Lindley and there join General Colvile, with a convoy of waggons, to which it was to act as escort. A forged telegram, which after-events proved to have been sent by the Boers, but which purported to come from General Colvile at Lindley on May 23, laid down the route to be followed. The Yeomanry left on the evening of the 25th and made a forced march to Lindley, which they reached, with their horses utterly worn out, early on the 27th. As the village was approached a party of horsemen were seen to ride out of it. They were at first taken to be Colvile's rearguard. But the scouts, pushing on ahead, sent word back that not only had Colvile gone, but that the horsemen were Boers. The convoy was left a mile from the village, and two companies out of the four cautiously entered Lindley. Almost at once the Boers showed in force on the heights round the place, and skirmishing began. Lindley was held till about 5 p.m., when the enveloping tactics of the enemy compelled Colonel Spragge to order a retirement, and under cover of the fire of two Colt guns he withdrew to the

The Yeomanry in difficulties.

[*Photo by Edgecombe, Beaufort West.*]

COLONEL SPRAGGE AND OFFICERS OF THE 45TH AND 47TH COMPANIES, IMPERIAL YEOMANRY, CAPTURED AT LINDLEY, June 26, 1900.

Colonel Spragge sits at the head of the table, to the right in the picture. On his right are (in order) Lieut. Stannus, Captain R. Robinson, Lieut. Villiers Stuart, Lieut. Du Pre, and Veterinary-Lieut. Fenner. On his left Captain Hadley, M.B., Lieut. Robin, Captain Lord Longford, Lieut. Wright, Lieut. Lane.

convoy. This convoy, however, he must subsequently have abandoned, as he stated in his messages to Rundle and Colvile that he had food only for one day. His men and horses were so exhausted that retreat to Kroonstad was out of the question, even if he had been able to fight his way through the surrounding Boers, now one or two thousand strong. Accordingly, confident in the belief that General Colvile would turn back to his aid on hearing the firing, he seized some kopjes near at hand, and during the night entrenched himself as best he could. He had succeeded, before the wires were cut, in telegraphing his situation to Lord Roberts, promising to hold out some days; he had also sent to Colvile a messenger who got through the enemy's lines and reached that general on the morning of the 28th at a point twenty miles from Lindley. But Colvile was himself hard pressed by the Boers. He had been skirmishing with the enemy daily since his departure from Ventersburg; moreover, he was under orders from Lord Roberts to be at Heilbron on the 29th. Heilbron is forty miles by road from Lindley, or three days' march. If he turned back, it was certain that he would not arrive at the required time, when some much larger and more important combination might fail. He therefore decided not to return, sent back a message to that effect, and advised Colonel Spragge to retreat to Kroonstad, authorising him to abandon his stores and convoy.

Fruitless appeals for help.

After a night's intermission, the Boer rifle-fire recommenced on the morning of the 28th, and continued all that and the two following days. The breastworks thrown up offered poor protection, and the losses were considerable. On the night of the 30th Colonel Spragge sent out two scouts with

F. J. Waugh.]

A CAVALRY PATROL SURPRISED IN A DONGA.

(667)

a fresh message, imploring assistance, to General Colvile, and yet another to General Rundle. One of the two sent to Colvile, on hearing that there was no hope of help from him, at once rode to Lord Methuen's column, which was at this moment marching on Heilbron. Lord Methuen acted with the most praiseworthy energy and decision. He immediately changed the direction of his advance, and moved so swiftly that within 25 hours of the moment at which the appeal reached him he arrived upon the scene of action. But he found a field tenanted only by the dead. There, before him, lay some forty of the Yeomanry who had fallen; the living had vanished, and it was learnt that the battalion had surrendered two days earlier—on May 31. The Boers had brought up two field-guns and a "Pom-Pom," the shells of which at short range inflicted heavy loss. The

Surrender at Lindley. white flag was raised by one of the four companies, holding an outlying kopje, and the other three followed suit and surrendered to prevent further effusion of blood. The total British losses are variously stated at 78 and 111, and, as no full and official report has appeared, it is impossible to say which figure is correct. The resistance was less strenuous than might have been expected of a force of such high quality—for some of

ENTRANCE TO THE PRISON ENCLOSURE AT NOOITGEDACHT, AND THE MEN WHO GUARDED IT.

It was at this spot that the Yeomanry captured at Lindley were confined.

YEOMEN INSIDE THE PRISON AT NOOITGEDACHT.

The young man standing in the centre of the picture and wearing a cap is Mr. Goschen, son of the (then) First Lord of the Admiralty. Lord Leitrim, son of the Chief Justice, is another member of the group.

the best blood in England was among the captured troopers. But, at least, it seems to illustrate the weakness of a hastily assembled, ill-disciplined volunteer force. Not less humiliating is the fact that the prisoners were seen by a British officer, who had escaped from the Boers, proceeding quietly north under the guard of only eight armed men. The Prussians, in 1866, wondered when two Austrian batteries, numbering 207 men, taken at Tobitschau, allowed themselves to be marched off under an escort of 25 cuirassiers.

A second mishap followed speedily upon this mortifying affair. Colvile's troops at Heilbron were short of food and ammunition, and had the enemy all about them. It was a matter of urgent necessity **De Wet captures a convoy.** to get a convoy through to them. Accordingly, 55 waggons left the railway at Vredefort Road on June 1, guarded by only 160 details of the Highland Brigade. Captain Corballis, of the Army Service Corps, was in charge of the convoy; Captain Johnson in command of the troops. Conflicting orders were received, directing the convoy to move on Heilbron, and advising it to wait. Under these circumstances it adopted, what is always a most dangerous course in war, the middle course, and halted on the Rhenoster, half-way between Vredefort Road and Heilbron, till the night of the 2nd, when it resumed its march. The infantry

s

escort for the most part got into the waggons and went to sleep—not that it mattered much what they did when a helpless and unwieldy array of oxen and waggons was calmly walking into the midst of 3,000 enemies.   On the afternoon of the 3rd signs of the enemy were seen, the convoy laagered, and a message was sent back to Vredefort Road, where was a force of about 1,000 men of all arms—details of various regiments with few officers—under Major Haig, asking for help.   The messenger returned at 8 a.m. of the 4th with the news that Haig had started, and was near the camp.   An hour later a message from the Boers reached the convoy.   It said: "I have 1,200 men and five guns.   Surrender at once—De Wet."   After some futile attempts at negotiation Captain Johnson capitulated.   A successful resistance was of course out of the question, and, as a matter of fact, Major Haig, when only a couple of miles from the convoy, had been compelled to return by

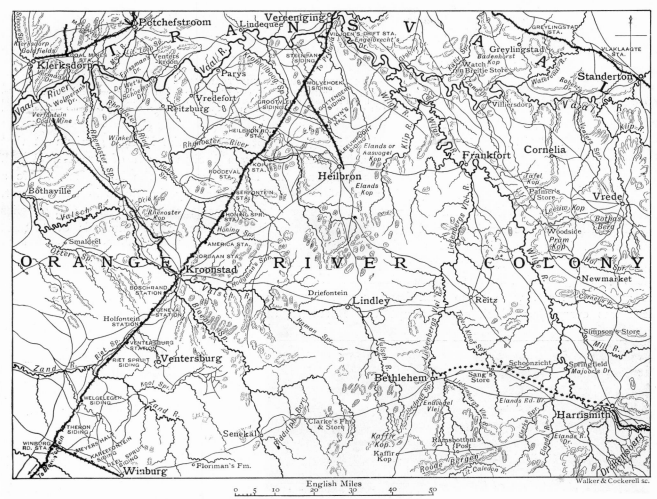

MAP OF THE SCENE OF OPERATIONS AGAINST DE WET, June, 1900.

the movements of a Boer force in his rear, which was threatening his line of retreat and the railway.   Nor was it possible for the convoy to withdraw.   But the consequences of its loss were extremely grave.   De Wet was supplied with warm clothing and stores of all descriptions; the Highland Brigade was reduced to desperate straits for food, so that it was for four days upon quarter rations; and the Boers were immensely encouraged by this second brilliant success.   Men who had taken the oath of neutrality flocked to De Wet's side, and his force grew almost miraculously in strength.   Who was responsible for the incredible mistake of ordering the convoy to proceed to Heilbron under such an escort has not yet been revealed; though General Colvile was sent home shortly after these incidents, it does not seem that he was to blame for them—at least, on the evidence which is accessible.   The affairs of the Yeomanry and the convoy help to swell the long tale of mysteries in this war.

Flushed with success, De Wet now turned his attention to the railway. His farm was in the region watered by the Rhenoster, and every inch of ground from Vredefort Road to Honing Spruit was in consequence familiar to him. It is a kopje-studded, spruit-broken region, where local knowledge must stand a soldier in good stead. On June 5 a raiding detachment from his force destroyed the railway bridge at Roodeval; on the 6th a large Boer force show-

[*Photo by Sergt. Haslam, R.E.*

A MONSTER GUN IN THE TRANSVAAL.

This huge weapon, of 9·2-inch calibre, is called "Kandahar." It was taken from a fort at Capetown, set upon a specially-constructed carriage from which it is fired, and manned by the Cape Garrison Artillery. The photograph was taken at Belfast in August, 1900. The reference in the text on this page is not to this gun, but to two howitzers of about the same calibre, which, however, being shorter and lighter, were independent of the railway.

ed itself near Vredefort Road, but, though it exchanged a hot fire with the British garrison at that place, made no serious attack. The railway, however, was again broken north of Vredefort Road.

Disaster on the Rhenoster.

The next stroke was aimed against the British post on the Rhenoster, where a new railway bridge, in place of the one demolished by the Boers in their retreat, was in course of construction. Here, too, a vast amount of stores and supplies for the army had accumulated, waiting transport to the front. There were hundreds of tons of ammunition, including lyddite shells for the as yet unused 9·4-inch howitzers, which had a place in Lord Roberts' siege-train; there were thousands of great-coats, blankets and winter uniforms, with stacks of forage and innumerable truck-loads of flour, beef, and biscuits; last, but in the eyes of the army not least, were 1,500 mail bags, containing letters and parcels for the troops. In fact, there was everything which could tempt the Boers to a raid. To protect the stores and the bridge the total force available was a company of railway pioneers and the 4th (Militia) Battalion of the Derbyshire Regiment, totalling about 600 men; of these, 150 were on the south of the river, and the other 450 four miles off on the north bank. There were no guns. An attack was known to be imminent, but appeals for help brought the disquieting answer from Kroonstad that no more troops could be spared, and that the post must do the best it could. The Derbyshires only marched in late in the night of the 6th, and were unable in the darkness carefully to examine their camping ground, which lay midway between the Rhenoster and a line of kopjes, about a mile away. In these kopjes the Boers were already lurking, so close at hand that they clearly heard the officers giving orders to the sentries and learnt the countersign. Two companies are stated to have been placed in the kopjes,

THREE BRAVE BOYS.

These three loyal boys, George Melville (aged 16), Sydney Melville (aged 11), and a Kaffir youth named Ramanana, living on a farm near Vredefort Road, one day noticed Boers placing dynamite about bridges and culverts on the railway. As soon as this work was completed to their satisfaction, the enemy went away; thereupon the boys seized their opportunity and worked for hours carrying the dynamite to the farm, where their father buried it. At dawn the Boers returned, only to find to their amazement that the explosive material had been removed.

though on this point the authorities are not all agreed. In the course of the night Australian scouts and Kaffirs warned the officers that the enemy were close at hand in great strength, but the warning was treated with ridicule. A few shots, however, were fired, upon which the outposts were strengthened, and then, as nothing more happened, the bulk of the force turned in. Their sleep was not for long; between 2 and 3 a.m. a terrific fusillade was poured into the camp from the high ground all round. Yet the militia, though subjected to one of the severest trials that can befall

soldiers in war, and though raw troops now for the first time under fire, behaved finely. They rallied from their surprise and made what reply they could. Their Colonel, Baird-Douglas, swore he would shoot the first man who raised the white flag, and not till he had been killed, with many of his officers, did anyone suggest surrender. At daylight the Boers opened with four guns and a "Pom-Pom," inflicting terrible loss. No entrenchments had been dug; little cover could be found; and it was known that there was no chance of reinforcements arriving. The only thing that could be done was to fight until sufficient loss had been incurred to take away any taint of dishonour from surrender. About 10 a.m. of the 7th this point was reached, the white flag was hoisted, and the battalion laid down its arms.

The small post to the south of the river was likewise attacked, but not till daybreak. Under cover of a flag of truce demanding its surrender, the Boers approached to within 800 yards and opened with a field-gun and with about 500 rifles. The first shell fired landed in the very midst of the British, killing and mangling four men and wounding three others. But with fine pluck and coolness the rest of the detachment faced the Boers,

CHRISTIAN DE WET.

General Christian De Wet, who was born about 1852, springs from the ranks of the better educated Boers. His life has been spent in farming, which in his case meant growing "mealies" (Indian corn) and forage for market. He amassed some fortune, but speculated rashly on the Johannesburg Stock Exchange and lost nearly all. He has taken part from time to time in minor native wars, but in no respect can he be said to have had anything approaching a military education. As a Free State burgher (he comes from the Harrismith district) he might have taken a prominent part in politics, but has preferred to remain comparatively aloof.

firing with such accuracy and steadiness that they were forced to remove their gun to 2,000 yards. A second gun came up and opened at 7.30 a.m.; and three hours later, just as the noise of firing ceased in the quarter where the rest of the Derbyshires were fighting, three more guns and another large force of Boers arrived. The detachment was shelled from the front and rear, and the enemy's marksmen succeeded in working in to within 500 yards. It was now mid-day, and the prospect was absolutely hopeless. "We had," says a Canadian officer engaged, "no hope of receiving assistance from Kroonstad . . . it was a hopeless struggle against tremendous odds, with no prospect of relief." The white flag was accordingly shown, and with 12 killed and 17 wounded out of 150 the detachment surrendered. The total British loss in these two actions on the Rhenoster was 35 killed, 111 wounded, and about 500 prisoners.

De Wet at once proceeded to destroy all the stores that he could not carry off. The mail-bags were ripped open, searched, and burnt with their contents; forage, provisions, and ammunition were collected in mountainous piles and set on fire; the almost completed bridge was thoroughly destroyed,

BOERS LOOTING THE BRITISH STORES AT ROODEVAL STATION.

De Wet wreaks destruction on the railway. and the line of railway was torn up from America Station to Leeuw Spruit—a distance of 30 miles. All the 8th and 9th he waited in the neighbourhood; but then, learning that Lord Kitchener with a strong force was marching down from the north and Lord Methuen up from the south, he promptly fell back from the line, on his way exchanging fire with Methuen's advanced guard, in an affair which the British reports pompously described as "a complete victory," but which in real truth was a strategic success for the Boers, since they got away with their prisoners and waggons, and did not lose more than one or two men. The two British columns effected a junction and set to work to repair the line. De Wet was not long before he gave fresh evidence of his activity and daring. Marching all the evening of the 13th, he struck the railway at Leeuw Spruit Station about midnight, and surrounded the station, in

Gordon Browne, R.I.]   [*From a sketch by a British officer.*

HIGHLANDERS SEARCHING AMONGST THE DEBRIS OF THE DESTROYED MAIL-BAGS AT ROODEVAL.

which were standing two trains with supplies and railway material. The working party, 200 strong, was taken by surprise; a hail of bullets was poured in upon them as they were mending the line, but in spite of the fact that there were only nine rifles at hand, the workers succeeded in holding off the enemy, though the trains and the new bridge over the spruit were destroyed. At the same time another attack was made upon Kopjes Station, near at hand, where Lord Kitchener himself was asleep in a siding, and where a construction train was at work under the personal supervision of Colonel Girouard. Only the opportune arrival of 150 mounted infantry with two guns saved the situation and compelled the retreat of the Boers, who managed to make a bag of 40 or 50 prisoners. After this exploit De Wet determined to keep quiet for some days, as he learnt that Lord Kitchener was taking the most vigorous steps to put a stop to his depredations. On the morning of the 14th another attack was made upon the line of communications, by a quite independent body of Boers, at the Zand River, south of Kroonstad. Here, however, the enemy were held in check till General Knox could come up from Kroonstad, when he scattered them in all directions. Unhappily this affair cost

the life of Major Seymour,* a distinguished American engineer, who had rendered brilliant service in the Railway Pioneer regiment.

Meantime, in the east of the Free State Generals Rundle and Brabant had been steadily pushing forward, flanking Lord Roberts' advance. On May 18 they held a line from Clocolan to

[*Copyright of the " Review of Reviews."*]

MRS. KRUGER LISTENING TO HER GRANDDAUGHTER MISS NETTIE ELOFF, WHO IS READING THE LATEST NEWS FROM THE FRONT.

The photograph was taken on the stoep of the Presidential residence in Pretoria, where Mr. Kruger left his wife to the care of the men whom he characterized as "brutal savages." Lord Roberts set sentries to secure Mrs. Kruger's safety and privacy, and himself paid her a ceremonial visit.

MR. KRUGER'S DRAWING-ROOM,
Showing the golden eagle subscribed for by American sympathisers.

Winburg with the formidable pass of Mequatling's Nek behind them. Here some hundreds of determined men could easily have delayed

Operations of Rundle and Brabant.

their passage for days or weeks, but De Wet had apparently decided to fall back, in alarm at Lord Roberts' progress. On the 25th Senekal was reached, while Brabant seized Ficksburg; but this was not achieved without some sharp skirmishing, the Yeomanry with Rundle suffering considerably. They were in advance when they were vigorously attacked by the Boers. Major Dalbiac and four troopers of the Middlesex Yeomanry were killed; four other troopers were wounded. Fortunately Campbell's brigade of infantry arrived just in time to prevent more serious loss. At Senekal, Rundle halted for supplies, but receiving news that Colonel Spragge, with the 13th Yeomanry, was in a

* See his portrait in the group on p. 372.

desperate situation at Lindley, he determined to strike at the enemy, in the hope of diverting their attention from the beleaguered detachment. It was impossible for him to reach Lindley in time to give help, as that town is forty miles from Senekal, and Spragge had reported that he had only food for twenty-four hours.

SENEKAL.

South African towns are wonderfully alike; there are always the same one-storey shanties of wood and iron, with corrugated iron roofs, apparently lost in the great expanse of veldt. In the photograph, the kopje in the left foreground is the one stormed by the Imperial Yeomanry, in which action Major Dalbiac met his death, May 25, 1900.

At one o'clock on May 28, therefore, General Sir Leslie Rundle led all his available force out of Senekal, marching along the Bethlehem road. Three battalions had to be detached to hold Senekal, leaving him only Campbell's brigade, composed on this occasion of the 2nd Grenadiers, 2nd Scots Guards, 2nd East Yorkshire, and 2nd West Kent, with the 4th and 7th Yeomanry Battalions, and the 2nd and 79th Field Batteries—a total of less than 4,000 men. From Senekal to the steep hills, known as the Tafelberg and Biddulphberg, which rise in an amphitheatre athwart the Bethlehem track, was about six miles of veldt, covered with grass, dry and inflammable, and in places so tall that a man was hidden in it. The British troops reached the foot of the hills before evening and carefully reconnoitred the Boer position, suffering some loss. From a farm flying the white flag a party of Driscoll's Scouts was fired at, and one man killed and another wounded. At sunset the men bivouacked under the height, in readiness to attack next day. The night was a miserable one for all, the cold being intense.

At dawn of the 29th General Rundle determined to turn the enemy's right. The infantry were marched five miles in a north-easterly direction till they faced the Biddulphberg.

Battle of Biddulphberg.

The crest of that mountain had been carefully watched by the scouts and officers with the help of strong glasses; at first a large number of Boers were seen, but then they seemed to vanish, and it was supposed that they had retired. The artillery was brought up to make certain, and the two batteries searched the mountain ridge with a hail of shrapnel. Not a shot was fired in reply; not a human being could be seen stirring on the desolate, stone-strewn summit. Meantime, great inconvenience had been caused the troops by fires in the deep grass, due to careless soldiers dropping matches. These blazed up in more than one direction, and compelled the Grenadiers to change position again and again. After thirty

[*Photo by W. H. Gill, Viljoen's Drift.*

INTERIOR OF A BOER HOSPITAL TRAIN.

A good deal has been said and written in disparagement of the hospital arrangements of both forces. The train here shown appears to be very comfortable and clean inside. The gentleman on the right is a member of the German Ambulance Corps. The one on the left is a well-known Free State doctor. The two nurses are ladies from the Continent.

minutes of bombardment, as there was still no sign of the enemy, the infantry prepared to advance. The Grenadiers in the most open order faced the Biddulphberg; four guns of the 2nd Battery went forward and opened on the farm whence the white flag had been shown the previous day, while the 79th Battery took post close to the infantry. A number of Yeomanry and several transport waggons collected just to the rear of the batteries.

At the second shot the Boers disclosed their presence. It has since been said that they were greatly inferior in numbers to the British troops to whom they opposed so stubborn a resistance. Suddenly a single quick-firing gun replied from a position close to the farm and began to place shells all round the 2nd Battery. The Yeomanry and transport at once were compelled to execute "a strategic movement to the rear." "I regret to put it on record," says the *Daily Telegraph* correspondent, "that the four guns of the 2nd Battery were unable to do the enemy's gun the least injury. Indeed, for a considerable time the one gun fired more projectiles than our four. Our ranging was wretchedly bad, and when shrapnel was used the fuses were so badly timed that the bullets pelted into the hillside behind the gun instead of into the gunners. So ineffective was Major McCree's Battery that General Rundle ordered up the 79th. It did much better, and in a few moments the Boer gun was temporarily silenced. All this time no rifle shot had been fired, and not a Boer was visible except the few serving the gun. It looked as if by some accident the gun had been left behind, and that we had nothing to do but go and take it."

In excuse for the British shooting, it must be remembered that the 2nd Battery was one of the scratch batteries, hurriedly despatched at the epoch of disaster, with half-trained gunners, and that

[*Photo by Argent Archer.*

MAJOR DALBIAC,

Killed at Senekal, was formerly in the Royal Artillery, from which he retired in 1887. He served in the Egyptian campaign of 1882, and distinguished himself at Tel-el-Kebir. He held a captain's commission in the Yeomanry.

the guns were inferior to the Boer weapon in pattern. While this artillery duel was in progress, the grass fires had spread, and now a roaring sheet of flame and a heavy pall of smoke rose between the two opponents. Before the flames could completely bar the road, the Grenadiers were ordered to dash forward and secure the gun. They sprang to their feet and swept up against the farm; at once the Boer weapon turned its whole fire on them and began to pelt them with shrapnel as fast as the gunners could fire, without, however, hitting a man. Then from the ridge came the crackle of rifles, above the roar

[*Photo by Rolph & Sons, Lee.*

A FAMILY OF YEOMAN BROTHERS.

These are six young men of Lee, brothers named Westley, all in the 62nd Company of Imperial Yeomanry. They were present at the relief of Lindley, the taking of Bethlehem, and other actions in the district; one was shot through the elbow, and another had his hat blown off by a shell. Whether they were known by numbers, or how otherwise they were distinguished, has not transpired.

of the flames, and it was seen that the enemy were there in force.   Many of the Grenadiers dropped, and to the horror of the onlookers, the flames began to creep towards these prostrate men. Some staggered to their feet with uniforms smouldering and flesh singed and managed to escape; others, more unfortunate, perished terribly in the conflagration.   The aspect of the battle-field was appalling.   The uproar of the artillery, the crash of bursting shells, the sputtering of the rifles, the heavy roar of the grass-fires, made up an infernal concert, while shrouding everything was the pall of white smoke, veiling a hell of suffering, out of which from time to time came stricken men, or the stretcher-bearers with their sad loads.   The Scots Guards and West Kents were put in to support the Grenadiers, but no ground could be gained.   The enemy had the great advantage of an enormously strong position.   The intended flank attack had become a frontal assault, which there was no chance of pushing home.   At this moment General Rundle received orders from Lord Roberts to move to the assistance of General Brabant, who was reported to be in difficulties further to the east.   A withdrawal was therefore necessary.   First the Scots Guards, then the West Kents, and last the Grenadiers fell back, keeping superb order. In this retreat Lieutenant Quilter of the Grenadiers heard that some of his wounded comrades were lying far to the front, in danger of being burnt to death.   With a squad of brave men he went back under a heavy fire from the enemy, and brought off six of the wounded. Private Daniel particularly distinguished himself by

[*Photo by H. W. Barnett.*

LORD CHESHAM,

Commanding Imperial Yeomanry, was born in 1850. Educated at Eton. Entered the Coldstream Guards, 1870; 10th Hussars, 1873; and the 16th Lancers, 1878. He retired from service in 1879; succeeded his father, the 2nd Baron, in 1882; and in 1900 was appointed Master of the Royal Buckhounds; the photograph represents him in this capacity.

A PEN-AND-INK AGITATOR.

Dr. Engelenburg is a Hollander journalist who at one time edited the Pretoria *Volksstem*, a violent Governmental anti-Uitlander paper. He is a fluent writer, a ready speaker, a consistent supporter of the ex-President, and a devoted ally of Dr. Leyds. His unscrupulous paper certainly did much to foster anti-British feeling amongst the Boers, who nevertheless did not like its editor. He managed, however, to feather his nest very well during his sojourn at Pretoria.

dashing into the flames and rescuing a helpless man. The British losses in this sad affair were heavy.   No less than 38 men were killed and 134 wounded, while the missing, among whom it is to be feared were many burnt to death, numbered twelve.   Nor was General Rundle's object attained.   The Boers, however, suffered as severely.   They had many killed and wounded, including among the latter their Commandant, De Villiers. For these wounded they sent in a flag of truce to General Rundle, asking medical aid and brandy, which the British general granted.   On June 1 Rundle closed up to Brabant, marching to Hibernia, while Brabant's troops were now extended from Ficksburg north-westward to Hammonia.   General Clements, with troops of the Sixth Division, took Rundle's place at Senekal.   For some time there was no forward movement in this quarter, as the whole energy of the British troops was required to prevent the Boers from working through this line of defence to the south.

s

R. Caton Woodville, R.I.]

ORDEAL BY FIRE.

At the battle of Biddulphsberg, near Senekal, on May 28, the Grenadiers, under General Rundle, were holding a position on the Berg, when, possibly by the carelessness of some of the men, the dry grass was set alight, and several of the wounded were badly injured by fire before they could be removed.

Meantime, in the western field of war, Sir Charles Warren, after his transference from Natal to the office of Military Governor of Griqualand West, had been busy pacifying that desolate and disturbed district. With a small mobile column of Colonials, Yeomanry, and Canadian Artillery he encamped on May 29 at Faber's Put, a farm to the west of Kimberley, on the Vaal. Here he was suddenly attacked by rebels at dawn of the 30th. They crept up to within fifty yards of the camp, eluding the outposts, and then poured a tremendous fire upon the British from three sides. The horses were stampeded, and heavy losses were inflicted upon the British troops. So deadly was the fire that the shield of the Yeomanry Colt gun was shattered. But the

Warren subjugates Griqualand West.

IMPERIAL YEOMANRY SCOUTS WITH RATIONS FOR TWENTY DAYS.

Canadian Artillery rapidly came into action, and the British, after the first momentary confusion of the unexpected attack, fought with the utmost coolness and determination. Sir Charles Warren showed great bravery, riding calmly to and fro with his staff, and three of the officers round him either were wounded or had their horses shot under them. At length the enemy lost heart and retired, leaving thirteen dead on the field. The British loss was about fifty killed and wounded, among the former being the gallant Colonel Spence, of the Duke of Edinburgh's Volunteers—a crack Cape Colony regiment. This affair was a death-blow to the rising in Griqualand West, though the Boer leader in this quarter, De Villiers, did not surrender to Sir Charles Warren until June 20, when he and 220 of his men came in and were made prisoners. Yet further to the west, at Kheis, Colonel Adye gained a victory over the rebels on May 27. He attacked their camp, and with a loss of only twenty-five, completely routed them, captured a hundred prisoners, large quantities of stock, and 3,000 rounds of ammunition.

[*Photo by J. Bowers, Pretoria.*

THE IRISH BRIGADE WITH THE BOER ARMY.

This brigade, commanded by Colonel Blake, was mainly recruited from the Irishmen resident in the Transvaal. They are said to have been the chief element of disturbance at Johannesburg, which led to the request for twenty-four hours' delay in the occupation of the town by Lord Roberts.

THE PORTION OF THE 10TH MOUNTAIN BATTERY WHICH ESCAPED FROM NICHOLSON'S NEK, AND AFTER THE RELIEF OF LADYSMITH FOUGHT WITH BULLER.

CHAPTER XXIX.

GENERAL BULLER'S ADVANCE INTO THE TRANSVAAL.

Boer stronghold at Laing's Nek—Conference between Buller and Christian Botha—Composition of the Fifth Division—Drakensberg Passes—Bombardment of the heights—Botha's Pass won—Struggle for Alleman's Nek—Boers retreat into the Transvaal—Buller's tactics—Securing the British right flank—Junction of Natal Army with Lord Roberts.

THE centre of interest now shifts to Natal, where, after considerable delay due to the need of repairing the railway, and after long preparation, General Buller was once more ready to move. The Boers held Laing's Nek with a force of some four or five thousand men, and, owing to the strength of the position, had to be manœuvred out of it. The first point was to divert their attention from the flank selected for attack. To accomplish this, and to clear the Boers away from the British right, where they menaced the line of communication, General Hildyard was directed to move on Utrecht on May 27, and General Lyttelton on the Doornberg, a mountain range which rises north-east of the battlefield of Talana Hill. Hildyard reached Utrecht and received the surrender of the town on the 29th, while Lyttelton cleared the Doornberg. This work achieved, both columns returned to take part in the operations against Laing's Nek.

Boer stronghold at Laing's Nek.

The Boer lines at Laing's Nek began on Mount Pogwana, to the east of the Buffalo River. Thence they followed the ridge, in which is the Nek, to Majuba, and from Majuba bent south-westwards to the Drakensberg at Quagga's Nek, following this mountain range to the south of Botha's Pass. The total length to be defended was about twenty miles; on the west the line rested upon the towering mountains which part Natal from the Orange River Colony; on the east it was not easily to be turned, as the country there is broken, roadless, and brush-covered. On Pogwana the Boers had mounted a big Creusot. The British troops held the summit of Inkwelo, which rises even higher than Majuba, and on its lower slopes, during the 29th, mounted two 4·7's and two naval 12-pounders. At this juncture, when all was ready, General Buller determined to approach his adversary, Christian Botha, brother of the more famous Louis, to try whether bloodshed could not

Conference between Buller and Christian Botha.

SANGAR, OR SHELTER, NEAR THE BOER CAMP, NORTH OF LADYSMITH.

be avoided by negotiation. On June 2 the two opposing generals met and Buller urged Botha to surrender his artillery, promising that the burghers should be allowed to go to their farms with their rifles, subject to Lord Roberts' consent. Botha asked for three days' armistice, in which the British troops were not to move, that he might consult the Boer authorities, but on June 5 sent word that he could not accept the terms.

It was thus necessary to expel the Boers by force. General Buller had available Hildyard's **Composition of the Fifth Division.** Fifth Division, composed thus:—

COKE. 10TH BRIGADE.
2nd Dorset, 2nd Middlesex, 1st Inniskilling Fusiliers, 1st Dublin Fusiliers.

WYNNE. 11TH BRIGADE.
2nd Royal Lancaster, 2nd Lancashire Fusiliers, 1st South Lancashires, 1st York and Lancasters.

HAMILTON. 2ND BRIGADE.
2nd East Surrey, 2nd West Yorks, 2nd Devons, 2nd West Surrey.
South African Light Horse.
7th, 14th, and 64th Field Batteries.
5-in. and other Heavy Guns. Naval Guns.
61st and another Howitzer Battery.
Three "Pom-Poms."

Aided by two Cavalry Brigades:—

BROCKLEHURST. 2ND CAVALRY BRIGADE.
18th Hussars.
19th Hussars.
A Horse Artillery Battery.

DUNDONALD. 3RD CAVALRY BRIGADE.
Thorneycroft's Mounted Infantry.
Regular Mounted Infantry (Composite Regiment).

With this force of about 10,000 men and 45 guns he had decided to attack **Drakensberg Passes.** the Boer right on the Drakensberg. There were two passes, either of which he might assail—Quagga's Nek to the north, and Botha's Nek to the south— both entrenched by the Boers; the first strongly, the second indifferently, and both difficult. The Drakensberg on its

[*Photo by* **L. Weinthal.**

GENERAL PENN SYMONS' GRAVE.

The photograph was taken during the Boer occupation of Dundee. A monument has since been erected over the grave. The picture includes a portion of the English Church.

eastern face hereabouts falls almost precipitously for 2,000 feet, and its long ridge is broken by no well-defined gaps giving ready passage. At Botha's Nek there is no depression; the ridge does not drop; but it is here easier of access than elsewhere, owing to the fact that the mountain spurs slope less steeply than to the north and south, allowing a bad road to zig-zag deviously up to the summit. Five and a half miles to the north-east of Botha's Pass rises Inkweloane, a summit 6,200 feet high, or 200 feet higher than the pass, the topmost level of which is 6,000 feet. Four and a half miles to the east of the pass is another mountain, Van Wyk's Hill, which is somewhat lower than the crest of the pass. On Inkweloane the Boers had guns; Van Wyk's Hill was as yet unoccupied by either side.

On June 6 the South African Light Horse were ordered to reconnoitre the summit of Van Wyk's Hill. They were supported by the 10th Brigade. With difficulty they accomplished the steep ascent and occupied the flat summit, where at once they came under the fire of a Boer gun on the slopes of Inkweloane, and of Boer riflemen who lurked on the western slopes of Van Wyk's Hill. Reinforcements were sent for, but could not arrive at once, and for four hours the South African Light Horse bore the brunt of the fight, repelling two Boer attempts to recapture the hill. Then the 2nd Middlesex and 2nd Dorsets came up and secured the position. The shell fire, however, continued to be severe, and by nightfall the troops on the summit had suffered a loss of 25 killed and wounded. During the night the Naval Brigade went to work to drag their guns up. First two naval 12-pounders and then two 4·7's were sent up to the summit. To place the 4·7's in such a

MAJUBA HILL AND O'NEILL'S FARM.
The historical spot where the convention of 1881 was signed, and where Buller and C. Botha met in 1900.

position was no ordinary task; the guns had to be removed from their fighting carriages, lashed upon waggons, and then dragged with treble spans of oxen, assisted by tackle, up the steep slopes. By the night of the 7th, these four long-range guns were ready to open fire. Meantime, two British 5-in. guns had been placed on the lower slopes of Inkwelo, the mountain which on one side faces Inkweloane and on the other Majuba; other naval guns had been mounted on a spur to the east of Van Wyk's Hill, and the whole force of infantry, artillery, and mounted men had concentrated at Yellowboom Farm, which lies just under the hill. From its new positions the heavy artillery would now be able to sweep the ridge of the Drakensberg with a cross-fire, from Inkweloane to Botha's Pass, and prepare the way for a frontal assault by the infantry.

J. Finnemore, R.I., R.B.A.]   [*After a sketch by an eye-witness.*

MEETING OF SIR R. BULLER AND CHRISTIAN BOTHA, June 2, 1900.

Early on the 8th the bombardment of the heights began. Sixteen long-range weapons, and all the howitzers and field guns, were quickly in action; then the South African Light Horse, supported **Bombardment of the** by the Second Cavalry Brigade, moved forward, and seized without resistance a **heights.** high, conical hill known as Spitz Kop, close under the Drakensberg and to the north of Van Wyk's Hill. Between it and Van Wyk's Hill wound the road up to Botha's Pass. Next the infantry deployed—York and Lancasters, Royal Lancasters, South Lancashires, East Surreys, 2nd Devons, and West Yorkshires—in a line five miles long from left to right, from Botha's Pass to the point where the line of the berg makes a sharp angle south of Inkweloane, advancing directly upon the berg, and scrambling up the steep, almost precipitous, slopes. The right was guarded by the 2nd and 3rd Mounted Brigades. Notwithstanding the immense difficulty of the ground, the climb was rapidly accomplished. Regiment raced against regiment, and the whole line seemed to spectators to breast the summit simultaneously as the guns ceased to pour in their

[*Photo by J. Wallace Bradley, Durban.*

THE BATTLE OF BOTHA'S PASS: INFANTRY GOING INTO ACTION.
This photograph was taken at the commencement of the infantry movements. With the aid of a glass the men may be made out advancing in open order over the foot of the hill and the level ground near the river, while individuals mount the hill beyond.

rain of lyddite and shrapnel, and the crest showed through the clouds of smoke from bursting shells which had enveloped it. No resistance worth mentioning was offered by the enemy in the centre and left. It was found that the fire of the British heavy guns rendered the crest quite untenable, but on the right Thorneycroft's Mounted Infantry were the recipients of a hail of bullets from trenches which had been dug half-a-mile back from the mountain ridge. It should be said that on the Orange River Colony side the berg does not drop sharply, but extends for miles in rolling, upland plains. From these trenches two Boer "Pom-Poms" and a 9-pounder shelled the British viciously. Two of the A Battery 12-pounders and the Colts of Dundonald's Brigade were, however, quickly on the ridge—the 12-pounders hauled up by hand—when the Boer artillery was speedily silenced, and the Boers compelled to retreat. Their withdrawal was accelerated by the rapid advance of the South African Light Horse up Botha's Pass. To cover their retirement the enemy fired the long grass on the uplands, and thus veiled the whole country in an impenetrable fog of smoke.

The crest won, the British bivouacked on the summit. The losses were insignificant—in all only sixteen killed and wounded. The Boer strength was estimated at from 1,500 to 2,000 men, though

Botha's Pass won. it may have been less, as the enemy had anticipated attack at Quagga's Nek, and had there concentrated the great bulk of their force, neglecting Botha's Nek. That night and the whole of the 9th were occupied in moving the transport and guns up Botha's Pass, while the troops remained encamped on the tableland west of the Drakensberg. On the 10th the advance was resumed. The division marched northwards through the Orange Colony, with the South African Light Horse acting as vanguard, and entered the Transvaal before noon. At midday the Light Horse reached a hill north of the Gans Vlei, whence they could make out a large force of Boers falling back from Laing's Nek. The Boers on their part, fearing attack, at once detached the Lydenburg commando to cover their retreat. It engaged the Light Horse, inflicting upon them a loss of six killed and eight wounded, but sustaining itself yet heavier casualties. However, it prevented any interference with the Boer retreat.

On the 11th General Buller once more turned east and headed for Volksrust, to regain the railway. The Boers had occupied a strong position in his front on a ridge running north-west from the Drakensberg, the only pass in which was Alleman's Nek —or as it is sometimes spelt, Almond's Nek — a narrow gap in a line of jagged cliffs. Fortunately they had not had

GENERAL J. TALBOT COKE AND THE STAFF OF THE 10TH BRIGADE.
General Coke sits in the centre of the group with Captain Phillips on his right and Captain Jervis Edwards on his left. The group contains the Post Office Corps, Military Police, servants, and orderlies.

time to excavate their usual deep shell-proof trenches in the slopes, or the task of dislodging them

Struggle for Alleman's Nek. might have been exceedingly serious. "In many ways," says the *Standard's* correspondent, "the enemy's position at Alleman's Nek was stronger than that at Laing's Nek. The pass at Alleman's is much narrower than that at Laing's Nek, and could have, and doubtless would have, been rendered impassable by rifle fire alone, had Botha only known General Buller's plan." General Buller, however, completely outwitted his adversary, who was waiting for him at Quagga's Nek, and there digging a splendid system of trenches.

When the British troops arrived in front of Alleman's Nek, the Nek and the heights on either side of it appeared to be unoccupied. But the Boers were not a second time to repeat the surprise of Colenso against General Buller. "A" Horse Artillery Battery was ordered up to an eminence facing the Nek, and began to search with shrapnel the ground at the foot of the cliffs; the naval guns followed; and presently the British fire drew a reply from a Creusot to the south of the Nek. The field batteries and howitzers now came into action, and a terrible fire was directed upon the Boer position. A little before 2 p.m. the order was given to the British infantry to advance. So far the enemy had not fired a single rifle-shot, notwithstanding the furious bombardment to which they were being subjected. But that they were there—and in some force—was indisputable. The 2nd and 10th Brigades deployed for the assault; on the right were the Dublin Fusiliers, heroes of innumerable stubbornly contested fields, the Middlesexes, and the Dorsets; on the left the West Surreys, East Surreys, and West Yorkshires, supported by the Devons, from right to left. The left wing had the help of two field batteries and two "Pom-Poms." The formation maintained was an open one. Rapidly the line of men descended the gentle slope which led down to the bed of a spruit under the cliffs held by the Boers, while over their heads hurtled the missiles from forty British guns in action. Then, at last, the Boer rifles opened with a noise as of hail beating heavily upon an iron roof. A "Pom-Pom" played on the East Surreys, but the British guns located it and speedily reduced it to silence. The artillery redoubled its fire; the infantry pressed forward without a halt or check, facing the Mausers as coolly as though manœuvring in a mimic engagement on Salisbury Plain. The advance was rapid till the spruit was passed and the point reached where the ground began to rise; then the pace was reduced, and the men began painfully to breast the slopes under the cliffs. The Dublins, Dorsets, and Middlesexes found themselves at the foot of the ridge where it was steepest; but if it was difficult for them to escalade the terrace-broken precipices, on the other hand the very sharpness of the declivity gave some shelter from the Boer rifles. Moreover, the

MAP ILLUSTRATING BULLER'S CAMPAIGN IN NORTHERN NATAL AND THE TRANSVAAL.

British artillery had greatly shaken the enemy's marksmen, who found that rocks and stones afforded little cover against the terrible projectiles of the howitzers and heavy guns. The Dorsets soon after 3 p.m. reached and carried a rocky kopje to the south of the pass, but from this kopje they found it difficult to advance along the broad, exposed crest which connected it with the main ridge. The Boers were in force on the ridge in this quarter, and by their fire kept back the infantry. When, however, the exact position of the enemy was made out, the whole mass of British guns turned its deluge of shells upon this one point; straightway the Middlesexes and Dublins, to the right of the Dorsets, gained ground. The East Surreys, with a cheer which rose above the din of cannon and rifles, reached the summit to the north of the pass, and the West Surreys carried a kopje yet further to the British left. The Boer guns limbered up and the Boer marksmen could be seen bolting for their lives. At this moment the Dorsets, with magnificent dash, rushed across the nek and struck the crest of the ridge.   The Boers facing them saw their glinting bayonets and did not wait.   Soon after 4 p.m. the enemy were in rapid retreat northwards and north-eastwards, firing the grass as they fled to preclude pursuit.   The infantry emptied their magazines into the fugitives at long range, and

a section of the 7th Battery shelled them for two miles, but the cavalry and mounted men were not available and night was already falling, so no captures of guns and waggons were made and few prisoners were taken.   But the last position between General Buller and Laing's Nek was now in British hands.

On the extreme right Dundonald's Mounted Brigade had had sharp fighting. The Mounted Rifles and Thorneycroft's Mounted Infantry, attempting to turn

[*Photo by J. W. Bradley, Durban.*

BOER TRENCHES AT LAING'S NEK.

the enemy's left flank, lost two good officers, and found themselves in a tight corner, until the Dublin Fusiliers took pressure off them by attacking on their left.   The 2nd Cavalry Brigade was not in action, having been detailed to guard the British left.   The British casualties in this battle were by no means heavy, except in the case of the Dorsets, who lost 9 killed and 55 wounded out of a strength which probably did not exceed 600.   In all, 26 were killed, 126 wounded, and there were 2 missing.   The Boers owned to heavy loss from the British shell and rifle fire ; they had no less than 140 killed, and probably twice as many wounded.   That same night they evacuated their position at Laing's Nek, retreating through

Boers retreat into the Transvaal. Volksrust and Wakkerstroom, and next day General Clery was able to march his men over the pass without firing a shot.   Buller, in the meantime, advanced to the neighbourhood of Volksrust, and joined hands with Clery on June 13.   The Laing's Nek tunnel was found to have been blown in at either end by the Boers, but the damage done was not of a serious nature, and by the 18th trains were able to run through into the Transvaal.

[*Photo by Sergt. Haslam, R.E.*

THE TUNNEL AT LAING'S NEK.

The Boers blew up the entrances to this tunnel, but it was repaired by the Royal Engineers.   Captain Headley, R.E., the Somerset cricketer, was one of the officers who superintended the work.   He is shown near the centre of the photograph, turning round towards the spectator.

General Buller on this occasion outmanœuvred the enemy **Buller's tactics.** at every point, avoided the mistakes which had been committed earlier in the campaign, and with a loss of about 200 men in all turned a position of immense strength, a frontal assault on which would probably have cost 2,000 casualties.

It now remained for the army of Natal to push up the railway to Johannesburg and join hands **Securing the British right flank.** with Lord Roberts' forces ; but before this could be done further operations took place to secure the British right flank.   On June 16 General Hildyard, with the 11th Brigade, the 3rd Mounted Brigade, and a powerful artillery, set out from Volksrust to march to Wakkerstroom, which place had revolted after making its submission.   Hildyard

29*

STANDERTON LOCOMOTIVE SHED, WITH SOME OF THE CAPTURED
LOCOMOTIVES.

entered the town on the 18th and received the surrender
of a number of burghers. Thence he returned to take
part in the advance up
the railway. On the
18th General Buller
had begun the march
with General Clery's
Division, leaving Lyttelton to guard the railway from Newcastle to
Volksrust. On the 21st Paardekop was reached; on the 22nd
Dundonald with his mounted infantry rode into Standerton, where
eighteen locomotives, but slightly damaged, and 200 trucks and
carriages were secured—a welcome addition to the rolling stock on
the railway. A halt of six days' duration was made to repair the
damage to the line; on June 30 Clery with a mobile column composed of the 4th (Cooper's) Brigade, Thorneycroft's Mounted Infantry,
Strathcona's Horse, which had just joined the army, and sixteen
guns, set out for Heidelberg. The enemy hung upon the flanks of
the column and persistently "sniped" the scouts and outposts. On

**Junction of Natal
Army with Lord
Roberts.**
July 2 Greylingstad was reached; on the 4th
the column encamped at Vlakfontein, while Major
Henderson, of the Intelligence Department, rode
forward to Zuikerbosch Spruit and there met
General Hart with the head of the 10th Division. The Natal army
and Lord Roberts' army were now at last in communication, and it
only remained to repair the railway and guard it against further
damage. The Boers, however, were still in considerable force between
Vlakfontein and Greylingstad, where is a defile three miles long. On
July 5th they vigorously attacked a squadron of Strathcona's Horse
and made six prisoners. Only the prompt arrival of Thorneycroft's
Mounted Infantry and the A Horse Artillery Battery upon the scene
prevented a grave mishap. Next day General Buller, who was proceeding to Pretoria to confer with Lord Roberts, left Greylingstad
and passed through the defile without incident, but a large convoy
which was following him was heavily shelled by two Boer guns. The
line of communications remained liable to interruption, and, in fact,
British control of the country did not extend beyond the range of
the guns mounted to protect the various camps.

[*Photo by F. Bremner, Rawal Pindi.*

GENERAL COOPER.

Major-General Charles Duncan Cooper commands the 4th Brigade, South Africa Field
Force. He joined the Dublin Fusiliers in 1868;
Captain, 1879; Major, 1888; Lieut.-Colonel,
1895; Colonel, 1899. At the head of his gallant
regiment he was the first to enter Ladysmith
at the state entry into the town.

R. Caton Woodville.]

DUNDONALD'S CAVALRY FOLLOWING UP THE BOERS IN NORTHERN NATAL

The enemy frequently set fire to the grass with a view to impeding pursuit.

EVENING PRAYER IN A BOER LAAGER.

[From a Boer photograph

CHAPTER XXX.

THE ADVANCE TO KOMATI POORT.

Military position in June—More cavalry wanted—Boers break the oath of neutrality—Geographical difficulties—Deficient staff—
Effect of the Chinese crisis—Movements in the Western and Eastern Transvaal—Refractory Boers—Johannesburg
plot—Attack on Nitral's Nek—Sergeant Rawdin's bravery—Prolonged but hopeless defence—Ruse of the enemy at
Derdepoort—Result of Johannesburg conspiracy—Scottish Yeomanry at Wolverkrantz—Second stage of the war ends
—Advance eastwards—Action at Honing Spruit—Operations in the Western Transvaal—Advance towards Komati
Poort—Transvaal unsubdued—Advance along Delagoa Bay Railway—Annexation of the Transvaal—Occupation of
Komati Poort—Flight of Mr. Kruger.

HOUGH the enemy, no doubt, had their moments of grave discouragement, the
successes of De Wet inspired fresh hopes, and even if they had not from the first
been resolved to fight on to the end, that course was now finally decided on. The
Boers had suffered but little in battle since Paardeberg and Pieter's Hill. There
had been no
pitched en-
counters and
no great British victories. Time
after time we had failed to envelop
the enemy's
Military position in forces and
June. deal them a
deadly blow. With each mile that
our troops advanced, the difficulty
of guarding the lines of communication increased. Men and horses
were exhausted by the desperate
exertions and short rations of the
march to Pretoria, and once more,
as at Bloemfontein, it was the
"wreck of an army" that Lord
Roberts commanded. Nor can
it be denied that officers and
men were weary of the struggle.
The vigour and determination
displayed in the initial stages of
the war no longer manifested

[Photo by the Biograph Co.

LORD ROBERTS AT HIS HEADQUARTERS, THE BRITISH RESIDENCY AT PRETORIA.

When Lord Roberts went to Pretoria he occupied as his headquarters the old British Residency, on
the steps of which he is here photographed, receiving a letter from his private secretary, Colonel Neville
Chamberlain, with one of his Indian N.C.O.'s in attendance. Later on he used as a private residence the
handsome villa built for Mr. George Heys, illustrated on page 696.

themselves. A similar phenomenon has been noticed in every modern army. It was the same with Napoleon's veterans, with the soldiers of the American Civil War, and with the German legions before Paris. Home-sickness pervaded all ranks, and there were no new brigades and divisions ready to relieve the men whose energy had expired under the trial of incessant marches and skirmishes. The prisoners they made to-day were released on parole to-morrow, and the day after were again fighting in the enemy's ranks. A good instance of the carelessness shown in dealing with our prisoners is recorded by one of the correspondents. "A Boer prisoner who had escaped from the prison camp at Simonstown," he states, "was caught again and 'pacified.' A third time he was caught in a small Boer laager, and, being recognised, he was good enough to inform his captor that he had been visiting some friends. He was put into the guard tent, and conferred the honour of an interview on a distinguished general next morning. Shortly afterwards the general said to his captor: 'What a nice

man you brought in last night! He speaks English like a native. I've given him a horse and sent him to his farm!' When he gets tired of home life that cheerful sportsman will probably go out and have a swipe at some poor Tommies who are paid to be shot by any-one—including 'pacified' Boers. Now and again we catch a 'pacified' Boer under arms. Concealment of arms is not by any

[Photo by H. W. Nicholls, Johannesburg.

HOW THE BOER PRISONERS WERE GUARDED AT CAPETOWN.

means an unknown crime. In such cases we inflict the farcical sentence of three or five years' imprisonment, and it is generally accepted that when things have quieted down there will be substantial remissions." Little wonder that a vague sense of depression and discouragement filled all ranks.

Above all, at this juncture, mounted men were needed. Day by day the hopelessness of dealing an annihilating blow to the Boers with a force composed mainly of infantry more and more obtruded **More cavalry wanted.** itself. The cavalry had never recovered from the heavy losses of February; the mounted infantry, organised with so much trouble and effort at Bloemfontein, had been greatly reduced in number by the hardships of the march to Pretoria. The Yeomanry were for the most part required in the Orange Colony. How rapid and continuous had been the waste of horseflesh in the cavalry can be seen from the record of the First and Second Brigades for June:

				1st Brigade.				2nd Brigade.
Nominal strength	...	...	about	1 800	...	...	...	1,800
Horses Fit	...	...	...	861	...	...	...	795
„ Unfit	...	...	...	90	...	...	...	168
Remounts	...	...	...	437	...	...	...	542
Horses in Hospital	...	...	...	367	...	...	...	324
„ destroyed	...	...	...	88	...	...	...	61
„ remaining	...	...	...	1,145	...	...	...	1,124

It will be observed that in each case, notwithstanding the arrival of remounts, the Brigades were reduced to half their nominal strength. Nor were the remounts supplied good for the work to be done in South Africa. They generally arrived in poor condition after a long voyage, and were put to service before they had recovered. Overladen and ill-fed, they rapidly succumbed. And thus, though on paper the mounted branches of the army made a fine enough show, in real fact they were numerically weak and vastly inferior to the Boers in mobility.

Lord Roberts was naturally anxious to effect the pacification of the conquered territory with all possible speed, but there were circumstances which prevented him from accomplishing his desire. In the first place, the kindliness and uprightness of his nature led him, as we have seen, into the mistake of allowing all prisoners who would take the oath of neutrality to go to their farms. In but few instances was this oath observed by the Boers, and the soldiers noticed with growing exasperation that the greater part of the enemy's men killed in the fights of July and August had British passes in their pockets. Our men had over and over again to fight and vanquish the same Boers.

Boers break the oath of neutrality.

Then the extent of territory to be subdued was immense. The area of the Transvaal and Orange River Colony is little less than that of France—in all about 185,000 square miles, and in by far the greater part of this no British force had ever yet shown itself. Nor was this country easy to traverse. Much of it was mountainous, almost Alpine in character; the roads were bad and supplies scanty. The British columns scouring it could not be certain of subsisting on the land, and must drag with them trains of cumbrous waggons con-veying food and forage. The Boers on their part knew every inch of the land in which they were fighting; the drifts over the rivers, tracks shown in no maps, caves and hiding places in the moun-

Geographical difficulties.

tains and kopjes. The inhabitants who remained on the farms and in the towns could always be trusted to supply them with food and full intelligence of British move-ments. Their leaders were per-fectly aware of what we were do-ing, while our generals had to grope in the im-penetrable fog of war. And when combined move-ments on a large scale had to be carried out, the want of a trained headquarter's staff made itself felt. "Order, counter-order, disorder" is an old saying, and

Deficient staff.

HOISTING THE BURIED FLAG AT POTCHEFSTROOM.

On June 15, 1900, was hoisted at Potchefstroom the Union Jack which had been carried by the 94th Regiment when nearly annihilated on its way to reinforce the garrison at Pretoria, in the Boer War of 1881. This flag was rescued by a woman who hid it under her dress and so carried it to Pretoria, where on August 2 it was solemnly buried opposite Government House, and the following epitaph inscribed on its tombstone: "In loving memory of the British Flag in the Transvaal, who departed this life on August 2, 1881, in his fifth year." The flag was afterwards removed, brought to England, and, on their departure for South Africa, entrusted to the Royal Scots Fusiliers, who hoisted it at Potchefstroom, as it was impracticable for them to do so at Pretoria.

it constantly proved true in the operations of the summer and autumn of 1900. Alone of the great European armies the British had never troubled itself with the formation of a general staff. "A general staff," Moltke wrote in 1890, "cannot be improvised on the outbreak of war, but it must be prepared long beforehand in peace." The saying proved true: in war we paid a bitter price for our neglect, our soldiers suffering in life and limb for the delinquencies of the nation, the Cabinet, and the War Office.

BOER WOMEN BRINGING IN FOOD TO THE BRITISH CAMP AT MODDER RIVER.
There is no doubt that much useful information was conveyed to the Boer leaders by women visiting the camps ostensibly to sell farm produce.

The Chinese crisis, news of which reached the Boers in June, had also some effect in stimulating **Effect of the Chinese crisis.** their resistance. They felt confident that sooner or later England would be involved in war with France and Russia, as the result of this crisis, and so prolonged their efforts in the field, hoping that when this moment came the British force in South Africa would be weakened, or Britain be compelled to grant them the only terms with which they professed their intention of resting content— their independence.

On his return to Pretoria from the battle of Diamond Hill, Lord Roberts issued a proclamation guaranteeing the non-combatant population of the Transvaal their personal safety and freedom; all **Movements in the Western and Eastern Transvaal.** who laid down their arms and took the oath of neutrality were to be given free passes to their homes. Unhappily, the disarmament here, as before in the Free State, was not strictly enforced. Especially in the Western Transvaal, the surrender of old elephant guns, Martini rifles, and even flint-locks, was accepted, and too many of the burghers were allowed to retain their Mausers. The British outposts to the east were at this date near Bronkhorst Spruit, but the army was reduced to practical inactivity by the want of remounts, which could only be sent up with difficulty, owing to the frequent interruptions of the railway in the Orange River Colony, and by the need of detaching strong forces to deal with De Wet and the commandos in the north-eastern corner of that colony. Ian Hamilton with his army was at first designated for this work, but, as he was so unlucky as to break his collar-bone, General Hunter took over the command. Hamilton had pushed down the Natal Railway from Johannesburg as far as Heidelberg, which he occupied on June 23.

WAR-WORN SOLDIERS.
The photograph, which represents a number of men of the Eighth (Rundle's) Division, shows the effects of an arduous campaign on the soldiers' clothing. It is to be remembered that June and July are mid-winter months in South Africa, when ragged clothes constitute an absolute peril to health.

Hunter with the 10th Division, covered by General Mahon's cavalry, had marched rapidly across the south-western Transvaal through Lichtenburg, Ventersburg, Potchefstroom, and Krugersdorp to Johannesburg. At the same time Klerksdorp was occupied and the surrender of the younger Cronje with a commando received there. From Johannesburg Hart's Brigade followed Ian Hamilton down the Natal Railway, and met General Buller's army at Vlakfontein. On July 1 Hunter with Ian Hamilton's command entered the Orange River Colony and occupied Frankfort.

Meantime Boer forces hovered round Pretoria and Johannesburg, and displayed growing audacity.

Refractory Boers. Their attacks on the railways and De Wet's raids in the Orange Colony had already compelled Lord Roberts to issue more stringent proclamations, announcing that where railways or telegraphs were cut, the farms in the vicinity would be burned, or heavy fines levied upon their occupants. On June 28 the

NATIVE DANCE AT SPRINGS
In honour of the Queen, and to celebrate the British victory.

town of Springs, east of Johannesburg, was suddenly attacked by the Boers, but the Canadians, who were in garrison there, offered an excellent defence and beat off the enemy. In Pretoria and Johannesburg there was great unrest among the civilians, who were almost to a man Boers or the most hostile and undesirable type of foreigner. They were in constant communication with the enemy outside, and it was not long before they began to hatch plots against the weak British garrisons. Some of the most refractory among them, the Hollander employés of the Netherlands Railway, who had destroyed railway bridges in British territory, disabled the locomotives abandoned at various points by the Boers, damaged the water tanks on the lines, and greased the rails on inclines to prevent trains from running, were ordered to leave the country on July 2. But they were only a small fraction of the undesirable element. The Boer women and children were especially troublesome. They had been left, like Mrs. Kruger, to the English, and they

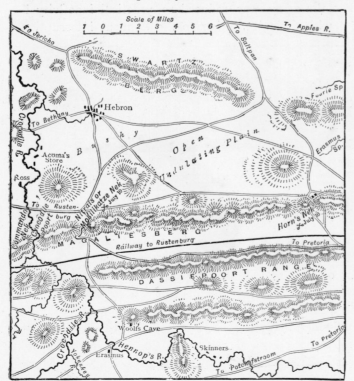

MAP OF THE MAGALIESBERG DISTRICT.

had to be fed and maintained while their husbands and fathers were fighting us at the front. It was their delight to insult the British officers and soldiers, who, of course, could not retaliate.

On July 5 Mahon and Hutton were directed to drive back the Boers to the south-east of Bronkhorst Spruit. A rising

Johannesburg plot. in Johannesburg had been planned by the foreigners and Boers. They were to arm themselves with rifles smuggled through the lines or previously buried; to attack the British officers at a gymkhana, which was to be held on a Saturday, to shoot them down, and then overpower the 600 troops in the city. Simultaneously Botha from the north-east and De la Rey from the north-west were to attack Pretoria, and if possible cut it off from all communication with the south. Probably the movement of Mahon and Hutton was intended to anticipate this design. They came into contact with a force of 4,000 Boers who were pushing south to Springs and engaged them with no decisive result. Fighting went on all the 6th,

s

7th, and 8th; the Boers were kept away from Springs, but they were not defeated. At the same time Pole-Carew's right in the neighbourhood of Pretoria was attacked without much result. The enemy, however, met with far greater success on the British left, and here were able to inflict upon our troops a small but regrettable disaster.

Eighteen miles to the north-west of Pretoria is a pass through the Magaliesberg, known as Nitral's Nek. It lies on the road from Pretoria to Rustenburg, and is an important point on the **Attack on Nitral's** line of communications between these two towns. A mile wide, with several **Nek.** small kopjes in it, it is bordered on the east and west by abrupt heights. In the nek were stationed two Horse Artillery guns of O Battery, placed on a hillock on the eastern side of the nek, and one squadron of the 2nd Dragoons. As a Boer attack was known to be impending these were reinforced by five companies of the 2nd Lincolnshires. Three

COMMANDANT DE LA REY AND HIS NEPHEW.

General De la Rey is certainly the politest, best mannered, and best educated among the Boer generals. He looks about sixty years old, but is only forty-eight. He sat in the first Volksraad for eleven years and always opposed Kruger, being ever on the side of liberalism and progress.

companies were stationed in the nek close to a small kopje some distance behind the Horse Artillery guns; two companies were a mile or more to the south. The high ground on each side of the pass was not occupied or entrenched, and no steps seem to have been taken to defend the British camps, although De la Rey was known to be near at hand with over 1,500 men, meditating attack.

At dawn of July 11 Boer sharpshooters opened on the British pickets and drove them in. They showed in some force on the eastern height bordering the nek, and thence were able to sweep the pass with their fire. The two Horse Artillery guns at once attempted to silence them with shrapnel, but, unluckily, the enemy were high up on the hill-side, behind perfect cover, practically invisible, and the guns could not be elevated sufficiently to reach them. Holes were dug in which to sink the trails; even then the 12-pounders would not bear. The Boer marksmen poured a simple hailstorm of bullets upon the gunners at quite close range. The battery and its escort of Dragoons made a stubborn and splendid resistance, but their position was desperate from the first minute of the attack. The cavalrymen with their short carbines were no match for the Mauser-armed Boers, who beset them on every side. There was no hope of repelling the enemy unless strong reinforcements should arrive.

Anxious messages had already been sent back to Pretoria, stating the circumstances. Meantime the three companies of Lincolns in the nek had moved to the aid of the guns, deploying to the west of the road through the nek, while the remnant of the Dragoons formed up to the east of the road; they held one of the rocky kopjes in the centre of the pass. The fight that ensued was an individual one—skirmishers and small groups of men engaging skirmishers and small groups of men—but the Boers had always the advantage of invisibility. Gradu-

A TRAIN-LOAD OF "UNDESIRABLES" DEPORTED FROM PRETORIA.

ally they worked round the Lincolns, as they had worked round the Horse Artillery guns. At this juncture Sergeant Rawdin, of the Lincolns, distinguished himself by the manner in which he handled his

Sergeant Rawdin's bravery.

Maxim. "The Boers," says Mr. Bennet Burleigh, "made it a target, and bowled over several of those serving the gun. Once the Maxim jammed, and Rawdin sent his comrades to the rear to take cover, for the Boer fire became hotter and more fatal. He stayed alone by his gun, deliberately took it to pieces, then replaced the parts in working order, and, single-handed, turned the deadly Maxim once more upon the enemy. By dint of steady courage, helped by the volunteer company of the Lincolns, the Maxim was saved." But this is anticipating events. The Lincolns displayed a spirit of resolute valour, and fought on obstinately, though the cover was not good and all hope of assistance was growing more and more remote.

The two companies to the south of the nek had

Prolonged but hopeless defence.

deployed and advanced towards the nek when the firing began. They were, however, too weak to effect much; they did not even succeed in joining their comrades. Presently they were reinforced by another squadron of the 2nd Dragoons, and by two more guns of O Horse Battery from Commando Nek, which lies further to the west; but even then their whole force did not

[Photo by Nicholls, Johannesburg.

MORE "UNDESIRABLES."

Boer women and children assembling at Pretoria Station with their belongings in compliance with Lord Roberts' proclamation that all the destitute families of fighting burghers were to be conveyed to the Boer lines.

exceed 250 men, and they could not fire on the enemy to the rear of the detachments in the nek without risk of hitting their comrades. They were themselves in considerable danger. De la Rey had brought up two guns and two "Pom-Poms"; his force was overpowering, and he was threatening their flanks. About midday they retired, leaving the men in the nek to their fate. Had the beleaguered Lincolns and the Dragoons forthwith surrendered, they could have been pardoned; but though abandoned—inevitably abandoned—they still fought on. From amongst the rocks they directed a steady fire upon the enemy, and the Boers dared not close with them or rush the hill. In command were Colonel Roberts and Major Scobell, both determined men. About 3 p.m. the Boer skirmishers worked forward, and, slowly approaching under cover of the shells from their "Pom-Pom," succeeded in capturing the two Horse Artillery guns, which, by some fatal oversight, had not been disabled. They now turned the guns upon the Lincolns. The shrapnel from these weapons proved far deadlier than the projectiles of the Boer weapons, which latter began to direct their shells upon the wag-

CORPORAL McKAY,
V.C.

Corporal McKay, the man in a helmet cutting bandage, is regimental medical corporal of the Gordon Highlanders, and at the battle of Doornkop so greatly distinguished himself by carrying wounded to safe places, and coolly dressing their wounds whilst he himself was exposed to fearful fire, that he was recommended for the Victoria Cross. On July 11th, at the battle of Wolverkrantz, seeing Captain Younger lying beside the guns exposed to certain death from the enemy's marksmen, he went out alone and carried the Captain to a place of safety. For this act he was again recommended for the V.C., which he has now obtained.

gons and men in reserve. Numerous officers and men were killed or wounded. Colonel Roberts himself was shot in the arm; Captain Maxwell and Lieutenants Connolly and Pilkington were among the casualties. Ammunition was running low. About 5 p.m., Roberts suggested to Major Scobell that surrender was necessary, the position being hopeless; but the Major declared that they were there under orders to defend the nek, and that these orders must be obeyed till the last cartridge was fired. Already a force had moved out from Pretoria to their relief. A thousand cavalry and infantry, with two guns, were at 4 p.m. only six miles to the south of the pass, when, by one of those errors of judgment so common in war, the officer in charge, instead of determining at all costs to go to the aid of his hard-pressed comrades, fell back, considering the enemy too strong to be meddled with. Thus a second time were the men in the nek abandoned. It was now growing dark, and the resistance could no longer be protracted, so about 6 p.m. the white flag was raised, and, after a defence the prolongation of which in the face of such odds does them all honour, the sorry remnant of the detachment surrendered. A small body of thirty men alone escaped; they had been at some distance from the main detachment, in the rocks, and they stole away under a heavy fire, favoured by darkness. There were some other marvellous escapes. Major Scobell managed to get away in the night. The Boers were so busy looting the British camp that he was able to bolt into the bush,

MAJOR-GENERAL SMITH-DORRIEN,
Commanding the 19th Brigade. (See the biographical note on page 413.)

Major-General Smith-Dorrien, in an earlier stage of the war, successfully co-operated with General Kelly-Kenny in investing Commandant Cronje at Paardeberg. Later on, he engaged in the operations near Bloemfontein, against Thaba N'chu, and Kitchener's-Horse Hill, and shared Lord Roberts' successful march to Pretoria. Like Generals Pole-Carew, Buller, Methuen, Rundle, and Kekewich, he is a West-country man.

and though pursued he reached Pretoria on foot. The British losses in this melancholy affair were 19 killed, 56 wounded, and 190 captured.

Nor was this the only British mishap on this day of ill-fortune. At Derdepoort,

Ruse of the enemy at Derdepoort. to the east of Pretoria, a squadron of the 7th Dragoon Guards approached a force of mounted men, uniformed in khaki and wearing helmets, which they took to be a regiment of British cavalry, and were fired upon with deadly effect by these cunningly disguised Boers. A lieutenant was killed, and several men were wounded. The Dragoon Guards found themselves sharply engaged with a thousand Boers under Grobler, and, though reinforced by the 14th Hussars with two "Pom-Poms," were compelled to retreat. As the result of these affairs our lines in the neighbourhood of Pretoria were driven in, and communication with Rustenburg was temporarily lost.

LORD ROBERTS' HOME IN PRETORIA.
This house, which Lord Roberts made his home during his stay in Pretoria, belongs to Mr. George Heys, an affluent resident who made his fortune by running coaches between Johannesburg and Pretoria before the advent of the railway. The house overlooks Burger's Park, and smacks of "money" from roof to basement.

Fortunately, full information had been obtained by the police as to the contemplated rising at Johannesburg, or fresh and grave embarrassments might have been the consequence. On the night

Result of Johannesburg conspiracy. of July 13–14 over 400 of the plotters were arrested, of whom about seventy-five were released on their respective consuls giving guarantees for their good behaviour. The remainder, for the most part Frenchmen, Germans, Hollanders, and Levantines, were treated with great leniency. Though they had planned wholesale murder, and had broken

AFTER THE BATTLE OF WOLVERKRANTZ: GORDON HIGHLANDERS HAVING A GOOD WASH-UP.

their parole, they were merely deported from the country. Most other armies would have shot them, or at least decimated them, and with good cause, since this lenity of the British authorities resulted in the hatching of fresh plots at Pretoria and elsewhere. The conspiracy, however, brought about one desirable result, as it proved to all that magnanimity was a dangerous policy. The Boer women, who had hitherto been maintained at the expense of the British taxpayer, while their husbands were killing the British soldier, and the feeding of whom, with De Wet loose on the line of communications, was no light responsibility, received orders to leave Pretoria and Johannesburg. They were sent to their sorrowing relatives with Botha's army.

Simultaneously with the affairs at Nitral's Nek and Derdepoort, a British column under General Smith-Dorrien was checked, moving north from Krugersdorp, at a place named Wolverkrantz.

Scottish Yeomanry at Wolverkrantz. The Scottish Yeomanry, with two guns of the 78th Field Battery, got into a tight corner; and the Boer sharpshooters closed on the guns, inflicting heavy loss on the gunners, Lieutenant A. J. Turner, a well-known cricketer, being among the severely wounded. Great difficulty was experienced in removing the guns, and many volunteers of the Gordons were shot down in their gallant attempts to limber up the weapons. It was only at nightfall that they could be withdrawn, with a total loss to the British of thirty-six men. Yet this affair in the official reports became a "successful engagement." As a rule, an action of this kind cannot be called successful when the troops have to retire. And though the Boers were supposed to have lost heavily, there was no proof of the fact.

That the Boers considered themselves victorious all along the line—as, indeed, they had a perfect right to do—was seen when five days later, on July 16, they again attacked the British left before Pretoria. They approached with great confidence and resolution, and closed with the Royal Irish Fusiliers, calling upon them to surrender. Their assault, however, was beaten off with a loss to themselves of about seventy; the British casualties were fifty-eight, and among the killed was the gallant son of the Canadian Minister of Militia.

With the actions about Pretoria in July the second stage of the war may be said to have closed. In the first stage we have seen the

Second stage of the war ends.

British Army fighting the enemy, generally with unsuccess, upon British soil. In the second stage we have seen Lord Roberts' rapid and successful advance from Modder River to Pretoria, through the enemy's country. The third stage of the war, the complete conquest and pacification of the Boer territory, has yet to be told. This stage is distinct and wholly different from the others. It is an affair of brigades and battalions rather than of army corps and divisions. Its events and incidents will be dealt with in detail in a subsequent volume, when the guerilla war in all its later phases will be fully described and related. Here we can only record the main events leading up to the annexation of the Transvaal by Lord Roberts.

After the affairs of July 16, Lord Roberts again prepared

Advance eastwards.

to take the offensive. He despatched Ian Hamilton

F. de Haenen.]   [*After a photo by Lieut. Elsner.*

HOW THE SCOTS AND COLDSTREAM GUARDS CROSSED DRYSHOD A SPRUIT ON THE WAY TO MIDDELBURG.

—now recovered from his accident—and Mahon to clear the country immediately to the north of the Delagoa Bay Railway, and on the 23rd began the general advance eastwards to Middelburg. Hamilton formed the left, marching to the north of the railway; Pole-Carew's Eleventh Division the centre, and French with the 1st and 4th Cavalry Brigades and Hutton's Mounted Infantry the right. The weather was bitterly cold, and the suffering of the troops, who had to bivouac in sleet and frost, severe. No serious opposition was attempted by the enemy.

DE WET'S FARM ON THE RHENOSTER RIVER, NEAR KROONSTAD, BURNT BY THE BRITISH.

The Boers uniformly retreated; Bronkhorst Spruit was reoccupied on July 24; and three days later French entered Middelburg, from which place the Boers fled in great disorder. The British casualties were insignificant, but one officer died of exposure on the night of the 25th. From Middelburg Lord Roberts hurried back to Pretoria, taking with him Ian Hamilton, whom he intended to despatch into the Rustenburg district with a flying column.

A word must here be said with reference to the operations against De Wet in the Orange River Colony. That bold leader, after his attack on the railway at Leeuw Spruit Station on June 13, remained quiet for the space of ten days. But on the night of June 22–23, he once more showed himself on the railway, this time ten miles south of Honing Spruit. Here he cut off an outpost of 11 Canadian Mounted Rifles, killing, wounding, or capturing them, and bombarding without result a camp held by 250 Canadians and Shropshires. During the night of the 22nd a train had been proceeding south to this very place. On board it were 400 of the released British prisoners from Waterval, under Colonel Bullock, armed with a promiscuous collection of odd weapons—Martinis and Sniders, with ammunition of the most wretched character. It is a characteristic and curious fact that while these old weapons had been preserved and issued to our troops, some hundreds of modern and excellent rifles, surrendered by the Boers, had been destroyed by the British authorities. No guns accompanied the detachment; two were to have been placed on board the train, but through some accident did not arrive in time. Nor was there any surgeon of the Army Medical Corps attached, though Lord Roberts' consulting surgeon, Dr. Cheatle, happened by some accident to be travelling south to Capetown to catch the steamer to England and was with Colonel Bullock. Thus, ill-equipped and altogether unprepared for serious fighting, this little force was entering the zone in which De Wet had performed most of his exploits. Its orders were to garrison Honing Spruit. Early on June 23 the destination was reached. At 5 a.m. the train drew up in the station, and the work of unloading it began. About 7 a.m. the troops were cooking breakfast, when suddenly three men were seen riding in from the north. Another three followed, and then a large force showed on the face of the veldt. A moment later a culvert to the north was blown up, and the detachment knew that the Boers were upon it. Simultaneously the telegraph to the north was cut. Fortunately the wire to the south remained open for a few

Action at Honing Spruit.

PRIVATE C. WARD, V.C.,

Obtained the coveted decoration for gallantry at Lindley, on June 26, 1900, when a picket of Yorkshire Light Infantry was surrounded by the enemy. The two officers in command were wounded, and only six of their men remained fit for duty, when Ward offered to carry a message asking for reinforcements to the signalling station 150 yards away, and actually returned through a storm of bullets, to report his success. On his return journey he was badly wounded.

minutes longer, and, before it too was severed, Bullock had time to inform the British commander at Kroonstad of his situation.   A few minutes later a culvert to the south was destroyed and the wire in that quarter cut.   At the first appearance of the enemy the troops had thrown themselves flat on the ground or sought what cover they could find.   No defences had been constructed beforehand, and there had been no time for Colonel Bullock's men to throw up earthworks.   The country was flat

and open; there were no stones or boulders of whose kindly shelter they could avail themselves.   A white flag advanced, and under cover of it a Boer emissary brought a note of the usual peremptory type from De Wet, demanding instant surrender.   But Colonel Bullock had once before, at Colenso, given proof of high courage; he now returned an abrupt refusal to De Wet's demand.   At once the enemy opened a tremendous fire. First the Boer rifles got to work, and then their guns began to shower shrapnel—and shrapnel from a captured British 15-pounder —upon the British force.   Our troops had the greatest difficulty

ARRIVAL OF A TRAIN-LOAD OF "UNDESIRABLES" AT BARBERTON, EXPELLED BY LORD ROBERTS FROM JOHANNESBURG AND PRETORIA.

This train contained Mrs. Kruger and Mrs. Louis Botha.

in replying to their fire.   The cartridges regularly stuck in the Martinis, and could only be removed by the use of the cleaning-rod.   The wounded, of whom there were soon many, were in a deplorable state; there were no instruments, no antiseptics, no dressings, and only one surgeon.   Fortunately some sheets were found in a house close to the line, and these were torn up and converted into

[*Photo by Rev. P. McQueen.*]

BOERS OF DE WET'S COMMAND.

The photograph was taken during a retreat and under fire.   The man in centre with square beard is General Kolbe; to his right in the picture is Commandant Pretorius.

bandages, but with nothing more than a pair of scissors and a pocket-knife it was impossible to perform any operations. Carbolic tooth-powder was the only antiseptic available.   The Boers steadily increased their fire; they were now shelling Honing Spruit with a 15-pounder, a 12-pounder, and a 9-pounder at a range of only 1,100 yards.   Short though it was, the old Martinis of the garrison were useless at this distance, but fortunately the Boer gunners set their fuses too long, and the bullets of the shrapnel they fired for the most part landed outside the perimeter of the defence.   At noon the bombardment grew more galling, the Boer rifle-fire more deadly.   Major Hobbs, who had been taken prisoner so far back as the skirmish at Willow Grange, was shot through the heart and killed; Lieutenant Smith was wounded; the Boers closed

in, and the British rifles jammed.   At this instant 40 of the British troops to the south, exposed to the enemy's fire from front, flank, and rear, became demoralised and bolted southward down the line in panic. Yet this rush of frightened men, by one of the curious chances of the battlefield, issued by no means disastrously. The British seemed to the Boers to be charging; a large party of the enemy left their cover to the south, and the runaways poured into them a fire at close quarters which shook the Boer courage; moreover, British guns appeared and opened on the enemy with shrapnel, and a relief force of 300 Yeomanry with the 17th Field Battery came on the scene. De Wet retired as suddenly as he had advanced. The British losses in this affair were 4 killed and 27 wounded. After this unsuccessful raid, De Wet seems to have fallen back to the south-east, upon which quarter British columns were now converging from all directions.

Meantime the Free State capital had been established at Bethlehem, after the Boer Government had been driven from Bloemfontein, Kroonstad, and Heilbron in succession. In the west, immediately

Operations in the Western Transvaal. after the relief of Mafeking, General Baden-Powell and Colonel Plumer had entered the Transvaal. Baden-Powell made Ottoshoop his base, and set to work to pacify the Malmani and Zeerust districts, while Plumer occupied Zeerust. Many Boers surrendered, took the oath, and were allowed to return to their farms, with the consequence that a month or two later they were again in arms. On June 16 Baden-Powell was able to occupy Rustenburg, whence he moved to Pretoria to hold an interview with Lord Roberts. Plumer at the same time advanced into the Eland valley. But the country was not carefully disarmed.

On August 16 General Paget with his brigade, which had been co-operating with those under Clements, Rundle, and Bruce Hamilton against De Wet, Olivier, and Prinsloo, arrived at Pretoria from Bethlehem,

BOERS SURRENDERING ARMS AT PRETORIA.

and was forthwith sent north along the Pietersburg railway with Baden-Powell, who

Advance towards Komati Poort. had arrived from Rustenburg. They marched as far as Warmbaths, taking a good many prisoners and skirmishing continually with the Boers, but were then ordered to retire, as all the available troops were needed to hold the lines of communication behind the main army, which was now moving eastwards to Komati Poort along the railway. Ian Hamilton and his men, who had been co-operating with Baden-Powell, were withdrawn to take part in this movement, and the Western Transvaal was left in a very disturbed condition to the care of General Carrington.

Thus by mid-August no material progress in the subjugation of the Transvaal had been achieved. Some 15,000 burghers were still in arms; 6,000 under De la Rey and De Wet in the west, at least as

Transvaal unsubdued. many under Botha in the east, and in scattered bands to the north and south another 3,000. In the Orange River Colony there were still about 5,000 men in arms, mainly in the north-east. About 12,000 prisoners were in the hands of the British, and at least another 5,000 men must have been killed, wounded, or incapacitated by sickness. Another 15,000 or more had taken the oath of neutrality, but proclamations of increasing stringency did not deter them from breaking that oath.

In mid-August the forward movement to open the line of railway which runs from Pretoria to Delagoa Bay was resumed. Since July 27, General French had held Middelburg; now Buller, with **Advance along Delagoa Bay Railway.** Lyttelton's Division, was to push up from Paardekop through Amersfoort and Ermelo to Belfast, where he would come into touch with Lord Roberts' army. The enemy had by August 23 concentrated on the mountain ridge between Belfast and Dalmanutha. It was decided to attack them both from the east and from the west. From the west Pole-Carew's division marched into Belfast and occupied the place without opposition on the 24th.

Early next day Lord Roberts arrived to take over the supreme control of the operations, and held a conference with Buller, French, and Pole-Carew. It was decided that French with two brigades of cavalry should advance to Lakenvlei, well to the north of Belfast, thus threatening at once the enemy's right flank and their line of retreat to Lydenburg. He was to be supported by Pole-Carew. Buller, meantime, was to assail the Boer left in the neighbourhood of Bergendal and Dalmanutha. The Boers were under Botha; they numbered about 6,000 men and had twenty or more guns, with the advantage of a position of quite exceptional strength. French may have had 2,000 men, Pole-Carew 6,000, and Buller 8,000; but it is difficult to determine the exact numbers, as there is no information as to how far losses from disease and action had been made good. The British troops had the support of a powerful artillery, including several heavy 5-in. "cow" guns.

On the 26th fighting with Botha began in earnest. The enemy offered a vigorous resistance to both Pole-Carew and Buller. Occupying the crest of the mountains in the loop which the railway makes between Belfast

[Facsimile of a sketch by Mr. Frank Stewart.

MOUNTED INFANTRY DRIVING THE BOERS FROM THE RAILWAY NEAR DALMANUTHA.

and Dalmanutha, with their trenches on the reverse side of the crest, the Boers were quite invisible. Buller, however, succeeded in forcing back their left in the neighbourhood of Bergendal farm, at a cost of only twenty-six casualties, and on the 27th carried their main position with a loss of a little over 100 men. Next day, August 28, Buller advanced to Machadodorp and occupied that town with only trifling resistance; on the 29th he reached Helvetia, a village on the Lydenburg road. On the **Flight of Mr. Kruger.** same day Mr. Kruger with what remained of his government fled to Nelspruit, where, however, he was not destined to remain long unmolested. The British columns pressed forward on all sides, and on the evening of September 11 Mr. Kruger, with his entourage, in two special trains, crossed the frontier into Portuguese territory and took up his residence with the Boer consul, Mr. Pott.

Annexation of the Transvaal. Meantime, on September 1, Lord Roberts from his headquarters at Belfast had issued a proclamation annexing the Transvaal. Thus the mistaken "magnanimity" of 1881 was at last undone. The enemy were vigorously pressed in all directions. No determined stand was made by them; they gradually fell back before the British advance until on the 17th they reached Komati Poort, where they destroyed their guns and

KRUGER'S TRAVELLING "CAPITAL."

Mr. Kruger, when he fled from Pretoria with some £2,000,000 worth of treasure, took up his abode in the saloon-carriage here depicted. From it he dated his State documents, and in the train, to which an engine with steam up was always attached, he is believed to have stored much of his "commandeered" treasure. At Machadodorp, at Nelspruit, and elsewhere, he established his travelling seat of government, until, on September 11, 1900, he crossed the frontier and arrived at Lourenço Marquez.

ammunition. About 700 then entered Portuguese territory and were disarmed; the remnant, some 2,000 or more, dispersed and scattered among the mountains, making their way north-west to Leydsdorp, or south into Swaziland. Komati Poort was occupied by the Guards under Pole-Carew on the morning of

Occupation of Komati Poort. the 24th, and there or at Hectorspruit were found two "Long Toms," eight field guns, four mountain guns, and a "Pom-Pom," all of which had been rendered unserviceable. On the Selati railway line was discovered an enormous quantity of rolling stock, stretching in a line for eight miles, undamaged or only slightly damaged, besides which there were many carriages and trucks that had been destroyed by means of fire. At Komati Poort also a large number of engines and carriages were found. Several bridges along the line had been blown up by the Boers, but these were at once repaired, and through-communication between Pretoria and Delagoa Bay was opened at last on September 29.

The capture of the Delagoa Bay Railway had now deprived the Boers of their last link of communication with the civilised world; their government had fled; their armies had been dispersed, and had lost the greater part of their artillery; but still there was no sign of a general and complete submission. Though British columns marched to and fro in all directions, the railways and small posts held by British troops were continually attacked. De Wet was still at large in the south and west, Botha in the east. What we had now to contend with was the obstinate resistance of a people in arms—the hostility, not of armies and commandos, but of men, women, and children.

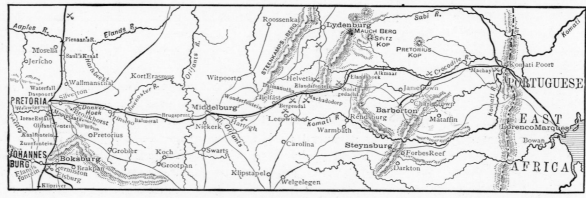

MAP OF THE LINE OF ADVANCE FROM PRETORIA TO DELAGOA BAY.

INDIAN WATER CARRIERS WITH LORD ROBERTS' ARMY.

CHAPTER XXXI.

SOME LESSONS OF THE WAR.

AVING travelled so far, we have now to apply the knowledge acquired by watching the British Army at work in the first serious struggle on a large scale in which it has been engaged since Waterloo. We have to ask why and in what respects it failed of complete success, and what are the lessons to be drawn from its failure.

In the first place it is incontestable that the problems of a conflict with the Boers had not been seriously studied by the generals who went out in the earlier period of the war. If we suppose that Germany had been in the same position in South Africa as England, we shall see what would have been done by her, and what should have been done by us. A section of her General Staff—in the British Army a General Staff does not exist—would have been told off to collect information about the Boer Republics and to prepare a plan of campaign. Every published work bearing on the Transvaal and Orange Free State would have been collected and examined. Secret agents would have ascertained the number of men available for military service in the Republics, the state of the Boer artillery, the organisation of the Boer commissariat. The theatre of operations would have been surveyed and mapped with scrupulous care. Meantime, a general of capacity, proved in repeated manœuvres, would have been designated for the command in the event of war, and with his staff would have made himself familiar with the problems likely to present themselves for solution. It is certain that with these precautions Germany would not have despatched an altogether inadequate force of cavalry and artillery, and have shipped these most needed arms the last of all.

Again, Britain, even in the era of defeat, did not put forward her whole energy. The conduct of the preparations at home was dominated by civilian ministers who had no knowledge of war, and who even failed to grasp the real lessons of the conflict in progress under their very eyes. They did not organise a sufficient reserve behind the eight divisions at the front. Fresh divisions did not leave England from time to time to replace the worn-out troops at the front; indeed, owing to the same lack of energy and foresight, there were no fresh divisions in existence.

Another cause of failure was the increasing aversion of the generals at the front to incur losses. Now war is a matter of life and death, and enemies of the calibre of the Boers cannot be overcome by mere manœuvring. No doubt smokeless powder and magazine rifles have immensely increased the delaying power of small forces in good positions; no doubt, also, the too precipitate frontal assaults of the earlier period of the war, and the outcry which the losses sustained in them had produced at home, tended to lead British generals to exercise great caution. But whereas at the outset we had boldly attacked the enemy, often when they were in superior force, now flank movements, which involved great delay, were substituted, to dislodge mere handfuls. Yet in the end the nation and the army had to lose by disease far more lives than would otherwise have been expended on the battlefield. The trained and disciplined soldier is not unready to give his life, where he knows that

that life will not be thrown away by incompetence. And while in the long run the loss-avoiding tactics pursued proved dear, they failed to break the spirit and determination of the enemy.

That the common soldier in this war has displayed high bravery and shown himself a gallant fighting man is not denied by any witness with the army, but it is a question whether that bravery —that fighting quality—is as great as it was in the days, say, of Wellington. The percentage of losses is the only certain test, and by this standard it does appear that on many occasions the capacity to face punishment is not what it was; and it may be doubted whether an army recruited, as ours is at present, largely from towns can show the same fibre as one drawn from country districts. The Colonial troops, who were drawn mainly from a country population, showed a tenacity which at times the British soldier seemed to lack, especially in the defence of detached posts. Some stories of tame surrenders must, however, be received with suspicion ; recent evidence, for instance, goes to show that the Yeomanry at Lindley (p. 668) made an honourable defence, and the statement that they were marched to Pretoria under the escort of eight Boers, although made by an officer, since retired, proves to have been a pure invention.

It has been concluded by many that the comparative success of the Boers against our armies proves that all that is required for national defence is a horde of civilians with rifles. We are to have thousands of men who do not own their own rifles, who are not expert in distance-judging—the first requisite for correct shooting—who have rarely fired a shot except through a Morris Tube, who are destitute of discipline and that instinctive obedience which it brings. And these, we are told, will suffice to beat off the attack of any invading army. Yet such a conclusion is calculated, if action be taken upon it, to lead Britain into deplorable disaster. When carefully considered, the Boer success will be seen to have been in great part due to the fact that their forces were infinitely more mobile than the British. On the other hand, the want of strict discipline in the Boer armies rendered them incapable of vigorous attack at the outset : the only instance of a determined assault delivered by them during the first six months of the war was at Ladysmith. An army which is good only for passive defence and which cannot deliver counter-strokes is not a model to be imitated.

The lessons of the war, then, may be thus stated : First, the absolute necessity for an organised and trained General Staff, such as is possessed by the German Army.

Secondly, that a considerable part of our home Army must be maintained in such condition that it will be able to embark on the shortest notice. Out of 47,000 men, nominally figuring in the various units mobilised for the Army Corps in 1899, no less than 21,000 had to be rejected. All this took time, and in the wars of the future time may not be given us. Natal was saved by the despatch of troops from India, where the units are maintained more or less in a condition of readiness for war. In conflicts hereafter India may not be able to spare a man, and may even need reinforcements.

Thirdly, the need for better training both of officers and men. Manœuvres must be held regularly every year, even if landowners are put to some inconvenience, and must not always take place upon the same old, familiar scene. Mistakes in manœuvres must be punished as severely as in Germany. After the naval manœuvres of 1893 the German Emperor retired compulsorily a vice-admiral, commanding-in-chief, a rear-admiral, a captain, and four lieutenants. It is by such unflinching strictness that a high standard of efficiency and duty is established. And if we are to have a voluntary army, which is also an efficient army, we must be prepared to pay both private and officer their fair market value. As matters stand to-day the poor and able man will shun the army, because it offers him no career. The British cavalry soldier must also be taught the art of caring for his horse in the open, and the infantryman must learn how to entrench himself and how to use cover.

Fourthly, it is certain that the proportion both of cavalry and artillery in the army needs to be largely increased. The formation of a mounted infantry division would seem to be a desirable step. It cannot be denied that mounted infantry has proved of the greatest value in the war, and that there are few fields on which it could not render good service. The present system of providing mounted infantry is the very worst that the genius of man could devise. It consists in taking one company each from certain infantry battalions, giving the men a certain amount of training, and then sending them back to their battalions till war is on the horizon, when they are combined under a commander who must be strange to most of them. To the artillery 43 batteries were added—on paper—in 1900, but further increase is required. The utter helplessness of infantry without an adequate backing of artillery was shown in the Modder River fight. Three batteries there averted disaster; ten would probably have enabled the British troops to assault with complete success.

Fifthly, better guns are needed; for when all is said and done, the rate of fire of our present field pieces is far slower than that of new models abroad. Long-range guns of position, mobile enough to accompany infantry, must hereafter form part of the equipment of the army.

Sixthly, in tactics the war has proved that the difficulty of reconnaissance has greatly increased. The work which falls upon the individual scout has become more hazardous and onerous, and the necessity of training a body of intelligent men for this special duty has been emphasised.

Seventhly, the Army Post Office and postal service require improvement. It is simply a scandal that parcels for the soldier, containing the little odds and ends which he dearly prizes, should often cost more for postage than the value of the contents, and should in many cases miscarry.

But the last and greatest lesson of the war is the need of a higher standard of duty in England. It is a fact to provoke indignation that while scapegoats are being removed from the combatant ranks, the Minister, to whom the arch-responsibility for the failure of the Army attaches, should have been not dismissed, but promoted from the War Office to the Foreign Office. Against Lord Lansdowne, personally, nothing can be said, but in his action as a Minister he fell far below the demands of his position. The nation, too, must rise to a loftier sense of its duty. It must realise that war is one of the necessary evils of this life of ours; like death it will be always with us. As the surest way of averting it we must be prepared for it, whatever sacrifice that preparation may involve.

VOCABULARY OF BOER AND KAFFIR WORDS AND NAMES,

WITH THEIR LOCAL PRONUNCIATIONS.

AASVOGEL (Ahs-fo'-gl)—Vulture.

AFRIKAN'DER—A man born in South Africa of European stock.

BASU'TOLAND.

BECHUANALAND (Betch-yu-ah'-na-land).

BERG—A mountain or considerable hill.

BILTONG—Strips of sun-dried meat.

BLOEMFONTEIN (Bloom'fontane)—*See* p. 544.

BOSCHVELDT (Boosh'-felt)—Country covered with bush.

BOTHA (Bo'-tah)—Com.-General. *See* p. 266.

BULUWAYO (Boo-loo-way'-o).

BUR'GHER (g hard)—Every Boer who possesses the franchise.

COMMANDEER'ING—The act of calling out on commando, or of requisitioning goods, etc.

CRONJE (Kron'-je)—*See* p. 15.

DAM—An artificial lake or water supply.

DELAGOA (De-la-go'-a) BAY—The finest harbour in South Africa. It belongs to Portugal, but England has pre-emptive rights.

DON'GA—A river bed, often dry.

DOP'PER—The ultra-conservative sect of the Boer church.

DORP—A village; equivalent to "Thorp."

DRAKENSBERG (Drah'-kens-berg)—"Dragon Mountains." North of Natal.

DRIFT—A ford through a river.

FONTEIN (Fon'-tane)—A spring.

GAT (Haht)—A hole or narrow passage.

GRAAFREINET (Grahf-ren'-net).

GRIQUALAND (Gree'-ka-land).

INSPAN—To harness up.

JOHAN'NESBURG (Yo-han'-nes-berg). *See* p. 11.

JOUBERT (Zhoo'-bare) GENERAL. *See* p. 37.

KLOOF—A ravine or a declivity on a mountain.

KLIP—A stone or diamond.

KOPJE (Kop'-pe)—A small hill.

KRAAL (Krawl)—Native village; cattle enclosure.

KRANTZ—A valley or cleft between two hills.

KRUGER (Kroo'-ger; g hard, as in "get").

LAAGER (Lah'-ger; g hard)—Boer camp.

LAAGTE (Lahg'-te)—A valley or slope.

LAND'DROST—District magistrate. [kwez].

LAURENÇO MARQUEZ (Law-ren'-so Mar'-

LEYDS (Laids), DR.—Transvaal Minister Plenipotentiary in Europe; formerly Transvaal Secretary of State.

MACHADODORP (Ma-hah'-do-dorp; the ch guttural).

MAFEKING (Maf'-e-king)—*See* Index.

MAGALIESBERG (Ma-hah'-liz-berg).

MAJUBA (Ma-joo'-ba)—*See* p. 4.

MA-SHON'-A-LAND—Part of Rhodesia.

MAT-A-BE'-LE-LAND—Part of Rhodesia.

MEA'-LIES—Indian corn.

NAAUWPOORT (Now'-poort).

NACHTMAAL (Nahkt'-mahl)—*See* p. 6.

NEK—The saddle connecting two hills.

NOOITGEDACHT (Noit'-ge-dahkt; g hard).

OUTSPAN—To unharness.

PAARDEKRAAL (Par-de-krawl')—*See* p. 7.

PALAPWE (Pa-lap'-che)—Town in Bechuanaland.

PIETERMAR'ITZBURG—Capital of Natal.

PITSANI POTHLUGO (Pit-sah'-ne Pot-loo'-go) —Starting point of Jameson "raid."

PONT—A ferry over a river.

POORT—A pass between hills.

POT'CHEFSTROOM—Oldest Transvaal town.

PRETOR'IA—Capital of Transvaal. *See* Index.

RAADZAAL (Rahd'-sahl)—Parliament House.

RAND—A ridge; also abbreviation of Witwatersrand.

REIM, or REIMPJE (Reem'-pe)—A hide strap.

REITZ (Raits), MR.—At one time President of the Orange Free State; afterwards State Secretary of the Transvaal.

ROOIBAATJE (Roy-baht'-che)—Red jacket. Boer term for a British soldier.

ROO'NEK (Roy'-nek)—Red neck. Nickname used by the Boers for Englishmen.

SCHANZE (Skahn'-tze)—An improvised shelter.

SCHREINER (Shrine'-er)—*See* p. 368.

SJAMBOK (Sham'-bok)—A hide whip.

SLUIT (Sloot)—A ditch on the veldt, usually dry.

SPRUIT (Sproot)—A small river or stream.

STAD—Native village.

STEYN (Stain), PRESIDENT—*See* p. 55.

STOEP (Stoop)—A verandah.

TAAL (Tahl)—Language of the Transvaal.

TREK—To travel by ox wagon.

TUGELA (Too-gay'-la)—River in Natal.

UITLANDER (Oot'-lander)—A resident in the Transvaal not of Boer origin.

VAAL (Fahl).—TRANSVAAL (Trans'-fahl).

VELDT (Felt)—The open plains.

VELDT-CORNET—A minor magistrate.

VIERKLEUR (Fear'-klooer)—Transvaal flag.

VILJOEN (Feel-yoon).

VLEI (Flay)—A pond or small lake.

VOLKSRAAD (Fokes'-rahd)—*See* p. 658.

VOORTREKKER (Fore'-trecker)—The older generation of Boers who "trekked" from Cape Colony across the Vaal River.

VRYBURG (Fray'-boorg).—VRYHEID (Fray'-hate).

WEP'-EN-ER.

WIT'WATERSRAND ("White Water's Ridge") —The district in the Transvaal containing the Main Reef Gold Belt.

ZARP—A Boer policeman, so called from the letters on his collar, ZARP, implying Zuid Afrikaansche Republiek Politie, or South African Republic Police.

[Photo by H. W. Nicholls, Johannesburg.

THE COST OF CONQUEST: GRAVES OF BRITISH SOLDIERS IN BLOEMFONTEIN CEMETERY.

CASUALTIES REPORTED SINCE THE BEGINNING OF THE WAR, UP TO AND INCLUDING THE MONTH OF OCTOBER, 1900 (OFFICIAL RETURN). *Concluded from Preface.*

Battle of	Date.	Killed.		Wounded, and died of wounds.		Prisoners and Missing.		Total Casualties.
		Officers.	Men.	Officers.	Men.	Officers.	Men.	
Monte Cristo (Colenso), &c.	Feb. 15–18	1	13	8	180	—	4	206
Paardeberg	Feb. 16–27	18	240	74	1,137	6	62	1,537
Ladysmith, relief of	Feb. 19–27	22	241	91	1,530	1	11	1,896
Driefontein	March 10	5	58	19	342	—	2	426
Karee, near Brandfort	March 29	1	20	9	152	—	—	182
Sanna's Post	March 31	3	15	16	122	18	408	582
Reddersburg	April 3–4	2	10	2	33	8	397	452
Senekal	May 29	—	38	7	127	—	12	184
Johannesburg and Pretoria, capture of	May 31– June 6	3	20	34	132	5	38	232
Pretoria, East of	June 11–12	8	6	16	128	1	3	162
Nitral's Nek	July 11	3	16	3	53	4	186	265
At Ladysmith during investment—								
Battle of Jan. 6	—	14	164	33	287	—	2	500
Other casualties	—	6	60	36	280	—	12	394
At Kimberley during investment	—	2	36	15	124	1	3	181
At Mafeking during investment	—	5	64	10	152	1	41	273
Other casualties	—	117	1,015	473	4,535	140	3,746	10,026

TOTAL REDUCTION OF THE FIELD FORCE, SOUTH AFRICA, DUE TO CASUALTIES.

	Officers.	Men.
Killed in action	302	2,902
Died of wounds	89	893
Prisoners who have died in captivity	3	90
Died of disease	155	6,115
Accidental deaths	4	145
Total deaths in South Africa	553	10,145
Prisoners and missing (excluding those who have been recovered or have died in captivity)	7	822*
Sent home as invalids	1,422	33,077†
Total, South African Field Force	1,982	44,044
		46,026‡

TOTAL REDUCTION OF THE MILITARY FORCES THROUGH WAR IN SOUTH AFRICA.

	Officers.	Men.
Deaths in South Africa	553	10,145
Prisoners and missing	7	822*
Invalids sent home who have died	4	208
Invalids sent home who have left the Service as unfit	—	1,030
	564	12,205
		12,769‡

OTHER CASUALTIES.

	Officers.	Men.
Died of disease in South Africa	155	6,115
Accidental deaths in South Africa	4	145
Invalids sent home:—		
Wounded	1,422	5,196
Sick		26,800
Not specified which		1,081

* This total includes a number of men reported "missing" who subsequently rejoined, but whose return has not yet been notified.
† Of these, 208 have died, 1,030 have been discharged from the Service as unfit, and 948 are in hospital.
‡ The difference between these two numbers is due to the fact that the great majority of the men invalided home have recovered and rejoined for duty. (*See note* †.)

INDEX.

The asterisk (*) denotes an Illustration or the footnote beneath an Illustration.

ERRATA.—p. 224, title to illustration, *for* "January 4" *read* "January 10."
p. 632, line 31, *delete the words* "Fresh from the campaign in the south-east."
p. 666, note below illustration, *for* "June 26" *read* "May 31."
p. 668, note below second illustration, *for* "son" (of the First Lord of the Admiralty) *read* "nephew," and *delete the words* "son of the Chief Justice." In correction of letterpress, see paragraph 2, p. 704.
pp. 693–6, Nitral's Nek is officially called Uitval's Nek.

EYRE AND SPOTTISWOODE, HIS MAJESTY'S PRINTERS, DOWNS PARK ROAD, LONDON, N.E.

S